Knowledge Management Tools and Techniques

Practitioners and Experts Evaluate KM Solutions

Knowledge Management Tools and Techniques

Practitioners and Experts Evaluate KM Solutions

Edited by

Madanmohan Rao

AMSTERDAM • BOSTON • HEIDELBERG • LONDON
NEW YORK • OXFORD • PARIS • SAN DIEGO
SAN FRANCISCO • SINGAPORE • SYDNEY • TOKYO

Butterworth-Heinemann is an imprint of Elsevier

Elsevier Butterworth–Heinemann
200 Wheeler Road, Burlington, MA 01803, USA
Linacre House, Jordan Hill, Oxford OX2 8DP, UK

∞ Recognizing the importance of preserving what has been written, Elsevier prints
its books on acid-free paper whenever possible.

Library of Congress Cataloging-in-Publication Data

Rao, Madanmohan.
  KM tools and techniques : practitioners and experts evaluate KM solutions /
Madanmohan Rao.
    p. cm.
  Includes bibliographical references and index.
  ISBN 0-7506-7818-6 (alk. paper)
  1. Knowledge management. 2. Organizational learning. 3. Knowledge
management—Data processing. 4. Management information systems.
  5. Information resources management. 6. Database management.
  I. Title Knowledge management tools and techniques. II. Title.

HD30.2.R356 2004
658.4′038—dc22
                                                        2004050698

British Library Cataloguing-in-Publication Data
A catalogue record for this book is available from the British Library.

ISBN: 0-7506-7818-6

For information on all Elsevier Butterworth–Heinemann publications
visit our Web site at www.books.elsevier.com

05 06 07 08 09 10   10 9 8 7 6 5 4 3 2 1

Printed in the United States of America

Contents

13

Hewlett-Packard: Making Sense of Knowledge Management

Bipin Junnarkar and Joan Levers

14

Knowledge Networking on a National Scale: A New Zealand Case Study

Paul Spence

15

Technology Applications of Communities of Practice: The Nursing Leadership Academy on Palliative and End-of-life Care

Cynda H. Rushton and Susan S. Hanley

16

KPMG: Leveraging KM Tools for Practice Areas and Clients

Hemant Manohar

17

Inter-organizational KM: The Experiences of Australia's National Office of the Information Economy

Luke Naismith

18

Knowledge Strategy in Small Organizations: The Office of Small Business, Australia

Christena Singh

19

A Day in the Life of a Rolls-Royce Knowledge Manager

Darius Baria

20

Creativity, the Knowledge Connector

Nel M. Mostert and Hilbert J. Bruins Slot

21

KM Tools in Human Resource Systems at the World
Bank: Promoting Empowerment and Knowledge Sharing 270
Michele Egan

Part II

22

"A Fool with a Tool Is Still a Fool . . ." 283
Ritendra Banerjee

23

Collaboration Software: Evolution and Revolution 293
Eric Woods

24

Competitive Intelligence and Knowledge Management:
Complementary Partners, Reinforcing Tools 302
Arik R. Johnson

25

Evolution of Knowledge Portals 311
Heidi Collins

26

From e-Learning to e-Knowledge...320
Jon Mason

27

Social Network Analysis in the KM Toolkit 329
Patti Anklam

28

Self-organization: Taking a Personal Approach to KM.........347
Steve Barth

Part III

Preface

As I write the preface to this book, I am going through my notes from the recent World Summit on the Information Society held in Geneva in December 2003, an unprecedented United Nations summit focusing on the global impacts and governance of information and communication technologies (ICTs). A number of provocative and profound questions were raised at the conference, which will be carried over into its second phase in Tunis in 2005.

How have ICTs affected productivity and learning? How have new media affected traditional media and international relations? How will ICTs affect the prosperity of a country? Will emerging ICTs widen the existing gaps between nations and communities or provide opportunities all around? What is the future of intellectual property in the Digital Age? How will ICTs like the Internet be governed? How have ICTs changed the way knowledge is experienced, created, shared, valued, and distributed?

The release of this book, the second in my knowledge management (KM) series of publications, seems timely in this context. With examples drawn from multiple sectors and countries around the world, this book shows how ICTs can profoundly strengthen knowledge management practices—provided, of course, that appropriate cultural and capacity foundations have also been built.

With a background in information technology (IT), media, and business and work exposure in Asia, Europe, the United States, and Latin America, my interests over the years have coalesced into the fascinating and compelling intersection between ICT adoption/creation on the one hand and (1) national cultures, (2) organizational cultures, (3) sectoral cultures, and (4) professional/vocational cultures on the other hand. This has led me to launch two series of books, drawing on contributions from dozens of experts around the world.

"The Asia-Pacific Internet Handbook" series explores the growth of the wired and wireless Internet and its impact on the technology sector, business environment, political climate, and cultural attitudes in the dynamic Asia-Pacific region. The series currently includes *Episode IV: Emerging Powerhouses*, *Episode V: News Media and New Media*, and *Episode VI: The Mobile Advantage*. (The titles borrow on the "Star Wars" movie series practice of structuring a set of narratives.) Future episodes will focus on issues like e-government; each book is a compilation and blending of perspectives from regional experts.

Shifting focus from a nation and region to an organization and sector as a unit of analysis, "The KM Chronicles"—of which this is the second book—consists of thematic compilations of essays about KM practices in different organizations and industry sectors. Each individual book is called a "travelogue" or a journey through a set of KM practices in clusters of organizations.

The first book in this series was *Leading with Knowledge: Knowledge Management Practices in the InfoTech Sector,* followed by "The KM Chronicles, Travelogue 2," which is called *Knowledge Management Tools and Techniques: Practitioners and Experts Evaluate KM Solutions.* The next travelogue in the series will be called *Cultures of Knowledge;* future travelogues will focus on KM in vertical sectors like government, manufacturing, and civil society.

Leading with Knowledge focused on IT companies, since the IT sector consistently dominates awards like the annual Most Admired Knowledge Enterprises (MAKE) awards across regions and across the past years. The most successful IT companies have certainly blazed a fiery trail on the KM front, and the book was an attempt to learn from and benchmark their KM practices. My educational and research background also includes a strong focus on IT, and I am particularly impressed by how innovative this sector continues to be and how it sets benchmarks for other industries as well.

Dozens of books have already been published about KM by consultants and academics, with expert analysis of KM practices in companies around the world—but not enough has been written by corporate KM heads themselves, who have been understandably too busy to write books. The "KM Chronicles" series of books fills that gap by bringing together perspectives, strategies, lessons, and recommendations straight from CKOs, knowledge managers, and KM heads. The clustering of books by vertical sector and horizontal themes also allows for intra-sector benchmarking and cross-sector transfer of learnings and best practices.

As importantly, this book series is a collection of *stories* about the growth of KM in organizations: about KM journeys, origins, destinations, roadmaps, speedbumps, gridlocks, and compasses. It brings KM to life as a human story, filled with a cast of characters, agendas, passions, and motives and even with confusion and conflict. The objective of the book series is to share these first-principles experiences and practical learnings with the entire KM community and, ultimately, to grow the KM discipline as a whole.

In my previous KM book, I classified business writers into four categories: *geek, genius, guru,* and *gypsy;* I fall in the gypsy category of writers who travel extensively, work with a wide spectrum of organizations, are exposed to all kinds of people and cultures, and blend multiple narratives together. This book is the second collection of my offline and online interactions with KM professionals in organizations and countries around the world.

In mid-2003, dozens of KM practitioners were contacted in person, via e-mail, or by phone in countries around the world, ranging from the United States and United Kingdom to India and Australia. Over 20 have graciously contributed entire chapters, and several others responded to a smaller questionnaire. Research insights were also culled from the Gartner Group; two sections of chapters were invited from KM consultants and vendors as well.

The diversity of perspectives and analyses in this book makes it a must read for a wide spectrum of the KM community: business professionals, CEOs, CKOs, CLOs, CTOs, CIOs, KM professionals, consultants, human resource professionals, academics, and MBA students.

All the contributors would like to thank their colleagues, families, friends, and well-wishers, and I myself would like to specially thank each and every one of the contributors for their painstaking efforts, time, and willingness in sharing details of their KM practices.

My thanks also go to the Butterworth-Heinemann team and the extended Reed–Elsevier network for their support of my various writing journeys. I am sure readers will appreciate the novelty and value of this book series and will join me in my various KM travelogues.

Questions? Fire away on the companion Web site of this book!

Madanmohan Rao
Bangalore
madan@techsparks.com
January 2004

To the struggle for knowledge, peace and justice

Overview: The Social Life of KM Tools

Madanmohan Rao

> The wise see knowledge and action as one.
>
> *Bhagavad Gita*

This is not the first book you should be reading about knowledge management, but it certainly should be your second.

Concepts and practices of knowledge management (KM) are soon approaching mainstream adoption, and this book focuses not on fundamental definitions of knowledge and strategy, but on more practical applications of KM tools and technologies in industry. KM tools, in a sense, are the "face and place" as well as the "nuts and bolts" of knowledge in the 21st century workspace.

"If the smart manager knows one thing, it is that knowledge management is not just about technology. But, if the smart manager knows two things, the second is that in today's age of technology-driven communication and information-production, the role technology can play to facilitate knowledge management should be examined," according to Koulopoulos and Frappaolo (1999).

Information and communication technologies (ICTs) play a key role in facilitating KM in today's globalized company, which operates in a complex web of partnerships and alliances. However, it is important to keep in mind that technology is not the panacea for a KM practice, though an easy-to-use knowledge-sharing infrastructure is an important enabler. Organization-wide access to KM architecture, Web-based applications, groupware, datamining tools, mobile devices, worldwide access, high performance, user friendliness, a standardized structure, and an easily administered controlling system are key requisites of the supporting KM infrastructure.

"We realized fairly early that the KM initiative has to be, of essence, people-centric. Nevertheless, technology has been an important dimension in our efforts to demonstrate the multiple possibilities of KM to our people, draw them to the movement, and help keep them committed. In this journey, a key lesson we have learnt is that unless people are able to see and experience the direct benefits of KM, no amount of incentives, rewards or recognitions are likely to elicit sustained enthusiasm, participation and involvement," according to Kris Gopalakrishnan, COO of Infosys, Most Admired Knowledge Enterprise (MAKE) award winner in 2003.

KM-enabling tools thus play a useful facilitating role in learning organizations, especially in dealing with the "info-glut" or information overload that is plaguing most organizations that have launched an intranet, enterprise resource planning (ERP), or business intelligence system.

While amplifying existing knowledge processes, information technology (IT) tools can also create new kinds of knowledge experiences in the long run, particularly among generations of users who grow up in IT-pervasive environments. "Technology enables new knowledge behaviours," according to Paul McDowall, KM advisor at the Treasury Board of Canada Secretariat.

Tools that currently fall under the KM umbrella have evolved in various phases since the 1980s, starting off with IT tools for computation and databases, followed by publishing and communication tools, and then accompanied by sophisticated platforms for collaboration, wireless delivery, search, and network modelling. From *automated agents* to *workflow tools*, KM technologies span almost the entire alphabetical spectrum.

Sidebar 1
KM Tools: The Alphabet Soup

Abstraction, agents, authoring systems, best practice repository, blogging, business intelligence, case-based reasoning, categorization, clustering, competitive intelligence, content management, collaboration, collaborative filtering, creativity tools, datamining, document management, e-learning, expert systems, expertise directories, expertise locators, groupware, heuristic software, idea management, intellectual property inventory, knowledge blogs, knowledge dashboard, knowledge discovery, knowledge mapping, knowledge mobilization, knowledge portals, knowledge visualization, meta-data, neural networks, online communities of practice, personal KM, profiling, P2P knowledge networking, search, semantic nets, Skandia navigator, skill inventories, smart enterprise suites, social net-work analysis, story templates, taxonomy, text mining, topic maps, validation, workflow, ...

While technologies and tools should not be the sole focus of KM efforts—culture and capacity building are as important—KM tools are finding increasing support from management in terms of being able to address some of their business pressures.

According to a new study by the consulting firm Bain & Company, companies are increasingly leaning on more and better methods of assessing economic uncertainty to reach elusive growth targets. "Most notably, CRM, contingency planning and KM rose through the ranks, both in usage and satisfaction," according to Darrell Rigby, Director of Bain & Company and founder of the "Management Tools & Trends" survey.

About This Book

This book situates KM tools in their right place as key enablers of knowledge behaviors and value in modern organizations, while also highlighting some of their limitations and shortcomings. While it does address the strengths and advances in KM tools, it cautions against the use of only KM tools for knowledge sharing; tools are identified as one of the many ingredients in the complex process of KM, but they work best only in the right supportive cultures.

"No matter how much we emphasise that cultural and organisational change is fundamentally what KM is all about, there remains the fact that KM today is IT-enabled and IT issues are of extreme importance," according to Srikantaiah and Koenig (2001).

This book is not intended to provide a detailed comparison of KM products or a competitive analysis of KM vendors. These are better dealt with by the various management and IT consulting firms and trade magazines. While some vendor and product names are identified, these are mainly in the course of narratives about KM implementation in an organization.

This book is targeted at organizations and communities that have decided to launch (or revamp) their KM practice and are looking at tools and technologies for implementing the practice. More precisely, the book is targeted at management professionals who are convinced of the importance of KM and are now looking for practical tips based on case studies, learnings, and recommendations from fellow KM practitioners in the field. So this is a book largely by peers for peers in the growing field of KM.

This chapter sets the stage for the book: it profiles KM tools in action, reviews recent literature on KM tools, provides a framework for analysis of tools in KM processes, captures the highlights of the KM tool case studies by the contributing authors, and identifies key learning areas and trends.

This chapter is followed by a journey through more than 20 first-hand narratives and case studies of KM tools in action in organizations around the world and in numerous categories: corporate, non-profit, government, independent professionals, and multilateral organizations. The narratives, from over ten countries, are presented directly by KM practitioners in delightfully different writing styles. The profiled companies include eight of the Top 50 companies in the world in the MAKE rankings for 2003: Accenture, American Productivity & Quality Center, Ernst & Young, Ford, HP, KPMG, Unilever, and the World Bank.

The next section of the book consists of seven expert commentaries on key KM tool areas: collaboration, portals, social network analysis, personal KM, e-learning, and blogging. The writers of these chapters are well-established consultants, market research analysts, or full-fledged KM authors in their own right, and they bring to the table years of experience and expertise in KM.

The last section of the book provides perspectives from six vendors in content management, expertise discovery, visualization, collaboration, competitive intelligence, and customer support. Each chapter provides a set of case studies of the benefits derived from deploying KM tools. Five of these vendors feature in *KM World* magazine's 2003 list of 100 companies that matter in KM: AskMe, Entopia, iManage, Inxight, and LexisNexis.

KM Tools in Action

KM can be defined as a systematic discipline and set of approaches to enable information and knowledge to grow, flow, and create value in an organization. This involves people, information, workflows, enabling tools, best practices, alliances, and communities of practice.

The 21st century business landscape is marked by increasing economic and political turbulence, a faster pace of innovation, an inter-networked organizational structure, a focus on intellectual capital, and an increasing employee churn rate. Within this context, KM is being interpreted as a critical discipline for risk management, increasing productivity, knowledge retention, and more efficient innovation.

According to IDC estimates, approximately 3.2% of corporate knowledge is incorrect or becomes obsolete every year. An estimated 4.5% of knowledge is lost or hidden due to employee turnover, information mismanagement, and knowledge hoarding.

While some of these are cultural problems, others can be resolved by properly aligning content management systems, information policies, and knowledge work.

This section profiles the following key sets of KM tools, as described in action in organizations around the world: content management, taxonomies, groupware, online communities of practice, portals, social network analysis, e-learning, storytelling, wireless platforms, innovation management tools, and inter-organizational knowledge-sharing platforms.

The material in this section is drawn from first-hand interviews with KM practitioners in the Americas, Europe, Asia, and Australia; consulting assignments for KM initiatives; and participation and reports from over two dozen KM conferences and workshops around the world in 2002 and 2003. (See the Online References section at the end of the chapter for links to full-length interviews, case studies, and conference reports featuring these tools.) Sidebars also provide analysis of KM tool usage in two industry verticals: infotech and pharmaceutical. Full-length case studies of KM tools in action are provided by other KM practitioners in another chapter of this book.

As these KM tools increase in popularity and intensity of usage, a growing body of literature is focusing on their adoption and strategies for utilization; this literature is reviewed in the next section. A framework for analysis of such tools in knowledge work and processes is presented in the subsequent section.

Content Management

A growing number of companies today have instituted content management systems for best practices, lessons learned, product development knowledge, customer knowledge, human resource management knowledge, and methods-based knowledge. Content teams, meta-data, knowledge maps, and a workflow contextualization can ensure effective reuse of content. Content-centric KM approaches like codification focus on efficiency and effectiveness of operationally focused value chains, while collaborative strategies focus on reinvention and advancement in innovation-focused value chains.

Advanced content management systems include features for seamless exploration, authoring templates, maintaining integrity of Web pages and links, periodical review, archiving, meta-data, version control, rule-setting, indexing, audits, authorized access, administration alerts, and flexible repurposing for multiple platforms and formats.

To begin with, an organization must conduct an enterprise knowledge audit to determine internal and external knowledge leverage points. Internal and external forces come into play here, ranging from customer knowledge to business intelligence via news media, according to Clare Hart, CEO of Factiva, which helps organizational KM initiatives via workflow design and newsfeeds.

Accenture implemented a Lotus-Notes-based KM system in 1992. In its early years, it was beset with problems like information overflow, duplication, and redundancies. Today, the Knowledge Xchange system has a standardized architecture and design and is accessed by 70,000 professionals to share information on project methodologies, sales cycles, current engagements, and other client learnings. Over 3,600 databases exist, and 250 knowledge managers are responsible for reviewing the content and selecting best practices. These are synthesized into special Web sections, and expert directories and external references are provided as well.

Chevron's KM strategy includes best practice sharing, internal/external benchmarking, technology brokers, networking, new planning tools, and work-tracking software. These are showcased via the Best Practice Resource Map, the Process Masters program, the annual Quality Conference, and the Global Information Link

Intranet. The Intranet even has areas called "Scratches" (for recording details on knowledge) and "Itches" (for recording requests for solutions to minor problems).

A well-designed content platform must be able to handle multiple content types, sources, and access patterns, according to Ryan Sciandri, Senior Systems Engineer at Interwoven. These content sources include corporate libraries, project activities, and personnel directories. Content can be structured or unstructured; some of it is generated and analyzed in real-time during various knowledge activities (e.g., online brainstorming).

Enterprise content can include videos, company policies, external Web sites, presentations, and press releases. An estimated 60–70% of portal content is unstructured, according to Sciandri. The content that is accessed via an enterprise knowledge portal is usually managed and maintained by a number of business users: marketing, human resources (HR), training, corporate communications, tech support, sales, and top management. All roles should be supported by a versatile content management system, advises Sciandri.

The KM system at Siemens is supported by a Global Editing Team which checks the quality of each document and provides support in writing powerful abstracts. Siemens' knowledge objects include successful practices, innovations, lessons learned, and methodologies. "It is important to launch with sufficient, valuable content and easy navigation. Disappointed users won't return a second time," warns Manuela Mueller, Director of Knowledge Sharing at Siemens Medical Solutions in Germany.

Meta-data features like classification, tagging, and validation are key in converting information to intelligent content. They help ensure compliance, relevance, proper categorization, and consistency. Content activities to factor in a KM system include authoring, management, and delivery of enterprise content. These should ensure that business content is consistent, of high quality, secure, timely, and meaningful.

Key features to consider in assessing products of content management vendors include customization to workflow, meta-data, tracking, integration, version control, archiving, and multilingual features. Portals and content tools are evident in many successful KM practices. For instance, the American Productivity & Quality Center's (APQC) KM infrastructure is based on Interwoven for content management and Verity for search. Bank of Montreal has an elaborate KM system based on an Intranet called MyBank, tools for social network analysis, a standardized lexicon, and a resource hub called K-Café.

British Airways launched its KM initiative in 1998; it included a high-level KM project board, regular knowledge fairs, a company-wide search engine, and tools for videoconferencing. BP Amoco has an expertise directory called Connect.

Sidebar 2
Industry Profile 1: KM Tools in InfoTech Companies

Through good times and bad, KM practices have been at the core of the more successful IT firms. Global IT firms are successfully leveraging KM to capture best practices, improve project management, nurture innovation, enhance customer service, reuse software code, and expand across boundaries of technology generations and varying maturity levels of markets. In fact, IT companies feature very prominently in the list of winners of awards like the annual MAKE awards, conducted by Teleos in association with The KNOW Network.

In the IT sector, software is often called the "quintessential knowledge industry," with software being an artifact which is purely a knowledge creation and which defies

Continued

Industrial-Age economics thanks to a zero cost of duplication and near-zero cost of distribution in the Internet Age.

Some other characteristics of the software industry include the relatively high degree of autonomy of the workers and their independence in career planning, a higher proportion of tele-work or remote computing, high degrees of churn as employees quickly move to other pastures or hive off their own start-ups, and the requirement of co-location in customer premises for contracts involving outsourcing (which can raise problems in terms of connectivity to remote systems and even cultural mismatch). Each of these throws up interesting twists for HR managers and KM planners of IT companies.

EDS has a vast architecture for knowledge sharing and innovation across its global force, which includes the Techlore technical knowledge repository and 114 communities of practice with over 28,000 members. **EMC**'s secure Web portal, Powerlink, facilitates collaboration between thousands of customer service agents who access more than 21,000 knowledge articles in the EMC Knowledgebase.

KM at **Fujitsu Consulting** is powered by the Knowledge Access System (KAS) portal and tools like ProjectFinder; it uses handheld wireless devices in the spread of KM at multiple "trigger points." **i2**'s Knowledge Base and Project Workbench help product developers and marketers in India and the United States improve upon software quality for their products and supply chain performance for their customers. Emerging KM trends identified in **IBM** include tighter linkage of KM to HR initiatives and enterprise content management; the biggest hurdles are culture, scale, and infrastructure.

i-flex's KM initiative is heavily based on process automation, as per the Capability Maturity Model (CMM) framework developed by the Software Engineering Institute (SEI) at Carnegie-Mellon University. i-flex has unveiled a plethora of schemes and tools on its i-Share KM portal, like the QuBase repository of methodologies, the Promotr project tracking tool, Project Closure Documents (PCD), the i-CleaR corporate learning repository, i-Suggest process improvement suggestion scheme, K-Forum for employees to seek solutions on unresolved issues, business intelligence monitoring contextualized with respect to i-flex's positioning, and K-Webcast conferences with i-flex experts hosted on the intranet called i-Opener.

Infosys' KM initiative for domain areas like software engineering is built on the KM Maturity (KMM) model and is promoted via the motto "Learn Once, Use Anywhere." The KM portal KnowledgeShop helps the company improve teamwork, refine software, reuse code, and meet growth expectations. A particularly useful incentivization scheme consists of Knowledge Currency Units (KCUs) whereby employees can award points to knowledge assets posted by their colleagues and can also earn points when their own posted knowledge assets are utilized. More than 99% of respondents in a survey expressed the belief that KM is essential for the company.

Lessons from **Inktomi**'s KM practice include the importance of not completely ignoring technology products (and underlying management decisions) like unused code and discontinued product lines. **J.D. Edwards** launched its intranet called Knowledge Garden in 1996 and a customer solution extranet in 1997. Unified through an enterprise taxonomy, knowledge assets in use include employee benefits content, technical and marketing briefs, presentations, multimedia, and applications. By 2002, 15% of customer queries were handled via self-service on the Knowledge Garden.

MITRE's KM initiative is powered by the award-winning Mitre Information Infrastructure (MII) and social network analysis to unearth pockets of expertise in real-time via the XpertNet. Interesting innovations include KM with partners via an extranet.

Open Text's corporate Intranet OLLIE hosts the global Knowledge Library and three key communities of practice: Competitive Intelligence Forum, Customer Dashboard, and Knowledge Centre. Open Text has also launched Livelink Wireless, which is being used by its knowledge workers on the road. Open Text launched an Extranet in 1997 to improve collaboration with its Affinity Partners. A key learning has been that KM solutions are always evolving, and there may be no "perfect" KM solution.

Oracle's formal KM-centered programs kicked off in 1997. Web-based project libraries have helped consultants readily find reference material and have decreased the number of technical assistance requests from customers. Technology is not just "another" enabler for KM, but a "key" one; technology-assisted platforms like My.Oracle.Com, GlobalXchange, Knowledge Areas, and Community Areas help KM concepts be put into action. Future steps include extending KM beyond the enterprise via the Oracle Technology Network (OTN) and Oracle Partner Network (OPN).

The Web site of **PMC-Sierra**, a leading provider of high-speed broadband communications, storage semiconductors, and MIPS-based processors, is rated by Cahners Research as one of the Top 10 "Manufacturer Web Sites Visited by Engineers." In addition to the company's Solution Advisor virtual sales tool, the site features a technical support Knowledge Base (KB) for customer support and collaboration between engineers.

SAS has a knowledge repository called ToolPool with loads of useful tips, tricks, and technical papers. An open culture, CEO support, human flexibility, responsiveness, internal marketing, commitment, and scalable technical infrastructure are important components of SAS' KM success.

Siemens Information and Communication Networks (ICN) devised a business development KM practice called ShareNet in 1999 to help share project knowledge across technologies and markets in different stages of maturity. Sales staff now find themselves playing the role of strategy-management consultants who have to be able to interpret trends and design new opportunities together with the customer. ShareNet helps tap and share local innovation in different parts of the world via project debriefings, manuals, codified databases, structured questionnaires, chat rooms, and hot lines. Technically based on OpenText's LiveLink, it is used by 7,000 sales and marketing staff.

Digital KM platforms can have a transformative power in environments where paper and face-to-face meetings constitute the bulk of knowledge transfer, as was the case when the **Sun Microsystems Philippines** (SunPhil) joint venture was formed between Sun Microsystems and erstwhile distributor Philippine Systems Products in 1999. Sun technology was used to launch the SunPhil Corporate Portal and its Knowledge Management System, with features like document rating, profiling and filtered search, and collaborative authoring. The time taken to prepare proposals and project documentation has been reduced tremendously, and innovative approaches are being explored to harness information mobilization and real-time expert contact via Personal Digital Assistant (PDA) and Short Messaging Service (SMS) (the Philippines, after all, is the world's SMS capital).

Architecturally, KM at **Unisys** is facilitated via the Knowledge.Net portal and Ask Knowledge.Net expertise location management application. Capacity building exercises like the KM@Unisys introductory e-learning course are available through Unisys University.

Xerox's **Eureka** practice for sales engineers is credited with solving over 350,000 problems annually with savings in excess of $15 million a year. Its Code Exchange initiative (CodeX) has now grown to over 1,000 registered users and saves over $3 million annually in software-license fees, servers, and other infrastructure costs.

Source: Data from Rao, 2003a.

"Referable and usable contributions from users must be culled, and irrelevant and unsolicited contributions must be filtered out," advises Ravi Arora, KM Head at Tata Steel in India.

"It is important to properly manage content up front so that costs of re-use can be kept down. Meta-data are important for content re-purposing," says Ben Martin, VP of Global Content Management at J.D. Edwards.

"However, it is important to remember that knowledge is not just a thing that can be managed but a flow that has to be nurtured, and this requires an understanding of the complex ecology of knowledge," cautions David Snowden, Director of the Cynefin Centre for Organisational Complexity at IBM UK.

In a nutshell, KM practice launch should begin with a systemic knowledge audit, which maps communication and information flows onto specific content repositories and validation processes. In addition to technology, costs will also be incurred in providing for and training content roles like content editor, knowledge steward, and subject matter expert.

Knowledge Taxonomies

Automated tools like computer-generated taxonomies can also assist in KM practices, especially in conjunction with human inputs and refinements. The info-glut or "digital sprawl" on corporate intranets has led to users not being able to find relevant information in time, and numerous taxonomy development tools are coming to the rescue.

"The knowledge taxonomy must fit the goals and strategies of the target business. It must reflect the needs, behaviour, tasks and vocabulary of the users as well, and be able to provide multiple paths and points of view," advises Marcia Morante of KnowledgeCurve.

Taxonomy-creating activities can be of three types: using tools with pre-built taxonomies, using tools with dynamically and automatically generated taxonomies, and using these tools along with human interventions. Verity offers Lexis-Nexis' pre-built taxonomies. Documentum has pre-built taxonomies for the financial services, energy, and life sciences industries, as well as for horizontal areas like sales, marketing, customer service, HR, IT, and legal. Autonomy and Verity use clustering algorithms to generate content types. Issues to look out for include managing node hierarchies, node memberships, and creating new nodes based on external market inputs.

Blue Cross Blue Shield of Florida uses software tools for taxonomy generation as well as automatic categorization (or assigning terms to specific documents). Such tools can identify important noun phrases, unused categories, uncategorized documents, and statistics on the degree of balance of the taxonomy, according to Dee Baldwin of Blue Cross Blue Shield. "An automated tool can significantly reduce the time for taxonomy development and maintenance, but humans are still required to review results," advises Baldwin.

"Effective tools can be used to build and test new taxonomies along dimensions of depth, breadth and detail. For administrators, the taxonomy should be easy to maintain, and users should find it easy to understand, navigate, and contribute," says Bryan Seyfarth, Senior Solution Consultant at Sopheon Corporation. He also cautions that no taxonomy is ever complete or perfect.

"A context-sensitive content taxonomy is needed to ensure workflow-oriented content structure for easy retrieval of knowledge," according to Siemens' Mueller.

A consistent content taxonomy, shared vocabulary, and effective governance system are important for maintaining relevance of organizational knowledge assets, keeping up with changes in the business domain, and adjusting to organizational growth.

Johnson Controls has an explicit taxonomy team charter whose mandate is to ensure that the right people can connect to the right information. "Common definitions are required to have cross-functional teams work together. Otherwise too many people will abandon searches after the first result," according to Jim Smith, Manager of Portal Content Services at JCI. Automatic and manual classification of content are needed, and meta-data requirements need to be clearly spelled out and agreed upon.

"Knowledge sharing can be hampered by lack of standardization. Standardization is particularly important in ensuring that the knowledge network can be accessible to new employees," according to Bill Wallace, Senior VP at construction firm CH2M Hill.

CH2M Hill launched formal KM efforts in the early 1990s, but quickly found that growth could outpace KM systems if governance of content, consistency of information, and better integration with IT tools were not properly handled. CH2M Hill now has a central office for the KM function and an advisory group for KM pilots like an expertise locator and CoPs addressing transportation and computer-aided engineering.

Companies specializing in tagging solutions for unstructured business data include Clear Forest, whose technology has been used for applications ranging from detecting insider tracking on stock exchanges to competitive intelligence in the chemical industry. Other vendors like The Brain and Inxight offer solutions for clustering and visualization as well.

Groupware

Desirable features for collaborative tools in the context of KM include affinity building, knowledge mapping, threading, polling, group document creation, rating, anonymity, notification, and access management.

A notable trend in tools for collaboration between networked employees is the convergence between asynchronous (e.g., collaborative document management) and synchronous (e.g., instant messaging) services, according to Timothy Butler, CEO of Sitescape.

Natural resources company Rio Tinto has set up 30 active communities of practice for business improvement, of which 11 are open to all employees, covering topics like environmental standards, underground safety, and dragline operation. The Rio Tinto Collaborative Forum (RTCF) was set up in February 2002, and a teamware tool was devised leveraging e-mail (particularly useful for people on the road) instead of direct Web access.

IBM's intellectual capital management (ICM) program, launched in 1994, marked a shift in focus from "big iron to big intellects." The framework is embedded in the policies, processes, personnel, values, and technology of the company. Key tools used include the ICM Asset Web (enterprise-wide infrastructure), Knowledge Café (for collaboration), and Knowledge Cockpit (for business intelligence and knowledge discovery).

Siemens Medical Solutions has an intranet-based portal based on OpenText's Livelink to support collaboration, knowledge sharing ("ShareNet"), and document management. The single-platform approach helps reduce the number of applications for similar purposes (e.g., e-Room, Sitescape, Hyperwave, Lotus Notes).

McKinsey has a culture where its professionals seem averse to reusing codified expertise of others and prefer unique solutions. Instead of searching for information on intranet databases, they prefer to meet and think creatively. Thus, KM professionals are part of the HR department and specialize in bringing people to people for collaboration.

In academic institutes like George Washington University, tools such as Entopia's Quantum solution are used to build content and collaboration platforms between faculty and students, building social links to tacit knowledge and encouraging knowledge sharing.

The challenge is moving through successful phases of integration of information, application and business processes for increasingly large networks (at the level of departments, enterprises and inter-organizational communities). Other trends to watch include the proliferation of P2P collaboration tools like Groove.

Sidebar 3
Industry Profile 2: KM Tools in the Pharmaceutical Industry

Pharmaceutical companies offer a wide array of solutions on numerous platforms (e.g., bioinformatics, combinatorial chemistry) to a diverse range of customers (e.g., pharmacies, hospitals, specialists, patients) in several therapeutic cate-gories (e.g., respiratory, cardiovascular). Deployed KM tools and activities in the pharma industry range from document libraries and mobile solutions to expert networks and e-mail mining. Quite a few notable successes have already emerged on the KM front in the pharmaceutical industry, particularly in terms of efficiency, process integration, and innovation.

Solvay has implemented an expert finder solution called X-Fert (cross fertilization) for almost 500 employees. It has over 3,000 personal pages. Thirty-five global communities of practice are connected to X-Fert, in countries ranging from the United State and Thailand to Portugal and Argentina. Solvay also has implemented a "KM-orientated document writing method" to recenter document creation on the strategic content of industrial processes, based on Robert Horn's Information Mapping method.

KM projects at Solvay fall into ten types: benchmarking, competitive intelligence, workflow, communities of practice, organizational modelling, learning, portals, skills, knowledge-based systems, and idea box systems. "From our learnings, I would recommend that KM practitioners work with motivated people, get top level support, and pay attention to individual learning issues. Technology is important, but should not be the first step. New technology + Old organisation = Costly old solution," jokes Emmanuel Vergison, Corporate Knowledge Manager at Solvay.

The Solvay intranet (called Faros) was based on concepts developed by INSEAD's Centre for Advanced Learning Technologies. Solvay's Idea Box Portal has 250 facilitators in Europe alone. Awareness campaigns about KM were started in March 2002, with focused presentations, in-depth training, and mock-up exercises.

KM at **Bayer** is facilitated via its knowledge portal called KIBIT (KM in Bayer's Intranet), hosted on its BayNet Intranet. Over five million documents are downloaded each month; employees are also given training on how to deal with information overload. The knowledge capture process is designed in such a way that learnings are captured from failures as well, not just successes.

Pharmaceutical companies today are still finding it difficult to retrieve discarded research, which becomes relevant again in new regulatory environments, or to locate appropriate expertise or to provide new employees with the appropriate information and tools quickly enough, observes Joel Miller, Manager of Learning Information Technology at **Eli Lilly**.

The company's mission statement is to provide its customers with "answers that matter" via innovative medicines, information, and customer support, and KM is an important strategy for linking people to other people, knowledge, and experiences. Eli Lilly's portal has subject guides, people look-up facilities, CommunitySpace, and a learning portal. Called myELVIS (Eli Lilly Virtual Information Service!), the corporate portal was launched in a 90-day focused effort.

Miller advises KM practitioners to establish governance structures early, use demos frequently, and ensure that search techniques work properly. "Scientists and researchers tolerate more complexity than business customers when it comes to information discovery," he observes. Challenges up ahead for Eli Lilly include staying focused on innovation and handling governance as the portal becomes truly global (the company has over 40,000 employees in 160 countries).

"Understanding of global rules and roles is critical for content management on large distributed portals," says Marianne Kohne, Global Intranet Content Manager at **Boehringer Ingelheim**. The company's intranet is called BIGnet (Boehringer Ingelheim Global Intranet).

Syngenta's KM initiative has focused on saving money in project management via solutions ranging from content formats and shared vocabularies to knowledge behaviors and a revamped intranet. "Buy-in is necessary from the IT department but KM is not necessarily high on their agenda," cautions Pauline Stewart, Knowledge Manager at Syngenta.

Techniques like automatic e-mail profiling can be used to identify business strengths in community users, says Jean-Marc Girodeau, from the Drug Innovation and Approval division of **Aventis** in France. The KnowledgeMail profiling tool for locating internal expertise scans e-mails and attachments and allows users to control their private and public profiles. Based on the Balanced ScoreCard approach, a tool called KnowledgeMail Navigator is used to evaluate the impact of the profiling system on time saving, productivity, and innovation at Aventis. "The adoption of this system is heavily dependent on trust," Girodeau cautions.

KM can be used to optimize the R&D value chain with workflow management in areas like regulatory claim submission, says Rudiger Buchkremer, IT head at **Altana Pharma**, whose wide-ranging KM suite also includes news spiders, PDA-based content delivery, collaboration with external universities, and social knowledge activities like management development circles and experience exchange groups.

"The speed of innovation is determined by experts' awareness of new direction and opportunity, their ability to integrate knowledge into a teachable framework, and the organisation's ability to mobilise it," says Victor Newman, CLO at **Pfizer** and author of *The Knowledge Activist's Handbook*. Companies should start thinking in terms of "return on experience" and not just "return on investment," he advises. A learnings database is a good start for a KM system, but it should also intuitively and visually model the way experts pay attention and think about work. e-Knowledge building and e-learning need to be put to work in tandem to create knowledge prototypes, stabilize knowledge assets, and mobilize the acquired knowledge.

"New technologies for mining and access can help deal with the problem of content under-utilisation. After lab work, information gathering and analysis are the most time-consuming activities in pharmaceutical research and development," says Ramana Rao, CTO and co-founder of Xerox spinoff Inxight. The company has developed automatic categorization tools for managing embedded concepts, topical categories, metadata, and linked concepts in documents; its clients include Pfizer, the European Patent Office, and Factiva.

Online Communities of Practice

Online communities constitute a growing part of the organizational landscape of 21st century global players, but businesses are still at the early stages of individual and organizational optimization of Web-based communities.

"The Internet is today's cave wall. The organisation is still adjusting to its newfound ability to provide open access to the Net's information, entertainment, communication and ideas within the work environment," according to Cliff Figallo and Nancy Rhine, co-authors of *Building the Knowledge Management Network*. The challenge is to create naturally and effectively scaled knowledge communities online.

More focused, task-oriented networks like communities of practice (CoPs) need to be carefully nourished and sustained, recommends Michael Fontaine, consultant at IBM's Knowledge and Organisational Performance Forum. Care should be taken to focus (especially during hard times for the economy) on CoP benefits and performance impacts on parameters like time savings, collective problem solving, and sales levels.

CoPs are known by various catchy names like Learning Networks (in HP), Best Practice Teams (Chevron), Family Groups (Xerox), COINS (Ernst & Young's community of interest networks), and Thematic Groups (World Bank). Corporate yellow pages have been known variously as PeopleNet (Texaco) and Connect (BP).

Online CoPs are emerging as a powerful tool for knowledge exchange and retention. APQC classifies CoPs into four types: helping (peer-to-peer sharing of insights, e.g., Schlumberger's Eureka, DaimlerChrysler's TechClubs), best practice sharing (sharing of documented verified user practices, e.g., Schlumberger's InTouch), knowledge sharing (connecting of members, e.g., CGEY), and innovation (cross-boundary idea generation, e.g., Siemens ShareNET).

CoPs also improve meta-capabilities—or the capabilities to generate capabilities—such as learning and collaboration, according to Debra Wallace of Clarica Life Insurance, which used online community techniques developed by CommuniSpace to create an Agent Network for knowledge sharing among 150 members.

Within online CoPs, an interesting debate revolves around whether or not to allow employees to post messages anonymously or to rank knowledge assets of their employees anonymously.

"Anonymity does not work in knowledge networks because accountability of knowledge contributions is important," stresses Hubert St. Onge, CEO of Konverge Digital Solutions.

Some organizations like Bain & Company actually do permit anonymity in employee rankings and ratings of knowledge assets. "But we can track the ratings behind the scenes so as to prevent abuse," says Robert Armacost, KM Director at Bain.

Participation levels in CoPs can be segmented into core, active, and peripheral. Success levels can be diagnosed via the application of knowledge, in the form of interviews, anecdotes, and employee surveys. Expertise directories are a useful way for connecting knowledge workers in such forming communities, but they must connect people and not just resumes, advises Drew Grimm, "digital activist" at Honeywell.

In addition to tools, however, care must be taken to address CoP governance, user support, communication plans, and realistic expectations of outcome, cautions Debra Wallace, co-author of *Leveraging Communities of Practice*.

Organizations like The Information Worker Productivity Council and The Centre for Research on Information Work conduct research and analysis on the nature of knowledge work in networked virtual environments.

Enterprise Portals

The enterprise portal is becoming the IT platform of choice for the interlinked e-workspace. "Context and aggregation need to be built around the role of each knowledge worker. Further personalisation should be made possible via customisation features," advises Jack Borbely, KM Director at management consultancy firm Towers Perrin, whose KM infrastructure includes Lotus Notes/Domino, BEA Weblogic, and Documentum.

Portals represent the "face" of KM, according to Steven Ng, Manager of Business Portals for IBM Southeast Asia, speaking at the KM seminar series, "Leading with Knowledge," held in Singapore, Kuala Lumpur, Mumbai, and New Delhi.

Portals help create the "on demand" workplace, customized to individual employee needs. A well-designed portal can serve as a delivery channel for KM applications any time, any place, and on any device. Knowledge portals are the single point of interaction and coordination for collaboration (calendaring, people finding), transaction (business intelligence), and information management (digital assets, data visualization).

Enterprise portals can have multiple target audiences: employees, partners, and customers (or B2E, B2B, B2C). A portal provides access to a wide range of applications, content, services, processes, and people. Key characteristics for assessment of portal vendors include scalability, security, customizability, navigability, and ubiquitous accessibility.

"IBM employees rate our portal, called W3, as the most credible, useful and preferred source of information today," according to Ng; the portal displaced employees' managers and co-workers as the primary source of information over the period 1998–2001. Two-thirds of IBM employees believe that the portal is now critical to performing their jobs and saves them valuable time. The portal also includes sections or "portlets" for working knowledge.

"We are now entering the era of the role-based workplace," says Ng, where the portal must provide multiple functionalities: employee-to-work (applications), employee-to-employee (collaboration), employee-to-company (yellow pages, HR, e-learning), employee-to-external (collaborative commerce), and employee-to-life (finances, leisure).

"An enterprise whose business processes are integrated end-to-end across the company and with key partners, suppliers and customers can respond with speed to any customer demand, market opportunity or external threat," advises Ng. To be effective, however, KM architecture must go hand-in-hand with organization-wide cultural initiatives for knowledge-exchange, content policies (e.g., document templates, validation processes), and communication policies (e.g., promptness of responses, adherence to threading tools).

Platforms for personalized access and interaction have evolved from chaotic intranets to more cohesive enterprise portals, says Tom Koulopoulos, President of Delphi Corporation. Delphi classifies enterprise portal vendors into the following categories: content management (Documentum, Open Text), collaboration (Microsoft, Lotus), search (Inktomi, Autonomy, Verity), KM (Intraspect), and ERP (PeopleSoft).

Enterprise knowledge portals have emerged as a foundational tool to bind together the various content and collaboration activities of a KM ecosystem. A well-designed enterprise portal site map can correspond meaningfully to the knowledge maps, communities, and expertise in an organization.

"The enterprise portal is a KM solution that brings a method to the madness. At the same time, KM professionals should beware of the 'portal in a box' myth. Portal maintenance can be expensive due to the frequent changes in people, processes and information," cautions Heidi Collins, author of *Corporate Portals* and *Enterprise Knowledge Portals* (2003). The enterprise portal is a way of context management, and the knowledge desktop should create an actionable environment for end-users.

Enterprise knowledge portals (a natural evolution of corporate portals, which themselves evolved out of corporate intranets and the consumer portal model) are useful platforms for tying together KM functions. These include features for content organization (for business intelligence and learning materials), presentation, search, integration, personalization, and collaborative activity.

Enterprise portals can help turn information into knowledge by facilitating the organization, navigation, visualization, and heuristic interaction of employees with one another and with information. "Business portals nurture a sense of community among users and provide access to knowledge and the experts who maintain that knowledge. They impact the supply side, demand side and organizational knowledge," Koulopoulos says.

From the industry side, a variety of alliances are being formed by vendors along the KM tool spectrum. For instance, IBM (Websphere portal) and Interwoven (TeamSite and MetaTagger content tools) have formed alliances for KM solutions for a number of clients in the public sector (e.g., state government of Utah), industry (Siemens, John Deere), finance (CSFB, Pacific Capital Bancorp), healthcare (Kaiser Permanente, Wellpoint), and distribution (Boston Market).

Sidebar 4
KM Tools for Knowledge Asset Rating: The Knowledge Currency Unit (KCU)
Scheme at Infosys

Bangalore-headquartered software services firm Infosys was the first Indian company to win the global MAKE award in 2003. One of the KM tools it has devised serves three major purposes: reward and recognition, measuring quality of knowledge assets, and measurement of KM benefits via knowledge currency units (KCUs).

Authors earn KCUs when their documents or artifacts are accepted for publication in the KM repository. Subsequently, each time a document is used, the user can award KCUs which accrue to the author's KCU account. The effort spent by subject area experts on reviewing documents for publication also earns KCUs. Employees thus build their KCU accounts, whose balance is a measure of their involvement in knowledge sharing. KShop, the Infosys corporate KM portal, supports interfaces that allow users to award KCUs while rating documents, and for KCU account management, as shown in Figure 1.1 on page 18.

However, a successful KM incentive program must go beyond material rewards, and public recognition is a powerful form of motivation. KShop features a KCU Score Board that gives visibility to top knowledge sharers. As a mechanism for measuring quality, the scheme associates with each document a composite KCU rating, which factors in the KCUs awarded by subject matter experts to the document at the time of reviews, those awarded by users over the document's life cycle, and also the frequency and recency of its use. The composite KCU rating is thus a market-determined indicator of document quality.

Content retrieved is displayed in decreasing order of composite KCU rating—the system thus aims to assist the user in sifting through a possibly large number of documents that may meet the search criteria specified. The content maintenance process uses the KCU mechanism to identify documents that potentially qualify for revision or "retirement."

The KCU scheme also provides a mechanism for quantitative management of the KM processes. One aspect of quantitative management is the composite KCU rating. KCUs are also used as metrics in the measurement of KM benefits and for measuring the level of KM activity within each organizational unit.

Source: Interview with V.P. Kochikar, KM Group, Infosys Technologies.

Social Network Analysis and Design

Within organizational settings, social network analysis (SNA) is emerging as a powerful tool for mapping knowledge flows and identifying gaps. SNA can be used to reinforce existing flows and to improve knowledge integration after activities like mergers and acquisitions. Methods used can be qualitative (e.g., employee surveys) or quantitative (e.g., analysis of transactions like e-mails or phone calls or information artifacts like documents and search strings).

Natural language techniques, visualization tools, and recommender systems can be harnessed here, leading to actions like identifying key individuals for retention or expanded roles or creating teams for cross-organizational and cross-functional projects. Direct applications of SNA include process redesign, role development, and improved collaboration between knowledge seekers and providers.

The focus on networks in the 21st century knowledge workplace is increasing because networks are where people engage, networks are where work happens, and networks are where knowledge lives, according to Rob Cross, author of *The Hidden*

Figure 1.1

Interface for rating knowledge assets (*Source: Infosys*)

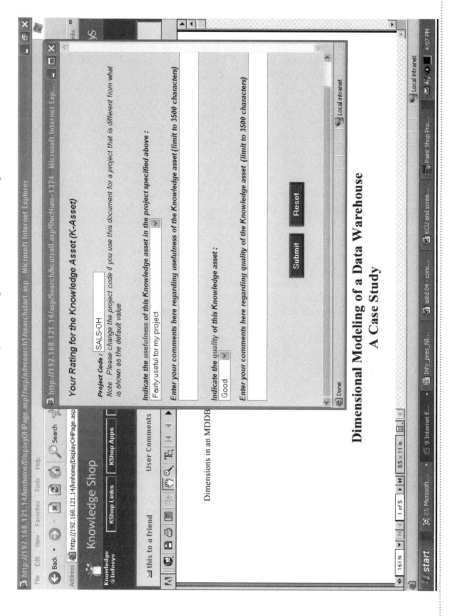

Power of Social Networks. Typical roles in organization networks include central people, peripheral people, boundary spanners, and knowledge brokers. "Network structure can facilitate or impede effectiveness of knowledge workers," Cross says.

SNA can help identify central people, connectivity levels of individual knowledge workers, diversity of subgroups, and level of organizational inter-connectivity. "Getting things done often depends less on formal structure than on informal networks of people," Cross observes. Many companies have top management teams, but not top management networks.

Successful SNA depends on meta-knowledge of employees, access to colleagues, frequency and intensity of interaction, and levels of trust. SNA has implications for organizational leadership, social ecology, relational development, and network planning. Tools like SNA can be used to analyze and improve numerous kinds of networks, such as advice networks and even energy networks. "Position in the energy network can be a much higher predictor of performance than expertise or use of informational networks. Employees connected to energisers tend to perform better," according to Cross.

"Social network analysis (SNA) can be used for addressing KM questions like frequency and value of knowledge exchange, and knowledge mapping. In organisational development, SNA can be used to reinforce decision making paths, trust and energy," says Patti Anklam of Hutchinson Associates, a firm which conducted SNA at Nortel Networks along with the Institute for Knowledge-Enable Organisations (IKO). "Graphical mapping, a product of SNA, is very meaningful to people, and can help conceptualise deeper organisational patterns," according to Anklam.

Mathematical concepts like degrees of separation between nodes, the number of connections to/from a node, centrality of the overall network, and density of possible connections apply here. Common patterns that can then be identified include clusters (dense groups), connectors (individuals linking to many others), boundary spanners (individuals connecting to other parts of an organization), information brokers (those who connect clusters), and outliers (peripheral specialists).

The number of ties and the strength of the ties reflect group membership and the strength of affinities in these groups. This information can be used to address knowledge problems (e.g., build better teams), communication problems (e.g., open more channels of dialog), or quality problems (e.g., increase the frequency of communication with experts).

"Networked knowledge is a force multiplier," says Bryan Davis, President of the Kaieteur Institute for Knowledge Management (www.kikm.org), and Joel Alleyne, CIO of BLG Canada. Networks help sustain the engine of knowledge. Companies should create rich connections inside and outside their organizations. The networked firm should have more synaptic connections so as to increase the power of the organizational brain, Davis and Alleyne advise. "The key is to make $1 + 1 = 11$," they advise. Tools like visualization, taxonomy, and search should be harnessed in this regard for knowledge mapping, and a "knowledge marketplace" for the exchange of knowledge should be supported.

E-learning

One interesting emerging development on the KM front is the growing convergence of viewpoints between the KM community and the e-learning community.

"There has been a disconnect between KM and e-learning because of different organizational lineage and varying vendor products. There is also a perception that learning is for new employees whereas KM is for experts," observe Edward Barnfield and Jennifer Wilson of Melcrum Research.

Actually, the concept of KM can be united with the goals of e-learning to create the larger ideal of a learning organization—via blended learning, skills directories integrated with course delivery, and the interleaving of working and learning. KM and learning management are two complementary disciplines that are continuously growing closer and support an innovative and agile enterprise.

"E-learning should be blended with communities of practice. Managers need to be able to anticipate training needs based on business goals and deliver those courses quickly to employees," according to Barnfield and Wilson.

"KM and e-learning are converging—managers and employees need to focus on doing while learning and learning while doing. Connected learning is the way to go," says APQC's Cindy Hubert.

Siemens blends KM and e-learning at its Siemens Learning Valley (SLV) initiative, founded in 2001 in Belgium and Luxembourg (branded as "Where Knowledge Shapes (Y)our Future"). Online courses can be taken via HorizonLive. A newsletter called SLV Gazette spreads awareness about this program and the associated Knowledge and Learning Index (KLIX).

Consulting firm Bain & Company has an elaborate KM system consisting of the Bain Virtual University (BVU) for online courses coupled with the Global Experience Centre (GXC). Its content assets include the core global toolkit (launched in 1999), codified insights into industry verticals (launched in 2000), sanitized summaries of client projects, video modules of case study reviews, staff profiles, and external market research.

"We have a number of dedicated knowledge roles, such as case team, regional knowledge broker and global topic specialists," says Robert Armacost, KM Director at Bain. The company launched the latest version of BVU and GXC in October 2002.

The corporate university and the KM department at the Bank of Montreal jointly funded the "kCafé," which acts as a bridge between classroom training and on-the-job tools, as well as an enterprise program called ideaNet to have employees identify and brainstorm on banking solutions.

Buckman Labs, another pioneer in KM, launched an online learning center in 1996, new IT infrastructure for KM in 1998, a TeamToolz toolkit for team creation in 2000, processes like After Action Review in 2001, and new people products in 2002.

Storytelling and Narratives

Building communities in business has become a priority in knowledge-sharing organizations around the world. Storytelling has become an effective way to mobilize change, according to Seth Kahan, President of the Performance Development Group and internal communications consultant to the World Bank.

"Personal storytelling builds community and can revitalise the way we do business. It brings us back to life and to our deeper purpose. How we share is as important as what we share," says Kahan, who has used non-traditional business communication techniques like art, theatrical tools, poetry, and even a Cherokee talking stick to improve internal and interpersonal communication.

"Springboard stories ignite action in organizations," says Stephen Denning, author of *The Springboard* (2001) and architect of the World Bank's KM initiative. "The most important challenge in this economy is creating conversations," says Tata Steel's Arora.

Models and theories from disciplines like complex adaptive systems can be deployed in this regard. Organizations like IBM's Cynefin Centre have developed classifications of knowledge work into categories like known, knowable, complex, and chaotic, focusing not just on storytelling, but on narrative analysis for collaborative sense-making and decision-making inputs. Tools like participatory observation, anecdote circles, deep immersion, organizational metaphors, and naive interviews are useful in this regard. Storytelling is used to promote knowledge sharing at NASA, via Transfer Wisdom Workshops and Project Management Shared Experiences Program conducted by the Academy of Program and Project Leadership (APPL).

In terms of narrative structuring, tools like "knowledge blogging" (or k-logs, a term coined by John Robb, President of Userland) have a lot of potential. "Stories are a good framework for sharing information, meaning and knowledge. Blogs encourage story-telling and foster understanding because they usually offer context," according to Darlene Fichter, library coordinator at the University of Saskatchewan Library. "Knowledge blogs help encourage brain dumps, exploration, and think-aloud behaviour. They create connected content, break down silos, allow comments, and can also be treasured as useful searchable archives," she observes.

Besides, over time, blogs are self-rewarding. "Often bloggers report that they discover their own interests and refine their perspectives. It leads to peer recognition," according to Fichter.

K-logs are also a useful, low-cost, and flexible tool for competitive intelligence (CI), says Arik Johnson, Managing Director of Aurora WDC. Well-designed CI blogs can help collect, analyze, package, and deliver current awareness and early warning of competitive and regulatory developments for sales staff and top managers. Blogs help write thought pieces to guide the organization on a strategic path. Bloggers can collect and connect information and provide useful overlays of context. "Blogging has enough critical mass and momentum, and will soon be integrated with other KM tools," predicts Johnson.

Wireless Tools for Knowledge Mobilization

One of the most notable emerging trends in workforce connectivity is the increasing use of mobile technologies to take "KM" to another dimension—"knowledge mobilization"—by bringing relevant knowledge directly to the fingertips of a company's road warriors and field-workers via cell phones, PDAs, industry-specific handheld devices, Wireless Local Area Network (WLAN), and Radio Frequency Identification (RFID) tags.

While personal computers (PCs) and workstations have come under some criticism for "tethering" knowledge workers to their desks, wireless technologies may be the perfect answer to "mobilizing" the workforce by letting them capture and harness key information and knowledge attributes wherever they are, whenever they want, and however they want.

"Knowledge anywhere, anytime and on any device is critical in this day and age. Wireless connectivity at the LAN level lets employees work creatively outside of office cubicles if they so desire. They can roam around and stay connected at the same time," observes Jeanne Holm, Chief Knowledge architect at NASA. "However, too much wireless interruption can be distracting at meetings as well," she warns.

"Wireless solutions can help employees communicate easily in real time and function across boundaries of space and time," says Robert Buckman of Buckman Labs, one of the pioneering champions of KM. In addition to wireless connectivity, ubiquitous bandwidth is key. Otherwise, information and applications will have to be designed for too many different bandwidths and devices, he cautions.

"We are now seeing the emergence of the *continuous economy*—across space and time, across organisational and personal boundaries," according to Gigi Wang, IDC

Senior VP for communications and Internet research. The continuous economy is characterized by ubiquity and mobility.

"Mobility-enabling technologies are emerging as drivers for the importance of knowledge," says Manuella Mueller, Director of Knowledge Sharing at Siemens Medical Solutions in Germany. Hundreds of mobile workers at Siemens Medical Solutions can stay connected and have access to crucial know-how via its Med2Go wireless solution on Compaq iPaqs.

Wireless will certainly bring great innovation to organizations, once stumbling blocks like inadequate standardization are resolved, according to Paul Hearn, Project Officer at the European Commission's Information Society Technologies Programme.

Boeing's engineers use laptops and WLANs to better access complex multimedia documents on the move. Bell Canada technicians use wearable computers and miniature cameras (Xybernaut Mobile Assistants) so that they can instantly tap office expertise even while they are on top of a pole, according to Keen and Mackintosh (2001).

Hotel giant Carlson's managers use iPaq handhelds with up-to-date information on room status and yield management. GM field technicians use voice-driven portable computers to record their activities, which are transcribed and analyzed.

Snyder Healthcare Sales uses a mobile-enabled KM system—devised by IMS Health Strategic Technologies—to give its pharmaceutical sales force automation tools for call reporting, sample disbursement, and signature capture accessible via handheld PCs. As compared to previous paper-based methods, accuracy of data capture increased and the time taken to provide reports to clients decreased from 60 days after a sales call to 10 days.

"Wireless service providers are ramping up broad ranges of services that are useful for any company's KM solution, ranging from SMS to broadband wireless service," according to Honeycutt (2000).

"80 per cent of our workforce is out in the field. Wireless technologies help us gather timely data which we can then harvest for information nuggets," says Carl Baptista, Head of R&D at Origin Exterminators, a rodent control company headquartered in Singapore, which uses wireless devices to seamlessly connect "white collar" and "blue collar" workers. Automatic wireless sensors and handheld devices operated by field technicians help the company sharpen its research and knowledge on key issues: Which rat baits are working best? Is the population of roaches increasing? What patterns can be detected in different seasons? "It almost puts a new twist to the acronym CMS (content management system)—cockroach management system," jokes Baptista.

As companies adopt Internet and mobile technologies, they will need to mature progressively across three phases: business process innovation, business model innovation, and ultimately business model creation, observes Noel Hon, Managing Director for NEC Singapore.

A wide array of portable wireless devices is emerging on the Local Area Network (LAN), Wide Area Network (WAN), and Personal Area Network (PAN) fronts, and these can plug in to productivity workflows and boost knowledge mobilization and real-time expert location as well. How to outfit the frontline and manage applications across multiple client platforms will be a key strategy and operational focus area for CKOs and CIOs in the coming years.

Innovation and Idea Management Systems

Online idea management systems have been deployed at companies like Bristol-Myers Squibb, Cadbury-Schweppes, and Mott's Apples. Managing an innovation pipeline, promoting an "idea central" or ideas marketplace, and creating the "hundred headed brain" are some creative approaches being adopted by KM pioneers, according to Mark Turrell, CEO of Imaginatik Research.

KM also helps organizations increase the efficiency of innovation by improving access to experts, tapping into past innovations, and creating conditions of "orchestrated serendipity," according to Kimberly Lopez and Darcy Lemon from APQC's custom solutions group. Boeing Rocketdyne, Millennium Pharmaceuticals, NASA's JPL, and 3M are good examples in this regard.

The spirit of innovation should be infused not just in R&D, but also in business strategy, organization models, and operating structures, leading to enterprise-wide "macro-innovation," recommends Mark McElroy, author of *The New Knowledge Management*.

At a global level, increasing connectivity, integration technologies, and collaborative filtering have led to the emergence of the "global brain," according to Ross Dawson, author of *Living Networks*. Drawing on numerous examples like Slashdot, Blogdex, NewsML, RosettaNet, IBM's Alphaworks R&D site, Eli Lily's Innocentive.com, PlanetFeedback, and InternalMemos.com, Dawson recommends that aspiring leaders in the age of the living network should create powerful knowledge-based relationships and develop a culture of responsible transparency and collaboration.

Tools for Extending KM across Organizational Boundaries

Online services such as dial-up bulletin boards and Web communities have actually helped network communities of interest across the globe for years. The World Bank has leveraged a strategy of "global knowledge, local adaptation" for brokering global knowledge exchanges.

This includes Web-based resources like case studies, Webcasts and videoclips from experts, world development indicators, knowledge toolkits (on topics like business climate and corruption), distance learning services, knowledge assessment methodology, and forums like Development Gateway.

The Latin American Urban Network is a good example of knowledge partnerships for better policy formulation between client CoPs in urban municipal staff in ten cities of Latin America and the Caribbean, according to Bruno Laporte, Manager of Knowledge and Learning Services at the World Bank. Civil sector organizations using Web-based KM networks on a global scale include Bellanet and Global Knowledge Partnership.

The North Suburban Library System (www.nsls.info), a multi-library consortium with over 650 members, uses KM to increase collaboration and improve the performance of its membership. The consortium uses expertise yellow pages, a consulting knowledge base, and after-action reviews called "hot washes," according to Christina Stoll, KM specialist at NSLS.

Professions Australia, the umbrella organization of professional societies (like Australian Computer Society, CPA Australia, Australian Physiotherapy Association, and Pharmaceutical Society of Australia), leverages its Web site (www.professions.com.au) as a KM platform for its members. "We have three components: Knowledge Base with resource links and syndicated content, Knowledge People with an expertise directory, and Knowledge Talk or online discussion," says David Stephens of Professions Australia. The objectives include addressing industry gaps, developing policy positions and advisory services which impact professionals, and encouraging debate on professional and ethical practice.

Literature Review

The rapid adoption of the above KM tools in enterprises and the proliferation of KM vendors and products have drawn the attention of a number of KM analysts, consultants, academics, and writers; we now review some of their literature on this topic.

Ruggles (1996) edited one of the first books to focus wholly on KM tools; the compilation of essays acknowledges that, although tools alone are not the answer to the difficult questions surrounding KM, if utilized effectively tools can open up new realms of innovation and efficiency for today's knowledge-driven businesses.

The lion's share of KM tool books focuses on content management, search, portals, and online CoPs, which will continue to be the bedrock of many KM projects. This section reviews over 30 books on KM, with a specific focus on their analysis and recommendations regarding KM tools.

The Importance of Web-based KM Tools

In a forthcoming publication, Nantel (2004) profiles over two dozen KM products in the following categories: business intelligence, workflow, collaboration, content, customer relationship management (CRM), data integration, enterprise infrastructure, expert systems, expertise location, portals, and search.

"Previous information technologies were much better suited to managing structured data, but the Web enabled the handling of unstructured text and graphic forms of information and knowledge. If not for their availability, KM would never have taken off," according to Davenport and Prusak (2003).

"Without the quality of connectivity and the simplicity and commonality offered by the software interface to application that is provided by an intranet, an organisation's ability to create, share, capture and leverage knowledge is stuck in the Stone Age, just above the level of typewriters, faxes and snail mail," says Rumizen (2002).

"Until recently, KM took a back seat to other management efforts, such as quality or performance management. However, as connectivity has improved and the economic leverage of knowledge has become valued, we have seen an increase in interest as management turns its attention to the value created by knowledge workers," according to Conway and Sligar (2002).

The broad acceptance of intranets and extranets as business process backbones, the growing sophistication of object technologies, the arrival of practical standards for data integration and meta-data management, and the entry into this space by the major IT companies are all collectively responsible for the increasing profile of Web-based KM initiatives, according to Natarajan and Shekhar (2000).

"The emergence of Internet and intranet technology has enabled knowledge management (KM) to acquire the kind of formidable possibilities that were previously not feasible," according to the authors. While KM is certainly much more than manipulation of technology, the possibility of effectively harnessing knowledge energies for better management has received a significant boost thanks to the rapid evolution in information, computation, and communication technologies. In Internet time and space, the speed of knowledge acquisition, transformation, and utilization has become critical for survival.

Success stories include Chevron's best practices conferencing mechanisms, Dow Chemicals' intellectual asset management system, PriceWaterhouse Coopers' AI-based tools for searching filings of public companies, Boston Consulting Group's Idea Creation Center, and Glaxo's internal benchmarking mechanisms.

The authors analyzed over 200 available KM tools. The XML family of technologies (via XSL, XLL, RDF, and DOM) is creating foundations of meta-data structures and standards that will ensure that multiple KM objects and KM initiatives are interfaceable at any point in time.

Web-flavored approaches to KM—based on intranets, groupware, and corporate portals—are presented by Applehans et al. (1999), Smith (2000), and Collins (2003).

In contrast to individual knowledge, organizational knowledge is a more complex and murky dynamic, involving socio-political factors of knowledge buying, selling, brokering, pricing, reciprocity, altruism, reputation, and trust, according to Davenport and Prusak (2003).

Successful codification is implemented via a knowledge taxonomy which is suited for different knowledge types and attributes and is aligned with business goals, as well as narratives and rhetorical devices for communicating knowledge behaviors. This can include external knowledge (e.g., competitive intelligence), structured internal knowledge (e.g., research reports), and informal internal knowledge (e.g., know-how databases).

Good examples include British Petroleum's Knowledge Highway, Monsanto's Knowledge Management Architecture for structured and unstructured content, Microsoft's Skills Planning and Development structure of knowledge and competencies, and various corporate yellow pages.

Technology like e-mail, groupware, digital archives, search engines, and videoconferencing are particularly important in knowledge transfer and innovation for globally dispersed organizations where the barriers of distance, time, and cost do not allow for frequent face-to-face meetings. Particularly in these contexts, "technology enables new knowledge behaviours."

"Networks and desktop computers, with their ability to connect people and store and retrieve virtually unlimited amounts of content, can dramatically improve knowledge market efficiency," according to Davenport and Prusak (2003).

"The availability of certain technologies such as Lotus Notes and the World Wide Web was instrumental in catalysing the KM movement. Since knowledge and the value of harnessing it have always been with us, it must be the availability of these new technologies that has stoked the knowledge fire," the authors explain.

Such technologies include artificial intelligence and expert systems, editorially annotated knowledge repositories, meta-data tags, and longer term analytical systems. Specific instances include HP's Network News and Chrysler's Engineering Book of Knowledge based on Notes, McDonnell Douglas's expert system for aircraft landing positioning, and Monsanto's distribution of external news updates via GrapeVINE.

The authors caution against a technology-centered KM approach, but argue that a technology ingredient is a necessary ingredient for successful KM projects. "Without an approach to managing structured knowledge, organisational learning is too conceptual and abstract to make a long-term difference to organisations," the authors explain.

Tools for Knowledge Processes

Gamble and Blackwell (2001) provide a useful KM matrix, a table with knowledge types on one axis (embedded, embodied, represented) and knowledge processes on the other axis (sense, organize, socialize, internalize). Accordingly, there are numerous KM activities (and enabling technologies) that arise, such as datamining, knowledge surveys, knowledge taxonomization, groupware, e-learning, and workflow analysis.

Keen and Mackintosh (2001) explore the use of handheld wireless devices in workflows to mobilize knowledge and provide "anytime anywhere any-device" access to intellectual assets and human expertise. "The knowledge mobilization opportunity using wireless technologies is so huge that no company can afford not to grab it fast and hard," according to the authors. This applies to external competitive/regulatory intelligence, structured internal knowledge, and especially informal internal knowledge.

"Mobile accessible information puts knowledge to work right at the demand points. Mobile technologies enhance communication, information and collaboration, the three cornerstones of knowledge building and usage," according to Keen and Mackintosh (2001).

"For knowledge workers, knowledge is simultaneously an input, medium and output for their work," according to Newell et al. (2002), who view modern firms more as "orchestras."

"ICT systems are increasingly widespread as enabling technologies for the processing of knowledge; furnishing knowledge *inputs* in the form of software systems; providing the *medium* for knowledge work through the development of email, groupware and intranet technologies; and becoming the means for capturing the *output* of knowledge work in the shape of ICT-based artefacts and presentations," the authors observe.

ICTs are simultaneously social and physical artifacts. ICTs play an important role in the globalization of business, inter-organizational networking, and cross-functional project teams. Structuring of KM architecture should allow for the complex nature of knowledge, which can often be uncertain, difficult to capture, dynamically changing, highly context dependent, expensive to codify, and too politically sensitive to make explicit. Care must be taken to roll out a KM system with a specific purpose in mind; otherwise there is a danger of information overload, increased bureaucracy, and excessive stockpiling of purposeless knowledge.

The authors identify different KM strategies and tools for the various phases of innovation. "Innovation involves different episodes. These can be identified as agenda formation, selection, implementation, and routinisation. These are not linear and sequential but are, more often, overlapping, iterative and recursive," according to the authors.

Each phase calls for different KM strategies and metrics. Key factors which play a role here include cognitive perceptions, social relations, and organizational politics. For instance, knowledge acquisition is a primary activity at the agenda formation stage and is based on a networking approach. Knowledge creation via a community approach is critical in the selection phase, and knowledge storage and reuse based on a cognitive approach are vital for the routinization stage.

Nonaka and Nishiguchi (2001) maintain that knowledge must be "nurtured" rather than "managed." New IT platforms and tools along with human-oriented approaches can help greatly in knowledge-sharing processes: CAD/CAM/CAE (which improve the efficiency of product developers' inductive, deductive, and abductive reasoning processes), simulation (to encourage experimentation), and prototyping (to refine solution models).

Cross-border knowledge creation within multinational companies involves IT platforms; identification of centers of excellence; customer/partner alliances; links with expert organization/universities/think tanks; and a mix of short-, medium-, and long-term movements of people across borders.

Dispersed innovation centers in countries around the globe are leading to joint knowledge creation at local and global levels in multinational corporations, which thus function as knowledge-creating networks. Nonaka identifies this cross-border synergistic process as "global knowledge creation" and sees it as the key process of globalization.

Dixon (2000) identifies five key categories of lesson sharing in large companies: serial transfer, near transfer, far transfer, strategic transfer, and expert transfer. They differ in terms of who the intended knowledge receiver is (same or different from the source), the nature of the task involved (frequency and routine), and the type of knowledge being transferred (tacit/explicit).

Examples of near transfer include Ford's Best Practice Replication in the vehicle operations division (each plant receives five to eight best practices per week via the intranet), Texas Instruments' Alert Notification System for wafer fabrication yields (managed via e-mail and newsgroups on the "ShareIt" intranet site), and Ernst & Young's PowerPacks (collections of best proposals, presentations, and articles pushed from the corporate KnowledgeWeb databases onto consultants' laptops).

Examples of far transfer include Chevron's Capital Project Management (with online forums as well as physical movement of project managers to spread learned lessons across the company).

Examples of expert transfer include Buckman Lab's TechForums (started in 1992, monitored by librarians and sysops, and supported by editorial help in producing weekly summaries of discussions), Tandem Computer's Second Class Mail (for tech support), Chevron's Best Practices Resource Map (a yellow pages of employee resources), the World Bank's internal help line, and Ernst & Young's Knowledge Stewards. Online infrastructure is critical here for multinationals, and there can be accessibility, affordability, and reliability problems on this front in emerging economies.

There are six key attributes of knowledge which must be factored into KM practices, according to Kluge et al. (2001):

1. Subjectivity (context and individual background shape the interpretation of knowledge)
2. Transferability (knowledge can be extracted and transferred to other contexts)
3. Embeddedness (knowledge is often in a static and buried form that makes it difficult to extract or reformulate)
4. Self-reinforcement (the value of knowledge increases, instead of decreases, when shared)
5. Perishability (knowledge can become outdated)
6. Spontaneity (knowledge can develop unpredictably in a process)

Best practice KM techniques for dealing with embedded knowledge include knowledge databases, corporate yellow pages, and co-location of staff. Finnish metal group Outokumpu has a solid IT infrastructure to make it easier to find knowledge among its staff. Self-reinforcement knowledge networking practices for jump-starting the knowledge value chain include online training, alignment with partner IT systems, and easy access for service data.

As for spontaneity in knowledge creation, it is certainly difficult to "create creativity," but quite possible to ensure that the frequency of valuable knowledge generation can be increased via creativity techniques, Internet access for all staff, and ideas contests. Ford lets its employees "log on and tune in" via the Internet—all its employees get free Internet access at home.

"The less successful companies do not realize the opportunities that a modern and open IT infrastructure can bring in terms of searching and scanning external knowledge pools," according to the authors.

"Just as no company will probably survive without taking advantage of the opportunities offered by the Internet, soon no worker will survive without actively using knowledge as a tool of their trade, whatever trade that is, and no company will succeed without tapping into the great potential of their employees' knowledge," the authors recommend.

"You must instil in your company a sense of caring for knowledge so that it becomes part of everyday life, rather than something that ebbs and flows as the mood suits," Kluge et al. advise.

Mertins et al. (2003) survey the numerous frameworks (e.g., benefits tree) that have evolved for tracing knowledge benefits to organizational benefits and for assessing intellectual capital growth (e.g., Celemi intangible assets monitor, balanced scorecard, Skandia navigator, value-chain scoreboard).

Their book has over a hundred pages of case studies of KM in action. Arthur D. Little's intranet, ADL-Link, serves as a portal for accessing case abstracts. At a continental level, the European Commission's Information Society Technologies Program calls for radical transformations of organizations in Europe to meet the KM challenge. It supports "innovation ecologies" via initiatives like the European KM Forum (www.knowledgeboard.com). It promotes knowledge co-creation in the public sector, as well as in NGOs and SMEs, in multiple languages. Workshops are held on topics like KM toolkits, with the message "If we share, we can win."

Content Strategies

Beerli et al. (2003) compare and contrast the codification ("stocks") approach to content management with the connection or personalization ("flows") approach of bringing employees together for project work. "Companies using the codification strategy are facing the problem of information overflow and the increasing difficulty of structuring the vast collections of documents. On the other hand, those adopting only the personalization strategy cannot cope with the challenge of speed in the new economy," according to the authors.

They also address the important issue of quality of information assets (via three parameters: comprehension, contextualization, valuation) in work environments of tight budgets, pressures on time, shortening half-lives of knowledge, and rapidly changing classifications or indexes. Information in such settings must be useful, usable, dependable, sound, well defined, unambiguous, reputable, timely, concise, and contextualized.

"Organizations are expanding their KM initiatives to provide meaningful and timely information to end users by creating processes that identify, collect, categorise and refresh content using a common taxonomy across the organisation," according to Hasanali and Leavitt (2003). The content templates and taxonomy must be customer driven and domain driven. The content architecture for KM must be devised by a cross-disciplinary team. Planners must keep in mind that technology implementation costs can run up to twice the application purchase costs, the authors advise.

Search

Sullivan (2004) addresses enterprise search tools. Knowledge workers typically search for answers in unstructured as well as structured information stores. Knowledge repositories range from e-mail folders and documents to databases and external Web resources. "Enterprise search requires an integrated architecture spanning content repositories, middleware connectivity, search engines and user interfaces," according to Sullivan.

Search engine technologies are becoming more sophisticated and diverse: popularity based, affinity based, context driven, Bayesian inferencing, natural language, case based, multilingual, multimedia, peer-to-peer, personalized, and visually mapped. Objects searched range from structured (e.g., presentations) to unstructured (e.g., e-mail, as in the case of Hill & Knowlton and Texaco, with vendors like Tacit, eManage, eRoom, and Intraspect).

Search systems can be either centralized or federated (with multiple search engines in a distributed environment). Search criteria include frequency of words, location of words, co-occurrence of terms, and presence in meta-data fields. Search quality is usually measured with two metrics: precision (focusing on relevant documents only) and recall (not missing any relevant documents). More sophisticated search systems will also keep track of a user's search behavior and even correlate it with that of other users, thus providing useful suggestions or recommendations where relevant. Such monitoring and tracking can also aid other KM tasks like refining knowledge taxonomies, knowledge gap analysis, expertise directories, peer networks, and social network analysis.

Tools and Knowledge Taxonomy

Data management vocabulary, descriptive taxonomies, and navigational taxonomies of an interactive and evolving nature are crucial components of knowledge taxonomy, according to Conway and Sligar (2002). "Maintaining a taxonomy is an oft-overlooked requirement and an underestimated cost," the authors caution. Sources of taxonomy can range from industry taxonomies and clustering technologies to search engine query logs and subject matter experts.

Change control measures are needed to keep the vocabularies "in sync" and in step with domain changes—for instance, via a taxonomy committee or advisory board. A mix of centralized and decentralized approaches ensures speed, interoperability, and elimination of redundancy.

Taxonomies can also improve search engine recall. For instance, Microsoft ranks most appropriate answers to user questions as "Best Hits." Microsoft in-house staff manage the bulk of taxonomy development and maintenance; some tagging is outsourced.

Networked KM

Allee (2003) addresses the growth of distributed webs of business relationships, increasing trends toward outsourcing, digital infostructure, and new ethical underpinnings of success. The enterprise webs of Cisco, Dell, and Nike and the referral networks of Amazon are good examples on this front.

Organizations must learn to deal not just with complicated systems, but with complex systems, which requires thinking with multiple lenses and multiple minds and resorting to the use of simplexities (or foundational elements of complex systems). Three levels of practice emerge: operational (e.g., using the Internet, portals, and databases of best practices), tactical (e.g., knowledge networking via CoPs), and strategic (e.g., via business modeling, intangibles, scorecards).

"The Internet is the backbone of the Knowledge Economy. It is a vast web of conversations and exchanges," says Allee; it is changing business in dramatic ways, and it collects as well as connects information and people. At the same time, the best technology infrastructure in the world cannot overcome other cultural and structural barriers to value creation.

Allee uses a "holo-mapping" technique in illuminating benefits of intangible knowledge and value exchanges such as sense of community, customer loyalty, and market savviness. This modeling can be used for exchange analysis (unearthing coherent patterns, imbalances, and optimal flows), impact analysis (creation of benefit), and value creation analysis (creation and extension of value).

An important function is programmatic, unobtrusive discovery of experts in networked environments, based on datamining of author submissions and communication. Microsoft uses the Netscan tool to display "sociograms" which relate users to those they reply to and those who reply to them. Newer approaches are based on Web services technology.

Web-based connectivity platforms have helped organizations develop extensive external collaborative links for knowledge work, as in the case of Intel, Dupont, Cisco, Sainsbury, and Embraer (what KM writer David Skyrme refers to as "k-business").

Collaboration

The key to successful KM is devising appropriate socio-technical systems, according to Davenport and Prost (2002). They profile KM practices and tools in the Siemens group of companies. Siemens Industrial Services, with 22,000 people in over 70 countries, uses a knowledge-sharing tool called Know-How Exchange to connect experts, employees, and their diverse project experiences. Areas of expertise here include engineering layouts, project structures, plant building, and contract negotiation for automotive and textile plants. The Knowledge Web learning portal includes abstracts of relevant literature and a Web board for discussion.

The KM practice at Siemens Medical Solutions, KnowledgeSharing@MED, involves the KnowledgeSquare know-how database, People@MED expert pages, and mobile solutions for sales representatives to access key information on handheld devices.

Knowledge Portals

The enterprise knowledge portal helps provide consistent views of the organizations, personalized access for employees, layered presentation, cross-media communication, improved involvement, and learning behaviors for quick adaptation to changed surroundings, according to Collins (2003).

Collins provides a sample questionnaire with 45 items covering issues ranging from success indicators and process improvement to mentoring roles and employee empowerment. These can then be cross-tallied and ranked in a table which includes IT-enabled tools (e.g., messaging, mining, balanced scorecard), depending on whether the features are viewed as *critical*, *must have*, *important*, and *nice to have*. The output of this analysis will be a request for a proposal to portal vendors.

Corporate portals offer a powerful capability for companies to embark on significant business model transformations and leverage collective intelligence, according to Terra and Gordon (2003). KM is a step beyond information management with respect to dimensions like context, validation, and human referencing. It involves components which are strategic (e.g., intellectual capital management, organizational core competencies) and tactical (e.g., knowledge creation and transfer mechanisms, KM roles, incentive measures).

The authors provide 11 KM case studies of portal implementation, where the goals for each case study are rated as primary, secondary, or not relevant, in 6 categories of intent: communications (internal and external), pushing information to employees (e.g., frontliners), knowledge reuse (e.g., expertise maps), collaboration (CoPs), human capital management (improve retention, get new employees up to speed quickly), and external relationships (reduce customer service costs).

For instance, e-business solutions provider Context Integration launched a KM platform called Intellectual Assets Network (IAN) in 1997, initially based on Lotus Notes and Verity. It has developed a client collaboration environment called PETE (Project Enablement Team Environment). Parts of the system can be downloaded to employee laptops. The portal links to introductory documents called roadmaps, learning documents called Curriculum Paths, and project artifacts.

Eli Lilly's KM team has 12 members for Web development, 6 members for process, 30 members for external content, and 7 members for architecting internal content. The portal called My ELVIS is based on Plumtree and Semio, vendors who were asked to develop prototypes. The KM effort for accelerated innovation cost $5 million and draws lots of repeat traffic. Subject matter experts play an important role in devising the content taxonomy.

Each business unit at public relations firm Hill & Knowlton has a KM coordinator and five regional KM executives. The intranet and client extranet were established in 2000, based on Intraspect. In 2001, portal integraton with CRM and other legacy applications was started. Employees can now come up to speed in a third of the original time. Best practices are archived as "Bestsellers" and help improve client focus and service. A key challenge is evolution of content taxonomy for local needs.

Brazilian government IT services firm SERPRO first conducted a knowledge mapping exercise over 2 months involving 30 internal consultants to identify macro processes, business themes, knowledge domains, and subjects. The portal is used to devise tailored HR programs for new hires.

Texaco launched a formal KM initiative called Knowledge Highway in 1999. The core application, PeopleNet, has 40 communities with inputs from 5,000 people. "Today's Featured People" profiles two individuals daily. Tacit's KnowledgeMail product is used to track employees' latest areas of conversation and expertise via e-mail profiling. Experts validate shared best practices, whose usage is tracked online; $100 million in benefits have been realized already. Knowledge continues to be "divulged and celebrated."

"Knowledge-intensive firms are becoming more and more like media companies. This means that content publishing is increasingly becoming a core skill and responsibility of not only communications departments but also of many knowledge workers and, ultimately, senior executives. Indeed, 'virtual publishing models' have emerged in very large organisations, such as Nortel, Motorola and Allied Irish Bank. They usually consist of a core dedicated team that sets editorial and technology standards and coordinates a wide team of publishers scattered across different departments, business units and locations," according to the authors.

"The enterprise information portal (EIP) movement can be seen as only the latest stage in a continuing trend toward achieving enterprise information or knowledge integration—a trend that has fuelled data warehousing and enterprise resource planning (ERP) sales, and is now beginning to fuel EAI, KM and EIP implementations," according to Firestone (2003).

"An EKP is a type of EIP. It is an EIP that is goal-directed toward knowledge production, knowledge integration, and KM focused on enterprise business processes and also focuses on, provides, produces, and manages information about the validity of the information that it provides," Firestone defines.

A true EKP would record the history of the competitive struggle among knowledge claims put forward to solve problems within the enterprise, whereas the EIP need not record such history. No product has as yet met the EKP definition requirements of Firestone, who decries the "cavalier" use of KM language by many IT vendors who view only a portion of the proverbial KM elephant.

Four chapters in Firestone's book cover evaluation of 23 enterprise portal products, divided into four categories: decision processing portal products (Business Objects, Cognos), content management portal products (Plumtree, Autonomy, Oracle, Enfish, Netegrity, Citrix, Verity, Sun ONE, Corechange), collaborative portal products (TheBrain, Open Text, Intraspect, IBM/Lotus), and decision processing portal products (Hummingbird, Viador, CA, Brio, Sybase, TIBCO, Hyperwave). Trends to watch in the future, according to Firestone, will be increasing multifunctionality, interface integration around cognitive maps, personalized workflow, XML-assisted connectivity, and collaborative commerce.

KM Tools and e-Learning

New technology environments—particularly the Internet, intranet, and wireless media—are transforming the very way knowledge is experienced and transformed, triggering a cascading cycle of reinvention of education (e.g., just-in-time learning) and organizational collaboration (e.g., tradecraft knowledge mobilization via handheld devices), according to Norris et al. (2003).

Within enterprises, the original concept of KM has evolved to broader notions of knowledge ecology, knowledge experiences, knowledge habitats, and knowledge marketplaces. Visualization tools, knowledge blogs ("klogs"), P2P (people-to-people) collaboration tools, and semantic searches are interesting developments on this front. "Over time, the strategic importance of fusing e-learning and knowledge management will become abundantly clear to policy makers and practitioners alike," the authors predict.

Today's vertical channels for e-content include book publishers, learning management systems (e.g., WebCT, Blackboard, Click2Learn, Outstart), universities, trade associations, and professional societies. These will be impacted by the activities of standards and consortia like the IMS Global Learning Consortium, Dublin Core, ebXML, and ODRL.

Professional societies like the American Association of Pharmaceutical Scientists have a knowledge portal which offers digitized journal content, e-mail news alerts, and online CoPs for lifelong learning. Industry-wide sharing is also emerging, as with the German manufacturing industry's CoPs partnership with the Fraunhofer Institute. Notable KM examples on the e-government front include the United Kingdom's e-Envoy knowledge communities and Australia's National Office of the Information Economy.

The University of Wisconsin offers portal-centric graduate learning, customized forms of learning and assessment ("e-pedagogy"), personal intelligent agents, lifelong access to a body of knowledge, greater involvement in professional societies, and fusion of internship experiences with formal learning. The Monterrey Tech System (ITESM) offers connected learning services to ten different countries in Latin America. The IEEE Computer Society offers e-knowledge marketplaces, blended learning, perpetual knowledge refreshment, and certification programs.

"Most persons in knowledge-rich enterprises will discover significant roles as both providers and consumers of e-knowledge," the authors predict. Organizations active in standards and meta-data for e-content, learner objects, and workflow specification include MERLOT, Open Knowledge Initiative, Learning Federation, Learning Objects Network, Global Knowledge Economics Council, HR-XML Consortium, IMS Global Learning Consortium, Open Knowledge Initiative, Workflow Management Coalition, and the Web services movement. The authors predict that horizontal e-knowledge marketplaces (e.g., SMETE, XanEdu) will achieve substantial market penetration by the end of the decade.

"Internet culture drives the e-knowledge industry," according to the authors; this includes academic, entrepreneurial, communitarian, and big-business cultures. "Communities of practice will become reorganised as the predominant organisational form in the e-Knowledge Economy. They will be the epicentre of autonomic learning and the development of individual and organisational capabilities," the authors predict.

Enterprise KM will be driven by "experience gateways" which can bypass knowledge silos and legacy IT systems. CoPs will seamlessly link to business processes. "The goal is to reinvent the conversational space of the enterprise," the authors advise.

Enterprises will have to reinvent their knowledge ecosystems, including infrastructure and cultures. Challenges will arise in overcoming the digital divide (e.g., between digital natives and digital immigrants), moving beyond digitizing and "Webifying" and creating new vocabularies and standards (technical, legal, financial).

Specialized KM Tools and Applications

Thanks to the rapidly falling costs of communication, the Web has been instrumental in catalyzing opportunities for knowledge sharing via connection and collection strategies and specialized applications, according to Ahmed et al. (2002).

Ford's C3P program (CAD/CAM/CAE product information management) aims at integration of knowledge bases right into the design tools, where design processes will be embedded with information related to costs and manufacturing.

The 200-year-old UK Post Office has conscious KM efforts that include expertise yellow pages and knowledge interviews (KIs) designed by psychologists, which are used to capture mental models of employees and processes. The interview maps cover employee contacts in the organization, learning points, values, information sources, views of changes in the economy and organization, and behavior.

Singapore Airlines, with a commitment to continuous improvement, uses KM in the form of dynamic modeling and operations research techniques to forecast demand based on historical travel patterns and current booking trends. A Staff Ideas Action Scheme ensures that feedback from frontline employees is put forward for service improvement.

KM Tools: Selection, Integration, and Deployment

Tiwana (2002) outlines a "Knowledge Management Toolkit," a practical ten-step roadmap to KM implementation. At the same time, KM is not a "fix-it-all" technology, not just a smarter intranet, not a seductive silver-bullet solution, not a canned approach, and not a one-time investment, Tiwana cautions.

The ten steps of Tiwana's KM roadmap can be grouped into the following four phases: infrastructure evaluation, KM system development, deployment, and evaluation. Technology enablers must be harnessed for knowledge finding (e.g., search, employee yellow pages), creation (collaboration), packaging (digital publishing), applying (classification), validation (CoPs), and reuse (project record databases).

A pilot deployment is highly recommended, followed by cumulative releases (according to the RDI or results-driven incremental methodology). An early proof of concept helps avoid a future goof of concept, Tiwana jokes. "Strive for iterative perfection and avoid over-engineering," he advises.

These points are illustrated with examples throughout the chapters, in sidebars and boxes. For instance, semiconductor company GASonics moved from paper to digital information to improve search and customization of research reports. Some companies tend to prefer codification methods (e.g., Gartner Group, Delta Airlines, Oracle, Dell, HP), while others prefer personalization (e.g., McKinsey, Boston Consulting, Rand Corporation) for knowledge sharing.

Texas Instruments invested heavily in content management systems and meta-data. Rolls Royce's migration from paper to digital documentation cut down paper costs, improved productivity, enhanced data processing, and reduced maintenance time for aircraft engines. Monsanto has deployed Plumtree's knowledge server product along with organization-wide process changes. Platinum Technology experienced information overload after multiple acquisitions and redesigned its processes for managing explicit and tacit knowledge. Enhancements were implemented upon user suggestions to improve sales force productivity.

Dow Chemical uses Microsoft NetMeeting for Web conferencing across 37 countries. British Petroleum uses videoconferencing for real-time transfer of contextual information between employees across continents. Procter & Gamble facilitates Web-enabled knowledge sharing via its MarketingNet digital library.

KM Tools: Implications for HR

On the technology front, IT plays a key role through real-time HR information systems (HRIS), ubiquitous access to information, expert systems, smart self-service, and customization tools, according to Lengnick-Hall and Lengnick-Hall (2003). HR can play a facilitative role in KM along two dimensions: the object view (codified knowledge or "knowledge stocks") and the process view ("knowledge flows" or CoPs).

Active management of knowledge assets and continuous learning among employees (along with a focused direction) need to be facilitated, and knowledge exchange needs to be brokered via online and offline (hi-tech and low-tech) mechanisms as well as incentive schemes. In an interesting case study, Westinghouse had to launch a crucial HR intervention to ensure that employees understood that a new ERP system was actually in the best interests of the company even though it disrupted its decentralized structure.

Sectoral and Regional KM

Quinn (2002) addresses KM potential and practices in the news media. He identifies a wide variety of approaches such as better newsroom design to facilitate easier communication between journalists and editors, learning from the habits of librarians and information scientists, a professional culture of teamwork and collaboration, software tools for sharing and repackaging of information (such as interview notes, contact information, source documents, news tips), a well-maintained intranet and digital library, use of structuring languages such as XML for multi-purposed content, and familiarity with new devices.

Useful tools in this regard include Xybernaut wearable computer gear (which allows reporters to plug into workflows at all times), Newsgear multimedia toolkits for journalists, NewsEngin's SourceTracker (to enable reporters to organize and index interview notes, e-mail messages, documents, reports), computer-assisted reporting, GIS-based analysis (to unearth regional trends via datamining and mapping), and IFRA's Advanced Journalist Technology Project (to research digital multimedia tools). The Newsplex at the University of Southern Carolina is a prototype news center showcasing the latest news tools and information management platforms.

Intranets can play an important role in archival management and collaborative activities for KM in newsrooms, says Quinn. It can assist in organization of research material, can help reporters in the field feel more connected to the newsroom, can cut communication costs for distributed workforces, and can share useful software tools. Many newspapers already leverage intranets to access their archives or feeds from partner news organizations, parliamentary transcripts, yellow pages, maps, news backgrounders, editorial guidelines, and even contact information for translators. "Knowledge management provides a tool for journalists to work smarter in the 21st century," Quinn urges.

Unfortunately, newspapers are generally conservative and have typically not been at the forefront of most technologies or of management approaches like KM. Many journalists tend to work individually rather than collectively. Managers of news companies have often found it difficult to engage in "coopetition" with rivals.

Rao (2003a) addresses KM strategies and tools in the infotech sector, as summarized in Sidebar 2 (KM tools in the pharmaceutical sector are covered in Sidebar 3). Wimmer (2002) charts new territory at the KM frontier in public sector and government agencies, in areas like smart citizen services and better administrative decision-making. Rao (2002) highlights the role of sectoral cooperation for collective knowledge generation by the IT industry in India. KM practices of some Asian IT companies are identified as well.

Rosenberg (2002) analyzes how "Silicon Valley clones" or clusters of knowledge industries are emerging and faring in Cambridge, Bangalore, Singapore, Helsinki, Tel Aviv, and Hsinchu. Many success factors of Silicon Valley are being replicated in these cities to nurture IT industries: business webs, IT-savvy local population, local "living laboratories," activities and organizations for communities of interest, merger and acquisition (M&A) activity for flow of skilled labor and intellectual property, local academic and research institutes, and commercial partnerships between academia and industry.

The collection of essays by Malhotra (2001) also offers broader insights into how KM practices can differ according to the nature of the organization: project based (e.g., construction industry), umbrella corporations (e.g., GE), virtual business communities (e.g., the Linux movement on the Internet), and the multidirectional network (e.g., lobbies of small and medium-sized enterprises (SME) in Taiwan). Knowledge capital can even be assessed at the national economic level, while planning for growth and performance for the entire country. For instance, going beyond measures of gross domestic product (GDP), a joint Swedish-Israeli study assessed Israel's intellectual assets in 1997.

Challenges to KM Tool Usage

One of the classic works in the field of computer-mediated workspaces addresses the "social life of information" (Brown and Duguid, 2000). The authors focus on the holistic context of social and technological systems within which any knowledge activities take place; "the way forward is paradoxically to look not ahead, but to look around," they advise. They caution against a "tunnel vision" focus only on tools and recommend that other knowledge ecology factors like work conversations and even office space design be included as well.

Though IT-based tools for KM can deliver significant benefit if properly planned, IT investments have not always been in lock-step with productivity increases, according to Malhotra (2001). For instance, ERP implementations led to an unprecedented level of information sharing across organizational functions, but straitjacketed the information flexibility of information processing for each of the locked-in functions.

Some current KM approaches have not dealt adequately with the "creative abrasion and creative conflict" that are necessary for business model innovation today. KM should embody the organizational processes that seek synergistic combination of data and information-processing capacity of information technologies on the one hand and the creative and innovative capacity of human beings on the other, Malhotra advocates.

Management strategies need to shift from command and control to sense and respond. KM processes should be focused on doing the right thing (effectiveness), not just doing the thing right (efficiency). KM is not merely about "bottling water from rivers of data," but about "giving people canoes and compasses" to navigate in these rivers of data. Instead of just codified best practices and enterprise portals, the emphasis should be on unlearning ineffective best practices and the continuous refinement and pursuit of better practices as well.

KM practices and tools can differ according to the nature of the organization: project based (e.g., construction industry), umbrella corporations (e.g., GE), virtual business communities (e.g., the Linux movement on the Internet), and the multidirectional network (e.g., lobbies of SMEs in Taiwan).

In terms of new approaches to knowledge work, Malhotra advocates a movement away from hi-tech hidebound KM systems to ones of more creative chaos, greater social interaction, playfulness in organizational choices, and strategic planning as anticipation of surprise.

"As the Web becomes more pervasive in everyday productivity, knowledge workers recognize intranet technology as a unique and fast way to gather, track and share information quickly. But the big picture should never be lost when combining information fragments into an enterprise KM system," according to Honeycutt (2000).

"Technology enthusiasts can be proud of what they have accomplished and of the number of successful Internet users, but deeper insights will come from understanding the problems of frustrated users and of those who have stayed away," according to Shneiderman (2003), who challenges IT developers to build products that better support human needs in areas ranging from creativity to conflict resolution. He provides a useful matrix of activities and relationships, with activities like informing, communicating, innovating, and disseminating on one axis and relationships with the self, family/friends, colleagues/neighbors, and citizens/markets on the other axis. This matrix can provide the basis for understanding current IT tools and projecting opportunities for new ones in various occupational settings.

In sum, social and IT tools have received significant attention in the KM literature. This book, however, is the first to pool together case studies, learnings, and recommendations about KM tools as told by KM practitioners themselves; it also draws overall lessons from these case studies and contextualizes them in the backdrop of the vast body of KM publications.

KM Tools: Uses, Impacts, and Frameworks

Having reviewed the literature on KM tools and surveyed various uses of KM tools in organizations around the world, let us dip into some detailed frameworks and methodologies for understanding the contributions and impact of IT platforms on knowledge work and use these frameworks to better contextualize the findings of the next section's practitioner reports on KM tool design and usage. Depending on organizational strategy, culture, technical skills, and knowledge requirements (in terms of knowledge assets, processes, and communities), a number of KM tools can be appropriately integrated and deployed.

KM tools and technologies are one of the many planks of successful KM practice. The KM analysis in this book series is based on the author's "8 Cs" framework (parameters which begin with the letter C, see Table 1.1): connectivity, content, community, culture, capacity, cooperation, commerce, and capital. In other words, successful KM practices can be facilitated by adequate employee access to KM tools, user-friendly work-oriented content, CoPs, a culture of knowledge, learning capacity, a spirit of cooperation, commercial and other incentives, and carefully measured capital investments and returns. While the bulk of this book focuses on KM tools, it should be stressed again that the analysis is within this overall framework of culture, cooperation, and IT platforms.

In work environments increasingly permeated by Internet, intranet, and wireless platforms, IT tools are becoming an important mediator in the way knowledge is experienced, described, gathered, processed, stored, retrieved, and distributed. Digital

Table 1.1

KM Framework: The "8 Cs" Audit	
1. Connectivity	What connectivity devices, bandwidths, interfaces, technologies, and tools do your knowledge workers access when they are in the office or on the road?
2. Content	What knowledge assets are relevant to the context of your workflow, and what are your strategies for codification, classification, archival, retrieval, usage, and tracking?
3. Community	What are the core communities of practice aligned with your business, and what organizational support do you have for identifying, nurturing, and harnessing them?
4. Culture	Does your organization have a culture of learning where your employees thirst for knowledge, trust one another, and have visible support from their management?
5. Capacity	What are your strategies for building knowledge-centric capacity in your employees, for instance, via workshops, white papers, mentoring, and e-learning?
6. Cooperation	Do your employees have a spirit of open cooperation, and does your organization cooperate on the KM front with business partners, industry consortia, and universities?
7. Commerce	What commercial and other incentives do you use to promote your KM practice? How are you "pricing" the contribution, acceptance, and usage of knowledge assets?
8. Capital	What percentage and amount of your revenues are invested in your KM practices, and how are you measuring their usage and benefits in monetary and qualitative terms?
Source: Rao, 2003a.	

Table 1.2

Properties of Knowledge Activities and Assets				
	Interactivity	**Bandwidth**	**Structure**	**Reusability**
Documents	Nil	Low	High	High
E-mail	Medium	Low-medium	High	High
Phone	High	Medium	Low	Low
Meetings	Very high	Very high	Low-medium	Low
Presentations	Medium	High	High	Low-medium
Workshops	Very high	Very high	Medium	Low
E-learning	Medium	Low-medium	High	High
Coaching	Very high	Very high	Low	Very low

Source: Adapted from Gamble and Blackwell (2001).

Table 1.3

IT Tools Classified by Time of Collaboration and Location of Participants		
	Same time (synchronous)	**Different time (asynchronous)**
Same place (co-located)	Instant polling, presentations	Shared infrastructure (e.g., workstations)
Different place (remote)	Chat, messaging, videoconferencing	E-mail, workflow

Source: Author.

assets (e.g., digital documents) and online activities (e.g., e-learning) in knowledge work differ in significant ways from their traditional ("analog") counterparts (e.g., paper books and face-to-face meetings), as summarized in Table 1.2.

Knowledge transfer cost versus efficacy trade-offs will necessarily need to be factored in with respect to interactivity, bandwidth, structure, and reusability in designing knowledge-sharing environments and activities. Most organizations use a blend of online tools and traditional knowledge activities in their KM practice, e.g., a mix of digital documents and print brochures or a hybrid model of mentoring with coaching and e-learning.

This is particularly true for the multilocation or globally dispersed organization of the 21st century, where employees often need to collaborate across multiple time zones. Depending on the time of collaborative activity and the location of the knowledge workers, a number of configurations of IT tools can be leveraged, as summarized in Table 1.3. For instance, e-mail is well suited for asynchronous remote communication; digital whiteboards can be used for synchronous co-located collaboration.

In addition to the level of structure and degree of interactivity required for transfer, knowledge has a number of other dimensions and facets which need to be factored in by IT tools, as outlined in Table 1.4.

Table 1.4

Knowledge Dimensions, Facets, and Implications for IT Tools		
Knowledge dimensions	Facets	Implications for IT tools
Complexity	Tacit, explicit	There will be limits to the efficacy of IT tools for KM, but they continue to push the limits.
Domain	Technology, business, environment, sociology, etc.	IT tools should be applicable to all workers in all domain areas of knowledge.
Focus	Operational, strategic	IT-enabled business tools should be made available for analytics as well as transactions.
Perishability	Near-term, medium-term, long-term	IT tools must provide for version control and expiry dates of knowledge archives.
Granularity	Coarse, fine	IT tools must allow for layered presentation and access to knowledge base.
Source	People (individual, group, organization, public domain); process; respository (e.g., structured transaction patterns)	A range of IT tools must be available for personal KM, group activity, organizational KM, and business intelligence.
Legal status	Proprietary, copyrighted, licensed, free	IT tools must allow for authentication, verification, and security of knowledge asset access.
Medium	Oral, handwritten, text/ graphic/multimedia, digital	IT tools must allow for knowledge exchange and repurposing in multiple media formats.
Audience	One-on-one, one-to-many, many-to-one, many-to-many	A variety of IT tools such as publishing, Webcasting, listservs, and instant messaging should be available for knowledge workers.
Exchange	Synchronous/asynchronous, co-located/remote	Synchronous and asynchronous e-communication tools should be available (e.g., e-mail, videoconferencing).

Table 1.4 *continued*

Knowledge Dimensions, Facets, and Implications for IT Tools		
Knowledge dimensions	Facets	Implications for IT tools
Importance	Relevant, useful, critical, indispensable, unique, irrelevant	IT tools must allow knowledge assets to be ranked and rated by knowledge users and creators.
Ownership objective	Gratification, personal or organizational gain, service to citizens, service to humanity	IT tools must enable knowledge sharing under varying degrees of control and dissemination.
Application outcome	Efficiency, effectiveness, innovation	Metrics must be built into IT tools (e.g., measuring access time, paths).
Relationship to personality, culture	Fact/document/system oriented, people/ relationship oriented	IT tools must support codification and personalization approaches to knowledge work.
Source: Author.		

For instance, the perishability of some kinds of knowledge assets implies that the relevant KM tools must provide for version control and expiry dates of knowledge archives. For knowledge assets of a highly confidential or proprietary nature, KM tools must allow for authentication, verification, and security of knowledge object access. Depending on the size of the audience for knowledge transfer, KM tools must allow for one-on-one or one-to-many knowledge dissemination. If knowledge claims are to be assessed and validated in the course of knowledge work, KM tools must be used which can enable knowledge assets to be ranked and rated by knowledge users and creators.

Knowledge has unique static as well as dynamic properties, captured in "knowledge stock" and "knowledge flow" strategies addressing knowledge assets and knowledge processes, respectively. Typical KM processes include knowledge extraction, codification, retrieval, distribution, and personalization. A range of KM tools can be deployed to enable such processes, such as knowledge discovery, search, visualization, and collaboration, as mapped in Table 1.5, which also lists sample vendors for each tool type. For instance, portals are useful KM tools for knowledge distribution; companies like Plumtree have enterprise knowledge portal offerings.

KM system design and deployment thus requires identifying the key knowledge assets and processes required for organizational excellence and enabling them via the appropriate KM tools, change management programs, and capacity building.

Another way of classifying these knowledge processes is via the classic "knowledge spiral" model of Ikujiro Nonaka, who traces the continual evolution of organizational knowledge (both tacit and explicit) via a set of interactions of four kinds of processes: socialization, externalization, internalization, and combination.

Table 1.6 identifies the relevant KM tools for these four kinds of knowledge processes, ranging from virtual reality tools (for transfer of tacit knowledge) and

Table 1.5

IT Tools for KM Processes		
KM processes	**IT-enabled tools**	**Sample vendors**
Knowledge creation	Business intelligence, knowledge discovery, e-learning	Business Objects, Skillsoft, Orbital,
Knowledge codification	Content management system, document management, categorization, abstracting, taxonomy	Interwoven, Autonomy
Knowledge retrieval	Search, visualization	Google, AskJeeves, Inktomi, Inxight
Knowledge application	Workflow, collaboration, help desk	eRoom, Intraspect, PeopleLink
Knowledge distribution	Knowledge portal, agents	Plumtree, AskMe
Knowledge validation	Online expert communities, contribution valuation, assessment/rating/ranking/scoring	IBM
Knowledge tracking (of human experts)	E-mail mining, corporate yellow pages	Tacit
Knowledge personalization	Expertise locators, communication, conferencing, collaboration	AskMe
Full-spectrum KM	Complete KM suites	Hummingbird, Open Text, Verity, IBM

Source: Author.

Table 1.6

IT Tools in the Knowledge Spiral Model	
Socialization (tacit→tacit)	**Externalization (tacit→explicit)**
Webcams Videoconferencing Virtual reality tools	P2P networks Expert systems Online CoPs
Internalization (explicit→tacit)	**Combination (explicit→explicit)**
Knowledge databases E-learning Visualization	Abstracting Classification Clustering

Source: Adapted from Nonaka and Toshihiro (2001).

Table 1.7

Lessons Learned from Content Management Systems in KM Practices	
Phase	**Lessons learned**
Planning and design	Business case should be mission oriented; taxonomies should reflect the way employees work; external content procurement is best centralized; content audits are key; provide users with templates; ensure quick wins; plan for cultural and training issues; define roles clearly; balance strategy with tactics
System implementation	Prioritize audiences and satisfaction goals; precisely define business rules; content stewards are important; work with early adopters in initial stages
Maintenance and upgrades	Content maintenance is as important as creation; provide multiple paths to information, but identify appropriate ones as well; build metrics for return on investment (RoI)
IT	Content management should be partnered with IT, but driven by business; provide tech support; there is no single tech solution; analyze costs well
Other	Content management is never completed: prepare for change in business needs and technology; enterprise content should be integrated, not isolated
Source: Adapted from Hasanali and Leavitt (2003).	

content clustering (for processing of explicit knowledge) to expert systems (for externalizing tacit knowledge) and e-learning (for internalizing explicit knowledge).

The previous two sections of this chapter have highlighted some of the commonly used KM tools by practitioners in organizations around the world. Content management systems, search, enterprise portals, and online CoPs constitute the lion's share of KM tools in the literature reviewed and the practitioner reports.

In the case of KM tools based on content management, it is important that taxonomies reflect the way employees work. A well-planned content audit is key in this regard. The rollout of content tools should also be supported by adequate training and user support. These and other recommendations for content tools are summarized in Table 1.7.

Portals and content management systems will constitute the "face and place" of KM in online knowledge workplaces. A number of authors have addressed the goals and requirements of enterprise knowledge portals (EKPs). An EKP must be able to improve knowledge reuse, support CoPs, empower knowledge workers, provide information about knowledge validity, and be context sensitive. Other related goals and requirements of EKPs based on the work of seven KM book authors are summarized in Table 1.8.

The rise of networked environments in virtual workplaces spanning the intranet, virtual private networks (VPNs), and the global Internet is spawning a variety of new configurations of knowledge environments, sometimes including suppliers, distributors, and customers.

KM analysts at Accenture have identified a number of such knowledge networks, as summarized in Table 1.9. Each has a different requirement of social and IT tools

Table 1.8

Knowledge Portal Goals and Requirements		
KM book author	**Recommended requirements for knowledge-oriented portals and architectures**	**Typical goals of knowledge-oriented portals and architectures**
Jose Claudio Terra, Cindy Gordon	1. Improve communication (top down, bottom up) 2. Push knowledge to employees 3. Improve reuse of knowledge 4. Foster collaboration 5. Improve human capital management 6. Improve relationships	Facilitate employee suggestions, codify knowledge, develop expertise maps, support CoPs, train new employees, improve customer satisfaction
Heidi Collins	1. Be organized around work processes 2. Facilitate knowledge communication 3. Focus on the future 4. Support business objectives 5. Promote innovation 6. Maintain a knowledge-creating organization	Develop success indicators, continuous improvement, collective understanding, training opportunities, empowered knowledge workers, mentoring
Joseph Firestone	1. Goal directed toward knowledge production/integration/management 2. Provide information about validity of knowledge 3. Provide business meta-information 4. Distinguish knowledge from mere information 5. Can produce knowledge from information 6. Orient users toward knowledge rather than information	Knowledge workflow orientation, personalized access, tracking of knowledge claims, knowledge validation frameworks, integration of disparate applications, access to external and internal sources, incentive schemes
Thomas Koulopoulos, Carl Frappaolo	1. Context sensitive 2. User sensitive 3. Flexible 4. Heuristic 5. Suggestive	Ability to handle multiple knowledge forms, predictive or forecasting support, system behavior improves with time and usage

Table 1.8 *continued*

Knowledge Portal Goals and Requirements		
KM book author	**Recommended requirements for knowledge-oriented portals and architectures**	**Typical goals of knowledge-oriented portals and architectures**
Dan Sullivan	1. Focus on business processes 2. Emphasize ease of use 3. Ensure deep integration of applications 4. Plan for scalability of services 5. Develop strong security models	Help solve real business problems, search structured and unstructured data, provide meta-data for content and applications, locate expertise

Source: Adapted from Terra and Gordon (2003), Collins (2003), Firestone (2003), Koulopoulos and Frappaolo (1999), and Sullivan (2004).

Table 1.9

Types of Networked Environments and Appropriate IT Tools				
Type of knowledge network	**Characteristics**	**Examples**	**Management tools**	**IT tools**
Experiencing network	Direct exchange of experiences and knowledge, small networks, personal contacts	7–11 Japan	Workshops, meetings, active listening, storytelling	Synchronous communication tools, media-rich channels
Materializing network	Focus is on explicating knowledge of experts, strong project focus	Sharp	Knowledge maps, knowledge reviewers, creativity workshops	Workflow, group decisions, skill mining, clustering
Systematizing network	Systematically manages explicit knowledge, knowledge is not tightly coupled to relationships	Accenture	Common language, forums, knowledge roles, rewards	Document management, messaging, filtering, portals, collaboration,
Learning network	Explicit knowledge transformed to implicit, learning is a key process	Buckman Labs	Scenario learning, mentoring, simulation	Computer-based training/Web-based training (CBT/WBT), community tools, conferencing, whiteboarding

Source: Adapted from Beerli et al. (2003).

for KM. For instance, a systematizing network has a strong focus on explicit knowledge and is powered by KM tools for document management and filtering. On the other hand, a learning network places more emphasis on activities like mentoring and relies on KM tools like e-learning. It is possible, of course, for an organization to have more than one such networked environment, thus calling for a multiplicity of relevant KM tools.

In addition to content and portal tools, mechanisms for harnessing communities of practitioners and experts are key for successful KM. CoPs are unique combinations of three fundamental elements: domains (scope, identity), community (which creates the fabric of learning via relationships and interactions), and practice (frameworks, tools, vocabulary, documents), according to Wenger et al. (2002).

The rise of networked virtual environments, especially in globally dispersed organizations, has led to the rise of online CoPs, which in turn throw up a number of challenges and opportunities for KM tools usage. For instance, participating in face-to-face communities can be more conducive to trust and high-bandwidth knowledge exchange, but online communities can work around some of the traditional obstacles like discomfort with public speaking or discrimination based on physical traits. Some of these contrasts are summarized in Table 1.10. Many organizations tend to use a blend of online and offline interaction for CoPs.

CoPs go through several stages of development: potential, coalescing, maturing, stewardship, and transformation. Different KM roles arise in these stages, for instance,

Table 1.10

Online versus Offline Communities of Practice		
	Online communities	**Offline communities**
Ease of participation	Depends on group dynamics, but is relatively easy—users can just key in their comments	Depends on community design, group dynamics, comfort level with public speaking
Usefulness for globally dispersed organizations	Extremely useful; in fact, it is often the only effective and affordable networking solution	Difficult and expensive; but occasional (e.g., annual) meetings can be extremely productive, synergistic, and important for building trust
Reusability of discussion, archives	Very high	Low; special steps need to be taken for documentation, archives (e.g., recording, transcription)
Development of trust, bonds	Difficult	Easier
Tools applicable for analysis of knowledge behaviors	Datamining, clustering, social network analysis (interviews + real-time digital analysis)	Social network analysis (interviews)

Source: Author.

Table 1.11

Roles and Tools for Online Communities		
Knowledge roles	**Activities**	**Tools**
Knowledge consumer	Search, browse, access, apply, learn	Portal, search engine, workflow
Knowledge creator	Publish, improve, classify, discuss	Content management, authoring, taxonomy, online CoPs
Knowledge editor	Interviewing experts, storytelling, content management	Content management systems, taxonomy
Knowledge expert	Validate, certify, legitimize	Online CoPs, ranking/rating tools, best practice repository
Knowledge broker	Locate experts/knowledge, identify gaps, organize, filter, coordinate CoPs	Enterprise portal, audit tools, online forums, organizational knowledge maps
Knowledge leader	Shape KM agenda, align with business objectives	Intellectual capital navigators, industry knowledge maps
Source: Author.		

coordinator, leader, and librarian. Each of these roles has a specific set of knowledge activities, and an appropriate set of KM tools corresponds to each of these activities.

For instance, taxonomy tools are important for knowledge editors and librarians, validation tools are key for knowledge experts, gap analysis tools are useful for knowledge brokers, and industry knowledge mapping tools are vital for knowledge leaders, as summarized in Table 1.11.

In an increasingly globalized and Web-based work environment, a plethora of tools and technologies supporting KM are emerging. These tools can be classified into various categories: corporate portals (e.g., IBM's Websphere, Hummingbird EIP, Cognos, Epicentric, OpenText's Livelink), search tools (e.g., Autonomy, AskJeeves, Google, Inktomi, The Brain), collaboration (e.g., eGain, eRoom, Groove Networks), expertise location (e.g., AskMe, Kamoon), content management (e.g., Interwoven, Documentum, FileNet, Sirsi), and business intelligence (e.g., Lexis-Nexis, Dialogue). Each has varying offerings for content aging, archiving, authentication, peer ranking, collaboration, and security.

At an activity level, these tools support a diverse variety of knowledge networking behavior such as videoconferencing, co-authoring systems, workflow management, online meetings, datamining, research, and e-learning. KM toolkits are now being offered by a number of second generation software companies such as Orbital Software, Sopheon, Stratify, BrainEKP (enterprise knowledge portal), BackWeb, Plumtree, Corechange, Epicentric, and Voquette.

In sum, a successful KM practice includes a blend of social and IT tools that are appropriately mapped onto the specifications of the knowledge audit, which covers issues ranging from people and process to technology and competitive strategy.

Knowledge gaps, assets, roles, communities, processes, and alliances need to be continually tracked over time, and the KM architecture needs to evolve in keeping with organizational priorities and capacities.

Practitioner Reports: Case Studies of KM Tools in Action

This section highlights some of the key findings of each of the case studies of KM tools, grouped into three categories: KM practitioner reports, expert commentaries, and vendor reports. The subsequent sections analyze these findings, draw overall lessons, and identify emerging trends.

For this study, in the middle of 2003, numerous KM professionals and experts around the world were approached in person, via e-mail, or by phone to narrate the story of their KM practices. The central focus was on the KM tools used but this was contextualized with respect to organizational profile, KM objectives, KM architecture, choice and design of tools, capacity building, cultural issues, tool usage anecdotes and impacts, learnings, and recommendations for other KM practitioners (based on the 8 Cs audit and the frameworks described in the previous section).

KM practitioners from over 20 organizations agreed to contribute full-length narratives, which form the bulk of this book. Others responded to brief questionnaires, which are also summed up in this section. Interviews were conducted with KM analysts at the Gartner Group, and some of their findings have been presented as well.

In addition to the practitioner reports, seven expert commentaries on key KM tool areas have been included: collaboration, portals, social network analysis, personal KM, e-learning, and blogging. Perspectives from six KM vendors follow: in content management, expertise discovery, visualization, collaboration, competitive intelligence, and customer support.

Let us now survey the salient features of KM tools in the profiled companies in alphabetical order (sorry World Bank!). The full narratives in the subsequent chapters are more informative, are open for further interpretation, and make for an interesting read as well.

Part I: KM Practitioner Reports

Accenture

Accenture's KM journey spans over ten years. The majority of knowledge workers in leading consulting firms today are well versed with IT tools in the workplace and have expectations of "one-stop shop" solutions for their knowledge needs. Accenture's KM system evolved through four phases: early enabling infrastructure, knowledge as byproduct, actively managed knowledge, and knowledge-enabled enterprise. The knowledge repository, called Knowledge Xchange (KX), hosts content ranging from proposals and client deliverables to white papers and links to experts. KM at Accenture has helped increase the rate of innovation, decrease time to competency, and improve productivity. A key observation is that information quality management will emerge as an important competitive differentiator in the future.

ABB

The ABB Group of companies uses KM tools for real-time collaborative activity; communication; meetings; and content preparation by employees, suppliers, and customers. ABB's KM team collects a wide range of statistics to monitor usage of the collaboration tools and their impacts on productivity and competitiveness. Real savings have also been delivered to the bottom line in terms of reduced travel costs and less paper documentation. Future plans include incorporating a Web interface for wider (though secured) access. A key learning has been that only by creating an adequate environment, culture, and infrastructure support will people adopt knowledge-sharing behaviors and enabling tools. The tools must have a strong link to the business imperative, will require continuous learning as the tools evolve, and must be integrated with systematic knowledge processes.

APQC

The Knowledge Sharing Network of the American Productivity & Quality Center (APQC) provides members with online access to a wide range of business resources on topics ranging from productivity to quality. The network includes a knowledge taxonomy, a portal platform, a template inventory, content management processes, community services, and authorization. Lessons learned from the project exercise include making a proper business case for KM infrastructure, involving the user in the requirements phase, having realistic expectations, assigning a full-time role to the project, and the importance of harmonizing new KM infrastructure with organizational culture.

Cable & Wireless

KM tools have played a key role in helping Cable & Wireless India coordinate round-the-clock teamwork across multiple locations, capture best practices, deliver e-learning services, and meet customer support requirements from all over the world. Features like Best Bets, incentive schemes like "Knowledge Dollars," and a taxonomy called Knowledge Index were devised. Key learnings include the use of Web-based tools for work processes to prevent e-mail overload, the importance of managing knowledge stocks to keep them relevant, the necessity of security, factoring in the unavoidability of a certain amount of knowledge hoarding by employees, and the fact that a KM solution is always a work in progress with multiple evolutionary paths.

Computer Services Corporation (CSC)

Social network analysis (SNA) was found to be a useful tool for intellectual capital research by unearthing social capital measures. Examples from technical communities in the global computer services industry demonstrate that the mining of relationship data from electronic logs of interactions or Web sites on the Internet can report on social capital in close to real-time, thus complementing existing methods of network analysis based on periodic interviews. Digital SNA also helps overcome one of the difficulties in developing social capital reports, viz. the time, effort, and cost required to collect data for accurate reporting. Challenges of an unforeseen kind, however, may arise via evolving privacy laws and social acceptance regarding monitoring activities.

DaimlerChrysler

Web-based KM infrastructure at DaimlerChrysler supports the Engineering Book of Knowledge (EBoK), where knowledge is captured and shared in the form of lessons learned, best practices, expertise directories, and discussion forums across the organization. DaimlerChrysler's TechClubs—CoPs in engineering—are built around robust business processes, capacity for knowledge behaviors, and sound Web infrastructure. Specific impact metrics for the KM system include decrease in time-to-talent, decrease in time-to-information, and increase in motivation. The DaimlerChrysler Corporate University plays a major role as a coordinator and facilitator of the KM CoP, with subcommittees for IT tools, measurement, culture, and marketing.

easyJet

Rapid growth and acquisitions have transformed the culture and knowledge infrastructure of easyJet from start-up to major player in just a few years, with many more changes ahead. To ensure scalability of operations and knowledge exchange, easyJet is dealing with "knowledge fracture" by augmenting its intranet with KM tools and an explicit KM strategy. Tool migration, training in new IT infrastructure, branding the intranet, dealing with infrastructure fragments, incorporating user feedback, and nurturing an attitude of continuous learning are some steps being taken. Lessons learned include the necessity to deal with potential challenges like inertia and even cynicism with respect to new KM tool usage.

Ericsson Research Canada

Ericsson Research Canada's KM initiative includes features ranging from the KM Advisory Board and vendor selection process to RoI approaches and technology support for online CoPs. Online CoPs were launched in 2000, with open Web-based support for knowledge networking (called XPERTiSE). Key learnings are the importance of starting off with a low-key design rather than an overengineered, overloaded, and confusing user interface design; allowing for a high degree of customization; the critical role of online communities to bridge geographical gaps in global organizations; the opportunities in blending offline and online community interactions; and strategies for quickly harnessing early adopters when new technology solutions are being introduced.

Ernst & Young

Ernst & Young is a pioneer in the field of KM and has evolved Web-based collaboration tools to enhance the relationship between e-business and knowledge management via EY/KnowledgeWeb (the intranet) and Ernst & Young *Online* (the extranet). Competitive advantage comes from the capability to most effectively integrate the tool with the right people, processes, and content. Knowledge managers within the firm's global Center for Business Knowledge™ (CBK) are responsible for integrating information, taxonomies, human knowledge, and technology into work practices. Key success factors include the ability for users to customize KM tools without developer support, the adoption of standards (e.g., for corporate branding), and high levels of security and legal protection.

Ford

Ford has always had a knowledge-sharing culture, and formal processes along with Web-based technology have extended this culture to the company's global operating units. IT support for best practice replication evolved from early "dumb terminals" and fax transmissions to a portal and knowledge-based engineering. Key lessons include the importance of documentation, professional usability design, adherence to content templates and taxonomy, optimization of infrastructure, automated alerting mechanisms ("nagware"!) to coordinate knowledge validation processes, and testing first via pilots.

Fuji-Xerox

The growth of IT-based tools for KM is leading to a shift in thinking in a number of Japanese companies, whereby explicit knowledge bases are being perceived as increasingly important in the future. Two key types of knowledge workers are identified: nomad and analyst. Analyst-type workers use IT most frequently and have a strong tendency to build new ideas through individual thinking; it is necessary for companies to increase their interactions including via virtual space in order to enhance the knowledge-creating process. A key learning is the importance of the seamlessness between the physical workspace and the virtual one for knowledge workers.

HP

Collaboration is now seen as one of the key KM priorities for HP after its merger with Compaq. The KM Tools and Technology Forum defines the standard tools and processes for KM within the company. KM technology building blocks include data-mining, groupware, knowledge repositories, and expertise locator systems. The Hewlett Packard "Community of Practice Handbook," a collection of instructions, tools, and templates to help organizations form CoPs, has been released. Collaborative knowledge networking will be used to join the "power of many"—the knowledge of the employees—with the "power of now"—instant access to information—to speed up the decision-making process. Key learnings include the importance of striking a good balance between tangible and intangible measures and sharing credit for KM successes.

Innovators Online Network, New Zealand

Small- and medium-sized businesses in New Zealand have been successfully using the Web-based Innovators Online Network (ION) for knowledge networking on issues like offshore research and marketing campaigns, thus overcoming constraints of distance and inadequate individual resources. The use of smaller subgroups and periodic face-to-face meetings helped foster trust, authority roles, and bonds between the practitioners. This case study also highlights some of the classic challenges in facilitating online CoPs and the means of tackling them, such as drawing user attention to fresh content, tools for easy publishing, secure access to confidential information, maintaining overall focus, training moderators, evolving rules regarding veto power and anonymous posting, and strong involvement of the overall project manager. In sum, electronic forums can indeed be a catalyst for driving intellectual discussion as well as delivering tangible gains on projects, provided adequate attention is paid to issues of capacity and culture.

KPMG

Employees at KPMG, one of the winners of the global MAKE study, can access KM tools like the KSource virtual library of knowledge, regional intranets, skills experience locator, and a universal search engine. The collaboration tool KClient provides client service teams a protected environment for sharing work in progress with clients. Extranet sites for clients and the kpmg.com Internet sites showcase the company's knowledge to larger audiences. Key lessons are that KM technology cannot work without communication and training; third-party KM tools can be more efficient than in-house tools; small-scale pilots are recommended for new initiatives; and templated Web sites are popular for creation on the intranet.

National Office of the Information Economy, Australia

Formed in 1997, Australia's National Office of the Information Economy (NOIE) has developed the Government Online Strategy and has leveraged Internet infrastructure for e-government services. NOIE uses KM tools not so much for achieving intra-organizational knowledge creation and sharing, but rather for promoting inter-organizational collaborative activities. NOIE considers KM to be a new socio-institutional framework and is represented on a Standards Australia committee that published an interim standard on KM in early 2003. One of the KM tools NOIE uses is similar to a best practices knowledge base: a collection of case studies (storytelling) of effective and practical applications of ICTs.

Nursing Leadership Academy for End of Life Care

The Nursing Leadership Academy for End of Life Care housed in the Institute for Johns Hopkins Nursing is leveraging KM methods and tools among nurses, physicians, medical specialists, and bereavement counsellors who are changing the culture of patient care. Such online CoPs stay connected for problem solving, providing member profile and patient support information, publishing photo galleries, and sustaining the momentum of face-to-face meetings. Close interaction between users and developers, ease of use, simple low-bandwidth design, minimum training needs, features for posting urgent queries, online discussions with experts, and indexing of Web content were other success factors in this platform for distributed CoPs.

Office of Small Business, Australia

Australia's Office of Small Business turned to KM as a way of dealing with voluminous knowledge flows, retaining knowledge of retiring employees, and rapidly changing information needs of small businesses in a globalized economy. SNA helped map knowledge sources and flows inside and outside the organization. A mix of codification and personalization strategies was incorporated in the KM practice, based on electronic file structure and the intranet. Lessons learned include the importance of conducting a knowledge audit before selecting KM tools and the significance of external knowledge flows for small organizations.

Rolls-Royce

Rolls-Royce launched its KM system in 1996. Knowledge communication occurs not just via the intranet, but also by traditional methods like manuals, posters, training courses, guidelines, presentations, and checklists. Structured Knowledge Auditing is used to provide visualization of key knowledge areas via group and individual interviews. The KM Lessons Learned Log has detailed procedures for knowledge validation and peer review; dedicated staff help maintain the log. People Pages capture expertise profiles of company employees. Key learnings include the importance of starting KM initiatives small and simple with proven tools that can ensure a successful pilot, promoting KM practices by word of mouth, and the use of surveys to assess and prioritize KM projects.

Unilever

IT-enabled creativity tools within overall idea generation mechanisms have been managed successfully in Unilever. Projects are continuously fed into the innovation funnel, and creativity sessions are supported by tools ranging from basic flip-charts and Post-Its to advanced IT tools like MindJet's Mindmanager and Invention Machine's TechOptimizer. These tools help researchers state research and engineering problems correctly, manage technical knowledge, make predictions about product evolution, and resolve potential technological contradictions by analyzing over 2.5 million patents. However, use of these tools must be augmented by measures of the success of creativity sessions, as well as identification and removal of potential barriers to innovation.

World Bank

Integral to the mission statement of the World Bank are the notions and practices of knowledge sharing and capacity building. HR's Web site—YourNet—was purposefully created as a "knowledge base" by applying KM principles to an HR system. KM tools in HR nurture a sense of empowerment and ownership. Automated notifications are delivered to the KM team for new content created by HR staff. Web-based tools are used for hiring professional associates, forming CoPs, and supporting knowledge networking among alumni. Expertise directories are created via the People Pages tool. Key lessons learned for sustaining a knowledge ecology include the importance of harnessing the familiarity of known tools and mediums in new ways and creating consistent narratives.

Part II: KM Expert Commentaries

KM Tools: Observations from the Quality Assurance Institute

First-hand research from the Quality Assurance Institute (QAI) India shows that KM tools have been successfully used in project management, brainstorming activities, and networking knowledge workers, but have been less successful in crisis management and large-scale organizational redesign. Challenges have been observed in failure to control KM infrastructure costs, inability to integrate multiple IT tools, developing solutions without seeking external professional help, and not properly aligning KM tools and solutions with business needs. Future trends include the use of systems thinking, pattern theories, and SNA.

Collaboration in Knowledge Work

In addition to the Internet and intranet, the emergence of tools for peer-to-peer communication, mobile access, instant messaging, and Web services having an influence on collaborative platforms and methods. Collaborative tools can facilitate a practice (how people work together to get the job done) as well as a process (the explicit or formal definition of how work should be done). Key observations include the proliferation of project-based collaboration tools in the market and the importance of a leadership role in encouraging collaborative solutions to knowledge work.

Tools for Competitive Intelligence and KM

There are numerous software applications, content aggregators, and service providers that can provide market intelligence to a company's knowledge inputs. KM methods and tools such as CoPs and SME networks lend themselves well to the competitive intelligence (CI) function. Of late, the CI function has embraced Web-based tools like collaborative technologies and even blogging (Weblogging). Blogs are emerging as a key low-cost component of building ad-hoc CoPs, while also creating a platform for delivery of market monitoring by the intelligence team to its customers. The increasing use of XML and RSS are emerging developments to keep an eye on as well.

Enterprise Knowledge Portals

Enterprise portals now appear in various forms such as enterprise information portals, enterprise process portals, and enterprise knowledge portals. Work environments need to be able to handle the growing diversity of content and applications, as well as increasing demands for flexibility by knowledge workers. Companies implementing portals need to understand how the various vendors and products design, architect, and support all of this functionality. To provide the complete range of functionality users will need, it may be necessary to settle on a set of overlapping or complementary product offerings. Change will be the most notable constant for the future in vendor space and throughout the design and implementation of the enterprise portal.

e-Learning and KM

The growing synergies between knowledge management and e-learning and the convergence of work and learning are leading to the importance of e-learning as knowledge scaffolding in the 21st century. Learning in KM-driven organizations can take place via mentoring in face-to-face CoPs, e-learning in digital environments, or blended learning. Web services and next generation Internet technologies will further enmesh knowledge and learning processes. Standardization is proceeding, thanks to consortia like the Workflow Management Coalition, the HR-XML Consortium, OASIS (Organization for the Advancement of Structured Information Standards), and GKEC (the Global Knowledge Economics Council).

Social Network Analysis

SNA, the tool of sociologists and anthropologists, can be used in the KM context to map teamwork, identify isolated individuals, balance workloads, devise better leadership schemes, and plan interventions for promoting knowledge networking. Automated data gathering and mapping tools can be supplemented with consultative interviews to get a better understanding of knowledge environments. Key learnings include the importance of having top-level management sponsorship and using SNA for identifying potential CoPs.

Personal KM

KM professionals need to answer tough questions about the direction of many KM initiatives today: Are they designed for knowledge managers or knowledge workers? Personal knowledge management (PKM) was a phrase barely whispered during the 1990s, but it is now assuming more importance in collaborative knowledge work. Leading academics and market research firms are identifying PKM as key in training knowledge workers to become more effective and efficient in their development and use of knowledge. There are hundreds of available tools for PKM, ranging from information access and evaluation tools to idea organization and collaboration tools. Issues like security and trust should not be overlooked in this context. PKM also includes values, skills, and processes that cannot be simply replaced by these tools.

Part III: Vendor Reports

Expertise Location in Large Organizations: Learnings from AskMe

AskMe's Employee Knowledge Network (EKN) builds profiles of employee expertise, manages escalation mechanisms for urgent queries, provides rating and validation support, integrates with other workplace tools, and routes and archives Q&A interactions for further reuse. EKNs have supported expertise discovery and CoPs in Intel, Procter & Gamble, Intec Engineering, Honeywell, Boeing, and CNA Insurance. Key learnings include devising the right reward and recognition schemes, designing business rules for handling critical queries, aligning taxonomies with work activities, making rating systems flexible or moving them to the background, and populating the EKN with content prior to launch so as to make it useful from the onset.

KM in Professional Services Firms: Tools from iManage

Knowledge is a primary driver of competitive advantage, and content is a key deliverable in professional services firms. Reuse of lessons learned is critical to productivity at every stage of the engagement. Integrated KM tools for content management and collaboration constitute the starting point for effective KM infrastructure in such firms. Key learnings include the difficulty of getting users to make a wholesale switch to a new way of working, balancing open access with security, the necessity of support from top management, the rise of near-real-time KM, and the pressing need of professional services firms to deal with new regulations governing records management.

Structured Knowledge: Optimal Contact Center Efficiency with ServiceWare

Knowledge—and quick access to it—plays a key role in today's contact center. A structured knowledge base, used in conjunction with a powerful search tool, can enable efficiencies across multiple contact channels. Metrics are provided to assess contact center efficiency. ServiceWare's Web-based KM solutions for customer service are used by clients such as Reuters, H&R Block, AT&T Wireless, Cingular Wireless, Green Mountain Energy, and Qualcomm. Powerful search technology helps querying by phrases and also weights queries depending on how often they are asked.

Integrated KM Solutions: The Experience of Entopia

Entopia has evolved a "3 Cs" philosophy of KM: collect, collaborate, and capitalize. Its offerings include content management, SNA, and dynamic search for clients like Gate5, Evesham Technology, and the U.S. Space and Naval Warfare Systems Center. The KM tools deployed were easy to use even for remote users with browser access, one-stop access solutions were provided for information assets, and dynamic profiles of experts were created. Key KM learnings include the importance of making knowledge sharing a strong part of organizational culture, focus on metrics, and start in a phased manner. Trends to watch include the growing use of XML in content management, better understanding of the human component of networking activities (e.g., via SNA), and the importance of PKM.

Content Visualization: Learnings from Inxight

Content continues to be an underutilized asset in large organizations today. Content applications need to focus not just on retrieval, but also on routing, mining, and alerting services. Companies like Inxight provide taxonomy and visualization tools for knowledge workers to provide a conceptual and perceptual map of the content collection. Information extraction technology has become mission-critical in government intelligence and is quite common now in the publishing and pharmaceutical industries. Key lessons learned include the importance of augmenting human skills with computational tools, factoring in natural use of language, the need for continually reprocessing text, and designing effective architectures in addition to algorithms.

Market Intelligence: Content and Services from LexisNexis

A range of market news, regulatory, and business statistics feeds are being provided to corporate intranets and handheld devices by value-added content aggregators like LexisNexis, Thomson, Dialog, and Factiva. The LexisNexis services combine searchable access to over four billion documents from thousands of sources, with useful tools for managing this content. These include portal integration with multiple platforms, premium tracking, e-discovery across multiple content formats, taxonomy management, and smart indexing. Alliances have also been formed to integrate such content services with workflow applications in domains like law and to extend competitive intelligence services to a myriad of Internet avenues like discussion groups and meta-tags.

KM Tools: Analysis of Findings

Having reviewed the key findings from the KM tool case studies, let us contextualize these findings via the following categories of analysis: success areas of KM tools, sophistication of KM tool integration, and lessons learned.

Success Areas of KM Tools

The practitioner reports and expert commentaries reveal that KM tools have been successfully used in project management, brainstorming activities, content management, networking of knowledge workers, and collaborative activity. They have been less successful in large-scale organizational redesign (e.g., after mergers and acquisitions) and crisis management.

Enterprise portals have been widely deployed among most of the profiled organizations, marked by creative branding as with Cable & Wireless India ("Phoenix"), Ernst & Young ("EY/KnowledgeWeb"), KPMG ("Kworld"), and World Bank ("YourNet" HR portal).

Content management tools have contributed to KM efforts via creation and use of a wide range of knowledge repositories, e.g., Accenture's client deliverables, APQC's white papers, Ford's best practices, DaimlerChrysler's lessons learned, NOIE's success stories, Nursing Leadership Academy's photo libraries, and Rolls-Royce's Project Reviews. Basic content management tools have been enhanced by other KM tools for taxonomy management, search, content clustering, syndication, repurposing for mobile delivery, personalization, and visualization.

Collaborative KM tools have been successfully used in process and practice areas by ABB (for content preparation), Cable & Wireless (for coordinating teams), Ernst & Young (for collaboration with clients), HP (to harness the "power of many"), KPMG (via the Kclient tool for client service teams), and the Nursing Leadership Academy (for widespread collaboration on palliative care). More sophisticated collaborative tools have helped extend teamwork from internal employees to external partners and customers as well.

Online CoPs have been deployed at DaimlerChrysler (TechClubs), Ericsson Research Canada (via the XPERTiSE tool), Ford (for engineering CoPs), the Nursing Leadership Academy (for palliative care), and the World Bank (e.g., for professional associates). Tools for online CoPs have helped break past traditional departmental and organizational barriers, to embrace globally dispersed participants.

Expertise locator tools have found use in Fuji-Xerox, KPMG, Rolls-Royce, and World Bank (via PeoplePages); tools have emerged for dynamic expertise profiling (e.g., e-mail mining) in addition to static approaches.

Idea management tools have helped creativity sessions for innovation in Unilever, such as MindJet's Mindmanager and Invention Machine's TechOptimizer. Application-specific KM tools are also used in areas like human resources (e.g., World Bank), e-learning, contact center operations, and professional services.

On the narrative tool front, KM blogging (or "klogging") is being increasingly adopted for uses ranging from corporate knowledge dashboard to competitive intelligence, and a number of tools for PKM are also emerging.

One of the newer tools to find growing acceptance is digital SNA, which has been used in large companies like Computer Services Corporation and associations of distributed organizations as in Australia's Office of Small Business.

At the same time, it should be noted that even a simple move to a basic digital platform for content storage has helped some companies realize significant efficiency increases and better knowledge sharing as compared to prior paper-based workflows (e.g., in the airline Go, which was acquired by easyJet).

Very basic tools for content hosting and e-mail alerting are also being used for knowledge networking by distributed communities of independent professionals (e.g., nurse practitioners) and small businesses (e.g., in Australia). This is probably due to lack of access to sophisticated IT platforms that larger enterprises can provide or due to lack of standardization of tools used by independent professionals. The growth of new P2P collaboration tools (e.g., Groove) is a promising development to watch in this regard.

Thus, KM tools ranging from basic digital content management to advanced knowledge discovery have found use in KM practices in a range of communities and organizations around the world.

Sophistication of KM Tool Integration

As can be seen from the previous section, a number of organizations or communities have just made the transition from paper and face-to-face communications over to digital documents and Web-based tools; others have deployed one or two KM tools, while quite a few have implemented a whole suite of KM tools. More sophisticated KM tools can also replace simpler ones (e.g., many companies now require the bulk of online communication to take place not via e-mail, but via workflow-related Web applications).

Among those who have deployed KM tools, some (e.g., Accenture) have evolved through four phases: early enabling infrastructure, knowledge as byproduct, actively managed knowledge, and knowledge-enabled enterprise. The majority of knowledge workers in leading consulting firms today are well versed with IT tools in the workplace and have expectations of one-stop shop solutions for their knowledge needs. IT tool support for best practice replication in Ford evolved from early "dumb terminals" and fax transmissions to a portal and knowledge-based engineering.

In somewhat general terms, we can classify KM tools into three families, based on their core functional focus: content, collaboration, and computation. Though lines between these tool areas can be somewhat blurry, the content family tends to be focused largely on the static document and information realm; the collaboration family tends to focus on messaging and workflow coordination; and computation tools are algorithm intensive or transaction oriented (see Table 1.12 for more details).

It is possible, of course, for organizations to employ all three families of KM tools (most large organizations in the world already do), but many smaller organizations (e.g., NGOs, SMEs) and distributed communities (e.g., freelancers, independent professionals, environmental activists) may have access to only one or two families of KM tools in their KM infrastructure. These ownership and usage patterns of KM tool families by an organization or a community can be captured in a Venn diagram as shown in Figure 1.2, which can then be used to classify KM architecture into three levels of complexity.

Table 1.12

Families of KM Tools	
KM tools family	**Sample applications**
Content	Document management, taxonomy, document templates, best practices repository, syndicated newsfeed
Collaboration	Cooperative document creation, whiteboarding, P2P, messaging, groupware
Computation	Search, clustering, SNA, visualization, business intelligence, commerce, enterprise portal
Source: Author.	

Figure 1.2

Groupings of KM tool usage and levels of organizational KM infrastructure complexity
(*Source: Author*)

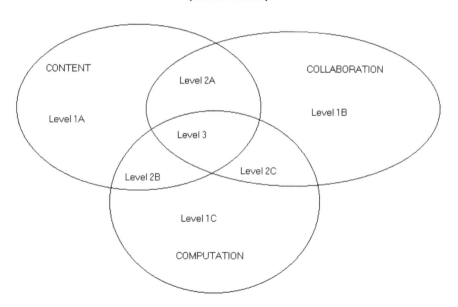

An organization or community can be said to be at Level 1 of KM infrastructure complexity if it uses not more than one family of digital KM tools. This includes the many organizations that have just made the leap from paper to digital document management systems (Level 1A, e.g., the airline Go which was acquired by easyJet) or the innumerable communities of professionals, hobbyists, and activists who use basic e-mail lists for knowledge networking (Level 1B).

Level 0 organizations use no digital KM tools, but instead use other traditional ones like paper documents, libraries, co-located collaboration, and face-to-face mentoring arrangements. This has serious implications for scalability, efficiency, and reusability of knowledge in such organizations and has caused a lot of concern, particularly in the emerging economies of the world. (More on that in the next section.)

If an organization or community uses two families of digital KM tools, it can be said to be at Level 2 of KM infrastructure complexity. For instance, the Unilever case study features the use of content and computational tools for creative brainstorming, but collaborative activities still take place largely face-to-face (Level 2B). Organizations which weigh in on different sides of the codification versus personalization debate may choose to place more emphasis on one or the other family of KM tools.

An organization or community which uses all three families of KM tools can be said to be at Level 3 of KM infrastructure complexity. Most of the larger organizations profiled in this book are at Level 3; they provide a wide range of tools for their knowledge workers around the world, but also invest heavily in technology integration, change management, and capacity building for using these tools. See Table 1.13 for a comparison of these three levels; more case studies and analysis would be needed to tease apart the distinctions among Level 3 organizations.

Table 1.13

Levels of Complexity of KM Infrastructure		
Level of complexity of KM infrastructure	Characteristics	Examples
Level 0	No digital KM tools are present	Paper documents, co-located collaboration, face-to-face mentoring
Level 1	Only one family of KM tools is present	Content management tools or messaging/ groupware
Level 2	Two families of KM tools are present (e.g., content and collaboration or content and computation)	Digital publishing + search, content management + groupware
Level 3	All families of KM tools are present	Content management + search + groupware
Source: Author.		

Key Learnings and Recommendations for KM Practitioners

Two sets of learnings can arise from the above case studies of KM tool usage: those directly related to the underlying technology of the KM tools (e.g., search algorithms, XML standards) and those related to management and cultural factors for tool selection and usage (e.g., change management, capacity building). Since the focus of this book is largely on the practice of KM and not computer or information science, we will skip discussion on esoteric topics like the Semantic Web and focus instead on the key success factors and challenges facing KM tool usage in organizational settings.

The range of success stories of KM tool deployment in this book is the result not merely of the technologies underlying them or their appropriateness for the targeted knowledge processes and communities, but also because of a host of other enabling factors. These include DaimlerChrysler Corporate University's training support for KM, Ericsson Research Canada's KM Advisory Board, KPMG's creation of roles for CKO and knowledge managers, HP's KM Leadership framework, and Rolls-Royce's corporate Community of Practice Leader to strengthen CoP activity.

At least 20 clusters of such lessons for successful design and deployment of KM tools can be gleaned from the case studies and recommendations provided by the KM practitioners in this book. The full-length case studies in the book are open for further interpretation and analysis by readers, of course, but let us survey some of the key learnings and recommendations below. They cover the following themes: culture, capacity, leadership, quality, knowledge taxonomies, alignment, knowledge workers, change, design, usability, standards, business rules, organizational communication, security, traditional KM mechanisms, IT project management, vendors, tracking, benchmarking, and future trends.

Culture

Create a culture of learning and knowledge. Provide appropriate reward, recognition, and incentive schemes to encourage employees to use KM tools. However, you may have to deal with a certain amount of knowledge hoarding attitude among some employees or inertia and even cynicism in moving quickly to new KM tools.

Sidebar 5
15 reasons why some KM tool implementations may fail to deliver

Leading KM with IT only
Lack of a common IT platform
Low trust in security of KM tool
Too many switches in IT platforms
Inertia in switching to new KM tool
Inadequate training in KM tool usage
Low usability and intuitiveness of KM tools
Lack of user participation in KM tool design
Inflexibility of KM tool with differing devices
Low performance of KM tools (e.g., slow speed)
KM tools unable to check information overload
Lack of maintenance and upgrading of KM tools
Lack of alignment between KM tools and workflow
Replacing key human interfaces with technological contact
Poor project management leading to improper KM tool implementation

---

Capacity

Create and circulate adequate documentation (e.g., handbooks) about the KM tools. Provide adequate helpdesks and a hotline. Bring in world-renowned KM experts and writers as speakers to share insights on global KM trends. Develop an online curriculum with courses and scenarios about KM. Get the corporate university involved in KM training, or form appropriate committees and task forces to address issues ranging from IT tools to KM marketing. Provide training on reflective behaviors, collaboration, and writing skills. Create a full-fledged role or a group for overseeing KM.

Leadership

Top management must themselves embrace KM culture, practices, and tools. They must demonstrate that they have internalized the KM message. This must be communicated with external audiences as well.

Quality

Pay attention to quality of knowledge assets. Ensure that the knowledge outputs and inputs of KM practices are of a high quality by devising mechanisms and tools for knowledge rating, validation, version control, and expiry of old assets. The KM tools should allow for anonymous ratings and postings as well. Manage your knowledge stocks to keep them relevant.

Knowledge Taxonomies

Align knowledge taxonomies with work activities. Choose KM tools which can balance flexibility as well as discipline in taxonomy structures. Be prepared for creation of new content categories as the domain of business evolves; create a taxonomy committee or task force.

Alignment

Link KM tools to the overall business imperative. Link KM tools to the business processes for each employee's workflow patterns as well. If a significant change in work pattern is called for, plan and sustain an appropriate change management campaign.

Knowledge Workers

It is important for companies to understand how knowledge workers actually create knowledge. Some Japanese researchers have identified various types of knowledge workers: nomad, analyst, agents, and keepers. Analyst-type workers use IT tools most frequently and have a strong tendency to build new ideas through individual thinking; it is necessary for companies to increase their interactions, including via virtual space.

Technology, Domain, and Organizational Change

Be prepared for change in KM infrastructure design as new technologies and tools emerge. Changes in organizational structure (e.g., due to M&A) may lead to integration of new KM infrastructure; these should also be anticipated where possible. Employees may demand more flexibility in work location (e.g., telecommuting). Shifts in competitive landscapes may call for new KM strategies. Finally, changes in government regulations regarding corporate governance may lead to new infrastructure requirements for documentation and e-mail audits. Remember, a KM solution is always a work in progress with multiple evolutionary paths.

Design and Rollout

Conduct a proper knowledge audit covering the domain, strategy, operations, processes, communities, experts, and existing infrastructure. Make a proper business case for KM infrastructure. Involve the user in the requirements phase. Assign a full-time role to the project. Begin in a phase-wise manner, start with a pilot, and target the right audiences. Quickly harness early adopters when new KM tools are being introduced. Use techniques like pre-population to make content repositories useful from the onset.

Usability

Start off with a low-key design rather than an overengineered, overloaded, and confusing tool interface design. Allow for a high degree of customization. Enable users to create content without needing technical support, e.g., via simple templates. Ensure consistency of KM tool interfaces and actions, and provide assurances of adequate performance levels.

Information Overload

Guard against information overload; KM tools can generate a lot of communication and publication activities. It is important to manage this within well-designed applications so as not generate unnecessary e-mail traffic.

Standards

Adopt standards for branding of intranet content, templates for knowledge assets (e.g., best practices, lessons learned), formats for a multiplicity of devices, and reliability levels of KM tools. Ensure discipline and adherence to these technical standards.

Business Rules

Clearly define business rules for publication of documents and communication of messages, especially alerting, escalation, and urgent queries. Integrate these with the appropriate "push" tools (e.g., e-mail or SMS notification).

Organizational Communication

Communicate the KM message, and circulate stories of successful KM tool usage. Showcase KM achievements to the outside world as well. Use regular communication vehicles like corporate newsletters. Host events, competitions, knowledge fairs, and award ceremonies to reinforce these messages. Pay attention to branding of the KM tools (e.g., via catchy but meaningful names).

Security and Privacy

It is important to balance openness of knowledge exchange with security of KM infrastructure and knowledge assets. Provide adequate IT tools and legal backing to secure company secrets or confidential client information. Challenges of an unforeseen kind may arise for KM tools like digital SNA via evolving privacy laws and social acceptance regarding monitoring activities.

Traditional KM Mechanisms

Blend traditional knowledge-sharing mechanisms with digital KM tools; do not ignore traditional knowledge networking techniques. Pay attention to the "social life of information" in online and offline settings. Tried and tested methods for knowledge exchange like personnel rotation across strategic groups still work. Blend online and offline interaction for CoPs; e-mail and print newsletters for corporate communication.

Online CoPs

Use tools that make it easy for users to publish content. Draw user attention to fresh content. Train moderators on technical issues like tool usage as well as overall issues like maintaining focus. The tools should facilitate evolution of rules regarding veto power and anonymous postings.

Large Organizations

Use a variety of appropriate KM tools, possibly from all three families of tools (see previous section). Use online communities to bridge geographical gaps in global organizations. Tools like enterprise portals, search, e-learning, digital SNA, and blogging may be particularly useful. Do not underestimate project management, capacity, and culture issues.

Small Organizations, Dispersed Communities

Use simple, low-bandwidth KM tools, with minimum training needs, e.g., basic text-based e-mail and simple Web formats. Blend online and offline tools. Use layered content (e.g., digests of headlines). Design and publish content with low graphical content where possible.

IT Project Management

Guard against cost and time overruns in IT project management for KM infrastructure. Familiarize yourself with outsourcing practices and contracts if relevant. Integrate multiple IT tools. Optimize KM infrastructure. Use a modular or component approach to devise KM solutions efficiently. Use third-party KM tools and outside KM consultants as appropriate.

KM Tool Vendors

Understand how the various vendors and products design, architect, and support KM functionality. Learn how to manage with overlapping or complementary product offerings. Be prepared for constant change in vendor space via new technologies, consolidation, or alliances.

Sidebar 6
Ten criteria for evaluating KM Tool vendors

Cost
Security
Performance
Future evolution
Client testimonials
Ease of integration
Monitoring services
Development environment
Ability to develop a prototype
Maintenance and upgrading of services

Track, Monitor, Assess, and Upgrade

Monitor and collect statistics of tool usage; tie these to user needs and business impact, and fine tune the KM tools as necessary. Also, collect anecdotes, stories, and case studies of KM tool usage; circulate them and make them easily retrievable. Conduct periodic polls and surveys of KM tool users. Set realistic expectations for KM tool impacts, and devise a proper mix of tangible and intangible measures.

Benchmarking

Benchmark your KM practice with those of your competitors and even with organizations or communities in other sectors. Areas of comparison range from tool design and usage to impacts and evolution. Form alliances and partnerships with industry associations and research institutes where relevant.

Trends

Pay attention to KM tool developments in areas like e-learning, blogging, visualization, discovery, wireless delivery, personal KM, digital SNA, open source, and Web services. Gear up for near-real-time KM and full-fledged organizational intelligence blending KM with business intelligence.

The Road Ahead

In this KM travelogue, we have surveyed over 30 first-hand case studies and expert commentaries on KM tool usage, reviewed over 30 books which address KM tool issues, and gleaned fresh insights about KM tools from KM practitioners at over two dozen recent conferences and workshops around the world. Emerging tool areas have also been identified.

KM as a discipline has crossed the "tipping point" and become a well-established business perspective and part of daily work, according to KM guru Larry Prusak. KM tools are on the cusp of nearing mainstream adoption.

"Technology is inescapably a part of all but a small number of knowledge management success stories. Technology is likely to play a strong role in the management of explicit knowledge, while its role in managing tacit knowledge will lie in facilitating interpersonal knowledge transfer. Additionally, technology will assume many of the routine work tasks of the past, freeing people to focus on knowledge-intensive activities which require human understanding and insight," according to Koulopoulos and Frappaolo (1999).

Sidebar 7
"Document and content management applications remain the most popular KM-oriented applications"

A conversation with Debra Logan, Research Director, Gartner Group

Q: What are some common mistakes companies tend to make when evaluating and implementing KM tools?
A:
1. Not doing thorough user requirements analysis and therefore selecting the wrong tools for the wrong users.
2. Failing to take into account the amount of time it will take users to change their ways of working.
3. Implementing collaborative tools in a non-collaborative environment.
4. Not creating real management objectives to enforce/encourage the use of KM or collaborative tools.

Other general shortcomings we come across include not aiming for quick wins; having IT involvement, but not enough business sponsorship; and not changing old ways of knowledge work (especially during M&A).

Q: What trends are we likely to see on the KM tool/technology adoption front in the coming year?
A:
1. Personal knowledge management tools will be adopted by individuals as enterprises fail to provide what users need.
2. Innovation management and idea management will be among the most talked about, but not the most implemented, systems in 2004.
3. There will be a resurgence of interest in expert system approaches to KM in 2004 and new start-ups will emerge in this area.
4. Document and content management applications remain the most popular KM-oriented applications.

Gartner has also used a "hype cycle" model to chart adoption paths of IT tools. Many KM tools have already reached a plateau of productivity (e.g., best practices programs, Web content management), while others are only at stages of enlightenment (e.g., virtual teams), inflated expectations (e.g., real-time collaboration, expertise location), or technology triggers (e.g., corporate blogging, P2P knowledge networking).

From an organization standpoint, we noticed in 2003 that some tactical issues (e.g., dealing with spam) were outweighing other priorities. Information Systems (IS) departments were able to demonstrate real value via more focused, shorter projects. Many organizations stuck to "good enough" solutions rather than expensive "best of breed" vendor offerings for KM. Employees used to personal "always on" wireless devices were expecting better offerings from IS as well.

Q: What are some notable case studies you have come across of successful usage of KM tools?
A:
1. The European Court of Human Rights in Strasbourg, France, used a content management system and workflow tool based on Hummingbird to save a million euros in its first year and improved process efficiency. It was able to respond to increased demand for its services (e.g., court case entry, tracking) despite limited resources. Its Web site provides access to all 44 member states of the Council

Continued

of Europe. Six months were spent in interviewing users prior to project launch to determine information and meta-data needs.

2. Engineering consultancy firm Arup used a thesaurus and taxonomy-based search tool to locate experts and draw on past project experience. For business bids, it needed to know whether similar projects were completed before and who had past experience in current challenge areas. Arup evolved from a card catalog to a Web-based index, created templates for future data entry, and focused on designing an appropriate taxonomy. This has helped in gathering references for winning new business around the world.

3. J.D. Edwards' Knowledge Garden initiative was launched initially with a combination of "knowledge storyboards" and content management systems for employee manuals and product catalogs. Based on Vignette, the systematic taxonomy helped avert the "knowledge jungle" problem, and the KM solution was eventually extended via the extranet to business partners as well. The $8 million annual investment on the KM system has been justified many times over via shorter marketing times and qualified leads; Web-based self-help has also reduced customer calls by as much as 15%.

Q: What are your Top Three recommendations for companies evaluating KM tools for their KM practices?

A:

1. Understand the various user groups. Engineers like tools that capture explicit knowledge; more creative types like pure collaboration tools.

2. Understand the dimension of collaboration and how various tools can affect the various dimensions.

3. Decide what the business objectives are and measure performance BEFORE implementation and after implementation of the KM tool. Do not expect RoI to be apparent before about 18 months, as behavior change takes time.

Source: Interview conducted in September 2003.

The META group predicts that by 2004, more than 85% of global organizations will be deploying enterprise portals. Ovum predicts that companies could spend $10.5 billion on KM services by 2004, and the enterprise portal software market will be worth US$7.04 billion in 2005. The market for e-learning products and services will grow to US$33.6 billion by 2005, according to Gartner research. Also, in 2000 alone, more than 100 books were published on KM.

Future KM initiatives will focus on high-payoff areas such as operations, R&D, sales, and marketing, according to Carla O'Dell, President of APQC, and co-author of *If Only We Knew What We Know*. KM approaches like collaboration, content management, expertise locators, and integrated learning systems will become increasingly institutionalized into business processes, predicts O'Dell.

Some analysts have classified companies into five types depending on their level of KM readiness: not ready, preliminary (exploring KM), ready (accepted), receptive (advocating and measuring), and optimal (institutionalized KM).

Given the rapid migration of the world's leading companies down this KM maturity path, it would be appropriate to conclude this chapter with two questions. (1) How exactly can the impact of KM tools be measured? (2) What are the challenges facing organizations and communities that have yet to embrace formal KM practices and IT tools in the 21st century, especially those in the emerging economies of the world?

KM Metrics

Several debates and discussions in the KM field revolve around metrics. What can be reliably measured in KM practices? How can they be measured on an ongoing basis? How valid are these measures? Should they even be measured? How should such measures be interpreted?

In the post-dotcom era and in a time of economic slowdown, measuring RoI in initiatives like KM is becoming a pressing concern at large organizations. The KM literature abounds with stories of successful RoI on KM investments.

For instance, metrics on RoI at consulting firm Bain include faster speed of operation, less time to build client presentations, lower training costs, and greater global consistency in service delivery. These are tracked via an Office KM Scorecard, Practice Scorecard, and VP ratings.

Dow's four-tier metrics framework includes knowledge store optimization (via meta-tags and filesharing), employee enablement (opinion surveys), KM capability metric (along dimensions like business sponsorship, KM roles, technology), and KM investment performance (hard RoI analysis).

"The KM measurement process must take into consideration the needs of all stakeholders," says Bruce Richard of HP Consulting. HP's goal is to improve profitability through KM and leveraging intellectual property, by recognizing and promoting desired KM behaviors through performance evaluation, development, coaching, and mentoring.

KM measurement at HP takes place at multiple levels—process, role, people, organization, and customer satisfaction—through measures including frequency of contributing, sharing, or reusing project material like profiles, snapshots, plans, and deliverables.

"We use a Knowledge Networking Environmental Assessment Tool (KNEAT) to assess our KM environment via surveys about leadership behaviour, individual behaviour, peer behaviour, organisational expectations, and IT tools," says Michael Burtha, Executive Director of the Worldwide Knowledge Networking Program at Johnson & Johnson.

In-process and end-process impacts and measures are an important part of KM metrics, according to Sue Hanley, Managing Director at the e-business solutions firm Plural. Measurement is needed for feedback, funding, follow-on, and focus and will ultimately help with organizational learning and industry benchmarks.

At Siemens, metrics for successful RoI include number of requests to the knowledge base, increase in orders, reusable R&D components, reduction in labor costs, reduction in production costs, lower training expenses, and reduced IT investments.

Tiwana (2002) warns against several traps in choosing metrics for KM: choosing too many metrics (20 should be more than enough), choosing metrics that are hard to control, choosing metrics that tear people away from business goals, and choosing the right answers to the wrong questions.

The metrics used must be company specific and robust; a mix of short-term, medium-term, and long-term measures serves well. Balanced scorecards, the Skandia Navigator, and benchmarking practices are also recommended for assessing KM vision translation, learning, business planning, and knowledge communication.

Hoffman-LaRoche used KM to efficiently manage the drug application process, cutting it down by several months at a savings of $1 million a day. New England heart surgeons have jointly collaborated to cut down the mortality rate for coronary bypass surgery. HP's case-based reasoning KM tool for customer support helped reduce call times by two-thirds and cost per call by 50%.

Buckman Labs reportedly spends $7,500 per person, or 3.5–4.5% of its revenue, on its knowledge efforts; a key metric is the faster pace of innovation. The global knowledge-sharing effort has helped increase the sales of products less than 5 years old, from 14% in 1987 to 34.6% in 1996.

Videoconferencing at BP led to savings of over $30 million in the first year of operation. Texas Instruments saved enough from transferring knowledge between wafer fabrication plants to pay for building a whole new facility. Chevron's KM practice reportedly reduced annual operating costs by US$2 billion in 2000.

Schlumberger reported a first year savings of $75 million through its KM initiative called InTouch, which improved operational efficiency by connecting technology centers and field-workers. As a result, technical query resolution time fell by 95% and engineering modifications update time was reduced by 75%.

Tata Steel reports significant savings in saleable steel costs to the tune of Rs. 3.41 crore (about US$700,000), thanks to its KM initiatives, and has even been guiding sister companies of the Tata group to implement KM.

However, it is important to classify these metrics into five kinds, depending on their focus: technology (or tool usage), business process, knowledge (stocks and flows), employee (cultural attitudes and performance), and business (overall economic impacts). Table 1.14 summarizes this break-up of KM metrics, along with sample measures in each category.

Far too often, metrics analyses stop short at only one or a few of these five categories. All categories of measures are needed together to ensure that KM practices and tools are steering the organization in the right direction and are indeed delivering value.

For instance, a mere increase in e-mail traffic (a technology metric) after KM tool deployment need not imply that users are communicating and collaborating more; this may be a reflection of e-mail overload. Many early BPR rollouts improved process efficiency (a process metric), but reduced knowledge exchange opportunities (a knowledge metric). Online CoPs may increase knowledge contributions (a knowledge metric), but may promote conforming behaviors and create cliques among employees (a people metric). Many organizations have extensive knowledge repositories (a knowledge metric) and high levels of motivation and retention among employees (a people metric), but are unable to convert this to market leadership and profitability (a business metric). True organizational success, therefore, lies in maximizing performance along all five dimensions of KM metrics listed in Table 1.14.

It is important also to choose the process and business metrics with care. For instance, the number of times employee contributions are successfully used is a better measure than simply the number of contributions in a database or discussion forum; actual customer satisfaction is a better measure than reduction in number of customer calls to a contact center.

Another way of analyzing these metrics is by their nature: quantitative, qualitative, or semi-quantitative, as summarized in Table 1.15.

In sum, KM metrics will continue to be a major factor in KM tool deployments in many organizations; debates will continue over definition, choice, accuracy, and interpretation of these measures. Other organizations, however, will accept KM as a fact of life and a way of working which need not be continually monitored and measured.

Table 1.14

KM Metrics (1)	
Scope of KM metrics	**Sample parameters**
Technology metrics	Number of e-mails, usage of online forums, number of database queries, Web site traffic, duration of portal sessions, number of search queries, number of blogs, number of alerts
Process metrics	Faster response times to queries, meeting international certification standards, more real-time interactions with clients, tighter collaboration with suppliers and distributors, more direct channels to customers, more accurate content taxonomies, more secure communications
Knowledge metrics	Number of employee ideas submitted, number of knowledge asset queries, number of knowledge assets reused, best practices created, rate of innovation, active CoPs, knowledge retention, quicker access to knowledge assets, fewer steps to distribute/repackage knowledge ("flow" and "stock" measures)
Employee metrics	Degree of bonding with colleagues, improved performance in CoPs, peer validation, feeling of empowerment, growth in trust, satisfaction with reward/recognition, retention in company, decrease in time to competency, more accountability, responsible risk-taking, increased motivation
Business metrics	Reduced costs, less travel costs, greater market share, increased customer satisfaction, customer loyalty, profitable partnerships, conversion of knowledge assets into patents/licenses, improved productivity, risk reduction, crisis management
Source: Author.	

Table 1.15

KM Metrics (2)	
Nature of KM metrics	**Sample parameters**
Quantitative	Reduced clerical work, less duplication of documents, reduced administrative costs, less paperflow, reduced telecom costs, lower travel costs, lower customer service costs
Semi-quantitative	Productivity (e.g., reduced training time, speedier information access) Satisfaction (e.g., improved morale, job satisfaction) Knowledge assets (e.g., usage of portal, reuse of best practices)
Qualitative	Better innovation, reduced knowledge hoarding, empowered frontline; stories/anecdotes
Source: Author.	

KM Practices and Tools in Emerging Economies

While much attention and development on KM practices and tools has understandably focused on large multinational corporations, multilateral organizations like the World Bank, and government agencies in industrially advanced countries, a major challenge is for emerging economies to bring the fruits of the Knowledge Society to their own organizations and communities—especially in rural areas, where most of their population lives.

Can a virtuous cycle of appropriate KM tools, local knowledge capacities, and revitalization of rural communities be stimulated? Are there models for leveraging localized IT platforms for preserving indigenous knowledge and harnessing social capital?

Globally networked knowledge communities like Bellanet, Development Gateway, and Global Knowledge Partnership have leveraged the Internet to create learning environments and to devise unprecedented development models, focusing on creativity and collective problem solving in emerging economies. The Open Knowledge Network initiative is another promising Web-based knowledge-sharing platform in this regard.

Sidebar 8
Bellanet: Customizing Tools to Enable Knowledge Sharing in the International Development Community

The **Bellanet International Secretariat** (http://home.bellanet.org) is an organization oriented toward helping people in the international development community work together more effectively. Bellanet has consistently found that strong communities are key for good learning, knowledge management, and sustainable information sharing. Fostering such collaboration is an art that involves a subtle understanding of group dynamics, the use of good facilitation techniques, and the use of appropriate tools.

1. Dgroups: Development Through Dialog
Dgroups (http://www.dgroups.org) is a jointly owned initiative between Bellanet, the Institute for Connectivity in the Americas (ICA), the International Institute for Communication and Development (IICD), OneWorld, the United Nations Programme on HIV/AIDS, and the Department for International Development (DFID) to broadly encourage and support online communities and dialogs in international development. The initiative is today the premiere international location to find, join, or launch online communities or discussions related to international development. As of October 2003, there were over 450 development communities with over 10,000 users (see Figure 1.3).

The design objectives for **Dgroups** include the maintenance of a simple, non-commercial, respectful of privacy, and low-bandwidth-oriented platform where e-mail-only participants in developing countries are first class "information citizens" in the groups to which they belong. In a **Dgroup**, participants can post documents in any format, post Web links and news items, share an event in a community-shared calendar, learn about other communities that are active, and send e-mail through their e-mail client or a Web form.

Dgroups can be used to build communities, develop proposals, design and follow up campaigns, and share documents and resources. Currently, the service is available in four roman scripted languages—English, French, Spanish, and Portuguese. With the possibility of developing this platform in an Open Source version, soon, this repository of knowledge will be accessible in several vernacular languages.

---

2. KM4Dev (Knowledge Management for Development)

KM4Dev (http://open.bellanet.org/km) brings together knowledge management (KM)/knowledge sharing (KS) practitioners working in international development to share ideas and experiences both face-to-face and online. It uses an Open Source application called **PostNuke** (http://www.postnuke.com), a Weblog/Content Management System (CMS) (see Figure 1.4).

Members can post news items, articles, documents, book references, polls, and photos. A Frequently Asked Questions page was built by the community itself using Wiki, an application which allows the organization of contributions to be edited, in addition to the content itself. The KM4Dev mailing list—the forum where discussions around issues relating to KM and international development take place—is archived on the Web site. As of October 2003, there were 300 KM4Dev members.

All-Important Common Denominator: The Mailing List

Underlying everything that Bellanet does is the belief that mailing list technology is still the most appropriate tool in supporting international development, providing dialog and information sharing space for those who have limited or no Web access. Bellanet has hosted hundreds of mailing lists over the last 8 years. Two mailing list software packages currently used are Lyris (http://www.lyris.com) and Mailman (http://www.list.org).

Source: Interview with Lucie Lamoureux, Bellanet, Canada.

However, in many emerging economies, lack of access to basic KM tools and Internet connectivity is a major obstacle, observes Afele (2003). The challenge for emerging economies is to harness new KM tools, build local knowledge capacities, and avoid the perpetuation of dependency or intellectual atrophy. ICT-enabled applications are transforming—though at a slower pace—commerce, education, healthcare, agriculture, and services organizations in many emerging economies. Interesting digital bridges are being formed via the Internet, linking diaspora populations of emerging economies into "global knowledge grids" for development via business and social entrepreneurship in their home countries.

Significant opportunities are emerging in countries like India, where major IT and biotech companies are flourishing, several organizations have become KM champions (e.g., Infosys was the first Indian company to win the global MAKE award in 2003), and the fruits of the Information Society are only now beginning to be extended to the rural areas. Related trends are also noticeable in other parts of the world, including Brazil and South Africa.

With proper planning, ICTs can indeed be integrated into the fabric of existing social, business, educational, and governance activities in rural areas. Such models may start off as the basic telecenter or cybercafe (in areas where many cannot afford to buy their own PCs and Internet connections), but have the potential to migrate all the way up the value chain to become full-fledged knowledge centers, where external knowledge is localized and contextualized and local knowledge generation is facilitated and then shared with external communities.

Key activities in such ICT-blended development models in rural areas include synergies between new media and traditional media, transactive activities (e.g., e-commerce, clicks-and-bricks commerce), and intellectual capital management (e.g., converting local intellectual property into licenses for revenue sources). So far, very few rural knowledge center initiatives have progressed all the way along this

Figure 1.3

Development communities at Dgroups *(Source: Bellanet)*

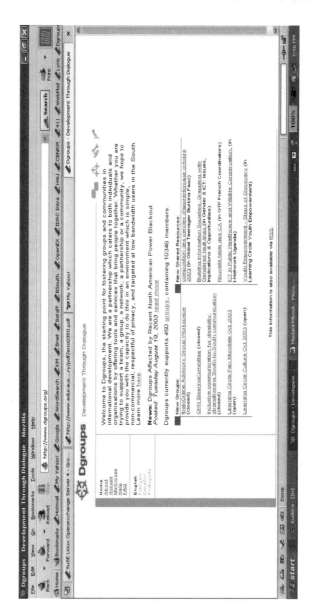

Figure 1.4

Knowledge Management for development site *(Source: Bellanet)*

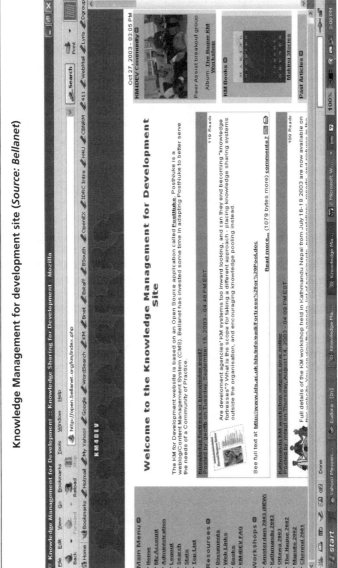

Table 1.16

Growth Path and Evolution of Rural Online Knowledge Centers	
Phase	**Characteristics**
Basic	Basic computer access, surfing Net, downloading forms
Interactive	E-mail, customization of forms
Publishing	Creating content and documents for the Internet, intranet, CD-ROMs
Transactive	E-commerce, job creation, marketing
Knowledge enabled	Digesting/localizing knowledge assets, creating local knowledge assets
Integrative	ICTs + radio + traditional media
Knowledge capitalizing	Leveraging intellectual capital for financial returns, gain
Globalizing	Exporting model/IP to other parts of the world
Transformative	Radical restructuring of rural economy, networks
Source: Author.	

value chain (see Table 1.16), with a few notable exceptions, like the M.S. Swaminathan Foundation's Village Knowledge Centre initiatives in south India.

Building a viable knowledge environment across the world is both a local and a global responsibility, and the story of its creation via appropriate KM tools, cultures, and energies will be the epic story of the 21st century.

References

Afele, J.S. (2003). *Digital Bridges: Developing Countries in the Knowledge Economy*. Hershey, Pennsylvania: Idea Group Publishing.

Ahmed, P., Lim, K.K., and Loh, Ann (2002). *Learning through Knowledge Management*. Boston: Butterworth-Heinemann.

Allee, V. (2003). *The Future of Knowledge: Increasing Prosperity through Value Networks*. Amsterdam: Butterworth-Heinemann.

Applehans, W., Globe, A., and Laugero, G. (1999). *Managing Knowledge: A Practical Web-based Approach*. New York: Addison-Wesley.

Beerli, A., Falk, S., and Diemers, D. (2003). *Knowledge Management and Networked Environments: Leveraging Intellectual Capital in Virtual Business Communities*. New York: AMACOM.

Brown, J.S. and Duguid, P. (2000). *The Social Life of Information*. Boston: Harvard Business School Press.

Collins, H. (2003). *Enterprise Knowledge Portals: Next Generation Portal Solutions for Dynamic Information Access, Better Decision Making and Maximum Results*. New York: AMACOM.

Conway, S. and Sligar, C. (2002). *Unlocking Knowledge Assets*. Upper Saddle River, New Jersey: Prentice-Hall.

Davenport, T. and Prost, G. (2002). *Knowledge Management Case Book: Siemens Best Practices*. New York: John Wiley & Sons.

Davenport, T. and Prusak, L. (2003). *What's the Big Idea? Creating and Capitalising on the Best Management Thinking*. Boston: Harvard Business School Press.

Denning, S. (2001). *The Springboard: How Storytelling Ignites Action in Knowledge-Era Organisations*. Boston: Butterworth-Heinemann.

Dixon, N. (2000). *Common Knowledge: How Companies Thrive by Sharing What They Know.* Boston: Harvard Business School Press.

Figallo, C. and Rhine, N. (2002). *Building the Knowledge Management Network: Best Practices, Tools and Techniques for Putting Conversation to Work.* New York: John Wiley.

Firestone, J. (2003). *Enterprise Information Portals and Knowledge Management.* Amsterdam: Butterworth-Heinemann.

Gamble, P. and Blackwell, J. (2001). *Knowledge Management: A State of the Art Guide.* New York: Kogan Page Limited.

Hasanali, F. and Leavitt, P. (2003). *Content Management: A Guide for Your Journey to Knowledge Management Best Practices.* Houston: American Productivity and Quality Centre.

Honeycutt, J. (2000). *Knowledge Management Strategies.* Englewood Cliff, New Jersey: Prentice Hall/Microsoft Press.

Keen, P. and Mackintosh, R. (2001). *The Freedom Economy: Gaining the m-Commerce Edge in the Era of the Wireless Internet.* New York: McGraw-Hill.

Kluge, J., Stein, W., and Licht, T. (2001). *Knowledge Unplugged: The McKinsey & Company Global Survey on Knowledge Management.* New York: Palgrave.

Koulopoulos, T. and Frappaolo, C. (1999). *Smart Things to Know about Knowledge Management.* Oxford: Capstone Publishing.

Lengnick-Hall, M. and Lengnick-Hall, C. (2003). *Human Resource Management in the Knowledge Economy: New Challenges, New Roles, New Capabilities.* San Francisco: Berrett-Koehler Publishers.

Malhotra, Y. (2001). *Knowledge Management and Business Model Innovation.* Hershey, Pennsylvania: Idea Group Publishing.

McElroy, M. (2003). *The New Knowledge Management: Complexity, Learning and Sustainable Innovation.* Boston: Butterworth-Heinemann.

Mertins, K., Heisig, P., and Vorbeck, J. (2003). *Knowledge Management: Concepts and Best Practices.* Berlin: Springer-Verlag.

Nantel, R. (2004). *Knowledge Management Tools and Technology 2004: 35 Systems to Maximize Your Organization's Intellectual and Human Capital.* New York: Brandon Hall.

Natarajan, G. and Shekhar, S. (2000). *Knowledge Management: Enabling Business Growth.* New Delhi: Tata McGraw-Hill Publishing Company.

Newell, S., Robertson, M., and Swan, J. (2002). *Managing Knowledge Work.* New York: Palgrave.

Nonaka, I. and Nishiguchi, T. (2001). *Knowledge Emergence: Social, Technical, and Evolutionary Dimensions of Knowledge Creation.* Oxford: Oxford University Press.

Norris, D., Mason, J., and Lefrere, P. (2003). *Transforming e-Knowledge: A Revolution in the Sharing of Knowledge.* Ann Arbor, Michigan: Society for College and University Planning.

Quinn, S. (2002). *Knowledge Management in the Digital Newsroom.* Oxford: Focal Press.

Rao, M. (2002). *The Asia-Pacific Internet Handbook, Episode IV: Emerging Powerhouses.* New Delhi: Tata McGraw-Hill Publishing Company.

Rao, M. (2003a). *Leading with Knowledge: Knowledge Management Practices in Global InfoTech Companies (The KM Chronicles, Travelogue 1).* New Delhi: Tata McGraw-Hill Publishing Company.

Rosenberg, D. (2002). *Cloning Silicon Valley: The Next Generation High-Tech Hotspots.* London: Pearson Education.

Ruggles, R. (1996). *Knowledge Management Tools.* Amsterdam: Butterworth-Heinemann.

Rumizen, M.C. (2002). *The Complete Idiot's Guide to Knowledge Management.* Wisconsin: Alpha Books.

SAP/PriceWaterhouseCoopers (2001). *The E-Business Workplace: Discovering the Power of Enterprise Portals*. New York: John Wiley.

Schneiderman, B. (2003). *Leonardo's Laptop: Human Needs and the New Computing Technologies*. Cambridge: MIT Press.

Smith, D. (2000). *Knowledge, Groupware and the Internet*. Boston: Butterworth-Heinemann.

Srikantaiah, T.K. and Koenig, M. (2001). *Knowledge Management for the Information Professional*. Medford, New Jersey: Information Today, Inc.

Sullivan, D. (2004). *Proven Portals: Best Practices for Planning, Designing and Developing Enterprise Portals*. New York: Addison-Wesley.

Terra, J.C. and Gordon, C. (2003). *Realising the Promise of Corporate Portals: Leveraging Knowledge for Business Success*. Amsterdam: Butterworth-Heinemann.

Tiwana, A. (2002). *The Knowledge Management Toolkit: Orchestrating IT, Strategy and Knowledge Platforms*. Upper Saddle River, New Jersey: Prentice-Hall.

Wenger, E., McDermott, R., and Snyder, W. (2002). *Cultivating Communities of Practice: A Guide to Managing Knowledge*. Boston: Harvard Business School Press.

Wimmer, M. (2002). *Knowledge Management in e-Government*. Austria: International Federation for Information Processing (IFIP).

Online References

Review of KM books, http://www.destinationkm.com/articles/reading_index.asp.

KM: Networks and Narratives (KM World 2003 conference, Santa Clara), http://www.destinationkm.com/articles/default.asp?ArticleID=1102.

Knowledge Management and Business Intelligence (Marcus Evans, Asia), http://www.destinationkm.com/articles/default.asp?ArticleID=1096.

The "8 Cs" of Successful Knowledge Management in the InfoTech Sector, http://www.zdnetindia.com/news/features/stories/83520.html.

Content and Community Strategies for KM (KnowledgeNets 2003, New York), http://www.destinationkm.com/articles/default.asp?ArticleID=1077.

A Decade of KM: APQC's annual KM Summit, Houston, 2003, http://www.destinationkm.com/articles/default.asp?ArticleID=1065.

KM in Australia (KM Challenge 2003 conference, Melbourne), http://www.destinationkm.com/articles/default.asp?ArticleID=1057.

KM in the pharmaceutical sector (Marcus Evans conference, London, Feb 2003), http://www.destinationkm.com/articles/default.asp?ArticleID=1037.

Braintrust KM 2003 Summit (San Francisco, February 2003), http://www.destinationkm.com/articles/default.asp?ArticleID=1040.

"Visions" paper for the ITU's World Summit on the Information Society, http://www.itu.int/osg/spu/visions/Conference/index.html.

Interview: KM at PMC-Sierra, http://www.destinationkm.com/articles/default.asp?ArticleID=1033.

Interview: KM at JD Edwards, http://www.destinationkm.com/articles/default.asp?ArticleID=1025.

Corporate Portals and KM (Hong Kong summit, December 2002), http://www.electronicmarkets.org/files/cms/40.php.

Case Study: KM in Tata Steel, http://www.destinationkm.com/articles/default.asp?ArticleID=1019.

Gartner Summit: Trends in KM, e-learning (Mumbai, September 2002), http://www.destinationkm.com/articles/default.asp?ArticleID=1007.

The 8Cs of Successful Knowledge Management (KM Asia 2002 review), http://www.electronicmarkets.org/files/cms/31.php.

Braintrust KM 2002 Summit, San Francisco, http://www.electronicmarkets.org/files/cms/18.php.

Interview: Knowledge Management at Infosys,
  http://www.destinationkm.com/articles/default.asp?ArticleID=982.
Wireless KM Technologies (KM Asia 2002, Singapore),
  http://www.destinationkm.com/articles/default.asp?ArticleID=973.
KM and content (Asia Intranet Content Summit, Singapore),
  http://www.indiainfoline.com/nevi/inwi/mm64.html.

Part I

Knowledge Management at Accenture*

2

Svenja Falk

> The execution of our entire business strategy to be market maker, architect and builder of the new economy is dependent on how we create, share and protect knowledge. Knowledge Sharing is the essence of how we bring innovations to change the way the world works and lives.
>
> *Joe Forehand, Managing Partner & CEO*

Introduction

I remember spending literally one whole term reading and discussing the first three pages of Hegel's Phenomenology of Mind in a university class. A total of five months spent on approximately 6,000 letters is a luxury of the past. In general, people do not like to read much to learn more these days. Especially in a knowledge-based business like consulting, the need to absorb tons of frameworks, strategic approaches, data, and blueprints has resulted in a changing attitude toward knowledge and information. This is reflected in their expectations on a truly effective knowledge management (KM) system. People want a "one-stop shop" solution with one user interface, one data repository containing a collaborative and content management functionality. To match those expectations, it is critical for a company thinking about the future of their KM solutions to keep one fact in mind: a system that is not used is a waste of money. In

---

* *Editor's Note:* This chapter covers key lessons learned from 10 years of knowledge management at Accenture. The majority of knowledge workers in leading consulting firms today are well versed with IT tools in the workplace and have expectations of "one-stop shop" solutions for their knowledge needs. Accenture's KM system evolved through four phases: early enabling infrastructure, knowledge as byproduct, actively managed knowledge, and knowledge-enabled enterprise.

The knowledge repository, called Knowledge Xchange (KX), hosts content ranging from proposals and client deliverables to white papers and links to experts. On a monthly basis, 400,000 orders for knowledge capital are generated and over 2,000 contributions for knowledge capital are made. Looking beyond the numbers, KM at Accenture has helped increase the rate of innovation, decrease the time to competency, and improve productivity. A key observation is that information quality management will emerge as an important competitive differentiator in the future.

order to cope with a system which has been in operation for 10 years, Accenture launched an organization-wide intranet portal in July 2001 to offer users a single gateway to the internal knowledge repository, called the Knowledge Xchange (KX).

Company Profile

Accenture is the world's leading management consulting and technology services company. Committed to delivering innovation, Accenture collaborates with its clients to help them realize their visions and create tangible value. With deep industry expertise, broad global resources, and proven experience in consulting and outsourcing, Accenture can mobilize the right people, skills, alliances, and technologies. With more than 75,000 people in 47 countries, Accenture works with clients in nearly every major industry worldwide. Through the integration of consulting and outsourcing, Accenture:

- Identifies critical areas with potential for maximum business impact
- Innovates and transforms the processes in those areas
- Delivers performance improvements and lower operating costs by assuming responsibility for certain business functions or areas
- Holds itself accountable for results

Accenture generated net revenues of $11.6 billion for the fiscal year ended August 31, 2002.

The Evolution of Accenture's Knowledge Management System

Accenture can refer to over 10 years of experience in KM. Way back in 1992, a Lotus Notes-based infrastructure was put in place to enable consultants to contribute and find knowledge capital across geographies and time zones. As was quite common for those days, the sponsors of the system thought that technology alone would make it happen. This, of course, was not true, and after a short while the system contained redundant or superfluous content which was difficult to navigate due to insufficient indexing. However, it was a notable way of starting to institutionalize global communication across borders and time zones. People began to appreciate the fact that they could learn collaboratively with their collegues from Stockholm, Johannesburg, or New York. The culture of knowledge sharing via information technology (IT) platforms emerged, but the architecture and processes needed some redesign.

Two years later, this problem was solved by standardizing the processes of contributing and retrieving knowledge which was now managed by dedicated knowledge managers. Today, a group of 300 people globally coordinate activities to ensure that the right knowledge is brought to the right people at the right time. Their role is focused on the "systematic progress of achieving organizational goals through the capture, synthesis, sharing, and the use of information, insights and experiences." The KM organization is now part of the learning organization to ensure seamless enabling processes within the firm (see Figure 2.1).

The Status Quo

Top-management sponsorship, necessary to have the best KM system in place, had always been the prerequisite for the improvements of architecture and processes. The wisdom that knowledge sharing is intrinsic to the execution of Accenture's business strategy has led the effort to constantly reevaluate the KM system.

Figure 2.1

The evolution of Accenture's KM system

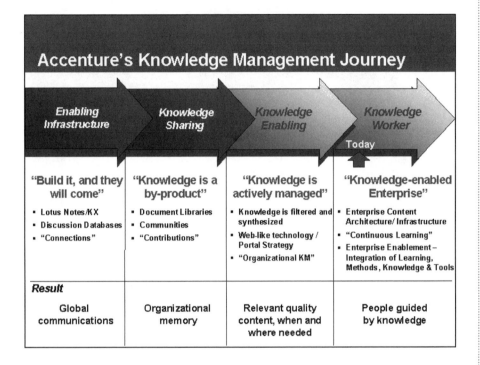

Approximately 7,000 databases cataloging Accenture employees' knowledge capital and client experience constitute the core of the company's KM system. These databases commonly center on Accenture's market units (e.g., communications and high tech, financial services, products, resources, government) and service lines (e.g., strategy and business architecture, customer relationship management, supply chain management, human performance). Some components of KX are global and others are unique to a client engagement or service line. Examples of items in these databases include:

- Proposals
- Client deliverables (sanitized if this is required by the client)
- Methodologies
- Thought leadership/white papers
- Links to external information
- Project plans
- Links to experts

Employees can access the Web-based KX from Accenture's more than 110 global offices or from remote locations such as client sites. The Web-based intranet portal, which has an intention-based home page, allows easy retrieval of knowledge without knowing which actually is the right database to go to (see Figure 2.2). It also provides access to Accenture's research organization to ensure that the data part of business questions is also covered. Furthermore, the find.expert page provides easy access to

Figure 2.2

Screenshot of the Accenture's KM portal

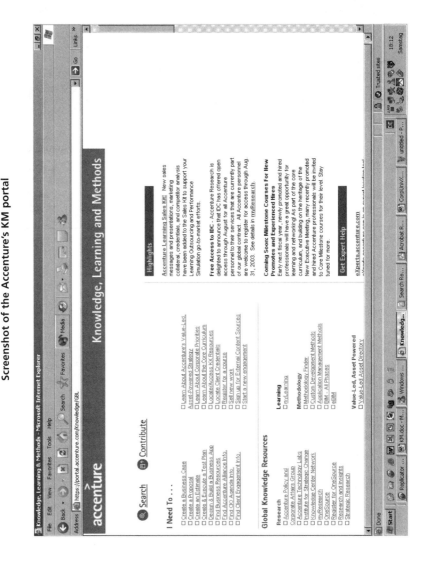

subject matter experts. "Communities of interest" can be joined online to foster online collaboration. The portal also provides access to firm-wide training opportunities; a wealth of courses can be taken online.

All enterprise knowledge is now aggregated, integrated, and personalized into an employee enterprise portal. The system is widely used. On a monthly basis 400,000 orders for knowledge capital are generated and over 2,000 contributions for knowledge capital are made. If printed, there would be over 2 million pages of knowledge capital available from KM managed applications.

What Is in There for Me? Benefits of KM

In consulting parlance, we call a situation "win win" if all participants benefit from an agreement. KM has to be in such a situation to be successful. For instance, imagine a German utility company facing the challenges of a deregulated market. The client team working with that company referred to experiences already made by consultants in the Nordic country where those markets have been liberalized for quite a while. They were able to adapt part of the Scandinavian solution to the German environment and helped the client to adapt to the challenges of an open market.

Apart from learning from each other's solutions—and of course mistakes—KM leads to:

- Increased rate of innovation
- Decreased time to competency
- Increased productivity

How Do I Get There? Learning to Share

To fully exploit the benefits of the system, consultants need to know how to navigate the system. Dedicated knowledge professionals provide on-site training just after people join the firm. If preferred, e-learning modules are available for self-training. However, the intention-based portal has taken away the mysteries of the past; the homepage is self-explanatory and easy to navigate. Furthermore, today's generation of consultants is accustomed to using information systems in a clever way without major instructions. Therefore, the enabling part of the KM role is becoming less important.

The Future

Knowledge is Accenture's market differentiator in ensuring that the company is perceived as an industry benchmark and thought leader. Through proper management of our knowledge capital, we avoid reinventing the wheel. Therefore, we will continue to ensure that we do have best practices in place. The following trends indicate the future of KM:

- Portals are taking center stage in the KM tool arena.
- There is a resurgence of interest in a single user interface and single data repository.
- Integration with collaboration is increasing.
- The adaptive workspace is emerging.
- People and processes are the core of every KM system, along with technology. KM is a business discipline rather than an application.
- Information quality management will emerge as an important competitive differentiator.

Building a Knowledge-sharing Network: Plan, Design, Execute . . . Reap?*

Farida Hasanali

> The productivity of knowledge has already become the key to productivity, competitive strength, and economic achievement.
>
> *Peter Drucker*

Introduction

Building a knowledge-sharing system to provide hundreds of organizations and thousands of workers with access to information that will help them do their job a little easier is a tall order to fulfill. The American Productivity & Quality Center (APQC) found out, as it built the Knowledge Sharing Network™, that the success of such an effort depends greatly on the ability of a knowledge management team to do its homework and then to make some wise choices.

The overwhelming driver for APQC, a member-based, non-profit organization, is to provide information, expertise, and opportunities that will enable an organization to make better decisions. APQC's formal mission is to work with organizations around the world to improve productivity and quality by:

---

* Editor's Note: This chapter is an excellent case study in implementing a KM infrastructure project and provides valuable and practical advice for KM practitioners. The Knowledge Sharing Network of the American Productivity & Quality Center (APQC) provides members with online access to a wide range of business resources on topics ranging from productivity to quality. In 2001, a top-level decision was taken to provide business content free to members over the Web. This chapter describes the interactions with the content management vendors, selection criteria, requirements analysis, knowledge taxonomy, modular development, phase-wise rollout, portal platform, interface design, template inventory, content management processes, community services, authorization, scalability, and testing.

Decisions and trade-offs like off-the-shelf package versus custom-built solution are discussed, as well as trickier issues like change management, use of new content categories, user training, transition ownership, and RoI considerations. Key objectives set for the knowledge networking project were to expand business, increase productivity, build customer loyalty, and expand employee goals and accountability. Lessons learned from the project exercise include making a proper business case for KM infrastructure, involving the user in the requirements phase, having realistic expectations, assigning a full-time role to the project, and the importance of harmonizing new KM infrastructure with organizational culture.

- Discovering, researching, and understanding emerging and effective methods of improvement
- Broadly disseminating research findings through education, advisory, and information services
- Connecting individuals with one another and with the knowledge and tools they need to succeed

In short, APQC provides organizations with access to content, to new ideas, and to each other. Since 1977, APQC has been fulfilling this mission through traditional channels. Networking and training events occur often, and APQC publishes guidebooks and benchmarking reports.

Its Web site was created in 1997 to disseminate marketing information on products and services. An important component of the site, however, was a members-only gateway to a repository of best practices. The best practices repository contained abstracts on articles found in business journals, periodicals, and industry trade magazines. The criteria for article selection was strict and had to provide information on an organization's effort to improve a process. The best practices database was a popular resource among the center's 500 members. Users depended on it for abstracts of the detailed results from a process or performance improvement initiative.

Organization Profile

An internationally recognized resource for process and performance improvement, APQC helps organizations adapt to rapidly changing environments, build new and better ways to work, and succeed in a competitive marketplace. With a focus on productivity, knowledge management, benchmarking, and quality improvement initiatives, APQC works with its member organizations to identify best practices; discover effective methods of improvement; broadly disseminate findings; and connect individuals with one another and the knowledge, training, and tools they need to succeed. Founded in 1977, APQC is a member-based, non-profit organization serving organizations around the world in all sectors of business, education, and government.

Today, APQC works with organizations across all industries to find practical, cost-effective solutions to drive productivity and quality improvement. APQC offers a variety of products and services, including consortium, custom, and metric benchmarking studies; publications, including books, white papers, reports, and implementation guides; computer-based, on-site, and custom training; individually sponsored research; and networking opportunities.

Rationale and Strategy for a New System

What prompted APQC to pursue a change? In 2000, APQC reassessed whether it was providing all that it could for organizations, especially members. The motivation to initiate a change was driven by a need to expand member benefits, create a central repository of all APQC research that could be disseminated easily and securely, provide staff with an outlet to publish material, reduce turnaround time on information technology (IT) requests, implement scalable technology and a consistent site architecture, and develop online content without assistance from an external provider.

In early 2001, APQC's executive team began to consider an e-business strategy. They knew APQC had years of research that resided untapped on its servers. This included electronic copies of benchmarking reports, case studies, presentations, surveys, tools, templates, metrics, measures, and articles. Several options were considered.

- Pay-per-view model—Create a repository of content that is open to the public and charge on a per-piece basis. This option was quickly dismissed because it did not fit with APQC's mission. Members were accustomed to access privileges, and pricing was another major issue. APQC creates its own content from primary and secondary research. The quality of the output is comparable to other major research firms, but the center's member base does not support a pricing structure similar to commercial research firms.

- Initial content provider model—This model initially was designed to provide members an all-encompassing portal (like Yahoo!) that allowed a member to set up a personalized page that would include news, weather, industry information, and APQC research. Upon further investigation, APQC found a number of reasons to not pursue this idea. In order to provide information from external sources, APQC would have to partner with several information providers to sublease their information on its site, and APQC had no past history on which to base the acceptability of this service from its members. Preliminary member feedback led APQC to its second or most important reason why it chose not to go with this initial content provider model: members wanted only APQC's research. They could get news and weather from many other sources, but APQC's research could only be found on its site. Their request was for APQC to focus on delivering its content to them in a personalized manner.

- Hybrid model—This model involved using natural language search engines along with intelligent agents to crawl APQC repositories and index content to create a repository that could then be displayed through a Web site. Search terms entered by members would continue to train the search agents and provide intelligent search results. The reason APQC chose not to invest in this option was that there was not a real business impact to their members in having this service. Although this option seemed very progressive, it entailed innumerable hours from both APQC and the software vendors. The technology itself was cost prohibitive for APQC. The total cost did not justify the benefits gained.

APQC's executive team had sat through months of presentations from different vendors. All options had some strengths and weaknesses, but none seemed to fit right. The executive team went back to the drawing board and again laid out the goals for this effort. The goal was adjusted to provide members access to APQC content in an organized and personal manner in order to provide more value to the membership.

The executive team then made a major strategic decision: to deliver all APQC's research to members as part of the membership benefits. In other words, published information that had previously cost up to $500 per unit would now be available free to members through the Web site.

This strategic shift caused APQC product groups to rethink their objectives and goals. For example, the publications department is charged with disseminating APQC research through the purchase of benchmarking reports. By providing content free to members over the Web, a large part of this group's customer base would disappear. They had to find new ways of reaching new customers to continue to support APQC's mission of information dissemination in fiscally responsible ways.

This new approach was proposed to the vendors who had already presented solutions to APQC, and surprisingly, their solutions easily adapted to the new requirements. (At the time, APQC did not realize that when a vendor said, "We can do whatever you want," that it actually meant, "That will cost extra!")

Figure 3.1

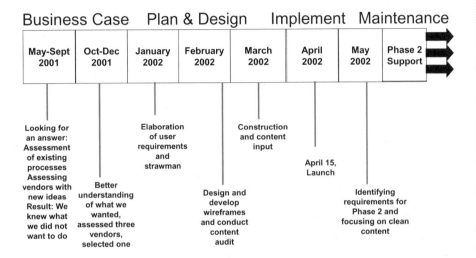

The executive team then appointed an executive champion, who in turn picked a team to design a solution. The core team initially consisted of an executive sponsor, a project manager, and the IT director. Their challenge was time. The decision was made in late October 2001, and the site had to be delivered in early April 2002 (see Figure 3.1).

Designing and Deploying a Solution

Vendor Assessment

The first step was to determine what the solution should look like. A critical requirements session was conducted with the executive champion, project manager, and technology director, as well as marketing and product group representatives. An external consultant in application and Web site deployment facilitated the session. The group identified two key elements: an initial set of functionality for the site and the realization that center staff would need external assistance in deploying the system.

With the requirements in hand, APQC again approached vendors. APQC's position to these vendors was, "We don't know what technology to use or what solution we should have. Here are the requirements; you propose a solution." Three solutions were proposed:

1. A custom solution based on software developed for other customers
2. Content management software, a search engine, and a custom portal for Web delivery
3. Content management software, a search engine, and a portal application for content delivery

To support the decision-making process, the vendor suggesting a custom solution created a prototype of the site so that the team could visualize what the application might look like. This was an eye-opening experience for the team. With no business analyst to guide the effort, the vendor created a prototype that was visually dismal.

There may have been adequate functionality in the background, but the delivery of the information was unprofessional.

The vendor suggesting the second solution seemed to understand what APQC wanted. Despite a more professional appearance, the team was wary of an absence of reputation for the vendor. Another consideration was that the solution had incremental costs that could not be determined up front. The risk was too high because APQC had a tight budget.

The vendor suggesting the third solution was selected by APQC. Several factors ruled this decision. First, the vendor came to the office prepared with two architects, one client manager, a business analyst, and the sales manager. They had done their homework, knew what APQC did, and came prepared to answer questions. Some of the key factors that affected the decision were:

- The vendor assumed some of the risk.
- The solution met the requirements and was bid at a fixed cost.
- The team and the vendor seemed to work well together.
- The vendor offered a proven solution that it had experience in implementing.

Gathering Requirements

APQC purchased the software based on the specifications provided by the vendor, and sessions began to capture detailed requirements for software and application development using use case modeling. A critical success factor in the sessions was the note taking by the business analyst. She captured all details and followed up on all requests. At times, team members would say something and completely forget about it, and she would bring it up the next day to make sure if the team had been serious about incorporating it or if it was just a passing comment. The status meetings with detailed lists of what was accomplished and what was slated for the next week were critical to keeping the project on target.

Once the requirements were reviewed and approved, development began. The sessions involved two weeks to create a complete HyperText Markup Langauge (HTML) shell. With that, the architects could begin to build functionality. With a clear-cut document, requirements did not alter as the initiative progressed.

Building a Taxonomy

At the same time that the team was gathering requirements, a subset of the team was also building the taxonomy. APQC has used two internal taxonomies for several years. APQC's Process Classification Framework is a hierarchical listing of processes. It serves as a high-level, generic enterprise model that encourages organizations to see their activities from a cross-industry process viewpoint instead of from a narrow functional viewpoint. The other taxonomy was its topic taxonomy. As APQC provided content to its members over 26 years, it gathered several hundred commonly used terms that members used to find information. That list, however, needed to be revised. Terms were collapsed into 16 categories and reviewed by APQC librarians. The final list was approved by APQC's president. This list forms the topic taxonomy for content in the system today.

Development

Because the time line was 16 weeks, the team could not follow the traditional approach of developing the whole system, getting approval, testing the system, redesigning, retesting, and then deploying it. The vendor instead built the system in modules. The team needed the content management piece first. This would allow team members to start inputting data into the system. The content management module was developed first, team members trained on it briefly, and they began to post content to the system.

Next came the development of search functionality. The decision had been made to use knowledge trees, which was a functionality provided by the search engine to form index listings of the content that matched the taxonomy. Knowledge trees enabled users to browse the taxonomy and view listings of content tagged with whatever term the user had selected to view.

Deciding how to display search results in a user-friendly format was challenging for APQC. The APQC team had viewed many popular sites for examples, and all of them displayed search results by relevance (i.e., the number of times a particular term appears in a document). APQC began with this model and then developed a slightly more complex version a few months after the Knowledge Sharing Network launched.

At launch, the basic search functionality displayed documents based on how many times the user's search term appeared in the document. This posed a special challenge. In all APQC's research efforts, there are certain processes that are always addressed. Information technology, measures, culture, and change management are some such terms. Throughout the reports, APQC addresses how these processes are affected by the topic being studied. For instance, what change management issues must an organization address while creating or deploying a new brand strategy? Because of this practice of addressing common issues, when a member conducts a search on a common term such as change management, he/she is likely to get all the reports in the system in the search results, making the search results ineffective. Once members started using the service and expressed concern with the search results, APQC modified the basic search functionality to look for search terms in the title first, in the brief description next, and in the full text last.

Refining search criteria is definitely an ongoing process for most information-sharing sites and, if adequate resources are allocated to it, can become a critical success factor for the usability of the site.

Alongside the development of the search functionality was the ongoing development of the templates that would display the content. The decision was made to build only one template for all content items. Although challenging at times because all content does not necessarily look good in one format, the decision to have one common template was a good one. This became evident when APQC conducted its first content management software version upgrade and was able to save a considerable amount of time due to standardization.

Testing

Three types of tests were conducted on the system. The developers conducted unit testing; that is, as they developed modules, they tested the modules to make sure they worked according to specifications. Typically, developers other than the ones who wrote the functionality are involved in unit testing. The second level of unit testing was testing the whole system together. In this effort, because three different software packages were involved, the real test was to hook it all up together and see how it worked. The vendor was responsible for this testing. The third test was user acceptance testing. This test involved the team, as well as a cross-section of APQC employees including power users and inexperienced users. The goal was to get feedback on ease of use, functionality, and intuitiveness.

The integrator provided test scripts for the system that mimicked tasks that a user might conduct on a system. This was a critical factor during testing. Without a script, it would be impossible to recreate problems or track how they occurred. Users were instructed to follow test scripts at first, to note all their experiences, if functionality worked, what errors were encountered, etc. Then they could browse the site free form and provide general overall feedback on their experience on using the site. The site was tested on personal computers and Macintosh computers, as well as with popular browsers such as Microsoft's Internet Explorer and Netscape Navigator.

In spite of efforts made by the vendor and the team, testing continued to bring to light errors or functionalities that did not work as designed. Testing was certainly a critical step in the deployment cycle.

Launch

As the launch date approached, the vendor realized all the functionality would not be ready. Because the launch date had already been published to members, the team devised an alternative plan. A "soft launch" would be deployed on the planned date to a core group of members who had been anxiously waiting for the new site. The soft launch also provided an opportunity to get initial feedback from advanced users and have time to make adjustments before the vendors left. The strategy worked well. Advanced users provided excellent feedback, which was incorporated before the final launch. The soft launch also provided input into where members would need the most assistance. This enabled APQC to ensure any staff supporting customers during the main launch were aware of the problems and apprised of solutions in the potentially troubled areas.

Tools

- Content management software—Content management software, at the very least, must support the life cycle of a content item. The content life cycle addresses issues of content acquisition, content classification and management, and content delivery (see Figure 3.2). In APQC's case, the software needed to provide a mechanism for users to submit content, tag the content using the taxonomy, send it as per workflow to an editor who could approve it, and then store the content in a repository that the search engine could access and index.

The software used by APQC enabled all three components, but none necessarily out-of-box as had been claimed by the vendor. During the requirements session, the idea of not requiring a content management system was brought up. Because the content being delivered was primarily APQC owned, the issue raised was whether APQC had enough content to warrant an industrial strength application. The team even considered getting the integrator to build a custom module to support APQC's content management requirements.

Ultimately, the decision was made to stay with the original choice. This decision was based on two factors. One, APQC did not have a sense of how fast this system would grow. It only catered to APQC content today, but tomorrow members could request other sources. Second, APQC was averse to the idea of custom software. Having experienced the dependency on contractors for its best practices database, the team wanted to make sure a similar situation was not created with this setup.

Figure 3.2

Pro-forma social & intellectual capital report

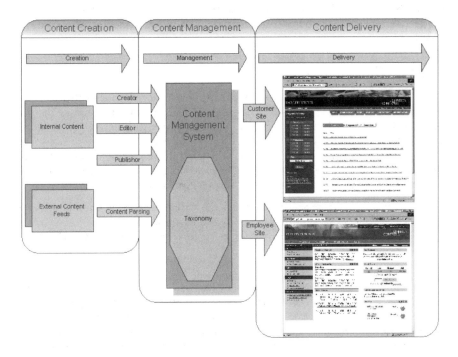

Looking back, however, the decision to go with a custom module may have been a good one. APQC would have saved $35,000 in the initial setup, and if members asked for more functionality, APQC could have hired a programmer to build it. The lesson learned is if your organization does not have in-house capabilities in the software you are buying, then you are going to have to pay a vendor whenever you want to make a change, regardless of whether the software is custom built or off the shelf.

Another factor to take into account when making the build versus buy decision is the scope of the functionality required and your organization's ability to control it. APQC was aware of the approximate number of content items it would put out on the site and the exact number of contributors to the site. Both these factors were within APQC's control, so even if the team had decided to go with the custom module, it could have planned the scope of the module accordingly. The primary reason that all these arguments fell through was that if the team had decided to go with the custom content management module, then the initiative would have to be delayed by at least a month. By weighing the total costs of the delay, the member impact, and the impact on resources involved in the deployment, the team decided to stick with the original plan and install off-the-shelf software.

No content management discussion would be complete without discussing XML (extensible markup language). XML is a markup specification language that enables the process of separating the content from the presentation layer in a system. Using standard XML schema enables organizations to share information across companies with partners and suppliers. The data is stored in component parts so that it can be delivered in a structured format, regardless of who is submitting content to the system. Although APQC is not using XML tags to define its content items at present, future plans involve reorganizing how content items are created and tagged in the Knowledge Sharing Network (KSN), using XML standards to make it easy to reuse parts of a content item for different purposes or to share content with external member sites if needed.

Portal

Purchasing the portal software was one of the best decisions made by the team. The same factors that caused uncertainty in the content management software decision were the ones that led to the certainty of the portal purchase decision. APQC did not know or have any control of how many people would access the portal or what functionality it would continue to build on it. Therefore, the decision was made to leave issues of scalability and response time to the professionals and purchase the software.

Three core functionalities made the portal very attractive:

1. The ability to create user profiles and allow users to provide a primary area of interest and deliver content based on the area chosen
2. The ability to target user groups for messages based on any demographic information in their profile
3. The ability to create communities

Communities in this context refer merely to technical functionality that would support the information-sharing efforts of a network of individuals that otherwise communicate with one another because they share a common interest. On the APQC portal, a community page allows a group of users to post content, create a community calendar, participate in discussion groups, and share a member directory.

Both the community pages and the ability to target content groups are truly out-of-box functionalities and require technical intervention only when special requirements are involved. All the above functionalities can be custom coded. An organization does not always have to buy a portal, but for APQC it was the right decision.

Change Management

Change is always difficult. In the case of APQC's rollout of its KSN, the change was big.

First, members had to reregister. A decision was made not to populate the new portal with the old data for two reasons. The information being required was different, and it was an opportunity to clean up unused user names and passwords that had been inactive for years. Second, members were used to having only one type of information: secondary research abstracts. Now they had access to seven other categories of information and were confused. To address this issue, APQC holds two orientation sessions for new users each month. These sessions have been very well received with an average of 15 users attending each session.

Internally, transitioning ownership of the content to various groups across APQC was more challenging than getting members to use the site. The premise behind purchasing the content management software was to decentralize content ownership across the groups. The first group to undergo training was marketing. Marketing is now fully responsible for information on the site concerning APQC's products, services, and upcoming events. The training has been slow and painful, partly due to the user unfriendliness of the software and partly due to the fact that it is a new process. The second set of individuals trained were the content publishers. This includes two groups of authors. The authors who write abstracts of articles selected from print publications, and the authors who write articles and white papers based on APQC primary research. The reasons for the slow transition were the same as the ones for the marketing staff with one added complication. The authors who submit abstracts are located remotely and require special setups to enable them to directly submit content. It is important to note that this was a major change for all the content contributors. They went from handing a content item to someone to get done to now being responsible for doing it themselves and being responsible for how it ultimately looked on the site. Although the transition was a bit rocky at first, some content authors agree that it is better for them to have control over their content than to run on someone else's time line.

Where change management is concerned, the APQC content management team considers it as an ongoing process that will evolve as user needs change. Change management is not a process that begins and ends with the deployment of a solution.

Return on Investment

RoI (return on investment), calculated by subtracting the total cost of a solution from the total benefits acquired, is a highly abused term these days in the technology arena. RoI is the new buzzword replacing older terms such as payoff or gains. That is not to say that it is not a valid concept. The premise of RoI is that an organization must undertake an initiative and spend money only if there is something to gain from it, not because it feels like the right thing to do or someone needs something to do. That said, the focus of RoI within organizations seems to have shifted from gains to "hard dollars" in great part due to the burnout of organizations that were victims of the technology boom and that lost millions in hollow claims made by vendors promising high returns on technology investments.

Although RoI has come to mean "dollar savings," RoI can be gained in soft savings as well as in dollars. Soft RoI refers to savings that cannot be easily quantified. A classic example of soft RoI is time saved. Although some may consider time saved as a quantifiable amount, such as dollars per hour paid to an employee multiplied by the number of hours saved, management rarely accepts this formula as hard-dollar savings. The argument is that time saved is not a measure of RoI, because employee salaries remain the same regardless of time spent. If that extra time leads to the generation of additional revenue, then it is a measure of hard RoI.

Different solutions lend themselves to different RoI expectations. An organization that is embarking on an initiative to convert its paper brochures into online searchable material does not have to worry about RoI. It is evident in the benefits gained from electronic distribution. The hard RoI is money saved because of not printing paper copies. The soft RoI is increased customer satisfaction in being able to search through all the literature at once and find information or in only printing the literature the customer is interested in. On the other hand, initiatives undertaken to improve access to information or to foster communication among employees have a far greater challenge trying to prove RoI.

The key is to think about RoI at the beginning of the initiative and not at the end. Regardless of whether your management required you to come up with a business case for your initiative, the measures of success for your initiative should be outlined at the start in order to get management buy-in and agreement on measures of success.

APQC's KSN had been a strategic initiative driven by the executive team. Although the reasons for pursuing the initiative were crystal clear, there was initially no request to prove RoI. As soon as the site was deployed, the term RoI started surfacing in executive meetings. Fortunately, some measures were already in place. They were not necessarily RoI goals, but rather growth goals. Measures included the number of new content items added each month, the number of new registered users each month, the number of active users each month, and customer satisfaction scores calculated quarterly through a survey administered to registered users.

The executive who championed the KSN recommended revisiting the initial reasons for deploying the KSN and building a scorecard* of measures around it. Four quadrants were set up to match APQC's strategic priorities for the year:

1. Expand business
2. Increase productivity
3. Build customer loyalty
4. Expand employee goals and accountability

The team reviewed several measures, picked the ones that were important to the executives and to the KSN, and categorized them in the above-mentioned categories. Expanding the business was measured through the number of leads generated by the network, revenue from network leads, the number of registered users in the networks that are also buyers of APQC products and services, and revenue from these registered users. Increased productivity was measured through the budget versus actual, the budgeted labor costs versus actual, and the budgeted external technology costs versus actual. There are several other measures for this quadrant that organizations can use, such as post-implementation maintenance and support costs versus present costs, time spent looking for information versus current time spent, and time spent recreating existing information versus reuse. To build customer loyalty, the team measured the number of community events, community members, registered network users, "KSN Updates" subscribers, orientations held, and orientation participants. Finally, to expand employee goals and accountability, the team measured employee achievements versus goals and the number of content items in the KSN.

The measures on the scorecard have shown increased activity in all the quadrants, except expenses. The KSN attracts 800 new users a month on average. There are more than 450 members in APQC's knowledge management community, an average of 1,500 active users each month, and conservatively 2 member renewal decisions each month influenced by the existence of the KSN.

It is important to note that these are measures of the network's impact, not RoI. The team came to the realization that nothing on the KSN would directly bring in dollars. Although the KSN is the platform on which all APQC publications and conferences are sold, and where consortium study proposals are posted, none of the revenue is attributed directly to the KSN. The argument is that marketing messages drive traffic to the site, which leads to sales. Therefore, the effectiveness of the KSN is measured in terms of activities undertaken to ensure that the content provided is valuable to the members and to increase traffic to the site.

---

* Adapted from Norton Kaplan's *Balanced Scorecard Approach.*

What Did the KSN Provide for APQC?

- A strong technical infrastructure to build on
- A repository of all APQC research and tools
- A personalized experience for registered users
- A tangible deliverable for membership
- A new content taxonomy
- A strong search engine
- A work flow to streamline the process for posting content to the repository
- The ability for employees to post content to the site by decentralizing content submission
- The ability to display targeted marketing content to viewers based on area of interest to generate leads

---

Lessons Learned

- Business case—While creating a business case for any initiative, take time to understand what management will ultimately look for in the system. Even if the system is a management mandate, make sure measures are in place. If possible, leverage other larger strategic initiatives in the organization by integrating the effort as part of the larger initiative.
- Design and development—Spend time on identifying the appropriate user representatives, and gather detailed requirements. Not involving the end-user is the primary cause for the initiative to fail, other than running out of money. If implementing a content management system, then conduct a content audit, and delete outdated or unused content. The more current the content, the more people will use it. If the system is being implemented enterprise wide, rollout should be in phases, which will provide value through lessons from the previous phase. A steering committee (group of executives who believe in the idea), when involved in the creation of the business case, is instrumental in breaking down barriers encountered during design and development.
- Communication—Do not over promise. Be realistic about what the system can do.
- Resources—Commit resources to the initiative. There must be at least one full-time employee who manages the whole initiative or else time lines will be difficult to meet due to lack of accountability.
- Change management—An organization's culture will not change because of the network. Design the system to match the culture as much as possible. Go with the people who support the effort, and the others will come along as positive results are reported. Also, always provide support. Support needs are generally high right after launch, but it is critical that users feel supported at this time. Good customer support will lead to avid evangelists who will market the system for you freely.

Conclusion

What did APQC do right while implementing the KSN?

- Vendors were fired when it was apparent the relationship was not going to work.
- Customers were asked what they wanted to see.

- APQC hired a consultant with experience in application deployment who had not bid on the job.
- An executive sponsor was completely involved in the project.
- The project had dedicated resources.
- The integrator's deployment methodology was closely followed.
- The team made decisions regarding functionality based on cost, time frame, and customer priorities.
- Numerous customer announcements forced the team to meet all deadlines.
- Projects were delivered on or under budget.
- Marketing was involved and had the ultimate say in the look and positioning of products and services.
- The team that gathered requirements represented departments across APQC, yet decisions were made only by three people. That avoided analysis paralysis.

In closing, the best advice may be not to get overwhelmed by the extent of the task, but to break it down into manageable segments and get started. Unless you get the ball rolling, many months will be wasted in contemplation. With technology, every month brings in massive changes in market players and functionalities. The longer you wait, the tougher the decisions will be.

Power to the People: Supporting Collaborative Behaviors for KM with Online Conferencing Technology*

Beat Knechtli

> In today's economy the most important resource is no longer labour, capital or land—it is knowledge.
>
> *Peter Drucker*

Introduction: The KM Context

The questions posed by the knowledge economy offer a unique opportunity to help organizations shift from the mechanistic, linear thinking of the Industrial Age to a more dynamic view of the world being ushered in by discoveries from a wide variety of scientific and human behavior fields. Business leaders must question and rethink underlying business models and practices in order to incorporate the new fundamentals for successfully leveraging knowledge to create value.

---

* *Editor's Note:* The Asea Brown Boveri (ABB) Group of companies operates in around 100 countries and employs around 135,000 people in the utilities industry. With such an extended reach in a high-pressure globalized economy, KM tools are required for real-time collaborative activity, communication, meetings, and content preparation by employees, suppliers, and customers. This chapter covers the use of tools like ABB eMeeting Center, rollout after pilot tests, and work impacts. ABB's KM team collects a wide range of statistics (as illustrated in numerous figures and tables) to monitor usage of the collaboration tools and their impacts on productivity and competitiveness. Real savings have also been delivered to the bottom line in terms of reduced travel costs and less paper documentation.

Examples are provided of the tools in action during the Dow Chemical/ABB alliance, preemptive action against the "Goner" virus outbreak, and team collaboration for a management education program. Future plans include incorporating a Web interface for wider (though secured) access. A key learning has been that only by creating an adequate environment, culture, and infrastructure support will people adopt knowledge-sharing behaviors and the enabling tools. The tools must have a strong link to the business imperative, will require continuous learning as the tools evolve, and must be integrated with systematic knowledge processes.

The knowledge questions go very deep into our underlying assumptions of how we create value. Leadership teams preparing for the new economy will find themselves engaged in challenging, provocative, and sometimes baffling and paradoxical situations. Those companies willing to live by these questions, however, will build the adaptive capacity and necessary tools needed for survival and prosperity in the "new" economy.

Company Profile

Asea Brown Boveri (ABB) is a global leader in power and automation technologies that enable utility and industry customers to improve performance while lowering environmental impact. The ABB Group of companies operates in around 100 countries and employs around 135,000 people. Headquartered in Zurich, Switzerland, its shares are traded on the stock exchanges in London/Zurich, Stockholm, Frankfurt, and New York.

More than half of ABB's revenues come from European markets and nearly a fifth come from Asia, the Middle East, and Africa, while about a quarter come from the Americas. The ABB Group was formed in 1988, when the Swedish Asea and the Swiss BBC Brown Boveri merged under the name ABB. Asea's history dates back to 1883; BBC Brown Boveri was founded in 1891.

ABB has streamlined its divisional structure to focus on two core businesses: power technologies and automation technologies. ABB Power Technologies serves electric, gas, and water utilities, as well as industrial and commercial customers, with a broad range of products, systems, and services for power transmission, distribution, and automation. ABB Automation Technologies delivers solutions for control, motion, protection, and plant integration across the full range of process and utility industries.

ABB's strategy is to offer more value for customers while building a leaner organization. To do this, we must know our customers well and, in turn, help them become more productive. We succeed when they succeed. The strategy in itself is not unique—how we deliver is. ABB is moving all of its offerings to a common architecture to deliver industrial information technology (IT)-enabled products and services that allow our customers to optimize their operations and link up in real-time with their suppliers and customers. The result is a leap in efficiency, quality, and competitiveness.

We are organized from the outside in to make sure our customers have quick and easy access to everything they need from ABB when and where they need it—whether they buy from us directly or through distributors, wholesalers, system integrators, or other partners. Our businesses work together to present one face, one offering, and one simple and seamless set of values to customers.

KM Practice: Online Conferencing at ABB

ABB's Online Conferencing Service based primarily on IBM's Lotus Sametime allows ABB employees around the globe to communicate instantly with their colleagues who also use the service. The application allows employees to find other people online; create personalized lists of team members and colleagues; schedule online meetings; and collaborate with colleagues simultaneously on the same document, presentation, or design. The service is maintained on dedicated servers in four regions: Americas, Asia Pacific, Europe, Nordic & MEA (Middle East and Africa).

Developed first by Lotus/IBM in 1997, Sametime surfaced as a pilot program in ABB Offshore Systems during the spring of 1998 and was quickly acknowledged by employees worldwide. A new trend toward real-time interaction and collaboration was established, leading to a full-scale global project. Today, Sametime is a standard Global Service in ABB around the globe. Current usage is in the office, at home, and on the road; future users will include external partners, customers, and suppliers.

Objectives and Benefits of the KM Practice

The objective of online conferencing is to provide the business with a cost-saving method of effective communication and to help develop a culture of communication and information sharing that will benefit ABB and increase productivity. For example, a design engineer in Norway can consult instantly with another engineer in the United States. The two employees can view exactly the same technical documents, allowing them to make alterations and suggest improvements in real-time, all without the delay that would be caused by sending the information back and forth via e-mail and clarifying the exact meaning of the information shared in the e-mails. This also greatly reduces the need for employees to travel to other offices for meetings, saving on the costs of travel, accommodation, and subsistence. The costs for the Online Data Conferencing Service are internally recovered through the group service catalog.

Most ABB offices have networks equipped with ABB's basic computing environment (BCE) which includes the Sametime tool. The Helpdesk teams have access to the installation software which can be downloaded from inside.abb.com. Users should always contact their local helpdesk to get the software installed. Each country also has a conferencing champion who can provide employees with the installation software, advice, and further information. No extra registration is required. Every Notes user who has set an Internet password is automatically qualified to use the service.

Success Stories

Since the introduction of Sametime in ABB, the service has produced many success stories. As soon as you discover the "power of presence" provided by the Lotus Sametime Connect client and the ABB eMeeting Center, you realize how it helps you and your team to stay connected and collaborate in real-time. What finally counts in today's challenging economic conditions is real savings to the bottom line.

Story A. Sametime Meeting on the Dow Chemical/ABB Alliance

This section captures some of the exchanges at the August 27, 2002, meeting between Arnold Allemang, Andy Berg, John Yost, and Dinesh Paliwal.

Arnold Allemang, Dow Executive Vice President, Member of Dow's Executive Committee, Corporate Operating Board and Board of Directors

> Our industry is 15–25% overcapacity in some product lines. It may take a decade to soak up that capacity. In commodity grades, our margins are razor thin. Even with our recent consolidation with Union Carbide, we struggle to boost profitability. It's a tough market out there, and there's no evidence things will change. So we need automation to increase productivity.
>
> To do this, we have to stop thinking about productivity as output, and instead think of it as input. What's the minimum level of input I can apply to these products to create and sell them? If we can make that shift in our thought processes, we will get the most out of our people resources, with the help of automation. And we will continue to make money.
>
> So our joint development with ABB in transferring our process knowledge from an internally developed system to a fully commercial system from ABB continues to be our key automation direction.

For instance, to maximize productivity, we don't want to take our production units down. So we need to work with ABB to make sure we can do "hot" software loads, on the fly, while the production unit is still running. There's real economic value here.

Another thing is security. Security is very important to us, especially after the terrorist attacks in the United States. There's very little general industry understanding of things like faultless process security. At the end of the day, you get there through process control.

Finally, our ability to maintain process control delivery schedules and meet the needs of our business units is extremely important to us. We tell the business units they have to get their process control from Dow corporate; they can't go shop around at Honeywell, Foxboro etc. So we have to meet their expectations.

We consider ourselves the best manufacturing people in the business. And the industry recognizes this. So the industry generally follows what we implement.

That's why our relationship with ABB is very important. We rely on ABB. And I am pleased to say that everything is working with the ABB relationship.

Andy Berg, Dow Process Automation Program Manager

We're very committed to our joint development with ABB. We believe when we're done with development, ABB's system with our process knowledge will be unique in the marketplace, which is good for ABB. ABB's team is leading the development effort, so we need him and his team to be creative and available. The Lotus "Sametime" tool has given us the ability to interact with ABB the same way we interact internally.

ABB's Industrial IT with the Aspect Integrator Platform is a great foundation for Dow. We are applying Aspects to our maintenance functions. We installed Industrial IT at our plant in Freeport, Louisiana, and now we are running Dow employees from other sites down there about every week because there's so much interest in seeing the equipment.

John Yost, ABB Group Vice President and Account Manager for Dow Chemical

Let me first state our mutual business objective. We're looking to boost profitability for both companies in a sustainable way. We've done a lot of work to break down the walls in areas that used to be proprietary. To help do this, we set up a "communications barrier" report. This helps tremendously to make sure everyone is communicating openly. And we have fun doing it.

Dinesh Paliwal, Executive Vice President, Head of Automation Technologies Division

Dow has our 100% commitment. We will do our utmost to keep open and honest communications. Dow means much to ABB, in many different ways, but especially in refocusing this company in a customer-centric fashion.

At our global management meeting in May, we focused on Dow. Not just to admire Dow, but because we don't have many customers with the culture of Dow, where we have joint kickoff meetings in different parts of the world to keep the entire global Dow/ABB team informed of our mutual direction.

We have never been as open before with a customer. To open ourselves up the way we have is not a trivial matter. It is the "next way of thinking."

Story B: Real-time Communication Helps Stop Virus Outbreak

Sametime once again demonstrated the benefits of instant real-time communication and collaboration within ABB during the "Goner" virus outbreak. ABB Notes administrators in the United Kingdom were alerted to a possible virus outbreak by an employee on Sametime. Within moments the Notes administrators in the United Kingdom had confirmed that the Goner virus had been released and that the e-mail system in the United Kingdom needed to be protected from the virus before infected e-mails started to arrive.

Having notified administrators in several countries, the UK administrators downloaded and applied a virus signature patch to their e-mail gateway. The first of hundreds of Goner-infected e-mails started to arrive at the UK gateway just 10 minutes after the administrators had completed the update of the virus protection.

The whole process from the first Sametime message from the user to the successful completion of the patch installation was a mere 15 minutes. Tony R. Sharp, one of the UK administrators involved in the work and a UK Sametime Champion, explained why Sametime had made the difference:

> We received the warning of the virus outbreak during the late afternoon. Before Sametime we would have relied upon mails being sent to colleagues in Sweden and elsewhere to share information and confirm steps that needed to be taken. In the event, some of the people we needed to contact were not in the office and would not have received the mails we would have sent them. We would have been waiting for a return receipt to confirm that our colleagues had seen our information and were able to act on it.
>
> However, using Sametime we were able to identify which colleagues were working late in Europe and we were able to inform them of the outbreak and get our strategy in motion within seconds. We were also able to draw on other resources within GP-IS in the UK to immediately assist us with the work that needed to be done. Using mail and phones only would have taken a great deal longer and been less effective.
>
> Had we not been able to work together in real time the virus would have certainly made its way onto our systems. And removing it would have taken some time and stopped us from doing other work. In the event, it did not happen that way. The use of Sametime saved us a great deal of time and effort.

In the UK's case, Sametime was proven to enhance the ability of people to do their jobs more quickly and effectively. It allowed administrators around the globe to communicate and assist each other efficiently, saving time and money.

Story C. Sametime: Better Communication, Lower Travel Costs

ABB's Sametime is one of the tools that can help the business reduce the need for travel, while providing a reliable platform for real-time collaboration and project management. It is being rolled out worldwide right now.

The communication possibilities and resources we already have in ABB are significant. If we all open our eyes to what is available, we will save time and money, as well as network resources, and we will increase productivity. "There is a positive impact both on the top and the bottom line," says Knut Meyn, GP-ISI Service Owner for Sametime Services. He continues, "Presence and availability are important aspects of a communication culture that can be enhanced considerably through the use of Sametime Services. Knowledge should be able to float freely in the organisation and information should be easily available and be part of our common resources from which we all may benefit."

ABB's activities have steadily become more and more global, which emphasizes the need for real-time technologies such as Sametime. The increase of daily users is climbing rapidly. From March to October of 2004, the number of worldwide Sametime users in ABB has more than doubled to well over 18,000. That number is increasing daily as ABB companies seek to take advantage of Sametime's cost-saving benefits.

Sametime offers online awareness and instant messaging, which also leads to group messaging. The software can be used to run e-learning and training sessions across the network. You can set up virtual meetings which are distributed across the world and hosted by regional servers. Sametime meetings can efficiently be held in combination with tools such as telephone conferencing. During such meetings people can share applications and presentations and remotely control programs and desktops. It is a highly effective collaboration tool.

Dispersed teams can therefore sustain a high degree of group activity, even being able to work on the very same document or file. It is also a very efficient form of collaboration, even if the participants are located across the globe from each other. Getting organized in logical online communities and groups makes it even simpler to instantaneously find people and groups.

All users in the United Kingdom are being given access to Sametime as part of a planned rollout. The roll out is being coordinated by the UK's Sametime Champion, Tony R. Sharp. He told us that it is important that ABB in the United Kingdom stay in the forefront of advances in such collaborative technology. "Some of ABB's competitors have shown that using Sametime in their organisation can deliver cost savings that enables them to gain competitive advantage. The UK is one of the larger parts of the ABB community so we have an opportunity to demonstrate what savings can be achieved by using Sametime."

All users will find Sametime very easy to use and will be impressed with the simple but comprehensive guides, tutorials, and tips available on the Sametime intranet site (inside.abb.gb.com/sametime). Sametime is monitored 24/7 by a virtual team in the four regional Information Systems (IS) centers in Sweden, Germany, the United States, and Singapore, so there is always someone available to ensure Sametime is working for ABB around the globe.

Departments or project teams can be grouped together logically in Sametime "Communities," and Sametime allows team members to collaborate simultaneously on documents without the need for multiple e-mails being sent back and forth. Managers are the priority for the Sametime rollout, quickly followed by all other users. Once people have experienced the benefits of Sametime, the use of the application will spread rapidly throughout all areas.

ABB's knowledge management team collects a wide range of statistics to monitor usage of the collaboration tools and their impacts: daily and weekly usage figures, maximum number of users, pattern of average hourly usage figures, growth of unique authenticated users, count of active ABB users in current year, number of meetings by day and month, and average numbers for meetings collected over the year (see Figures 4.1 and 4.2).

Service Extension: The ABB eMeeting Center

With the integration of more actual and potential customers of ABB, the use of IBM Lotus Sametime Connect was reaching its limits. In order to be more flexible and open, while securing the investments already made at ABB, a new tool had been selected, tested, and implemented to enhance the existing practice.

IBM Lotus Team Workplace: Instant, Secure Team Workspaces for the Web

IBM Lotus Team Workplace, a Web-based collaborative team workspace, integrates with existing applications, such as Lotus Notes 6 and Notes R5, Lotus

Figure 4.1

Actual meetings by month

Year	Month	Meeting	Number of Meetings	Average of Duration	Number of Participants	Average of Participants
2002			2'788	136	6'264	2.2
	12		2'788	136	6'264	2.2
		Instant	2'182	59	4'394	2.0
		Scheduled	606	413	1'870	3.1
2003			32'339	99	80'375	2.5
	1		4'824	90	10'468	2.2
		Instant	4'059	59	8'134	2.0
		Scheduled	765	255	2'334	3.1
	2		6'453	96	14'863	2.3
		Instant	5'576	59	11'367	2.0
		Scheduled	877	326	3'496	4.0
	3		6'139	108	16'145	2.6
		Instant	4'990	62	10'546	2.1
		Scheduled	1'149	311	5'599	4.9
	4		6'117	105	15'639	2.6
		Instant	4'973	59	10'655	2.1
		Scheduled	1'144	304	4'984	4.4
	5		5'351	97	14'085	2.6
		Instant	4'485	56	10'155	2.3
		Scheduled	866	307	3'930	4.5
	6		3'455	97	9'175	2.7
		Instant	2'837	56	6'407	2.3
		Scheduled	618	288	2'768	4.5
Grand Total			35'127	102	86'639	2.5

Sametime, and Microsoft Office XP, to help communicate in real-time, present ideas, and create and edit documents using familiar tools. IBM Lotus Team Workplace is a self-service application, so once administrators install the software on the server, users can take responsibility for creating a new team workspace and managing users for the workspace.

IBM Lotus Team Workplace has the customization capabilities that allow companies to maximize their investment in Web applications. Web designers and developers can customize the look and features of IBM Lotus Team Workplace to fit either horizontal or an industry segment's specific requirements. Changes to the look and functions of multiple IBM Lotus Team Workplace can be propagated simultaneously through centralized administration and template designs. IBM Lotus Team Workplace can also be integrated in a Web portal using the IBM Lotus Team Workplace Java/XML API.

Figure 4.2

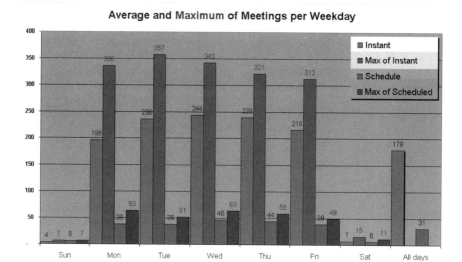

Average numbers for meetings collected since November 2002

ABB Quickplace Services: The Birth of the ABB eMeeting Center

In December 2002, the successful pilot phase for best utilization of Quickplace (QP) at ABB was finalized. This pilot, driven by Global Web Management (GWM), has proven QP to be the first choice to meet most of ABB's collaboration needs. QP has outstanding advantages to cope with the high and still growing demand for Web-based collaboration in projects, customer relations, task forces, and all other kinds of workgroups.

In January 2003, IS Applications Germany started to extend the services for QP and build up the ABB QP Service Center for the whole ABB Group. The migration phase during the first quarter of 2004 successfully relocated more than 70 QPs from Norway to Germany.

As of today, the new ABB QP Service Center provides QPs with enhanced services and features for everyone in ABB. A dedicated QP Service team with experts from ISA, ISI, and Helpdesk in Europe and the United States will ensure the productive and efficient collaboration based on QP.

What the eMeeting Center Offers to ABB Employees

Managing projects, accelerating and supporting internal processes, or simply safeguarding and intensifying relationships in today's business environment is increasingly dependent on continuous communication, exchange of knowledge, and ongoing self-organization within teams across organizational boundaries. Furthermore, facing the fact that communication and collaboration nowadays takes place among team members and business partners spread all around the world, the capability to work together at anytime from anywhere is absolutely crucial.

ABB's tool of choice to fulfill these requirements is QP, which can be set up easily and instantly and supports many kinds of collaborations right from the first day.

The newly designed ABB eMeeting Center (see Figure 4.3), based on QP, improves your ability to interact with people from all over the world without having to leave your desk. Its services include screensharing, document attachment to whiteboards, instant messaging, and polling. Combined with an Audio Conference, Lotus Sametime and its Meeting Center is a cost-and-time efficient solution that puts the world at your fingertips and helps ABB reduce unnecessary travel cost.

The ABB Meeting Center (as displayed in Figure 4.3) combines various tools in one window. The main part of the window hosts the area for screen/application sharing and the whiteboard (see Figure 4.4). On the right-hand side, a frame displays the meeting participants and their current Sametime status. On the bottom left, the interaction tab is displayed; it allows the moderator to send Web sites to the participants or poll them on any issue.

New data and drawings on the whiteboard, as well as the meeting room chat, can be saved by the meeting moderator. Letting another person drive the mouse on the screen has never been so easy and secure—grant or withdraw access with a single mouse click or even change the moderator during a session. To protect all meetings, all data transfers are encrypted and all meetings require a meeting password.

Purpose and Target

QP targets project teams, task forces, account teams, and all kinds of working groups, especially where external partners are involved. These teams can use QP as a community home during interactive phases of their projects and tasks.

During a project it is necessary to create and revise documents and presentations, work on draft concepts and discuss working progress, provide useful information links to people, and execute joint action planning as well as follow up open issues. This can become complicated and confusing via e-mail exchange, especially if the working group consists of many parties such as customers, consultancies, external agencies, vendors, and suppliers.

Therefore, it is useful to have one common workplace, where all of the work in progress can be stored, shared, and reviewed and where people can "meet" online and collaborate, discuss, and keep each other informed at the same pace and level at any time. QPs are established following a certain process, which evaluates that the intended use fits into the above profile.

QP does not replace ABB standards for maintaining and publishing information and material about products or for marketing (as within inside.abb.com/ www.abb.com, ABB Library, EDMS), but rather helps to bring this information plus all other specifics right to team members in the shape and functionality they need for their specific work. Table 4.1 compares benefits of QP usage across a range of activities.

Future Plans

Obviously, we will continue to try to leverage from our investments in Sametime and Quickplace/ABB eMeeting Center for the benefit of the customers and ABB. In mid-2003, we had an alternative option for ABB Sametime users to go along with a browser-based client, so that remote access to Sametime services from basically any place in the world is possible. Due to the very strict security guideline, these clients are

Figure 4.3

The eMeeting Center

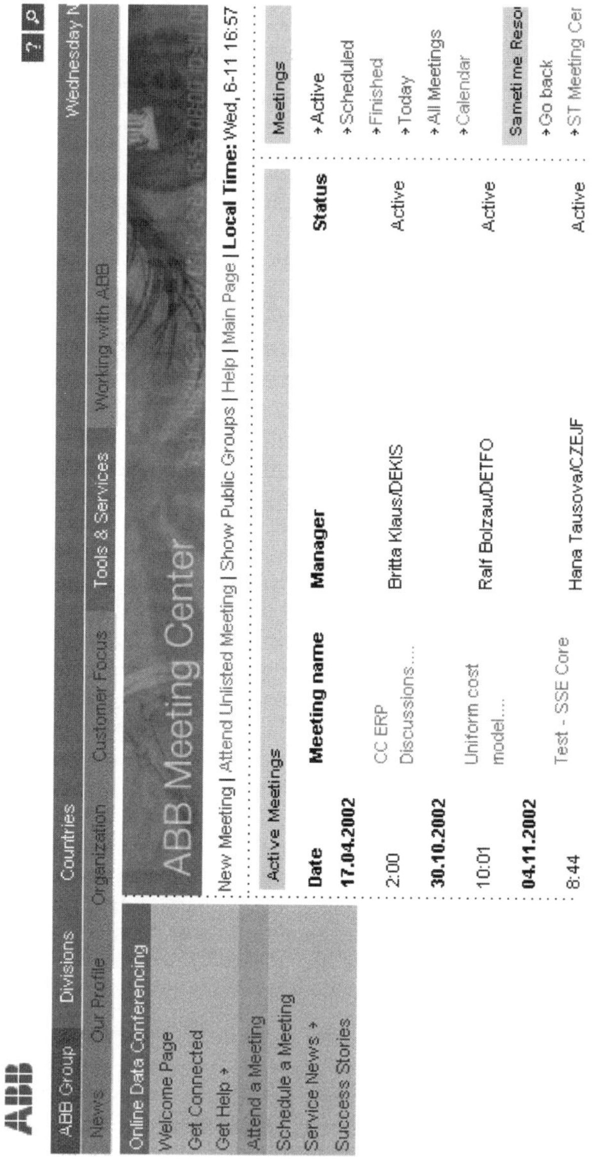

Figure 4.4

Features of the e-Meeting Center

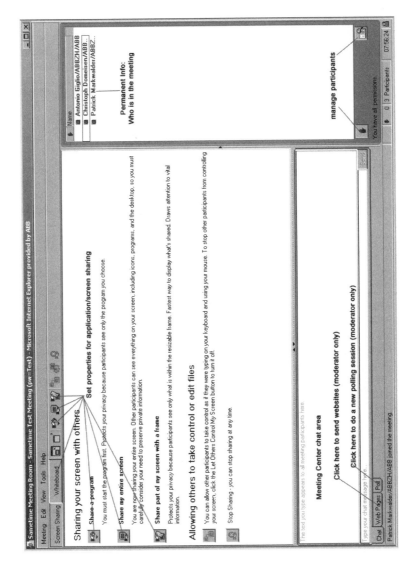

Table 4.1

Benefits Delivered for Collaborative Activities			
Activity	**Name**	**Description**	**Benefits**
Project collaboration	Sitra	Three teams located in Germany, on site and in Abu Dhabi	Less paperwork; latest and reliable information; reduced handling of technical documentation; reduced workload for back office
Online conference	Baan Conference	Participants from Europe, Australia, China, and Latin America	Reduction in travelling costs
Team collaboration	ABB Academy	Project workspace for the International Management Program	Allows participants from ABB to communicate and collaborate with each other and with external tutors and teachers; participants can work on specific tasks and projects between the IMP modules

not opened up for use by external partners, as they are located on the intranet of ABB. Nevertheless, a further integration of suppliers and customers in the online collaboration at ABB will be a target to reach for the near future.

Lessons Learned at ABB

When trying to use technology for the purpose of knowledge management (KM), a business need is an absolute must and prerequisite. In our KM approach, people and their interaction are key success factors. Logically, the need for interaction is first and the system or solution is second. We at ABB call that principle "systems on demand," instead of an approach where the solution is implemented first and, with a high probability, not used afterwards ("systems on supply"). Only then can IT systems and solutions be a real enabler for the business and a key element of a successful KM strategy.

When we started the process with the simple question of how to best organize a community and interaction, we quickly concluded that we should *not* organize it, but rather focus on how to create conditions for a community and interaction to exist. Only by creating an adequate environment and culture will people change and develop to a "Knowledge Sharing" concept. At the heart of KM, intensive communication and the sharing of knowledge are the main issues; leadership and leadership behavior are key. Knowledge needs brains and teams and a shared context (e.g., projects and business activity) to succeed. We should always remember that we cannot substitute the "human interface" by a technological contact.

Recommendations for KM Practitioners

To sum up, the following critical success factors are necessary for implementing and harnessing collaborative tools for KM:

- A strong link to business imperative
- Compelling vision and architecture
- Knowledge leadership
- Knowledge creating and sharing culture
- Continuous learning
- Well-developed information and communication technology (ICT) infrastructure
- Systematic knowledge processes

Conclusion

One should always remember that knowledge does not behave the same way as other resources. Knowledge, in the form of ideas, replicates endlessly. It is an infinite resource. Natural resources deplete with use. Knowledge expands with use. If a natural resource is sold or given to another, it is at the expense of whoever had to give it up. However, sharing knowledge allows both parties to not only retain the resource, but to amplify and expand it through the exchange process itself. This multiplier effect of knowledge as a resource means that significantly different economic equations must be brought to bear.

This infinite resource of knowledge that resides in and is largely controlled by individual workers and professionals cannot be managed with traditional Industrial Era methods. Prior to the recent focus on knowledge, most explorations of knowledge and organizations focused on information and data flows, being more concerned with the manipulation of documents and data "objects" than with the conversion of knowledge to value. In the heart of their KM strategy was ICT.

We still have much to learn about what this really means for the way that we will manage our organizations in this new economy—the knowledge economy. As more and more individuals appreciate the value of their knowledge, the ability to forge creative partnerships with each other becomes critical. People will only build knowledge together in an environment of trust and appreciation. This requires new management principles and a new ethic for knowledge sharing that is built on fairness and openness, yet it is a key leadership issue much more than a technical problem.

Resources

Allee, Verna (1997). *The Knowledge Evolution: Expanding Organizational Intelligence.* Boston: Butterworth-Heinemann.

Amidon, Debra (1997). *The Ken Awakening: Innovation Strategy for the Knowledge Economy.* Boston: Butterworth-Heinemann.

Buckowitz, Wendi and Williams, Ruth (1999). *The Knowledge Management Fieldbook.* Englewood Cliffs, NJ: Prentice-Hall.

Davenport, Tom and Prusak, Laurence (1998). *Working Knowledge*. Boston: Harvard Business School Press.

Krogh, George Von, Ichijo, Kazuo, and Nonaka, Ikujiro (2000). *Enabling Knowledge Creation: How to Unlock the Mystery of Tacit Knowledge and Release the Power of Innovation*. Oxford: Oxford University Press.

Nonaka, Ikujiro and Takeuchi, Hirotaka (1995). *The Knowledge-Creating Company*. Oxford: Oxford University Press.

Senge, Peter, Roberts, Charlotte, Ross, Richard B., Smith, Bryan J., and Kleiner, Art (1994). *The Fifth Discipline Fieldbook*. New York: Doubleday, Currency.

Skyrme, David (1999). *Knowledge Networking: Creating the Collaborative Company*. Boston: Butterworth-Heinemann.

Wenger, Etienne (1998). *Communities of Practice: Learning, Meaning and Identity (Learning in Doing: Social Cognitive and Computational Perspectives)*. Cambridge, UK: Cambridge University Press.

A Work in Progress: The Phoenix K-ecosystem at Cable & Wireless*

Tharun Kumar

> "There is no use trying," said Alice. "One can't believe impossible things." "I daresay you haven't had much practice," said the Queen. "When I was your age, I always did it for half an hour a day. Why, sometimes I've believed as many as six impossible things before breakfast."
>
> *Lewis Carroll on 'dreaming big'*

Introduction

Achieving it seemed like a dream. You are inundated with customer support requirements from all over the world. On top of that, you also need to coordinate with multiple teams—in-house, as well as global—to cater to the clients. Top this with challenges of the connected economy, economic uncertainty, Internet time, organizational restructuring, and changing customer expectations. How do you get hold of a solution to cope with this? This is the situation that Cable & Wireless India was in. We dreamt that we could solve this with knowledge management (KM). Let us see how we pursued our dreams and realized the vision.

---

* *Editor's Note:* KM tools have played a key role in helping Cable & Wireless India coordinate round-the-clock teamwork across multiple locations, capture best practices, deliver e-learning services, and meet customer support requirements from all over the world. The KM portal has helped provid a real-time cockpit view of the current projects by all stakeholders. The gigantic task of organizing, sharing, and searching huge amounts of information very fast in a user-friendly manner was facilitated by a "K ecosystem" called Phoenix. Features like Best Bets, incentive schemes like "Knowledge Dollars," and a taxonomy called Knowledge Index were devised.

Phoenix was integrated with day-to-day primary work processes so that the KM system became part of regular work processes. Key learnings include the use of Web-based tools for work processes to prevent e-mail overload, the importance of managing knowledge stocks to keep them relevant, the necessity of security, factoring in the unavoidability of a certain amount of knowledge hoarding by employees, and the fact that a KM solution is always a work in progress with multiple evolutionary paths.

Company Profile and KM Context

Cable & Wireless India is a 100% owned subsidiary of Cable & Wireless p.l.c UK. The company provides enterprise network solutions, such as high-end system integration, network design, and management. The company supports C&W Europe, C&W UK, and C&W Americas in addition to India-specific customers. Cable & Wireless has several departments within the organization, such as the design, projects, customer front office, and enhanced solutions departments. These teams work collaboratively to design, deploy, and manage the network infrastructure of enterprises. They have to coordinate tasks not just within the team, but also with Cable & Wireless teams across the globe.

Global Network Design & Professional Services, Global Project Management, and Enhanced Solution Support (ESS) are the major three activities being handled by Cable & Wireless from its India center. A technical team working around the clock in three shifts, catering to their global clientele, executes the ESS operation. Since the shifts change, troubleshooting and lessons learned are the major activities; these are automated with our KM system, Phoenix. There is also a lot of information like contact details, escalation procedures, and vendor support details that needs to be available online when required. Creation of a "problem & solution" database was also a major requirement. This was the foundation for creating an automated system for supporting operation division.

The challenges faced by the Global Network Design & Professional Service were similar to those faced by companies who handle clients where the engagement starts from requirement analysis until the implementation of the design. In the India center context, there were three main challenges: smartly managing huge amounts of data that existed in disparate forms, sharing of information and coordinating activities among different departments within the center, and easy update of new information.

The Global Project Management team executes global projects from India, which means cross-border coordination on a massive scale. The need was for a real-time cockpit view of the current projects by all stakeholders. Having the right information at the right time makes all the difference for this team; collaboration is their lifeblood.

To ensure that these teams access the latest available information, a fast and efficient knowledge network was needed. What this basically meant for Cable & Wireless was the gigantic task of organizing, sharing, and searching huge amounts of information very fast. It required a full-fledged user-friendly solution for document management, KM, and collaboration. Tacit knowledge also needed to be captured as soon as the engagements were completed. For us KM is not a "nice thing to have," but an essential business imperative. We had to create our own "K ecosystem" which was best suited for our business needs and which would enable us to provide smart solutions to our customers. Thus, Phoenix was born (see Figure 5.1).

Key Requirements for Phoenix

- Document sharing—Sharing of design documents, as well as the project plans and status, was critical for on-time delivery of the solution. The Cable & Wireless team, working on a solution either from a single department or multiple departments, needed to coordinate tasks based on these shared documents.
- Single point of reference for all customer information—Cable & Wireless has specialized teams which perform certain tasks during various project phases. There was a need to hand over and share customer information from one team to another, as the project moved through different phases.

Figure 5.1

Phoenix Knowledge Portal

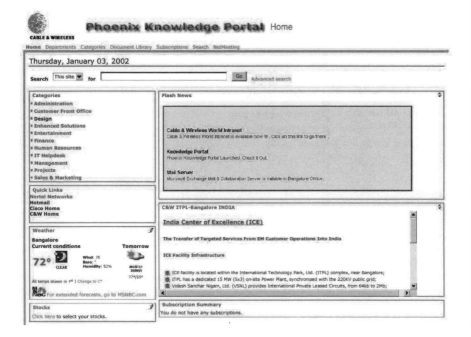

- Management of complex networks—With an exhaustive client list spanning various industry verticals, Cable & Wireless was managing complex networks that were vastly different from one another and unique in terms of their individual servicing requirements. A repository where problems and solutions can be archived was a key requirement.
- Connecting teams—For teams working on different portions of the same solution, facilitating easy and cost-effective communication to connect disparate islands of information was critical. Lack of an effective communication channel led to inefficiency in the system.
- Reporting—It was important for the team manager to be informed of time spent by the team on various aspects of a project.
- E-learning—All the team members needed to keep abreast of upcoming products and technologies, as well as telecom regulations of different countries, on an ongoing basis. This was essential in enabling them to offer the latest features to customer solutions, so that they were compliant with the regulations.
- Virtual teams—The various local and global communities of practice needed a home to interact.

Phoenix Evolution

We started with a proprietary Web-based document management system that was developed in-house and was named "Phoenix Portal" (see Figure 5.2). This was upgraded to a robust KM and collaboration platform based on Microsoft®

Figure 5.2

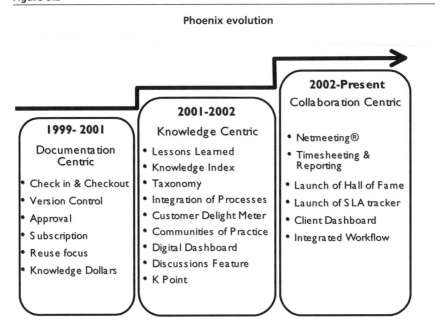

Phoenix evolution

1999- 2001

Documentation Centric

• Check in & Checkout
• Version Control
• Approval
• Subscription
• Reuse focus
• Knowledge Dollars

2001-2002

Knowledge Centric

• Lessons Learned
• Knowledge Index
• Taxonomy
• Integration of Processes
• Customer Delight Meter
• Communities of Practice
• Digital Dashboard
• Discussions Feature
• K Point

2002-Present

Collaboration Centric

• Netmeeting®
• Timesheeting & Reporting
• Launch of Hall of Fame
• Launch of SLA tracker
• Client Dashboard
• Integrated Workflow

SharePoint™ Portal Server, Exchange 2000, & Windows® 2000. A navigational tab at the top of the Phoenix Portal page organizes information by topic, event, or community and includes a powerful search function, which produces context-specific search and produces "best bets." Best Bets provide guidance to users by directing them to documents considered particularly relevant to their search. A Best Bet is a document selected as the best recommendation for a category or specific keyword. SharePoint™ Portal Server displays Best Bets at the top of a search results list.

For Cable & Wireless India, Phoenix is a central intranet-based knowledge repository, where all the work process is integrated and is tightly coupled. C&W global document management system is based on the Livelink™ platform. Phoenix serves as the portal, which has access to various other repositories like Livelink™ (see Figure 5.3).

Phase 1: Documentation Centric

This was our first step; the main objective in this phase was to reuse design, proposals, and project documents. In addition to the standard document management features like Check-in & Check-out, we also had the "subscription" feature enabled so that subscribed individuals get an e-mail message when documents of interest are added to the repository. During this phase we also launched an aggressive "Knowledge dollars" campaign to create knowledge where employees were given incentives to gain expert level knowledge. The evidence of this is usually achieving expert level accreditations of vendors. Before launching the "K dollar" campaign, we conducted a gap analysis and identified the knowledge needed to achieve our business goals.

Before we launched this centralized managed documentation system, it was difficult to share documents with others, control access to those documents, and publish documents. Important documents sometimes were lost, overwritten, or hard to find.

Figure 5.3

Phoenix Central Knowledge Repository

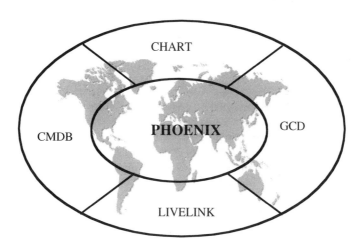

We also badly needed a solution to dam the information flood. Phoenix provides a number of features to help streamline our document management, such as version tracking, meta-data, publishing control, automated approval routes for reviewers, online discussion of comments, and access control.

Subscriptions notify personnel about new or updated information on topics that match ones of interests. One can subscribe to useful content: a specific document, all documents in a folder, all documents assigned to a category, or a set of search results. After one subscribes to content, Phoenix notifies the subscriber when the content is modified, if a new document matching the criteria is available, or if Web discussion comments about the content are added. Subscription notifications can happen on the dashboard site or via e-mail notifications.

Phase 2: Knowledge Centric

In this phase we moved to the "K-centric" mode and created our organizational memory. A Knowledge Index was created so that the users could navigate easily and drill down the content in the communities of practices (CoPs), best practices repository, and reusable content. We worked on different taxonomy models, but we found them not suitable to our needs. Most of the documents are unique. They are tagged with "key words," which form the meta-data. An informal undocumented taxonomy evolved as a result which achieved the end objectives. Globally dispersed virtual teams do most of our engagements. To facilitate the virtual team collaboration, dedicated dashboards were created for our CoPs.

The technology that played a major role was the Digital Dashboard. Web portals are quickly becoming a popular means of aggregating information from many different sources into one convenient place. The Phoenix dashboard site uses Microsoft Digital Dashboard technology to organize and display information. A digital dashboard consists of reusable, customizable Web Parts that can present information from a wide variety of sources, including Office documents and Web sites. One can add or remove Web Parts to customize the dashboard site. This helped us to add pages like the "Hall of Fame" easily. Also in this phase we integrated Phoenix with day-to-day primary work processes so that the KM system became part of day-to-day life and was not viewed as "another system to log on to." Other modules added in this phase were:

- K Point—This is where the collective knowledge of the team is archived. Lessons Learned, Tacit Knowledge, Reusable documents, and Expertise Locator form K Point.
- Customer Delight Meter—This is a dashboard where all customer feedbacks, star ratings, and service improvement plans are hosted.
- Discussions Feature—It is a well-known fact that the biggest enemy of any KM system is good old e-mail. Instead of using e-mail to discuss a document or trying to capture conversations about a document, authors and reviewers can communicate with each other through Web discussions. Web discussion features allow us to conduct online discussions about a document by modifying the document on the portal rather than the usual practice of sending e-mail attachments. Simultaneous discussions about a document can occur even if one person has the document checked out. Comments are stored as threaded conversations, grouping comments and replies together. With all comments grouped into a single place, document authors no longer need to compile handwritten comments from reviewers or comments sent through individual e-mail messages.

Phase 3: Collaboration Centric

In this phase we moved to genuine collaboration. Collaboration is the interaction of people, enterprises, or systems that are connected and working in concert on a shared goal, in a shared environment, through shared experiences, and using shared media. The embedded NetMeeting® server in SharePoint™ helped us integrate virtual teams by becoming a true collaboration hub. The interactive portal helps consultants globally to interact online for conversation and whiteboarding.

Some of the other tools that we incorporated into Phoenix at this phase are:

- Online Reporting & Timesheeting—Employees punch timesheets and weekly reports online into this module. It also includes a knowledge tracker, with queries like "Knowledge gained during the week."
- Self-service SLA tracker—This module can be viewed by our clients globally and displays the SLA and "work status" information in real-time. This is a classic self-service model—customers can input work requests online via this module. The system instantly e-mails the request to the designated team, and the work status is updated on the portal in real-time.
- Integrated workflow—Documentation workflow was implemented at this stage. Note that until now every employee had publishing rights—this was necessary to get buy-in from the user. Once we managed the maturity curve, documentation workflow was launched. Approval routes are an easy way to ensure that a document is adequately reviewed before it is published. When an author chooses to publish a document, it is sent automatically to one or more people for review before publication. The approvers receive e-mail notification when a document requires review.
- Client Dashboard—This is a dedicated Web page for each premium customer listing the customer's business, networks, and contacts. This is the all-in-one source of information for that particular customer, which ensures that all

Figure 5.4

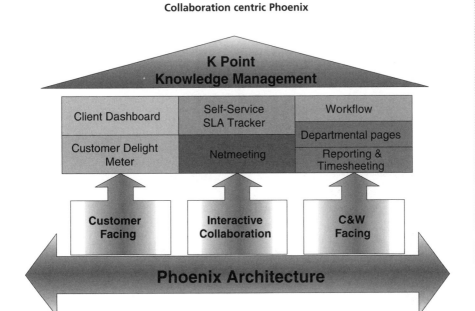

Collaboration centric Phoenix

departments are on a single page with respect to the specific customers (see Figure 5.4).

Future Plans

Our future plans include:

1. To move to the next level of collaboration and integrate people, processes, and technology into a seamless proposition. The end goal is to make Phoenix a utility service with knowledge on tap!
2. To enhance the user friendliness of KM infrastructure to store the knowledge so that the knowledge can be reused, maintained, and published on demand.
3. To raise the awareness of the importance of KM among all departments. Currently, the usage is high among Type A (tech savvy) departments.
4. To enhance the customer self-service features of the Knowledge Management System (KMS) to improve operational efficiencies.
5. Convert our Knowledge Assets (KA) into Business Intelligence Assets (BIA) so that cutting-edge relevant knowledge is available to everyone in the organization in real-time.

Phoenix Physiology—The Four Management Aspects

So far we have covered Phoenix evolution and architecture. Any KM system is a "work in progress." It is an ongoing journey, and one can lose all the benefits accrued if not managed carefully and diligently. Many KM rollouts in the industry have failed because KM practitioners focused on what software to use and what content to include, rather than the processes required to generate, capture, use, and maintain

Figure 5.5

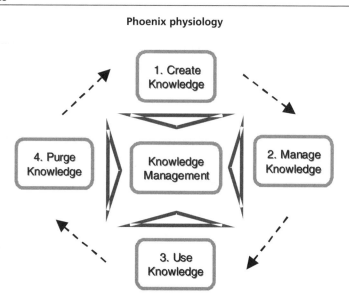

Phoenix physiology

content. There are *de facto* best practice information technology (IT) management standards, based on the Information Technology Information Library (ITIL). ITIL is a public-domain methodology for managing IT infrastructure and operations as a unified set of integrated processes. Our KM system management is based on the ITIL framework. For example, it is basic KMS Tool Management 101 to conduct regular load testing to see how many concurrent users can access the KMS. This is taken care of by the "availability management" processes of ITIL, which are different from "capacity management" processes.

Adhering to standards like ITIL helps avoid snags in IT management and service delivery and creates a compelling and integrated technology platform that automates KM processes. Let us now take a look at what it takes to manage the Phoenix Portal, via the following four processes (see Figure 5.5).

Creating Knowledge

We can "manage Knowledge" only after creating knowledge. We conducted a gap analysis and identified the K-needs to achieve our business goals. Once this was identified, an aggressive Knowledge Dollar program was launched to fill the gaps. Some of them were quick wins, whereas some knowledge assimilation took its time and could not be hurried. Challenges of the connected economy, economic process uncertainty, Internet time, organizational restructuring, and changing customer expectations have to be managed to achieve this constantly moving target. Instead of taking an ostrich stance, we are accepting these challenges seriously and working on them. Keep in mind that this is a journey, not a destination.

Managing Knowledge

This includes managing relevant content. The key here is to plan a methodology to continuously evaluate the knowledge categories that have high business relevancy.

Figure 5.6

System security and user acceptance

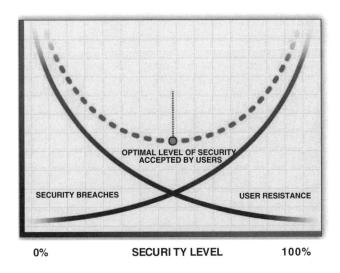

Phoenix has two logical partitions: the "Document Library" (document management system) and K-Point (knowledge management system). Developing and maintaining the taxonomy and meta-data architecture are also important. Taxonomy can be a tricky issue. We practice an informal one which is continuously monitored and evolving, and this approach seems to suit our business needs best. A key success factor for our KM initiative was user involvement from the very beginning. Though Phoenix is centrally controlled, there is no permanent full-time staff to run the show. The representatives from the communities of interest manage the solution on a rotation basis. The team also measures KM usage. Metrics measured are usage, CoP activities, workflow, downloads, reuse, and contributions to K Point.

An often-overlooked factor in KM is information security (see Figure 5.6). If you are not careful, your hard-earned knowledge can walk away. KM systems need to be handled differently, unlike applications such as enterprise resource planning (ERP), where access rules can be enforced. If you put in too much security, the system may be shunned by users; however, if you make it very open, you are inviting hackers. Remote access is granted only via secure HyperText Transfer Protocol (HTTPs). We have also implemented an IDS (Intrusion Detection System) so that we are alerted if there is a hacking attempt. Research in organizations around the world has shown that in many cases contractors or internal disgruntled employees are responsible for many of the successful attacks. A recovery plan to cope with disasters was also designed and tested at C&W Wireless.

Using Knowledge

There are knowledge contributors and users in the knowledge chain. We have to work diligently toward the goal of every employee contributing quality content to the system. Research firm Gartner (Gartner Perspective: 2002) has studied the knowledge-sharing behavior in consulting companies. On average, only 35% of the professional employees actively contributed to the KM system: the highest contribution came from businesses that have been in the business the longest. Note that consulting companies are often the torchbearers of KM. It is also important that the employees use available knowledge to their advantage. There is no simple answer to the knowing-doing dilemma (Pfeffer and Sutton: 2000) since it is culture dependent. We regularly conduct evangelizing campaigns to create a culture that places value on information sharing.

The KM awareness program is an ongoing activity, and some users need to be reminded periodically to use the system. We formed a virtual team comprising members from all departments, who act as the local champions for awareness creation, often on a one-to-one basis. This distributed leadership model helped increase the reach of the KMS. Knowledge sharing was also made part of the performance objectives for all personnel. This carrot and stick policy helped us manage the culture barriers effectively.

The other aspect of knowledge work concerns knowledge usage. Interlock knowledge activities with work processes are essential to ensure "knowledge pull." Currently, most of our processes have a Phoenix component built in. The goal is to make Phoenix part of our corporate DNA. This is again "work in progress."

Purge Knowledge

Content often starts to age immediately after knowledge capture. In a heavily used system, there is always a risk of knowledge workers reusing obsolete templates or documents. This is a time-consuming job. We have to guard against the tendency to clean up only the customer-facing pages and ignore the internal white papers and other documents. Deleting content is an often-underestimated job. For example, if you delete documents with links with meta-tags, to maintain database integrity we have to change the linkages; however, searching for the roots can be very time consuming.

Return on Investment

Once again, that clichéd phrase comes up—"What is the RoI?" Return on investment is based mostly on "intangibles" like customer satisfaction, productivity gains, and the like. For Phoenix, we estimate a time saving of 25% after Phoenix was launched, since we used to spend a lot of time searching for information. Our measuring metrics mentioned earlier help us to gauge our RoI. Note that typically "KM Integration" costs a lot, sometimes more than the software costs. RoI also depends on the "buy-in" of the team and the efficacy of the tool. It is a fact that people often tend to resist systems not established by them.

Phoenix was designed, built, and managed by the team with little help from vendors. This ensured a low-cost rollout, besides getting the buy-in from the team. This was a double whammy! The bang for the buck has been very high, though we have not yet worked out the hard numbers. Like most consulting organizations, we have not undertaken an RoI justification program: KM is a no brainer for us and a given in this sector! It is an essential business imperative which needs to be undertaken. Period.

To quote Timothy Wallis, Director, Business Development, Cable & Wireless UK: "There are many benefits from the Phoenix Knowledge Management rollout but for me the top one is the ability to view information on what the customer thinks of our service. The 'Customer Dashboard' portal, with all customer information archived on a single page, enables the global team to view the most current feedback from Customers and use this in the way they interact in future engagements. Coupled with the ability to view information on the services and solutions, we are building Knowledge Management around the Customer."

Lessons Learned and Recommendations for KM Practitioners

1. You have heard this before, but it is worth reiterating the top three success factors for an organization-wide KM rollout: the famous 3Cs—culture, culture, culture!

2. E-mail is the biggest enemy of KMS. Make your KMS as friendly as possible and make it as ubiquitous as e-mail. Current industry research indicates that knowledge workers spend at least one hour a day managing e-mail and that nearly half of all corporate knowledge is passed directly or indirectly through e-mail (Conway and Sligar: 2002).

3. Make KMS part of your internal work processes so that it becomes part of your DNA. Interlocking with work process is essential to ensure knowledge pull.

4. KM is not an IT department job. Communication, information, and collaboration are the keys here and not merely technical solutions. One needs to drive culture change and create incentive programs. Usually, this is not an IT department cup of tea.

5. If possible, build the KM system jointly with the team. People tend to resist systems not established by them.

6. Do not get carried away by the tacit knowledge conversion challenge. Accept the fact that hoarding knowledge is natural. Making "sharing behavior" a part of performance appraisal and incentivizing will help a lot. Sharing knowledge will happen only if there is a "give and take" culture. Also, make sharing knowledge easy. People resist going extra steps to share knowledge.

7. Ensure K-etiquette while adding documents. Using keywords and the like are very important as they form the meta-data used by search engines. A well-defined taxonomy will certainly help. Most KM systems are overengineered, so do not overengineer, but plan the architecture well. Beware of feature scope creep!

8. Most KM platform vendors sell hyped up features as add-on modules which increase the complexity (read complex maintenance). Vendors have played this game a thousand times and they know how to fool you! Implement the features YOU need and which will be accepted culturally within the organization. Many managers are technophiles, craving the latest PDAs and operating-system upgrades. However, tried-and-true technologies are sometimes the most effective—and least expensive—way to go. Keep it simple and user friendly.

9. Do not ignore the security challenges to your knowledge repository. The collective organizational knowledge can walk away. You also have to be prepared for disaster recovery and business continuity.

10. There are many paths to choose from the KM technology perspective, depending on migration paths. Choose the path that best suits your culture and business needs.

KM Architecture Paths

Careful planning is essential before you choose the right tool. Choose the path that best suits your culture and business needs. Eschew one-size-fits-all prescriptions. KM systems can be as simple as a file folder or business intelligence tools which use

Figure 5.7

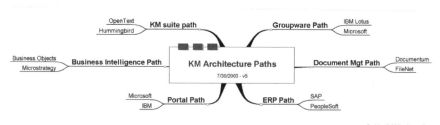

KM architecture paths

advanced data visualization and artificial intelligence to look for patterns that human users might not look for (see Figure 5.7).

We can learn from the hype around customer relationship management (CRM) and supply chain management (SCM). According to IDC, approximately $44 billion (http://dmreview.com/master.cfm?NavID=193&EdJD=3695) was spent worldwide on customer relationship management initiatives in 2000. How is it possible that, after billions of dollars invested to improve customer relationships, the average customer feels that enterprise-wide CRM is worse than ever? The answer is actually quite simple: assumptions that the "tool" will do magic and the lack of true enterprise integration.

The same is true for KM tools. KM tools can be broadly classified into different categories or evolutionary paths. Note that the differences between them are blurring, and we might see the paths converging. Note that there is no recommended path; it all depends on your needs and your definition of KM. Do not fall victim to the fallacy of assuming that you can have a KM system once the tool is "installed." In addition to culture issues, the tools need to be meta-data enabled for them to work effectively. Most of the tools are application development "environments" or middleware that require customization. KM tools are like a stone block. It is up to you to carve your own KM story.

GroupWare Path

This is one of the oldest KM architecture paths, and many organizations swear by this original collaboration tool. Lotus Notes® is a classic ex-ample. There is a school of thought that argues that GroupWare Path is not a true KM path, and there are many who are true believers in this (http://world.std.com/~rkarash/GW-OL/). As we all know, the success of any KM system comes from user acceptance, and GroupWare tools score high here as users are accustomed to them.

Document Management Path

Many organizations have reaped big benefits out of Document Management Systems (DMS). DMS are also morphing to Web Content Management systems. Documentum® and FileNet® are examples of focused DMS. Content is not just docu-ments, but artifacts, imaging, workflow, and the like. DMS products specialize in managing unstructured content. Library services (check in, check out, and versioning) and content search are the two basic features of all DMS.

ERP Path

Traditional ERP software providers are branching out to e-learning and KM; mySAP™ and Oracle Collaboration suite are examples. Theoretically, this is a powerful proposition—to marry the KM space which is "unstructured data" to the "structured" data: the high value human resources and financial data of your ERP database. If integrated well (which is a real technical challenge), they can cull "knowledge" and "insights" from your ERP database and can be a powerful business enabler, as the ERP vendors understand your business processes well. If your organization is already living on ERP systems, it is worthwhile to pursue the ERP path of KM.

Portal Path

Portals like Microsoft SharePoint™ and IBM Content Manager® can aggregate contents from multiple sources and present it through a single access point. It is easy to create customized pages via Dashboard technology. Portals are very popular, as they can be quickly rolled out and are very user friendly, which is necessary for KM success in organizations. They also usually have strong search capabilities. Some organizations have moved from the GroupWare path to the Portal path, as Portals can be a unifying framework for the enterprise. Once the much hyped "Web services" become popular, the Portal path will get a big boost.

Business Intelligence Path

Some KM practitioners argue that this is the next evolution of KM. There are distinct differences between KM systems and business intelligence (BI) systems. BI involves Data Mining (discovering relationships among data points), OLAP (Online Analytical Processing, or online analysis of transactional data), Querying & Reporting (viewing and manipulating data via multiple report formats), and Proactive Information Delivery (receiving information on a scheduled or event-driven basis via Web, wireless, or voice device).

Business Objects® and Microstrategy® are examples of BI software providers. Most of the BI products are point products; do not expect them to have an e-learning module or a DMS. It is expected that future BI systems will combine KM, collaboration, ERP, and CRM applications. The goal of BI systems is to enable synchronization of the entire enterprise around the customer, rather than just synchronizing data around the customer. The meta-data of a BI system are "rules," which are defined in the Business Rules Repository where all business rules are stored. The BI triggering engine then can be used for "what if" simulations, which can give you insights about your customers or business.

KM Suite Path

Hummingbird® and OpenText® Livelink™ are examples of "all in one" frameworks which span the entire gamut: collaboration, document management, KM, e-learning, scheduling/calendering, virtual team space, context-sensitive brokered search, connectors to interface with ERP/CRM, workflow, LDAP, desktop application integration, Native Language support, wireless access to the repository, and so on. They are XML centric. The pricing is modular, as you pay for features like cross-repository search, meta-data management, automatic content classification, and the like. These modules may look good on brochures, but you must be mentally prepared for long lead times in installing these complex features. This form of framework that provides all the KM puzzle pieces is getting popular, but still there could be holes that need to be plugged by specialized point products.

References

The Official ITIL Webpage: http://www.ogc.gov.uk/index.asp?id=2261.

Conway, Susan and Sligar, Char. (2002). *Unlocking Knowledge Assets: KM Solutions from Microsoft*. Englewood Cliffs, New Jersey: Prentice Hall/Microsoft Press.

Gartner Perspectives (2002). "Knowledge Management to thrive in professional services." (authored by Dennis Wayson, purchased from Gartner as PDF). Stamford, CT: Gartner.

Pfeffer, Jeffrey and Sutton, Robert L. (2000). *The Knowing—Doing Gap*. Boston: Harvard Business School Press.

Schemes and Tools for Social Capital Measurement as a Proxy for Intellectual Capital Measures*

6

Laurence Lock Lee

If you have knowledge, let others light their candles in it.

Margaret Fuller

Introduction

The need to better manage a firm's intellectual capital (IC), including the reporting and disclosure of IC performance, is now well accepted. The major difficulty has been the effort required to compile such IC statements and the difficulty managers have in effectively using them. Much of the difficulty spans from the non-standard way in which IC is reported. This chapter introduces a different tact for managing IC, through the lens of social capital (SC). SC is proposed as a unifying concept for IC that can provide a simpler and more usable measurement scheme. Examples of SC reporting based on social network analysis (SNA) techniques and Web

---

* *Editor's Note:* This chapter explores the potential of social network analysis (SNA) as a tool for intellectual capital research by unearthing social capital measures (see also Chapter 18 about SNA in Australia's Office of Small Business). Statistical calculations on the number and nature of ties can provide measures like network size, density, and heterogeneity, which can be used to infer community dimensions like degree of formality, spatiality, and relationships. SNA can be used to identify important brokers and coordinators in communities, particularly geographically dispersed communities.

Based on examples from technical communities in the global computer services industry, this chapter demonstrates that the mining of relationship data from electronic logs of interactions or Web sites on the Internet can report on social capital in close to real-time, thus complementing existing methods of network analysis based on periodic interviews. Digital SNA also helps overcome one of the difficulties in developing social capital reports, viz. the time, effort, and cost required to collect data for accurate reporting. As employees and citizens become increasingly Internet-savvy, the use of sociogram tools for mining intranet and Internet communication and publication patterns will only continue to increase. The ubiquity of the Internet is clearly going to provide a rich source for social capital reporting. Challenges of an unforeseen kind, however, may arise via evolving privacy laws and social acceptance regarding monitoring activities.

mining are provided to illustrate how an effective SC/IC reporting scheme might operate.

IC measurement has proven problematical for many organizations. Typically, organizations, both public and private sector, have looked for scorecard approaches based on intangible asset monitor (Sveiby, 1997) and Balanced Scorecard (Kaplan and Norton, 1996) approaches. Deciding what attributes to measure, which categories, how many, how to organize them, and, significantly, how they are eventually interpreted into organizational actions is proving a challenge. Some progress has been made on trying to establish standards for IC reporting. The majority of proposed IC statements are variants or expansions of Sveiby's original intangible asset monitor (Ordonez de Pablos, 2002, 2003; Edvinsson and Malone, 1997; April et al., 2003). Typically, these reports could cover 100+ individual measures broadly categorized into human, structural, and relational areas. The Danish government has gone as far as publishing a guideline for IC statements based on the contribution of 17 Danish company submissions (Mouritsen, 2000).

The cost of designing and collecting IC data and information over extended periods of time is not insignificant. This chapter proposes the use of SC as an effective proxy for IC measurement, taking advantage of mature SC measurement schemes. SC is introduced as a unifying concept for IC. An SC sample measurement scheme is provided. Examples of SC reports using SNA tools generated from Web-based information are provided to illustrate the potential for regular SC reporting, "mined" from intranets and the Internet. Finally, a discussion is provided on the current utility of an SC reporting technique using Web-mined information, with some learnings to date from their application.

Social Capital as a Unifying Concept

SC can be defined as, "The stock of active connections among people: the trust, mutual understanding and shared values and behaviours that bind the members of human networks and communities and make co-operative action possible" (Cohen and Prusak, 2001). SC as a concept has its roots in the field of sociology, being largely applied to describe organizational effects developed through socially derived connections in the broader communities, societies, and cultures (Baker, 2001; Nahapiet and Ghoshal, 1998). Traditionally, the context of SC for private sector firms is seen as their contributions (usually financial) to the communities within which they operate. While often seen as corporate philanthropy, claims have been made that such good corporate citizenship can contribute to improved business performance (Allee, 2000; Roman et al., 1999).

The traditional view of SC, as described above, is "Industrial Era" thinking. Many commentators have argued that we are currently transitioning from the Industrial Era to a Knowledge Era (Drucker, 1993; Savage, 1996), where the traditional factors of production of land, labor, and capital are being replaced by the creation of value through knowledge. In the Knowledge Era, firms are becoming embedded within a complex web of interconnections that span markets, governments, and communities. In this world the concept of SC can take on a whole new dimension for the "firm."

Table 6.1 identifies common themes for SC, as identified by the Australian Bureau of Statistics discussion paper on measuring SC (ABS, 2000), and a potential corporate interpretation:

The increasing importance of intangibles was initially identified by Swedish researcher Karl-Erik Sveiby in his work on "Company Knowhow" (Sveiby and

Table 6.1

Traditional versus Corporate Context for Social Capital	
Traditional societal context	**Potential corporate context**
Social networks and support structures	Communities of practice, industry bodies.
Empowerment and community participation	Membership of communities of practice or industry bodies.
Civic and political involvement	"Bottom up" initiatives; industrial body initiatives.
Trust in people and social institutions	Trust in management.
Tolerance of diversity	Cross-functional teams, cross industry initiatives.
Altruism and philanthropy	Investment in local communities, environment etc.

Risling, 1986). Since this time a plethora of literature has been published in support of new methods for measuring and managing intangibles (Sveiby, 1997; Edvinsson and Malone, 1997; Lev, 2001; Johanson et al., 1999). From Sveiby's Intangible Asset Monitor (Sveiby, 1997) and Kaplan and Norton's Balanced Scorecard (Kaplan and Norton, 1996), increasingly sophisticated scorecards have been built (Wall and Doerflinger, 1999; Liebowitz and Suen, 2000; Mouritsen et al., 2000). Intangible capital has been decomposed into intellectual capital, structural capital, human capital, customer capital, innovation capital, external capital, stakeholder capital, knowledge capital, and so on. Clearly, many of these concepts are interdependent and difficult to measure and operationalize. As an adjunct to the traditional balance sheet or profit and loss statement, they may eventually become useful analytical tools. However, in order to operationalize these concepts, a suite of simplifying intangible asset management heuristics needs to be developed.

The literature to date has been very much focused on expanding the concept of intangibles into ever-increasing subcomponents. Very little research has addressed the need to reduce this suite to the smaller set of heuristics that mangers will need to manage intangibles on a day-to-day basis.

The proposition is that SC is a leading driver and source of managerial heuristics for creating increased intangible asset value, subsuming a majority of other intangible concepts. An organization exhibiting excellent SC would be seen as one where internal departments are heavily interconnected, sharing a common vision and language. The firm would also exhibit similar traits externally, easily forming profitable alliances and partnerships to improve its overall market performance. Human interaction is a fundamental premise for building SC. It has also been argued that the human dimension accounts for at least half of all IC value to an organization (O'Donnell and Berkery, 2003).

Figure 6.1 summarizes SC measurement schemes derived from the literature (Stone, 2001; ABS, 2000; Borgatti et al., 1998; World Bank, 2003).

SC measures have two dimensions: structure and quality. The quality of social relations can be divided into social trust, which is personal and institutional trust, that works at an organizational level. Reciprocity refers to "in-kind" exchanges that are not necessarily economically based, typically "returned favors." Measurement constructs form the basis of SC survey instruments, where typically respondents are asked

Figure 6.1

Social capital measurement schemes

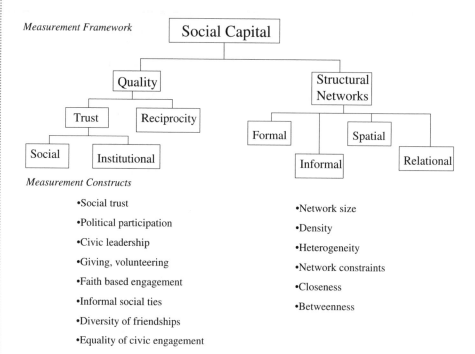

Measurement Framework

Social Capital

Quality

Trust   Reciprocity

Social   Institutional

Structural Networks

Formal   Spatial

Informal   Relational

Measurement Constructs

•Social trust

•Political participation

•Civic leadership

•Giving, volunteering

•Faith based engagement

•Informal social ties

•Diversity of friendships

•Equality of civic engagement

•Network size

•Density

•Heterogeneity

•Network constraints

•Closeness

•Betweenness

to rate these dimensions along a qualitative scale. The constructs provided are just a sample typical of those used in an SC quality survey.

The structural network measures are based on measuring connections. Survey respondents are typically asked whom they connect or interact with (i.e., nominate their "ties"). Often, the relative strength of a tie, e.g., strong, moderate, or weak, is also collected. A social network map can be generated from the data collected to assist with visualizing the nature of connections. Statistical calculations on the number and nature of ties can then provide measures like network size, density, and heterogeneity. Using demographic information collected about the respondents, the networks can be studied at the individual or aggregate (firm, organization, or national) level. These measures, in turn, can be used to infer dimensions like degree of formality, spatiality, and relationships.

Collectively, the structural and quality measures provide a snapshot of SC (and potentially IC) of the population under study. The SC report would have two parts, covering the quality and structural dimensions (see Table 6.2). The quality part of the survey would ask respondents to provide a rating for questions reflecting support for dimensions like collaboration, inter-business unit trust, and quality of alliance partnerships. The survey data would be processed to provide a picture of the state of SC (and therefore IC) for the population under study.

While the report in Table 6.2 is overly simplistic, its intent is to demonstrate the style of reporting that could be possible from SC surveys. The levels of IC are inferred

Table 6.2

Pro-forma Social & Intellectual Capital Report	
Example Social and Intellectual Capital Report	**Example Pro-forma**
	Structural Network Report This map illustrates the current relationships between Business Unit (BU) A, BU B, BU C, and Alliance Partner (only a subset of data included for clarity). The thickness of the lines denotes relative strength of the relationship. This particular population shows strong interconnectedness. One could infer from the relatively high density of ties and the absence of strong clusters or cliques that the level of SC between the BUs and alliance partner is quite high. The potential for new IC generation is generally high. **Social Quality Report** This particular population demonstrates relatively high levels of community of practice (CoP) participation, alliance partnership trust, and networks participation. Levels of interdivisional trust and volunteering (with the exception of BU A) are at moderate levels only. BU A demonstrates high levels of CoP participation and leadership in company social events and volunteering, but lower levels of tolerance for diversity and trust of other BUs. IC could be enhanced by engaging BU A more actively in these areas. On average across both structural and quality dimensions, relatively high levels of social (and intellectual) capital are evident.

through the levels of SC. Identifying specific IC-related actions would ensue from initially looking at areas of strength or weaknesses in SC. For example, where Business Unit (BU) A is seen to be trailing on inter-BU trust, the IC-related action would be to investigate what IC elements could have an effect in raising the level of engagement of BU A with other BUs. Developing a formal cross-divisional project between BU A and other BUs to develop a new product or service, i.e., new IC development, could be an example of an IC action. Anecdotal examples of IC creation, e.g., patents achieved, collaborative R&D results, and educational initiatives, could be added to the report to augment the SC commentary above and to provide a stronger IC flavor to the report.

The following sections provide some example applications of SC reporting that draw data from electronic repositories like the Internet, electronic discussion spaces, and collaborative tool usage logs.

From Surveying to Surfing (the Internet) Example

While SC surveys may be easier and cheaper to compile than IC statements, they both suffer from the same problem of only periodical reporting. Ideally, one would like to monitor the dynamics of SC and IC in close to real-time. For IC reports the data collection and monitoring systems would be prohibitive. For the SC surveys some level of semi-automated surveys could be designed and perhaps delivered over the Internet, which could give more regular reporting as different but complementary groups are surveyed.

An alternative, complementary, and somewhat novel approach for generating social/intellectual capital statements is to look for patterns of interaction on the Internet, at least for the structural dimension of SC. There now exist many sources of data on Internet usage, and the trend is clearly a global one. Recent statistics from Global Reach (www.glreach.com/globstats) show that the proportion of non-English speaking Internet users has reached 63.5%, of which European languages make up 35.5% and Asian languages make up 28.3%. As the sheer volume of data and traffic on the Internet grows exponentially, and most organizations develop a Web presence, it becomes possible to use patterns of activity and the content available to create an expansive picture of market-wide IC. The new discipline of "Web mining" analyzes both traffic flows and content to derive and interpret patterns of interest (Sundaresan and Yi, 2000; Paltridge, 1999). To date, a number of researchers have demonstrated how cyber-communities can be identified by tracking Internet activity, be they electronic discussion groups or simply e-mail traffic analysis (Lock Lee, 2003; Boudourides et al., 2002; Kumar et al., 1999). By following Web links between the Web sites of firms, one could infer connections which could be reinforced by content discovered through the use of intelligent search engines.

Laurent (2002) has used a combination of link analysis and content analysis to characterize the network of relationships that exists among the leading computer services organizations in North America (see Figure 6.2). He shows that IBM and HP are the most connected in the industry. The thickness of the links represents the strength of the relationship inferred from the link and content analysis. The sizes of the arrowheads indicate who is driving the relationship.

Research to date has clearly demonstrated that "cyber-patterns and content" mined from the Internet can strongly mimic reality, to the extent that some authors now consider electronic communications as an inherent part of social activity (Wellman, 2001).

While it is still early days with Web mining, as the techniques mature and the IC and SC Internet content continues to grow globally, the ubiquity of the Internet is clearly going to provide a rich source for IC and SC reporting.

Reporting on Social Network Evolution over Time Example

The following example reports on social network changes over time. The selected electronic data source was an active electronic discussion group of a global engineering network. The data source was selected over e-mail, as it was thought that participation in an electronic discussion is principally for knowledge-sharing purposes, whereas e-mail has many other purposes. The discussion activity was reported quarterly, with a focus on BU level connections and their changes over time.

Figure 6.3 describes the evolution of the discussion group over its first two years of operation. The arcs represent BUs, with the satellites showing intra-business contacts. Links between arcs within the main circle are inter-business contacts. Links are

Figure 6.2

Inferred relationships between computer services companies

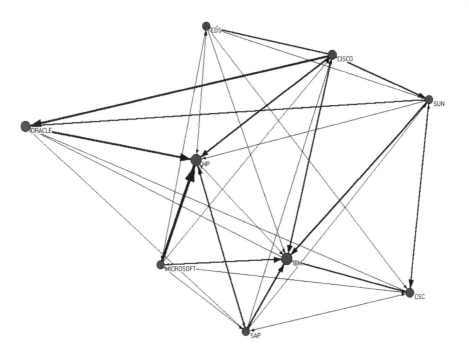

Figure 6.3

Evolution of discussion group activity

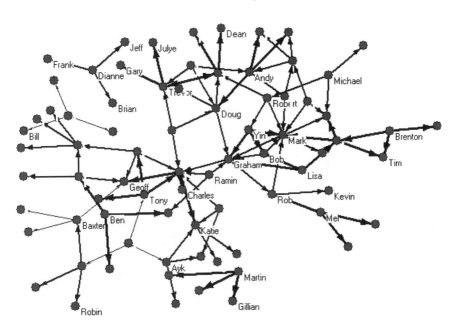

basically a discussion post. A discussion thread will create a number of links either linked back to the original post or to other res-ponses to the original post. Only major BUs are shown (GMNFT is the network facilitating team).

The reports were provided to the network's core facilitating team (GMNFT) for evaluation against their perceptions of network activities. Overall, the facilitating team found the interpretations and results quite plausible. In several cases they could identify events or situations that had occurred within the network that could explain or justify the interpretations. The reports also showed clearly the relative participation rate of the different BUs and the impact of the facilitating team, seeding discussions when activity quietens. One common characteristic was the increase in discussion activity following a major face-to-face conference.

Social Network Digital Identification Example

This example relates to another global network's use of a custom-developed community of practice (CoP) support tool, compared against a traditional SNA assessment of the network. This global network was divided into several topic-specific CoPs, each making use of the electronic space provided by the electronic CoP tool. Network members were free to volunteer to join the "electronic CoPs," but clearly not all CoP members joined the electronic CoPs. It is estimated that about 60% of network members had joined the CoP electronic space. Some are members of multiple CoPs.

The traditional SNA analysis was conducted across the network to assess inter-office interactions and connections within particular professional disciplines (see Figure 6.4). Around 40 network members were interviewed, basically being asked to nominate their key "trusted advisors" within their specialty domain. The resulting sociograms described the connections among some 70 members, approximately half of the total network membership.

The digitally derived sociograms were developed by looking for network members who tended to join the same electronic CoPs; hence inferring a relationship of common interests.

The directional links in Figure 6.5 indicate nominated "advisers," with the thickness of the arrow indicating the level of perceived value. Of the 125 online members and 77 members in the traditional (offline) study, there were 33 common members. The analysis was therefore restricted to this subcommunity.

Table 6.3 compares the top 10 (out of 33) rankings for both the offline and the online networks. For the traditional SNA the rankings were determined based on centrality, i.e., the number of input links from colleagues. For the online community the relationships were inferred by the number of different colleagues a member shares more than one CoP membership with, e.g., Mark is a member of two CoPs of which both Charles and Gary are also members.

The results show that 70% of the top 10 participants are common between the online and offline communities, which would suggest that those well-networked members who choose to join the online world are happy to participate in multiple CoPs. Rank orders within this grouping do not correlate that well, suggesting that there is a limit to how well networking behavior might map from the offline to online world. The top two ranking members for the online community do not figure in the top ten of the offline community. Charles is the network's leader and clearly plays a facilitative and oversight role in the online world, but is perhaps regarded more as a "manager or information broker" than a discipline specialist in the offline world.

Figure 6.4

Traditional SNA characterization of the network

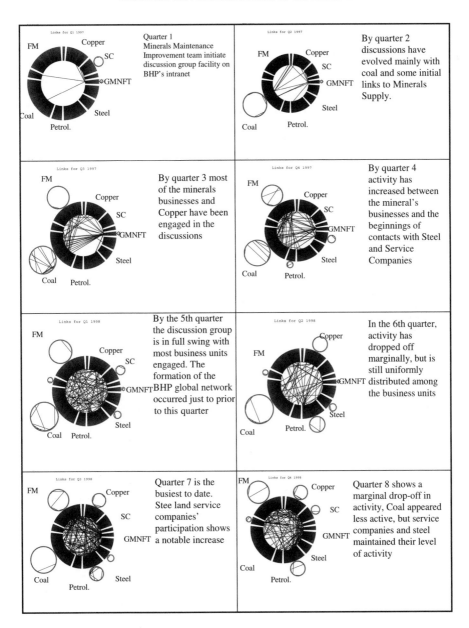

Figure 6.5

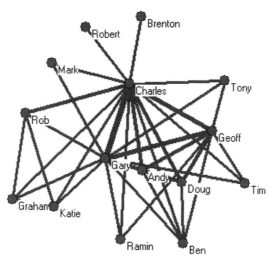

Online community

Table 6.3

Offline versus Online Comparison	
Top 10 "Online" participants (in rank order)	Top 10 "Offline" participants (in rank order)
Charles	**Mark**
Gary	**Graham**
Geoff	**Geoff**
Doug	**Andy**
Andy	Trevor
Graham	**Katie**
Katie	**Doug**
Rob	Tim
Ben	**Rob**
Mark	Bob

Note: Boldfaced names indicate members who participate in multiple CoPs.

This example demonstrates that data drawn from electronic tool usage logs can indeed provide an idea of networking patterns that mimic non-computer-based interactions.

Discussion

Based on the above examples and scenarios, the following observations can be made about digital tracking and identification:

- Web mining for relationships on the Internet will typically identify multiple links between companies. To better delineate the strength of the ties there is a requirement to delineate differences between relationships inferred from, say, a news article than, for instance, a joint research report. Reciprocal Web links on the respective corporate Web pages and their relative "distance" from the corporate home page is another example of measuring strength of ties.

- If we are interested in knowledge sharing in support for SC/IC development, the best electronic data will come from activities that are uniquely for knowledge sharing, as opposed to, say, administration tasks. For example, discussion group activity is likely to be more representative than e-mail or telephone data, as its use is almost exclusively for knowledge sharing.

- The use of sociograms for mapping discussions adds an extra dimension above simple counts of postings. By showing the source of each link, one can reasonably infer intra-organizational linkages, especially if the discussion is active.

- It should also be noted that the discussion group analyzed was mostly a "request for help" on operational issues group, meaning that responses were often drawn from a broad range of respondents—perhaps more representative than if the group was discussing more conceptual issues.

- Clearly, comfort with the online world is going to have an impact on how representative electronic activity will be of offline activity. In both cases under study, the level of information technology (IT) literacy was relatively high.

- While an electronic discussion response is clearly not as strong as an explicit link nomination in a survey, with sufficient data and looking at the data aggregated at the BU level, it does provide some insight into inter-BU interactions.

- In the online world, the activities of facilitators become visible, e.g., seeding discussions, joining electronic CoPs for oversight. In the offline world analyzed by SNA, facilitators are likely to appear as information brokers, rather than as "advisor" links.

As for the effectiveness of digital tracking, outcome measures typically capture benefits accruing from specific projects or the development of new artifacts, e.g., new processes or procedures. SNA-type measures are more related to assessing structural aspects of communication patterns within an organization, i.e., in-process metrics. By identifying "trustful" relationships in the interviews, SNA does more than just identify coordinator or broker roles, it also infers that highly connected individuals possess valuable and sought after tacit knowledge. Despite the clear differences between interview-based SNAs and digitally derived SNAs, digital tracking was still seen as effective at:

- Identifying the major communication patterns between membership groups, e.g., formal departments or BUs and professional disciplines within the community. The author has conducted several interview-based SNAs where the subjects were asked to differentiate between knowledge-based contacts and information-providing contacts. Largely, the patterns for knowledge contacts and information contacts were similar when viewed at the aggregate level. This also appeared to be the case with digital transactions.

- Identifying important brokers and coordinators in the community. These members may take the form of discussion group moderators or content managers, but in general it was observed that active members in the "offline" community would also be active if they choose to participate online as well.

- In geographically dispersed communities, one can identify key, remotely located contributors that would not be otherwise identified in an offline-only community.

A number of sociology-inspired studies have been conducted to try and understand the level of community that can be generated through participation in online forums. Eminent sociologist Barry Wellman (Wellman, 2001) argues that online communities should not be studied in isolation, but as an integrated component of everyday life. Wellman suggests that online community participation increases an individual's SC, through increasing the breadth and frequency of contacts. Therefore, the effectiveness of digital tracking should be judged by the added value that it brings in understanding social constructs within organizations, more so than its value as a substitute for interview-based SNAs.

It is worth noting that very few communities would be "Online only" or "Offline only." With online communities it is common practice for side discussions to occur either by e-mail or by telephone. It is also unlikely that offline communities will not use some level of e-mail or telephone communications (which could potentially be tracked).

Future Prospects

As with most data/Web mining activities, the acquisition and cleansing of the source data is the most costly and time-consuming task. However, as more experience is gained in understanding which forms of data are most strongly predictive of SC/IC development and performance, the source applications can be designed to provide the appropriate quality of tracking data.

Comfort in the online world is currently an issue that will undoubtedly diminish as the "generation X-ers" start to dominate the workforce. The Internet Age is still relatively young, so those that have "grown up" in the Internet Age are mostly in their teens. However, already this group will have generated one of the richest data sets for inferring social connections, i.e., the database of SMS messages.

The growing sophistication of the Web mining tools and advanced content analysis engines would suggest that the availability of effective digital tracking tools for measuring community performance will not be far away. For those communities that begin online and largely operate online, e.g., Yahoo Groups, one could anticipate that SNA tools could become a value-added service for community leaders/facilitators. However, for those communities established offline but with an online presence, the largest potential "show stopper" is a non-technical one, i.e., the evolving privacy laws that could potentially outlaw the use of digital tracking data without the explicit permission of all participants. There is also the issue of social acceptance of what amounts to a "big brother" monitoring activity. Communities may indeed object to having their activities monitored, even if it is in the name of increased efficiencies or effectiveness.

Conclusion

This chapter aims to make two contributions to IC research. The first is the recognition that SC and IC are highly interrelated, and, therefore, SC measures could provide an effective proxy measure for IC within a firm. Additionally, SC could provide a simpler unifying concept by which managers can operationalize IC concepts, i.e., if we optimize our SC we will be in effect optimizing IC. The second contribution is the demonstration that the mining of relationship data from electronic logs or Web sites can provide the facility to report on SC in close to real-time. One of the difficulties in developing both SC and IC reports is the time and effort required to collect data for reporting. Even in instances when this has been achieved, the effort to sustain the level of IC reporting is often not forthcoming. The ability to partially automate reporting through the use of tools for mining electronic communications spaces will only get better as the breadth and depth of information continues to grow exponentially. The promise is that firms will in the future be able to monitor their intangible asset performance at the same frequency that they monitor their tangible asset performance.

References

April, K., Bosma, P., and Deglon, D. (2003). IC Measurement and Reporting: Establishing a Practice in SA Mining, *Journal of Intellectual Capital*, 4(2), 165–180.

ABS: Australian Bureau of Statistics (2000). Measuring Social Capital: Current Collections and Future Directions, www.abs.gov.au.

Allee, V. (2000). Return on Knowledge, *Executive Excellence*, 17(9), 8.

Borgatti, S., Jones, C., and Everett, M. (1998). Network Measures of Social Capital, *CONNECTIONS*, 21(2), 36.

Boudourides, M., Mavrikakis, M., and Vasileiadou, E. (2002). E-Mail Threads, Genres and Networks in a Project Mailing List, Association of Internet Researchers International Conference, Maastricht, Netherlands, Oct. 13–16, 2002.

Baker, W. (2001). Social Capital, *The AVENTIS Magazine*, February 2001 (see www.corp.aventis.com/future/fut0102/social_capital/printversion.htm).

Cohen, D. and Prusak, L. (2001). *In Good Company: How Social Capital Makes Organizations Work*. Boston: Harvard Business School Press.

Drucker, P. (1993). *Post Capitalist Society*. New York: HarperCollins.

Edvinsson, L. and Malone, M. (1997). *Intellectual Capital: Realizing Your Company's True Value by Finding Its Hidden Brainpower*. New York: Harper Business.

Johanson, U., Eklov, G., Holmgren, M., and Martensson, M. (1999). *Human Resource Costing and Accounting Versus the Balanced Scorecard*. Stockholm University, School of Business.

Kaplan, R. and Norton, D. (1996). *The Balanced Scorecard: Translating Strategy into Action*. Boston: Harvard Business School Press.

Kumar, R., Raghaven, P., Rajagopalan, S., and Tomkins, A. (1999). Trawling the Web for Emerging Cyber-Communities, *Computer Networks*, 31, 1481–1493.

Laurent, D. (2002). Understanding External Relationships in the Knowledge Era: An Exploratory Study that Applies Social Network Analysis to the World Wide Web, unpublished Honours Thesis, School of Information Technologies, Sydney University.

Lev, B. (2001). *Intangibles: Management, Measurement, and Reporting*. Washington, DC: The Brookings Institution.

Liebowitz, J. and Suen, C. (2000). Developing Knowledge Management Metrics for Measuring Intellectual Capital, *Journal of Intellectual Capital*, 1, 54–67. Liebowitz: Volume 1—R. Kumar, P. Raghavan, S. Rajagopalan, and A. Tomkins. Trawling the web for emerging cyber-communities. Computer Networks, 31:1481–1493, 1999. Conference version at Eighth Internation World Wide Web Conference, 1999.

Lock Lee, L. (2003). Does Your Community Leave a Digital Footprint?, KM Challenge 2003, Standards Australia Conference, Melbourne, April.

Mouritsen, J., et al. (2000). A Guideline for Intellectual Capital Statements, Danish Agency for Trade and Industry (see www.efs.dk).

Nahapiet, J. and Ghoshal, S. (1998). Social Capital, Intellectual Capital, and the Organizational Advantage, *Academy of Management Review*, 23(2), 242–266.

O'Donnell, D. and Berkery, G. (2003). Human Interaction: The Critical Source of Intangible Value, *Journal of Intellectual Capital*, 4(1), 82–99.

Ordonez de Pablos, P. (2002). Evidence of Intellectual Capital Measurement from Asia, Europe and Middle East, *Journal of Intellectual Capital*, 3(3), 287–302.

Ordonez de Pablos, P. (2003). Intellectual Capital Reporting in Spain: A Comparative View, *Journal of Intellectual Capital*, 4(1), 61–81.

Paltridge, S. (1999). Mining and Mapping Web Content, *Journal of Policy, Regulation and Strategy for Telecommunications, Information and Media*, 1(4), (August), 327–342.

Roman, R., Hayibor, S., and Agle, B. (1999). The Relationship between Social and Financial Performance', *Business and Society*, 38(1), 109–125.

Savage, C. (1996). *Fifth Generation Management* (www.kee-inc.com).

Stone, W. (2001). Measuring Social Capital, Australian Institute of Family Studies, www.aifs.org.au.

Sundaresan, N. and Yi, J. (2000). Mining the Web for Relations, *Computer Networks*, 33, 699–711.

Sveiby, K. and Risling, A. (1986). *Kunskapsforetaget (the Know-How Company)*, Liber, Malmo.

Sveiby, K. (1997). *The New Organizational Wealth: Managing and Measuring Knowledge-Based Assets*, San Francisco: Berret-Koehler.

Wall, B. and Doerflinger, M. (1999). Making Intangible Assets Tangible, *Knowledge Management Review*, (Sept/Oct).

Wellman, B. (2001). Computer Networks as Social Networks, *SCIENCE*, 293 (September).

World Bank on Social Capital (2003). see http://www.worldbank.org/poverty/scapital/index.htm.

Knowledge Management in Practice: Making Technology Work at DaimlerChrysler*

Gopika Kannan, Wilfried Aulbur, and Roland Haas

> Knowledge is like money: To be of value it must circulate, and in circulating it can increase in quantity and, hopefully, in value.
>
> *Louis L'Amour*

Introduction

The management of intellectual property and of knowledge challenges in a highly competitive, innovation-driven, and global environment such as the automotive industry provides an exciting opportunity for today's knowledge manager. Dealing with fast-paced and complex changes in business models, customer preferences, and the like requires new organizational forms rather than the traditional command-and-control chain prevalent in a manufacturing environment (DaimlerChrysler Corporation; Haas and Aulbur, 2003; Kannan and Akhilesh, 2002; Wenger and Snyder, 2000). While

---

* *Editor's Note:* Dealing with fast-paced and complex changes in the global automotive industry requires new knowledge-based organizational forms rather than the traditional command-and-control chain prevalent in a manufacturing environment. Web-based KM infrastructure at DaimlerChrysler supports the Engineering Book of Knowledge (EBoK), where knowledge is captured and shared in the form of lessons learned, best practices, expertise directories, and discussion forums across the organization. This chapter describes how DaimlerChrysler's TechClubs—CoPs in engineering—are built around robust business processes, capacity for knowledge behaviors, and sound KM Web infrastructure.

Examples are provided of KM tool usage by the Composite Materials (CFK) Tech Club at German Airbus. One of the best practices in promoting knowledge networking at DaimlerChrysler is the "Austauschgruppe" for personnel rotation across strategic groups. Specific impact metrics for the KM system include decrease in time-to-talent, decrease in time-to-information, and increase in motivation. The DaimlerChrysler Corporate University plays a major role as a coordinator and facilitator of the KM CoP, with subcommittees for IT tools, measurement, culture, and marketing. The company provides training on writing skills to engineers and has schemes to improve motivation. This chapter also provides useful tips for selection and evaluation of KM tools, such as build/outsource, usability across domains, embeddedness, and fundamental/strategic use.

meeting knowledge challenges requires a variety of tools, we have found communities of practice (CoPs) to be an efficient means to achieve business process improvement and manage complexity. Here, we describe hands-on experiences with CoPs: why they are useful, why you may want to use them in your corporation, what makes them work, who should be involved, and some of the lessons learned. We also speak of the evolution of Knowledge Management (KM) technologies to knowledge-based engineering solutions and the added value we achieved from them. Technology is used widely for knowledge sharing and transfer in this culturally diverse and geographically distributed organization, to enhance productivity and innovation. The KM practices and techniques used are briefly described, issues and constraints faced are discussed, and solutions are presented.

KM at DaimlerChrysler

DaimlerChrysler is a leading automotive, transportation, and services company, with its car, truck, and financial services businesses all ranked at or near the top of their respective industries. The company's purpose is to be a global provider of automotive and transportation products and services and to generate superior value for its customers, employees, and shareholders. With a strong presence in North America and Europe, DaimlerChrysler is currently aggressively expanding its presence in Asia. DaimlerChrysler also has large equity holdings in EADS Airbus [European Aeronautic Defense and Space Company, a multi-national merger of DaimlerChrysler Aerospace (Germany), Aerospatiale Matra (France), and CASA (Spain). BEA Systems holds a 20% share of Airbus]. DaimlerChrysler Research and Technology India is a 100% subsidiary of DaimlerChrysler AG and supports the group in research, development, and business process consulting.

Knowledge distribution is one of the biggest challenges faced by a global company such as DaimlerChrysler, especially from a technological and cultural point of view. Systematic and sustained knowledge transfer requires top-management support and coordination, especially in the context of transnational integration. Knowledge is captured and shared in the form of lessons learned and best practices across the organization. Best practices in knowledge sharing will be presented later in this chapter.

Recognition of knowledge as the only resource that increases with use would be a first step in the right direction. The author's guesstimate is that 30% of the Fortune 500 companies and 60% of the Economic Times 500 companies (in India) believe that KM is a stand-alone information technology solution. We wish to emphasize the importance of the *people* and *processes* components of KM initiatives. Organizations which have been successful in KM initiatives are those that have understood and implemented people and process changes. At DaimlerChrysler, we believe that people contribute to 80% of the success of the KM initiative.

KM like the establishment of CoPs ensures that knowledge flows quickly between isolated knowledge islands in the company. Within DaimlerChrysler, CoPs are groups of employees charged with business process improvement within a given knowledge area or domain. Their agenda, scope, and composition is determined by the business processes and underlying knowledge areas. For example, an engineering CoP—which is known as a Tech Club at DaimlerChrysler—may involve all brake engineers. Their task is to conduct brake design and supplier reviews across several product development groups. An e-learning CoP not only includes training providers, but also information technology and infrastructure experts. Typical topics for such a community include the definition of a common learning management system, agreement on standards for e-learning objects, or coordination of a common supplier policy.

The CoP approach is built around optimizing business processes by involving every member in the community. The key elements of the DaimlerChrysler KM initiative are listed in Table 7.1. Handling the different aspects of our KM framework requires very different capabilities and approaches as summarized in Table 7.1. One of the key tasks of a CoP is to document knowledge.

Recent research has shown that organizational processes have a direct relationship with employees' value addition and replaceability. Organizational culture, top management support, knowledge-sharing practices, opportunities for learning and development, and rewards and recognition were found to have a positive effect on employee value addition. At DaimlerChrysler, we emphasize the importance of systems and processes for effective management of people and their knowledge. We build our software and technology solutions around process interventions and have found that to be effective. Off-the-shelf stand-alone products such as Microsoft's Share Point Server have been used by several organizations, but they have been most effective only when integrated with organizational processes and when supported by the top management, a case in point being Motorola's One Team solution. At DaimlerChrysler, this has led to the development of robust KM solutions which are based on the CoPs approach. We will discuss these solutions, the key facilitators, and inhibitors in this chapter.

Table 7.1

Key Elements of the Three Building Blocks of the DaimlerChrysler Knowledge Management Framework: People, Process, and Technology			
	People	**Process**	**Technology**
Key Competencies	• Leadership • Ability to affect behavior	• Know-how and experience • Persuasion	• State-of-the-art technology • Accuracy
Approach	• Empirical with extensive discussion and participation	• Analytical and empirical with extensive discussion	• Strong user involvement • Iterative
Support	• Culture of knowledge-sharing • In-house responsibility • Top management involvement • Reward system	• Internal support structure leverages Best Practices • Stakeholder involvement to identify processes that meet knowledge needs	• IT capability • Often support from outside of the organization
Other Considerations	• Tolerance for imperfections • Open-ended	• Some tolerance for imperfection • Continuous improvement	• Minimum tolerance for errors • Clear milestones

EBoK—The DaimlerChrysler Solution

CoPs and Books of Knowledge are an effective and probably the best-known example of knowledge-sharing activities at DaimlerChrysler. The Engineering Book of Knowledge (EBoK) refers to an electronic, hierarchical, secure, and interactive repository of DaimlerChrysler core knowledge (e.g., best practices, lessons learned, Yellow Pages). It is a virtual one-stop technology solution to facilitate knowledge sharing from the engineer's desktop. EBoK is an information technology (IT) support solution for enabling CoPs in DaimlerChrysler. A screenshot of EBoK is presented in Figure 7.1.

The EBoK is a Web-based system for collecting and distributing knowledge. It is user friendly, secure, efficient, and flexible; it does not require any user skills apart from Internet browsing. The EBoK stores knowledge in the form of "lessons learned" and "best practices." EBoKs are a useful part of an engineer's work and average at least one read per day.

The EBoK comprises several books. By clicking on one of the book icons, the user enters the next level of detail, where he/she finds substructures (like chapters and sub-chapters) while finally reaching individual documents. There are three basic ways to use the CoP tool:

- The user can browse the books and their substructures, reading best practices and lessons learned randomly.
- He/she can use the structure to navigate through specific books or chapters.
- He/she can retrieve information on a specific topic by searching for key words.

The EBoK also provides for peer/expert review of documents. The readers can provide feedback on a chapter/subchapter by sending e-mails to the authors and book owners. After providing feedback, the author and the book owner must be notified and react to the feedback. Figure 7.2 depicts the EBoK life cycle and Tech Club roles.

The EBoK system's architecture is presented below.

Figure 7.1

EBoK: the IT tool that facilitates Tech Clubs in DaimlerChrysler by providing a virtual forum for sharing of lessons learnt and best practices

Figure 7.2

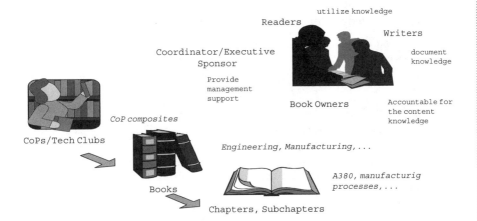

CoPs and EBoK: the life cycle

Challenges Faced

Two key challenges were faced in deployment of the books of knowledge and have been resolved over time.

- Challenge #1: To deliver integrated knowledge to the engineer's desktop. The organization's response was to collaborate with the engineering information provider community.
- Challenge #2: To motivate and support EBoK authors. We incorporated aging agents to keep the repository up to date. The organization also provided training on technical writing skills to engineers and supported and encouraged knowledge sharing. A streamlined and systematic review process was put in place to increase transparency and thereby motivation. Further news groups were created to motivate usage.

KM Best Practices: Communities of Practice and Knowledge Sharing

The amount of literature on KM, in general, and CoPs, in particular, is large and growing. Nevertheless, it is difficult to find first-hand reports on how CoPs start, thrive, and die in modern corporations. As a consequence, we will focus on describing existing, well-functioning CoPs within DaimlerChrysler rather than on theoretical ideas and frameworks about communities. In the following, we describe two types of knowledge-steering communities: the well-known Engineering Tech Clubs and the Corporate KM CoP that leverages KM practices throughout DaimlerChrysler. In addition, we will present an innovation community: the so-called "Austauschgruppe" or exchange group. These communities have recently been recognized as outstanding examples of efficient CoPs within global corporations (American Productivity and Quality Center Best Practice Report, 2001). As a matter of fact, DaimlerChrysler was chosen as a Best Practice partner of the American Productivity and Quality Center's benchmarking study on "Building and Sustaining Communities of Practice." The post-merger integration department also recognized "Tech clubs as a best practice among DaimlerChrysler business units."

The "Austauschgruppe": Personnel Rotation around Strategic Knowledge Domains

The mission of the "Austauschgruppe" (ATG, or exchange group) is to integrate DaimlerChrysler's business and functional units across regions through strategic knowledge transfer. The focus of this knowledge transfer is the individual, and the main tool is personnel rotation around strategic knowledge areas, which normally lasts two years. The main focus is the transfer of technological advances and innovations from DaimlerChrysler's Research and Technology division into Engineering, Manufacturing, Sales, and Marketing. Knowledge about changing customer preferences and tastes is communicated back to Research and Technology to continuously adapt and redirect research efforts. Members of the ATG are challenged not only to build bridges between strategic knowledge domains, but also to be entrepreneurs within DaimlerChrysler.

The ATG is composed of members from 21 countries around the globe and has a strong international and intercultural competence that it leverages efficiently to support the integration and further globalization of DaimlerChrysler. The effectiveness of the ATG has been established through other measurements. For example, rotation and networking should decrease time-to-talent, decrease time-to-information, and increase the motivation of a member of the ATG compared to average employees. While members of the ATG rate themselves as 20% better in these three areas than average employees, their management sees a 30% improvement.

Tech Clubs and EBoK

The Composite Materials (CFK) Tech Club at German Airbus (DA) faces the following business challenge: the quality of the material must be improved and errors in handling composite materials must be reduced. In particular, this requires close communication and efficient information exchange between manufacturing, engineering, and services. These units are located in different cities (e.g., Stade, Bremen, and Hamburg), which complicates communication further. In addition, competencies have to be managed, for example, in the form of "Yellow Pages." Yellow Pages list experts, their area of expertise, and contact information. The CFK CoP consists of people within German Airbus who are working with composite materials. They share a structured knowledge pool through the EBoK, which consists of three books that mirror the communication needs: one each for manufacturing, engineering, and service. For this particular CoP, there is no further substructure (i.e., chapters or subchapters); lessons learned and best practices are entered directly into each book. For example, Quality, Services and Engineering noticed some problems with the tightness of composite materials that had been produced. For small components there is a simple, non-destructive solution to quickly check the tightness. This was written down as a Best Practice in the following form:

> Tightness of sandwich parts shall be checked after manufacturing by dipping parts in warm water. Increased porosity of CFRP sandwich parts may cause water ingression in service. Sandwich parts may suffer defects after manufacturing. Before delivery, water tightness shall be checked. This test can be done by dipping these parts in warm water; air bubbles will show possible defects. This test can easily be

combined with NDT (Non-Destructive Testing) done in final inspection. If water soak is not possible, X-ray is an option to detect water after NDT.

The message quickly spread. Soon after publishing the Best Practice in the Engineering Book, the method was routinely applied within Manufacturing.

Corporate Knowledge Management Sharing Forum (KMSF)

The transfer of knowledge-sharing processes needs organized support and facilitation. To facilitate knowledge and experience transfer across regions and between business and functional units, the Corporate KM CoP was founded in late 1999 based on the model of the Auburn Hills KM Sharing Forum. One to two representatives from each business and functional unit meet about four times a year to discuss KM Best Practices and Lessons Learned, as well as to recommend corporate KM guidelines. Meetings are facilitated by the DaimlerChrysler Corporate University (DCU), which plays a major role as a coordinator and facilitator of the KM CoP. The mission of the Corporate KM CoP is to help DaimlerChrysler build, share, and apply the best knowledge available to achieve superior business results.

To fulfill this mission, the KM CoP started subcommunities centered around important components of the DaimlerChrysler KM framework, such as IT tools, measurement, culture, and marketing. The responsibilities of the Corporate KM CoP include establishing corporate KM guidelines such as metrics for KM benefits or IT tools. Other tasks are the internal and external promotion of KM activities, the leveraging of Best Practices and Lessons Learned, and the provision of start-up support for CoPs at the business and functional unit level.

Knowledge-Based Engineering Solutions

Engineering knowledge is dynamic and does not often have one standard solution to a problem. Engineering problem-solving switches between analysis and synthesis (real) phases. The latter modifies the solution by adding new information to it. Analysis results in new requirements and in control knowledge about how to proceed and is dependent on common sense knowledge, which can be modeled. Patterns are identified and formal knowledge modeling is used to automate design updates and improvements, thus leading to large-scale savings in cycle time and performance effectiveness.

Knowledge is structured using ontologies. Ontologies are systematic, comprehensive, reusable knowledge repositories. They facilitate communication between people and organizations; translation of modeling methods, paradigms, languages, and software; are reusable and sharable; provide for search and retrieval; and are highly reliable.

Knowledge-based engineering (KBE) makes knowledge accessible, usable, and reusable to designers and engineers; formalizes knowledge modeling, acquisition, documentation, and management; and relieves experts from routine work allowing them to review and update their work. KBE solutions also allow the designer to directly apply the rules to their CATIA models and capture best practices in the form of rules. The KBE tools support the knowledge value chain for engineering and facilitate large savings in cycle time and rework.

Choosing a Tool: Roadmaps to Success

The journey toward effective management of knowledge has been a long and successful one for DaimlerChrysler. Our philosophy of building practices around people and processes and of embedding technologies within processes has had distinct advantages. Technological infrastructural support was a prerequisite for an organization of our size and geographic distribution, yet the building blocks of success lay in localized efforts, top-management support, and creating a culture of knowledge sharing. This section presents a method toward building effective KM solutions.

Methodology for Choosing a KM Solution

The success of a KM tool is dependent on its effective usage. Hence it becomes imperative to garner knowledge regarding the users' knowledge needs. Needs may be collected through extensive interviews or through discussions in weekly meetings or through a CoP. Challenges faced by the potential users need to be understood and built into the tool in order to increase the return on investment (RoI). The expressed needs need to be consolidated and prioritized on the basis of the effort required (systems vs. organizational) and the criticality to the organization (ease of availability of the knowledge, core competency, importance or business criticality, and performance in that domain). Barriers to usage are analyzed—these could be structural, boundary, or cultural—and factored into the solution. Ease of implementation is then assessed, and a solution is then designed, which may be developed in-house or bought off the shelf. "Make-buy" decisions are based on several factors, such as "fit" between needs and available tools, cost of development, and whether development requires outsourcing company core knowledge.

Evaluation Criteria

The tool may be further analyzed on the basis of its usefulness and distinctiveness. Usefulness across the company refers to the number of core competencies that it pertains to. This could be transversal, multiple, or narrow. A tool that is widely applicable across the business—independent of process, industry, and cultural bounds—is said to be transversal. A tool that has an impact across at least three knowledge domains is classified as multiple, and one that can be applied across only a limited set of conditions is narrow.

Distinctiveness refers to the potential value that can be created from a given tool. This could be rated as fundamental, advanced, or innovative. Fundamental refers to basic applications that may be available across several tools already in existence in an organization. Advanced tools have a strategic advantage and offer more than fundamental information management features like database management, archiving, and search and retrieval. These are tools that are customizable and match the organization's specific needs. Innovative tools are those that need to be developed, as they offer new and unique features and meet proprietary knowledge needs of the company. Usefulness may be plotted on the "X-axis," and distinctiveness may be plotted on the "Y-axis."

Tool assessment and selection should also be based on the type of knowledge being addressed. Is the knowledge widely spread across the organization or available to only a few? Is it collectively shared? Collectively shared knowledge may be easier to capture and transfer, as sharing is not perceived as a "threat," and will require fewer organizational incentives. Consolidated knowledge—or knowledge that is regularly used within the activities for which it is directly intended but not elsewhere—is easy to formalize and codify. Such knowledge is easily captured and shared through groupware or collaborative IT solutions. Embedded knowledge, on the other hand, is tightly integrated into all activities in which it is useful. It has been well formalized, except in cases where the nature of the knowledge makes this infeasible. In this case, the knowledge has been integrated into work through other means (e.g., culture, training). Such knowledge cannot be transferred through IT solutions, but needs to be integrated into practices. Embedded knowledge may be captured and reused through KBE solutions.

Measurement and Metrics

Performance measurement is an essential part of the process of getting things right. Measurements inform us about the effectiveness of a solution, whether it is meeting the needs and objectives, and also help us take corrective actions, whether they be process redesign or technology enhancements. Some common metrics used for collaborative lessons learned (LL) solutions include:

- Number of processes or tools replaced
- Number of total users
- Number of different customizations
- Number of log-ins to the tool for viewing
- Number of locations of the tool
- Number of proposed answers
- Number of actually reused LL/viewed
- Number of reworks that have been avoided thanks to right-in-time information
- Time to find originator and context of a comment
- Time to talent
- Time taken to access the tool
- Time to find relevant information
- Problem-solving time
- Diffusion time
- Reaction time
- LL creation time

Some tools have a built-in provision for these statistics and thus enable assessment. Continuous assessment and measurements result in proactive behaviors, which lead to a competitive advantage. RoI and financial baseline measures of tool effectiveness should be incorporated at later stages of evolution.

EBoK has resulted in the elimination of printing, shipping, and storage of written operational manuals; led to more knowledgeable employees, increased productivity, and improved dealer and customer satisfaction; and generated quantifiable savings. Further knowledge and ideas management has resulted in a savings of *62 million* Euro/year and a total of 69,000 suggestions in the year 2001, supported by a Web-based solution known as Idee.com.

Recommendations for KM Professionals

The authors' diverse experiences in DaimlerChrysler have taught us some lessons and shown us some best practices for effective management of knowledge. The golden rules to follow, in our opinion, are:

- KM initiatives can be successful only when they take people into consideration. All KM issues are people driven and need to address the employees' knowledge needs and show a direct relation between the initiatives and performance. KM professionals should keep this in mind while designing an initiative.

- People, process, and technology, in that order, are the key mantra.
- Incentivize knowledge-sharing activities. Link initiatives to performance and rewards.
- Build processes around knowledge flows.
- Facilitate and encourage cross-departmental knowledge sharing, discussions, and collaboration.
- Link knowledge reuse to innovation and measure.

Knowledge—as well as its efficient dissemination and reuse—is of central importance to any global company and ought to be a strategic function that is linked to performance management systems.

Conclusion

KM works in DaimlerChrysler as it revolves around people, processes, and technologies. People's knowledge needs are first ascertained through knowledge audits and needs analysis and then built into organizational processes and "ways of doing things." These processes are built around knowledge flows to ensure success. The technology solution is then built around the process. CoPs have proved to be an effective method toward knowledge sharing in our organization. EBoK, the technological support solution for CoPs, has shown sustained value addition in the form of lower cycle times and higher reaction time, as well as more effective decision-making. Several technological solutions such as Yellow Pages and e-learning solutions and KBE tools like ICAD have been deployed through the organization and have also shown consistent returns. The critical success factor has been the need for such a solution and its adoption as part of the methods and processes, thus overcoming cultural resistance. KM has become a norm or a way of doing things within the organization and is used as a tool for performance effectiveness. In DaimlerChrysler, knowledge sharing is part of the LEAD appraisal systems, and DaimlerChrysler Research and Technology India is also involved in intangibles measurements.

References

American Productivity and Quality Center (2001). Building and Sustaining Communities of Practice, American Productivity and Quality Center Best Practice Report (http://www.apqc.org), March 2001.

Haas, R. and Aulbur, W. (2003). Enabling Communities of Practice at EADS Airbus, in *Sharing Expertise: Beyond Knowledge Management*, Ackerman, M., Pipek, V., and Wulf, V., Eds., Cambridge, MA: MIT Press.

Kannan, G. and Akhilesh, K.B. (2002). Human Capital Value Added—A Case Study in InfoTech, Haas, R. and Kannan, G. 2002, *Aspects Of Knowledge Sharing In Distributed Design Build Teams*, 9th European Concurrent Engineering, Madena, Italy.

Ryckebusch, M. (1996). "*Chrysler Through the Years*", Corporate Communications, Chrysler Corporation, 1000, Chrysler Drive, Auburn Hills, MI-48326.

Wenger, E.C. and Snyder, W.M. (2000). Communities of Practice: The Organizational Frontier, *Harvard Business Review*, January–February, 139–145.

Ready for Take-off: Knowledge Management Infrastructure at easyJet*

8

Ben Goodson

> Never doubt that a small group of thoughtful, committed citizens can change the world. Indeed, it's the only thing that ever has.
>
> *Margaret Mead*

Company Profile

easyJet is Europe's largest low-cost airline at the time of writing, offering point-to-point services between 38 major European airports. The company has grown exponentially ever since it began running services between London and Scotland just over seven years ago, with two leased Boeing 737s. From a small orange port-a-cabin on the outskirts of London Luton airport (called "easyLand") and a roomful of people led by the enigmatic entrepreneur Stelios Haji-Ioannou, easyJet has grown to over 3,000 people and 67 wholly owned Boeing 737 aircraft.

During the year 2002–2003, our growth has been reinforced as the airline reacted to changing market conditions in the sector by acquiring "Go," the low-cost airline started by British Airways and subsequently owned by the investment group 3I. Massive amounts of commercial and cultural change have been embraced enterprise

---

* *Editor's Note:* Written in a delightfully candid and straightforward manner, this chapter covers some of the challenges that have faced knowledge-sharing infrastructure in Europe's largest low-cost airline, easyJet. Rapid growth and acquisitions have transformed the culture of the organization from startup to major player in just a few years, with many more changes up ahead. On the KM infrastructure front, a key challenge was the acquisition of the airline Go, whose processes were very heavily dependent on hard copy documents, thus making it difficult to smoothly create organization-wide processes based on digital publication, communication, and workflow.

To ensure scalability of operations and knowledge exchange, easyJet is dealing with such "knowledge fracture" by augmenting its intranet with KM tools and an explicit KM strategy. Tool migration, training in new IT infrastructure, branding the intranet, dealing with infrastructure fragments, incorporating user feedback, nurturing an attitude of continuous learning, and communicating messages of open, transparent culture are some steps being taken. Lessons for the KM community from this chapter include the necessity to deal with potential challenges like inertia and even cynicism with respect to new KM tool usage.

wide since the integration. Managing this change, as well as our existing business, has proven challenging, thought provoking, and emotive. The experience has fortified the business for the next major commercial and cultural challenge: integrating Airbus into the easyJet network. The transition from Boeing to Airbus will be one of the primary factors in enabling easyJet to become Europe's best low-cost airline, not just its biggest.

The Early Years: Document Management and the "Paperless Office" at easyJet

Until 2002, easyJet did not have a fully defined knowledge management (KM) strategy and was not actively pursuing one at a senior level. Certainly, there were themes and projects going on around the organization that reflected the principles and discipline of KM. Just like most other businesses, human networks and small communities of practice evolved from the initial management frameworks and hierarchies. These were particularly strong operationally, where the interdependencies between processes and people were and are essential to our business model. They were also strong culturally, with consultative communities and social architects coming together to develop and maintain our identity.

However, in terms of "hard" knowledge distribution, storage, and management, we were slightly more disjointed. Critically and oddly, for a business that explicitly states and tries to create an "open" culture toward information, most of these projects and networks were growing up in isolation from each other.

Early on, we decided that our information and communication strategy would revolve around the paperless office concept, which has been culturally at the heart of documentation intentions. To support the vision, easyJet had been using the document management tool Keyfile. Owned by Lexign Corporation at the time of writing, Keyfile provides full document management functionality, from distribution and storage to records management and basic workflow. It is used throughout the business to capture and distribute all of the paper that comes in from external sources. However, the acceptance and belief in the paperless vision from the organization is not what it was six years ago. Times have changed. "Paperless?" people chuckle, "Have you ever walked around easyLand with your eyes open?" Of course, I answer "no" and laugh warmly back before launching into my well-rehearsed song and dance routine (no show tunes; top hat and cane optional) on the fabulous benefits of living the paperless lifestyle.

The first thing to realize about the paperless office is that the term has become slightly misleading at easyJet; that is our fault. It really describes the nirvana of what we are trying to achieve, and in some ways it is accurate. We *are* trying to run an airline and an office (and in some respects an aircraft) with less paper. However, it does not accurately describe the day-to-day environment at easyJet.

Charting a Knowledge Strategy

I define knowledge as **the insight, experience, and creativity that exist within people expressed through explicit and tacit communication events.** By being efficient and effective with our knowledge, we can reduce our associated costs and increase our competitiveness in a sector that is becoming ever more challenging to operate in. It is the trinity of people, processes, and technology that defines how successful we are at being paperless and how successful we can be in managing our knowledge. Our people need to understand the paperless office concept, and as a business we need to define and communicate it successfully. We need to identify, capture, and communicate the right behavior that will allow the paperless concept to add value to our business.

Explicitly, our knowledge strategy focuses on:

- Centralizing our KM repository and our electronic communication
- Developing two-way networks into our entire knowledge base across the enterprise
- Identifying, capturing, and disseminating the right behaviors for using what we know effectively
- Culturally growing an organizational environment that allows and encourages effective KM
- Supporting our KM with effective training and development

Our strategy needs to be able to adapt to the needs of an organization and a market sector that is constantly changing. It needs to be able to support the airline in its stated aim of becoming the biggest and best low-cost airline in Europe. It must allow for the creation and management of simple, highly scalable, and intelligent processes that enable the business to be as lean as it can be. Critically, it must be able to deliver on its potential to nearly every single area of the organization (see Figure 8.1).

KM Infrastructure: Grappling with "Knowledge Fracture"

Crucially, we need to get our technology right. We have been using Keyfile as our document management system of choice for the past six years and it has done an admirable job of supporting the company in getting us to where we are today. However, in many ways its functionality has been superseded by other business systems (like Microsoft Outlook) and that has seriously reduced its effectiveness.

This knowledge fracture is one of the primary reasons for developing a viable, workable KM strategy. Most people involved in any sort of information or KM discipline are using a combination of Outlook and network drives to manage their work. Why? Why do people choose not to use our document system as their primary information management tool? It comes down to a combination of factors.

First, people are familiar with the windows and Microsoft product interface. While Keyfile uses a very simple Graphical User Interface (GUI), using Outlook feels comfortable. Sending and receiving information is easy. Network drives are a part of everyday life. "Right Clicking" has become an accepted part of the language.

Second, there has been a shocking lack of training and product marketing on the Keyfile system for users. Historically, line managers or knowledgeable individuals conduct Keyfile training when it is needed. There is little in the way of consistency and practically nothing in the way of user support. Certainly, the electronic document message, while defined initially, suffers from a lack of reinforcement as people come into the organization.

Third, our merger with Go, an organization that conducted most of its business (process, workflow, and management) in hard copy, means that we have had a sharp increase in people who have never worked with an electronic document management system.

To support the understanding of the "paperless" concept, we have therefore begun to provide as much training on the Keyfile system as possible for individuals. We have also tried to reinforce the paperless message by taking time to market and distribute as much information as possible. We made posters, wrote magazine articles, and

Figure 8.1

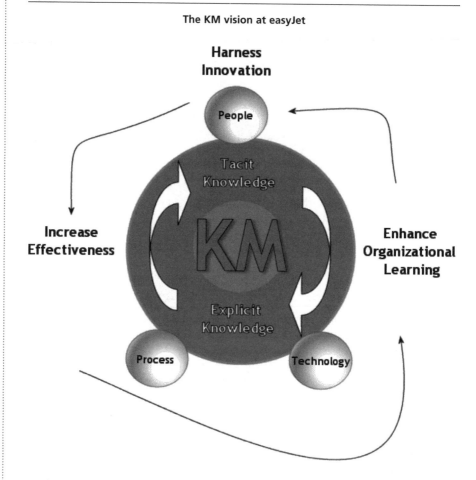

The KM vision at easyJet

conducted face-to-face small group discussion forums. These feedback sessions were extremely effective in man-aging the change process. Reactions to the paperless concept were varied. Some were more willing to go with it than others. Ultimately, the merger provided the spark in kick-starting the training and marketing process on the paperless office.

Launch of the Intranet: Branding and Content

In 2001, easyJet launched **http://inside.easyJet.com,** an intranet designed to propagate easyJet's cultural value system around the growing organization. The recognition that Luton was the cultural epicenter was the first step to understanding that those values were less well accepted the further away from Luton you went. The intranet was really designed to try and bridge that understanding and behavioral gap. As such, it was led by the man responsible for easyJet's culture, Chris Goscomb. In collaboration with our Web team, we built an intranet that was bright orange in every sense. It was designed to be fun and packed full of features that people really wanted to use and become involved in. It was also designed to have a serious business function.

We started with daily news content, for sale and wanted boards, orange pages contacts, message forums, and a staff travel function. We now have a reward and recognition mechanism, staff party booking functionality, sales figures piped directly from our reservation system, and so much more content that I could, quite literally, take up the rest of this chapter talking about them. In a way, we were offering some technical knowledge management functionality without really defining it or, perhaps, realizing it.

Certainly, providing a Web interface into our human resource (HR) database so that we could display a common list of contacts (complete with funky photo) is information management. It becomes KM when someone uses that mechanism in either distribution or creation. Similarly, providing our marketing managers with direct sales information allows them to then use their experience, insight, and creativity to make our business more effective.

Leap forward to 2003 and easyJet has an embedded document management system, a thriving intranet, and a heavy dependency on Microsoft Outlook. All of these systems could claim to be very worthy KM projects. How they all grew up to be big and strong without working together is a little harder to explain.

Choosing a KM Tool Vendor

At the time of writing, we are replacing Keyfile, our document management system, with a new KM system. From the ground up, we will have the opportunity to review and challenge every single assumption we have made about our system, people, and processes over the past six years. Twelve months ago, before the integration with Go, a small project team was assembled and led by our company secretary (who has corporate responsibility for information) to look at replacing Keyfile. We knew that the current system was no longer capable of supporting the business. We also knew that not many organizations were using technology to support an enterprise-wide paperless concept. Certainly, we knew that nobody else used Keyfile like easyJet.

So we set about examining our system functionality, defining the core requirements of an easyJet system, and identifying the areas we needed to improve upon. Ultimately, we had to centralize our electronic communication and the knowledge base, migrating all of the existing data in our virtual drives and Keyfile into the new system. Then we had to understand exactly what parts of Keyfile were effective. What was working for easyJet? What sort of things would we like our new system to do? What was the scope of our project? Were we simply replacing Keyfile or were we doing something far more dramatic?

Using the research and advisory firm Gartner, we produced a short list of potential vendors, including the incumbent. We asked for detailed submissions from each potential vendor on how they might meet our core system and process requirements. Then, over a period of several months, we met them, viewed their products, and spoke with them at great length to understand the potential cultural as well as technical fit. We then narrowed down our potential list and went into further detail on each selected vendor, visiting reference sites and examining how the product was working in a live environment. At the time of writing this, we have been in extensive negotiations with the selected vendor and we hope to conclude and announce a deal soon.

KM Tools and Cultural Challenges

Getting the technology right is important. However, at easyJet, that is really the easy part. As an enabler, our new KM system will allow departments to create simple, scalable processes. The system will centralize our knowledge base and our electronic communication function. But what will motivate people to use it effectively? What role will people play in the creation of new processes? What will the system mean to them? How do we avoid creating the cynicism and negativity that has arisen with our current technology? There are many questions that surround the human element of a successful knowledge strategy.

The approach that we will take focuses on creating understanding, providing support, and reinforcing the messages. Organizational workplace culture is a complex animal. In our enterprise, as with many others, our organizational culture is made up of very distinct groups that all need to be managed, developed, and working hard to make our business successful. Our workplace culture is very powerful, having evolved from the entrepreneurial spirit and energy of the individuals who founded easyJet. One of our corporate strengths lies in our brand awareness and the marketing of the color orange to mean "low cost" or "great value." Our brand is now considered a "super brand," something more akin to a lifestyle choice.

With such a powerful external brand it should come as no surprise to learn that we have an equally powerful internal brand. To our people, being "orange" means living to a defined set of values that they themselves were involved in developing, transcending the cultural subset. If people feel ownership and responsibility toward their culture, they are more likely to proactively demonstrate those values.

With the Go merger now complete, easyJet has to reflect once again on the cultural model needed to support the new business going forward. This is a process being led internally. In terms of creating an environment suitable for maintaining an effective knowledge system, easyJet has laid the foundations. Certainly, there has long been a focus on building openness and trans-parency, fostering learning and organizational development.

For our knowledge strategy, we will focus on building or adding content to programs that feature elements of inner and external understanding (for both individuals and groups). We will create an effective model for technical system support, and we will constantly reinforce our cultural and behavioral messages through our various communication channels. Doing these things and combining them with a product that is truly focused on managing knowledge (not just documents or data) should allow us to elicit the right kind of behavior from our people, leading to an effective and efficient knowledge utilizing organization.

The challenges to evolving the cultural model from entrepreneurial to something slightly more traditional are many. We must retain the spirit, energy, and values of our model, while applying them in a much larger context. The airline nearly doubled in size during 2002–2003. The merging of Go and easyJet into the new easyJet has led to individual changes in ideology. Processes have changed. Personnel have changed. Things that were once certain are now open to question. It is inevitable that the increase in the size of the business will also see a strengthening of the structural framework. However, we must be careful not to confuse strength with unnecessary bureaucracy.

The impact that our cultural evolution will have on our ability to manage knowledge effectively is not underestimated. Our intranet has quickly grown into an effective KM tool. While technically we will be consolidating our hard information management and distribution through Outlook and Keyfile, there is the question of whether we will integrate our intranet. This has yet to be agreed on (or really discussed) organizationally. My personal thoughts are that full integration with our KM system makes little sense at this stage. While some areas could benefit from the power that a KM system would bring (for example, the setting up of a virtual crew base), there are other areas that would not benefit.

Also, there are good reasons for keeping them "separate." The intranet was built specifically to propagate our cultural values. The fact that it does some KM functionality as well does not mean that it should automatically fall under the KM umbrella. We will continue to work on this issue until we resolve it.

Recommendations for KM Practitioners

If you are leading or being asked to lead a KM solution in your organization, there are so many things that will affect the successful outcome of your project that I could quite happily write an entire book on the subject. But I will not; instead, I will limit myself to four or five hundred words.

Do you really know your organization? Does your organization really know itself? Does it have a strong workplace culture supporting its commercial framework? Is that culture receptive to nurturing creativity and organizational development? Does it have to be in order to grow good KM behaviors?

Take our example, for instance. Running a KM program or strategy at easyJet will differ from delivering a successful project at British Airways. Even though the two organizations compete in a similar sector, they are very different places to work. At easyJet, there are several ways of getting things off the ground. Our offices are open plan. Our chief executive sits in the corner. Admittedly, he has two computers (where most others only have one), but there are no walls or closed offices. If you want to talk to him about anything, then you go and talk to him. The same goes for managers and people at every level of the organization. New ideas are actively encouraged. Talking about things openly and frankly is encouraged.

Creating an environment where it is okay to be honest and challenge those around you is important. How people feel is important: about themselves, about their peers, and about the business they work for. Let us not beat around the bush here; I do believe that ultimately there is a direct correlation between organizational culture and good KM. I do not believe that KM can be an enabler if it is stifled by an organization that cannot (or will not) learn new things. You cannot leverage any kind of return value from KM if your organization does not like sharing its tacit and explicit knowledge.

Really, the first step is to reflect on your organization and to try to understand it and the people who work for it. Because guess what? They all belong to unique cultural subsets, and each and every one of your people is different. So you will need to use a variety of methods to get your messages across.

This segues nicely into how you market and promote your project. Quite frankly, if you do not have management buy-in from most levels of your business, then the risk to your project is increased. The exposure to that risk increases the higher up the management food chain you go. Ideally, the need for KM would be spread from the top throughout the organization. Your MD or CEO would be the main vehicle for realizing KM throughout your business, espousing the benefits from the highest hilltop at every board meeting. Directors and senior managers would be authorizing cultural change and backing it up with hard cash.

However, the reality is that KM is often seen as a "soft" discipline. KM projects generally begin because there is a realization that things could be better. At a corporate level, *where* KM is sponsored is fundamentally important. Generally, there is the need for serious information technology (IT) buy-in, as you are going to deploy or change a system for managing knowledge. However, that does not make it an IT project. As I have hopefully tried to get across, the best IT system is redundant if you do not have a culture that will allow you to get the most from it.

Good KM programs are littered with real success stories across many market sectors. How you measure that success is directly applied to your particular audience. If you are talking to people who have 65% of their budget spent on just *managing* physical paper, then they are going to be interested in how your project might save them time and money. Equally, if you are talking about revisiting and challenging lots of existing processes, then you must come to terms with the fact that people will feel ownership of them. Ultimately, there are elements of change management theory, organizational and behavioral theory, and communication theory present in any good KM project.

Finally, you must retain flexibility in your work. The project must be able to cope with the changing needs of the business and should be as forward-looking as possible, while focusing on the present environment. Use some "good project manager" discipline. Create a scoping document stating the business case and outlining the perceived costs and resources. Outline the structure of the project team, and identify the right people with the right skills to lead each part of it. Create a top-level project plan and break things down into manageable bits and pieces.

Reflect upon your organization and its people, and make sure that whatever KM scheme and technology you put in place supports the business. That is, after all, what you are.

Resources

Collinson, C. and Parcel, G. (2001). *Learning to Fly: Practical Lessons from One of the Worlds Leading Knowledge Management Companies*. Capstone Publishing: Oxford.

Kluge, J., Stein, W., and Licht, T. (2001). *Knowledge Unplugged: The Mckinsey Global Survey of KM*. Palgrave Macmillan: New York.

Pfeffer, J. and Sutton, R. (1999). *Knowing-doing Gap: How Smart Companies Turn Knowledge Into Action*. Boston: Harvard Business School Press.

Ark Group (2003). Various articles in *Knowledge Management*. London, UK.

SuperBrands, http://www.thebrandcouncil.org.

Building and Sustaining Communities of Practice at Ericsson Research Canada*

Anders Hemre

> A leader who does not allow himself time to think may turn into a thoughtless leader. Likewise, an organization that does not allow itself time to think may turn into a thoughtless organization.
>
> *Anonymous*

Company Profile

Founded in 1876 and headquartered in Sweden, Ericsson has a long and illustrious history as a leading provider of products and services for telecommunication networks worldwide. Telecommunications is an innovation-based industry, and R&D is therefore a core function in telecommunication companies. Hence developing new products and services and moving these effectively and efficiently to market are the main functions of the business operation.

Ericsson Research Canada is located in Montreal as part of the worldwide R&D organization within the Ericsson group and is responsible for the provisioning of specific products and services for wireless communication networks. With over 1,700 employees (July 2003) the company is the largest single Ericsson R&D site outside of

---

*   *Editor's Note:* Telecommunications is a heavily innovation-based industry, and knowledge management forms a key plank of R&D in companies like Ericsson Research Canada. This chapter highlights features of the company's KM initiative ranging from the KM Advisory Board and vendor selection process to RoI approaches and technology support for online CoPs. From the beginning, an exploratory approach to KM implementation was adopted. Online CoPs were launched in 2000, with open Web-based support for knowledge networking (called XPERTiSE).
    Key learnings from the KM tools point of view are the importance of starting off with a low-key design rather than an overengineered, overloaded, and confusing user interface design; allowing for a high degree of customization; the critical role of online communities in bridging geographical gaps in global organizations; the opportunities in blending offline and online community interactions; and strategies for quickly harnessing early adopters when new technology solutions are being introduced. Through technology, the concept of the "Digital Employee" is emerging, which will challenge traditional notions of "headcount," "resources," "competencies," and "productivity."

Sweden. In 2003 Ericsson Research Canada rated among the top ten companies in Canada with respect to R&D investment.

KM at Ericsson Canada: Context and Objectives

During the mid- to late 1990s, the Montreal organization grew rapidly and took on new product and technology mandates. The upside of this is obvious. The downside was increased fragmentation, difficulties with communication, and a growing lack of cooperation and collaboration within the organization. Also, the continuously increased need for new product development speed implied less time available to execute the business process and certainly no time available for duplicating efforts or reinventing the wheel. With many new products and technologies being developed during a relatively short time period (e.g., open systems, third generation wireless, mobile Internet), it was becoming increasingly obvious that successful market introduction of new products also involves effective transfer of knowledge.

In 1999 it was decided that the opportunities offered by knowledge management (KM) should be explored to help address the issues mentioned above. Two activities were conducted in the early stage of the KM initiative: an organization and culture study and a technology assessment. Even though the former pointed to the importance of the social side of KM, the initial focus was certainly on technology. The first technology assessed was a system for guided knowledge discoveries in organizations. This involved applying a "what—how—why" structure to the operation, thereby capturing (in one tool) not only process activities, but also strategy and knowledge.

A KM Advisory Board was formed in the summer of 1999 to oversee and guide the effort involved in moving the initiative forward. Members included the CKO, CIO, CTO, HR Director, and Systems Research Director. A KM support team was also assembled, with representatives from human resources (HR) and information technology (IT) to directly assist the CKO.

One of the first decisions was to not do "KM" in general, but to focus on some important and relevant organizational aspect. It was decided to develop and promote "knowledge sharing." This, in turn, pointed in the direction of collaborative technologies, people networks, and social exchanges for knowledge sharing. The vision was that it should eventually be possible to innovate or solve problems using the best available knowledge resources wherever present in the local or global organization.

In general, the following benefits were expected from knowledge sharing: raising the level of innovation, retaining and leveraging existing knowledge, accelerating product knowledge transfer, identifying and effectively deploying best practices, speeding up problem solving, integrating and exploiting new expertise, and accelerating learning.

Realizing that the original technology assessed, despite its considerable merits, was not addressing the actual needs of the organization, it was decided to abandon this approach and continue to explore other possibilities. At this time (1999) the main KM technology offerings were still in the areas of portals, search engines, document management, and the like. Knowing that such technologies were already available within the company (e.g., Autonomy and Documentum), the search for something different continued.

A few vendors had positioned themselves in the collaboration and knowledge-sharing area with expert locating technologies and question and answer (Q&A) systems. These solutions appeared to be better suited to further exploration. At this point there were two choices: invite several vendors to submit their technologies for assessment or preselect one vendor and focus on building a strong business relationship. For several reasons the latter approach was chosen, and, subsequently, an industry leader agreement was concluded in early 2000 with Orbital Software (now Sopheon) for the installation of their Organik product.

The original software installation was on a Compaq Deskpro computer running Linux and a separate Oracle database on a Sun Ultra5 machine. Eventually, the system was ported to a Windows 2000 environment on a server grade machine. During the program this system evolved from a Q&A and people-finding application to an online community builder.

It should be noted that there was no need for a return on investment (RoI) to make a decision to move forward. The feeling was that this is good and we will go ahead, but let us not forget to demonstrate value down the road. It was also felt that there was not enough insight at this early stage to produce a very credible RoI case. It was also understood that if one of the benefits of knowledge sharing is time savings, it would be difficult to measure, as, like in most other organizations, we could only account for time spent but not for time saved.

Therefore, the initial argument was based simply on plausibility by underestimating the benefits. Statements such as "if the average user can save only 2 hours of time *over the entire lifetime* of the system it will pay for itself" and "suppose we can (through effective knowledge sharing) make 1000 knowledge workers appear as if they are 1001 the system will be paid for through a mere 0.1% improvement." These kinds of statements along with a limited financial exposure were sufficient to build initial confidence and support.

A more formal RoI was done later, primarily to help guide the continuation of the effort and engineer the program for value. This, in fact, turned out to be useful later when many IT initiatives came under scrutiny during a corporate "efficiency improvement" program.

Even though at this point there was a potential solution identified, it was necessary to examine the situation rather carefully to avoid ending up with a solution looking for a problem. It was also clear from the beginning that just introducing a piece of technology was not going to be an effective approach. Another insight involved earlier work performed by the organization in the areas of competence development and empowerment. It was felt that *competence → empowerment → knowledge* constituted a "critical maturity path" in organizational development such that *competent people can be empowered and empowered people can put knowledge effectively to use.*

KM Program and KM Solution Architecture

One of the early insights of the KM team was simply that *"this is not a project, it is an exploration."* The initial project-based approach was therefore abandoned fairly quickly in favor of an evolving approach with considerable room for change in direction and accommodation of new discoveries.

In the summer of 2000 the program discovered communities of practice. Interestingly, it was the technology vendor who introduced this concept, as their solution had developed from an expert locating system to a more full-blown community builder. A relationship was established with McDermott Consulting to help develop the concept of communities. This was a turning point for the entire program, which was now able to offer a complete KM concept *anchored* in the people domain and *supported* by a suitable technology. At this point it was decided to move forward and actually engage the organization. Community domains were approved by the KM advisory board, and it was decided to launch only a few to begin with. The first community of practice was launched in late 2000 followed by a few more in early 2001. It had thus taken well over a year from the initial exploration to the moment of truth.

These communities were launched using a one-day facilitated workshop guided by a generic straw model for community design provided by McDermott, in the following phases:

- Review straw model
- Decide what kind of knowledge to share
- Define community structure
- Define roles
- Identify events (meetings)
- Decide membership
- Develop guiding principles
- Review/adopt online technology
- Formulate vision and success

This served the additional purpose of initial bonding of core members and creating a feeling of joint accomplishment. Even though the program was well grounded in theory, it quickly turned out that things do not always go according to the book.

The first community stalled shortly after launch due to the fact that the community leader relocated. This clearly demonstrated the crucial role of the community leader. It was decided to try shared community leadership with two individuals involved and later to use a small core group to plan community programs and prepare meetings. The role of community meeting facilitator was also introduced.

By mid-2001 confidence had grown enough to try virtual launches via NetMeeting and teleconferences. Such launches were conducted as two to three shorter sessions over a one- or two-week period still using the straw model approach.

As initial community activities were not associated with any specific company objectives, it became important to conduct value assessments as part of the program. These assessments were conducted as structured interviews with community leaders to identify value contributions from community activity.

Early examples of value added included identification and use of a database for improved quality of business cases, identification of new business opportunities, design of a new security feature for a network product, and finding a third party technology provider for a new product offering. Other and softer benefits such as improved information sharing and stronger influence on methodology development were also stated.

A third way of designing and launching communities was introduced in 2003. This approach involved deliberately using team aspects such as purpose and objectives to get off the ground and then gradually add community aspects like learning, collaboration, and sharing. This was useful in avoiding the inevitable self-questioning that usually occurs during the early stage of community building (what is the purpose of this; why are we doing this; what is our expected contribution). Communities launched this way were referred to as forums and were targeting disciplines such as project and portfolio management and measuring and managing product in-service performance.

These forums were guided by small core groups of members who had accepted the role of planning, preparing, and facilitating community meetings, as well as developing a more long-term outlook and plan.

Figure 9.1

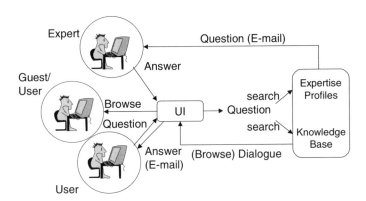

Accolade Knowledge Network

The selected technology—Accolade Knowledge Network by Sopheon (originally Organik by Orbital SW)—was not used by all communities, but primarily by local groups promoting and sharing their product technologies and by more loosely formed global networks where the only option was to operate online. Later, the technology was also used for a Knowledge Board application where selected reports and articles could be posted. The overall system architecture is depicted in Figure 9.1.

The system was left open for access through the intranet and focus was on building global connectivity rather than quickly loading the system with a maximum number of users. It integrated well with the intranet and Outlook. Even though some users would have preferred an even more seamless integration with e-mail, it was felt that a mixed user interface had the advantage of underlining the public nature of the system (viz. answering through a browser-based Q&A user interface).

Evolution of KM Strategy

The company's KM strategy developed over time as the program matured and involved the following aspects:

- Research & Pilot to learn, review, and validate concepts; screen and customize technology
- Focus on collaboration and knowledge sharing
- Voluntary participation, no conscripting of knowledge
- Start opportunistic, move toward a more deliberate approach
- Identify knowledge domains in Business/Technology and Management/Engineering
- Deploy locally, design for global outreach from the beginning
- Align with corporate knowledge networking program to solicit interest and support
- Build on existing business and knowledge networks with global participation
- Establish cost/benefit model and demonstrate value
- Build strong, value-added business relationships with concept & technology providers

The critical success factors for the KM initiative include:

- Comprehensive research, planning, and preparation
- Deployment was *not* heavily engineered and used a low-key approach
- Coaching and support of communities
- A high degree of freedom and customization
- Management support and community leadership
- Value propositions and operating scenarios prepared for communities
- Focus on individual value
- Build organizational value gradually
- Soft engineering of events (social or online)
- Simplification of the technology, in particular the user interface

Business Case for KM

The business case was prepared primarily for the technology investment and rested on five fundamental assumptions.

1. Collaboration and knowledge sharing have business benefit.
2. Technology adds value to KM solutions.
3. Global participation determines the overall value of the network.
4. Individual value must materialize for organizational value to build.
5. Turning a (online) knowledge base into a *useful* knowledge base requires human intervention.

It was further assumed that hardware depreciates at the normal rate used for servers in corporate computer networks and that it should be possible to recover software license fees by individual value gained through time savings alone.

The numbers used in this business case represented conservative estimates of value gained, thus demonstrating that even a relatively low usage could deliver sufficient value, assuming a minimum number of active users. Twenty percent penetration of a particular domain population was used as an upper limit estimate for active involvement in collaborative knowledge sharing (of any kind).

The following model was used for cost/benefit calculations:

- 1,000 registered (R&D) users
- Single site installation
- Current (2001) functionality level
- Registered user/guest user ratio = 1/3 (three guest visitors for every registered user)
- 0–5% improvement is realistic for most initiatives
- Managing the knowledge base requires one dedicated knowledge manager
- 15–25% of overall benefits may be attributed to technology

Implementation

Table 9.1 shows the basic outline and value engineering of the KM program (called XPERTiSE), with respect to three parameters of people, process, and technology.

Customizations

The following general technology requirements were established for the KM system XPERTiSE.

Table 9.1

KM Program 2002–2005

Area	Program activity	Outcome	Investment	Benefit	Long term capability
New Product Development (NPD process)	Assess NPD process and develop NPD KM applications Expand knowledge desk Value assessments	Increased productivity Improved information access and sharing Improved knowledge transfer Time savings	Time consulting	Improved product quality Smoother new product introductions	Technology management Organizational learning Capability Maturity
Community (people)	Community launches and support Value assessments Training and awareness HR development (roles, positions, reward, and recognition)	Improved decision making Increased/improved collaboration and knowledge sharing Speed up problem solving Developing and sharing good practices	Time consulting Training Industry events	Improved product marketing and technical sales support Stronger Company Value Proposition Increased employee satisfaction Increased customer/ sponsor satisfaction	Project management Software engineering (Smart) innovation (Complex) problem solving
Technology	Install Accolade Version upgrades Feature upgrades Grow number of system users	Support for virtual communities Increased people-to-people and people-to-information connectivity	Software license and maintenance Server and data-base System administration and support	Improved access to global expertise Reuse of knowledge Bridge geographical distance	Knowledge networking

XPERTiSE shall support on-line knowledge sharing and collaboration in a large, global organization populated by a mobile workforce. The system shall be easy and intuitive to use and require minimum administration. The system shall be able to bridge geographical distance, provide a collaborative domain for people-to-people connections and create a knowledge base, which is searchable for information content as well as people. The system shall employ a dynamic algorithm for creating knowledge profiles based on user activity. The system shall provide sufficient means to manage the knowledge base with respect to its usefulness. The system shall provide information about user behaviour and statistics relevant to the operation of the system.

XPERTiSE shall integrate with e-mail and intranet environments and shall co-exist with other collaborative, knowledge management and document management systems.

As for the selected technology, the initial impression was that the user interface was overengineered. Changes were introduced to hide features such as expert ratings and showing average response times. This would have caused too many questions about how these features actually work and how the information was supposed to be used instead of focusing on getting the basic system going. Advanced features could always be reintroduced later.

A registration process whereby users could submit their initial knowledge profile through the user interface was also added. This was interesting as the profile (checkbox menu) was based on an organizational knowledge map that was done in the early stage of the KM initiative, but never used for its original purpose.

Another change was to remove the capability for threaded discussions and instead just use sequential scrolling. Again, this was for simplicity reasons and from observing that most dialog involved less than five contributions and few involved up to ten contributions.

The people finder function was expanded to include more search parameters, and the product evolved to support uploading of photos and changing the initial knowledge profile.

Sidebar 1
Case Study: Development of a Server Product

One design team decided to use the KM technology as a way to facilitate knowledge transfer for a new J2EE server product being developed. The method used involved the translation of a technology blueprint to a Q&A format to populate a knowledge base with sufficient information and then the addition of expert teams to form a knowledge desk.

This was initially intended to support application developers, but was eventually re-directed to support product deployment in field trials and first office applications. The line manager initiated this with the additional purpose of accelerating team learning, as many team members were new to the technology being developed.

Benefits of this solution included less time spent by design engineers answering repetitive questions and fewer resources needed for product introduction support.

The difficult part involved changing people's work behavior and drawing users into the solution. Also, accessing the knowledge desk from field locations outside the intranet firewall required special access and security considerations, which were not always possible to easily accommodate. All in all, this solution ended up somewhat underleveraged.

Experiences with Knowledge Communities

One could say that communities are built with "magnets" and "glue"—domain interest and content value *attracting* people and relationships *bonding* members.

Implementing communities requires attention to diverse areas such as people relationships, social networks, business processes, organizational behavior, change management, and technology implementation. In terms of approach, it is clear that one size does *not* fit all (plenty of room for customization needed). Also, an overall low-key approach leaves more room for adaptation and lowers the risk for "campaign fatigue."

Even though people generally like to network, it is necessary to nurture and guide the *process* of networking. The role of the community leader is critical. Community facilitation and support are also required and often underestimated. Organizational change and movement of key personnel can be disruptive and need to be accommodated by sufficient community design and contingency planning. Top experts do not always have the best social skills. They do not like to ask questions or be asked questions that "waste" their time. For these reasons, inclusion of experts in communities requires special consideration.

Communities have life cycles (see Figure 9.2), and it is important to identify points where community design requires special attention, such as at launch, when losing steam, and when entering a mature stage. Organizational value should not be expected too early in the community life cycle, but for it to materialize individual value must be perceived by community members for them to continue to participate and contribute.

Communities may start opportunistic or deliberate. Keeping a balance between these components is important in order to both encourage new ideas and maintain sufficient focus on purpose and objectives.

In virtual (online) communities it is easy to participate (e-mail, intranet), but difficult to develop relationships and a feeling of community. Online dialog is non-real-time, and there is no verbal or body language communication involved. It is therefore particularly beneficial to complement online community activities with teleconferences/NetMeeting and "back-channel" work, i.e., contacting members over the phone and not missing opportunities to meet in person.

Figure 9.2

Community life cycle

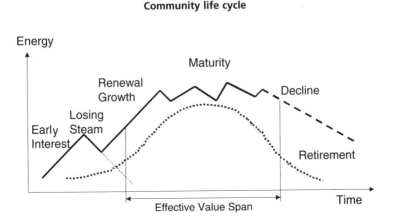

It is easier for people to respond to a question if notified by e-mail (more personal and convenient). Also, good questions get good answers, and it is beneficial to have a moderator who can follow up on unanswered questions and also initiate community dialogue and keep the "pot boiling."

When new technology solutions are being introduced, the targeted users or participants typically fragment into three groups: early adopters, early rejecters, and neutrals. Energy is better spent using the early adopters as pilot users helping to draw in the neutrals rather than trying to convince the non-believers. Content value is critical (as with any Web site), and it is necessary to regularly purge the knowledge base of incorrect or obsolete information.

Participation by recognized thought leaders is helpful, but if experts are reluctant to join and participate, there is certainly value in tapping into and leveraging the "second tier" of knowledge, particularly in a large organization.

Good community recruiting policies include recruiting people who are active in other discussion forums (chances are they will continue to be active) and inviting someone to respond to a particular question or discussion as part of joining a community (it increases purpose and relevance).

Future KM Developments

Collaboration in the 21st century organization is expanding across the extended enterprise (customers, partners, suppliers). Processes will become more people- and information-centric than just describing "workflows." This will put increased emphasis on people relationships, communication, information, and knowledge-sharing activities as being part of the process.

Modular processes should be able to execute on different computing devices such as desktop, laptop, PDA, and mobile phone with seamless integration and synchronization. Just as a PDA can synchronize with the parent desktop for calendar, contacts, and e-mail, it should be possible to synchronize process information modules, e.g., customer requirements or project status, with the main process information environment.

Through technology the concept of the "Digital Employee" is emerging—an information and knowledge worker who is technology enabled, networked, shared, associated with information and knowledge, and "always on." This will increasingly challenge managers to think beyond the more traditional view of "headcount," "resources," and "competencies."

Technologies will continue to support value chains and communities, as well as the individual knowledge worker. Despite the usefulness of technology, it will be necessary to develop a better understanding of how personal productivity improvements actually translate into organizational value.

Conclusion

Many firms recognize the need for collaboration and knowledge sharing across organizational boundaries and realize the benefits of such activities. A prerequisite for being a knowledge-based organization is the appreciation of knowledge and understanding the role of knowledge in the business. The greatest organizational KM potential is in leveraging tacit knowledge. Tacit knowledge sharing is accomplished through social exchanges or people networking.

Large global organizations benefit from also utilizing some form of technology to bridge geographical as well as organizational distance. A technology closely emulating how people share knowledge seems to offer the most promising potential. A particular technology may not be crucial to the overall success, but technology in general is certainly useful and has its place in the KM space. Effective solutions must solve real business problems and stay close to the business process—it makes more sense to people. Even so, it is necessary to support and promote the solution to draw in users and build critical mass.

Technology must not involve a steep learning curve, particularly if usage is on a voluntary basis. When assessing KM technologies, it is particularly important to include people and organizational aspects as knowledge sharing is a social phenomenon and user acceptance of the technology is a prerequisite for value creation.

Resources

Accolade Knowledge Network. www.sopheon.com.

Magnusson, M. and Davidsson, N. (2001). *Knowledge Networking at Ericsson—A Study of Knowledge Exchange and Communities of Knowing*, Department of Innovation Engineering and Management, Chalmers University of Technology, Gothenburg.

Hemre, A. (2001). *Implementing Communities to Promote Collaborative Knowledge Sharing*, Delphi summit on collaborative commerce, San Diego.

Hemre, A., McDermott, R., and King, I. (2001). "Communities of Practice—If We Build It Will They Come"?, KMWorld conference & exhibition, San Jose.

Hemre, A. (2002). "XPERTiSE—A Knowledge Sharing Initiative at Ericsson Research Canada," IQPC conference "Creating Value from Knowledge in R&D," London.

Hemre, A. (2002). "Acts of Knowledge in New Product Development," University of California, San Diego, Knowledge Application Conference.

Hemre, A. and McDermott, R. (2003). "A Natural Step—Applying KM Solutions in New Product Development without Launching an Initiative," Braintrust Conference, San Francisco.

Wenger, E., McDermott, R., and Snyder, W.M. (2002). *Cultivating Communities of Practice*. Boston: Harvard Business School Press.

Success at Ernst & Young's Center for Business Knowledge: Online Collaboration Tools, Knowledge Managers, and a Cooperative Culture*

James Dellow

> The great end of knowledge is not knowledge, but action.
>
> *Thomas Henry Huxley*

Introduction

In 1997 Tom Davenport wrote a classic case study on the evolution of knowledge management at Ernst & Young where he documented its beginnings back in the 1990s. Today, his case study still serves as an excellent introduction to knowledge management at Ernst & Young. Rather than summarize that early history here, I will pick up where he left off by quoting his concluding point that:

---

* *Editor's Note:* Ernst & Young is a pioneer in the field of KM, has won many awards for KM excellence, and has been written up in many KM texts already. This chapter focuses on the role of Web-based collaboration tools in enhancing the relationship between e-business and KM for Ernst & Young and its clients, via EY/KnowledgeWeb (the intranet) and Ernst & Young *Online* (the extranet). While such tools can indeed be deployed by other companies as well, Ernst & Young's competitive advantage comes from its capability to most effectively integrate the tool with the right people, processes, and content. Knowledge managers within the firm's global Center for Business Knowledge™ (CBK) are responsible for integrating information, taxonomies, human knowledge, and technology into work practices.

Key success factors for deploying such tools include an easy to use interface (*de facto* Web based), the ability for users to customize it without developer support, adequate tech support, the adoption of standards (e.g., for corporate branding), and high levels of security and legal protection. Success stories about usage of such tools in client engagements are adequately documented so that a virtuous cycle is created for future knowledge collaboration. Cultural issues may arise in other organizations not used to online collaboration, and hence a change management initiative may be necessary to spur adoption of such tools.

> *While John Peetz, Ralph Poole, and the growing number of E&Y knowledge managers were pleased with the firm's progress thus far, they felt that they were still in the early stages of their efforts. The only thing of which they were certain was that there would still be many changes and challenges that they would have to face in the future.* (Davenport, 1998)

Despite these challenges—which included the then unthinkable acquisition of Ernst & Young's consulting business by Cap Gemini in 2000—knowledge management at Ernst & Young remains strategically important to our business. Today, one of the current challenges for Ernst & Young's knowledge managers is at the intersection between e-business and knowledge management—to make possible a knowledge-based strategy using our global extranet, known as Ernst & Young *Online*.

One of the most sophisticated components in the extranet is a software application developed by IBM Lotus called Quickplace. This software application is a secure, Web-enabled collaboration tool. Reflecting somewhat the views of Michael Porter (2001), we know that while Quickplace technology provides Ernst & Young with an electronic workspace that it can share with its clients, this feature alone does not differentiate us from our competitors. Instead, our competitive advantage comes from our capability to select the right work technology and integrate this with the right people, process, and content.

This collaborative capability is the central theme to this chapter. It aims to provide a background to Ernst & Young's approach to knowledge management in order to understand the following key issues:

- Why Quickplace was selected as the tool to enable collaboration with our clients
- How this approach contributes to the successful diffusion of a new information technology innovation into the business
- How it has helped us to manage the risks that exist for organizations that implement Web-based collaboration
- To provide a framework that can help other organizations to understand how they can develop the capability to collaborate online with other organizations

Knowledge Management at Ernst & Young

There is no doubt that Ernst & Young's particular approach to enterprise knowledge management has contributed to our success with using technology as a knowledge work enabler. To understand how we went about selecting and using IBM's Lotus Quickplace specifically for online collaboration, it is helpful to first understand Ernst & Young as an organization and our broader approach to knowledge management. As one of the largest business advisory firms in the world, we are a globally disbursed organization with over 100,000 people located in more than 141 countries with an annual turnover of US$12 billion. The firm has more than 500 offices in Europe and the Americas, 65 in the Middle East and Africa, and more than 100 in the Asia Pacific.

In terms of knowledge management, Ernst & Young is well known as one of the early pioneers in this field, and it continues to win accolades such as the Most Admired Knowledge Enterprise (MAKE[SM]) award. The firm's global Center for Business Knowledge[TM] (CBK) is at the heart of its knowledge management program, although it works closely with other supporting business units and practice areas to provide tactical support for service delivery. At an operational level, these tactical services include business research, analysis, and competitive intelligence, as well as knowledge navigation and technical support for both EY/KnowledgeWeb (the intranet) and Ernst & Young *Online* (the extranet).

Because of Ernst & Young's early investment in knowledge management, the people in our business take for granted a standardized knowledge management tool set and a truly global intranet infrastructure. The Far East region (which includes countries such as China, Hong Kong, and Singapore) is the latest practice area to expand its local knowledge management initiatives under the umbrella of the global CBK. That region has subsequently become a member of the Global Knowledge Steering Group that is responsible for developing common goals and objectives for local implementation.

It is important to point out that the CBK is more than just a cleverly branded corporate library or intranet site. The extra piece that makes it different is the role of knowledge managers within the CBK and out in the business who are responsible for integrating information, human knowledge, and technology into work practices. On a practical level they dissect processes, categorize industries, map knowledge, and help practice staff to understand where and how they can apply the organization's knowledge resources. This integration function is an important factor to consider when deploying any kind of collaboration technology—not only must your staff know how to use it, they must also understand how to apply it to their business.

Quickplace as a Collaboration Tool

Now that the role of the CBK is understood, it can be seen that while Quickplace is an important technology component of the current generation of knowledge management at Ernst & Young, the CBK's theme of helping to integrate people, process, content, and technology continues with this new tool. However, focusing for a moment on the technology of Quickplace, we should also recognize that this software application has specific attributes that have made it useful as the main collaboration tool within the Ernst & Young *Online* extranet. IBM, who developed this particular product and now refer to it as Team Workplace, describes it as:

> *The Web-based solution for creating team workspaces for collaboration. With IBM Lotus Team Workplace, companies give users a way to securely work with colleagues, suppliers, partners and customers. IBM Lotus Team Workplace provides teams with workspaces where they can reach consensus through discussions, collaborate on documents and coordinate plans, tasks and resources. (Source: www.ibm.com)*

The choice of Quickplace over other Web-based collaboration tools was in some respects made because of convenience. Davenport (1998) identified the benefits to the Ernst & Young knowledge management strategy that came from a common software and hardware platform because "these standards meant that programs and documents could be exchanged easily around the firm." With its Lotus Domino origins, Quickplace was an easy choice to make. Since Quickplace is accessed using a Web browser, it was simple to integrate this tool into the overall Ernst & Young *Online* portal interface, and with the implementation of a new single-sign-on system users can access this particular tool without needing to log in again. It has also been straightforward to integrate user information from the firm's Global Directory system into Quickplace. This means an automatic Ernst & Young team listing can be created for the external users that includes information such as location, telephone, and e-mail address.

Of course beyond compatibility with our existing information technology (IT) infrastructure, Quickplace does also have particular features that make it a suitable tool to support inter-organizational collaboration. These benefits are not necessarily unique to Quickplace, but whatever collaboration software you choose to use these features are critical to successful inter-organizational collaboration.

1. Quickplace is Web based so users only need a Web browser to access the shared workspace (of course, in practice, it's not quite as simple as that). This makes Quickplace, and in fact any Web-based collaboration tool, an excellent choice for business-to-business collaboration since it does not require any additional software to be purchased or installed by the external users.
2. Quickplace's Web-based interface allows each collaboration space to be changed to suit the need of different groups of end-users. In fact, depending on organizational IT policies, it is possible for a Quickplace collaboration space to be entirely driven by its users from its initial creation through to its eventual deactivation.

Quickplace allows users to customize the workspace using a combination of import functions that can convert a word processing document or presentation file into a Web page and step-by-step configuration menus. Users can easily create made-to-order collaboration spaces without needing to involve a developer. The level of customization available includes look and feel, information architecture, workflow, and security. Of course, if greater levels of customization are required, developers can be used to create more sophisticated programmatic or non-standard information architecture customizations.

It is important to note that while this same functionality is available in Lotus Notes, end-users have limited and less direct control over these types of changes. This lack of end-user control may be acceptable for internal collaboration projects, where it is possible to identify an information architecture to suit their common business processes. In fact, Ernst & Young has successfully used this approach with EY/KnowledgeWeb standard knowledge base designs and standardized project databases known as Engagement Team Databases (ETD). However, for collaboration between two different organizations, traditional information technology approaches for software selection and development need to be challenged. This is because a tool with a fixed information architecture leaves no room for co-development by the intended group of internal and external end-users. This is particularly important for inter-organizational collaboration, where the evolution of requirements is a natural outcome of working across organizational boundaries; that is, until you start the actual collaboration process, specific requirements are unknown or uncertain.

In summary, there are two key benefits to using Web-based collaboration tools like Quickplace:

- Accessibility over the Internet using a Web browser
- User-driven development

The Ernst & Young Experience of Using Quickplace

The benefits of user-driven development and Web accessibility that Quickplace provides are evident in the success stories that demonstrate how it has helped Ernst & Young to win new clients and deliver services online in new ways to our clients. Our experiences show that, for our line of business at least, clients value our use of Quickplace because of:

- Cost and time savings
- More effective project management

- Process and information transparency
- The partnering approach it enables

In each instance, a customized Quickplace was developed to meet the specific needs of each client and the account team who works with them. Of course, our successes with Quickplace did not happen overnight. We have taken specific measures like:

- Introduced systems and procedures to deal with the new risks that a Web-based collaboration tool as introduced into our organization
- Systematically approached the task of diffusing this collaboration capability into our organization

These new risks relate to issues such as corporate branding standards, liability for incorrect or misleading content, copyright, and mistakes with access control that could break confidentiality and privacy requirements. Some of these risks can be managed at the technology level. For example, before any user (internal or external) can be granted access to a Quickplace, he or she must first be registered into a central user list. While this control creates an inconvenient two-step enrollment process for Quickplace managers, it is an important risk mitigation process. Each new Quickplace is also created using either a CBK or practice areas developed template to ensure it meets corporate branding guidelines.

In addition to the security controls described above, the Internet operating environment is not always as universally consistent and standardized as we would like. Such technical problems can affect the accessibility of the collaboration space, and we have discovered over time many reasons why this might be the case.

- Internet access speed from the client site
- Firewall configurations
- Internet browser settings
- Hardware
- Other software conflicts or incompatibility

The only way to avoid accessibility issues is to include the external organization in testing and learn to work with their IT group to resolve technical issues as early as possible. You should also consider using standards-based document formats such as Portable Document Format (PDF) or ensure you agree on document format protocols with your external users as part of the development of your collaboration space.

From the CBK perspective, these issues are IT issues that in most cases are best left to technical experts to manage and resolve. However, as part of the innovation process, it is still helpful that knowledge managers are aware of the reasons, if not the details of the technology implementation, for the security-related restrictions and controls. This way they can play a role in explaining the limitations and managing the expectations of end-users.

This is critical to a user-driven collaboration tool because at the next level of control, responsibility passes from the IT specialists to the end-users of the Quickplace. At this level, the CBK has a key role to act as a relationship manager to the business to explain why Quickplace should be used and how it should be used. The CBK does this by providing knowledge managers with access to a variety of different support resources. For example,

- Business researchers and analysts are available to identify existing content or to create new content for use in the Quickplace.

- Staff can log in to demonstration sites so they can become familiar with the navigation scheme and explore the functionality provided.
- The Ernst & Young *Online* Community HomeSpace (an intranet site on the EY/KnowledgeWeb) contains documented Quickplace success stories and other materials that can be used by knowledge managers.
- Second level support is available to Quickplace managers from any of three helpdesks located in Cleveland (U.S.), London (U.K.), and Sydney (Australia).
- New Quickplace managers are provided with training that covers functionality and expectations.
- An online Quickplace help database provides Quickplace managers with guidance on functionality and recommended development approaches.

Once the sponsors and potential managers of a new Quickplace have grasped why the tool should be used, then training becomes an important aspect of developing their ability to take ownership of the tool. However, we are a large business with staff dispersed in different offices around the world, and like many other organizations, we take advantage of a range of training options—from face-to-face Quickplace manager mentoring sessions to on-demand multimedia e-learning modules that deal with a particular Quickplace management issue. Teleconferencing and Web conferencing are also used on a routine basis—the ability to share a screen with a Quickplace manager in another office makes its easy to show as well as tell.

This comprehensive support infrastructure again reflects the overall approach of the CBK to provide guidance and resources that help the business to integrate technology with people, process, and content. Our collaboration capability is supported by an effective collaborative infrastructure. A collaborative infrastructure is described by Evaristo and Munkvold (2002) as consisting of three levels:

1. A totally implemented and tested technical infrastructure
2. Software readiness, as evidenced by installation, testing, and final availability to users
3. The availability of guidelines

As a knowledge management function, the role of the CBK at Ernst & Young permeates through all levels of this collaborative infrastructure and provides significant support at the guidance level. In practice, the role of the individual knowledge manager is therefore to help the account team and the client to co-develop a Quickplace environment that meets their particular needs, while not exposing the business to unnecessary risk. So far, this knowledge management-orientated support model has resulted in the successful deployment of Quickplace into many of our client engagements around the world.

Assessing Your Capability for Online Collaboration

If your organization is only just beginning to consider or experiment with online collaboration with your partners and customers, you should not take for granted that everyone will immediately understand the value of virtual teaming and online collaboration. In the United States, the concept of virtual collaboration—using a variety of technologies including the telephone and e-mail, as well as Web-based tools—is already well understood and accepted as a business practice. However, IDC has commented that the success of online collaboration software "remains largely a North American phenomenon" (Levitt and Mahowald, 2002). In fact, the implementation of Quickplace at Ernst & Young follows the familiar course of information technology innovation. However, it is not enough to rely on word of mouth to drive the adoption of a new knowledge management tool across a global business. We have also had to recognize and manage the paradox between the need for user-driven development and the need to mitigate the risks from user-driven development in a business environment.

Unfortunately, like other aspects of enterprise knowledge management, there is no blueprint for deploying online collaboration into your organization. The approach taken by Ernst & Young worked well in our business because we built on the foundations of a knowledge management function (the CBK) that has evolved over the last decade. It is quite likely you will need to follow a change management process in order to develop an online collaboration capability in your organization. In order to do this, you will need to understand where your organization is now and where it will need to be in the future.

To provide us with some structure for discussing the development of an online collaboration capability, we will use the elements described in the Australian interim Knowledge Management Standard (Standards Australia International, 2003): people, process, technology, and content.

This framework has a good fit, if not an explicit one, with Ernst & Young's underlying conceptual understanding of knowledge management. It is also fair to comment, and Evaristo and Munkvold (2002) also make this point, that most guidance on virtual teaming focuses on the dynamics of the individual teams and not the organizational environment that is wrapped around these virtual teams. It is only once the collaborative infrastructure is in place that recommendations such as those from Lipnack and Stamps (2000) can be applied.

In each of these knowledge management elements you need to consider issues such as:

- Do your people know how to collaborate?
- Does your organization understand the value, benefits, and risks of collaborating online with partners and clients?
- Are your IT people ready for user-driven development of a Web-based collaboration tool?
- Do you have the right processes in place to diffuse both a collaborative capability as well the processes that would form your collaborative infrastructure?
- Have you implemented the appropriate IT systems to help minimize the risks your organization is exposed to from online collaboration with your partners and customers?
- Is your technology infrastructure adequately prepared to support a Web-based collaboration tool?
- Do protocols exist for testing the online workspace before collaboration begins?
- What data, information, and knowledge do you intend to share online?
- Are guidelines available for knowledge managers and end-users to learn about the leading and recommended approaches to online collaboration?

This is not intended to be a complete list of questions, but as a first step in developing your collaborative capability, it is your responsibility as a knowledge manager to apply this knowledge management framework in the context of collaboration in your own organization.

While it is not always mentioned directly within many knowledge management methodologies, change management is an implicit part of any knowledge management project or strategy. James Carlopio (1998) has developed Roger's Diffusion of Innovation theories into a model designed for change management related to technology. A key step in the change management model described by Carlopio is to create organizational, group, and individual level awareness of the technology innovation. Organizational awareness can be addressed in a number of ways. Conceptually, there are typically three types of IT knowledge that can create the required awareness (Nambisan et al., 1999): context free, industry specific, and firm specific.

IT innovation in organizations requires the integration of context-free IT knowledge to its eventual application (firm specific) in that business. We would expect context-free and industry-specific IT knowledge to come from outside the organization. However, in large businesses, this type of IT knowledge might also originate from other business units—again here is a role for enterprise knowledge management. This knowledge can be shared through customer support units, user groups, user labs, and relationship managers (Nambisan et al., 1999). Ernst & Young has used all of these knowledge-sharing channels in its collaborative infrastructure.

Finally, as part of the process of creating a collaborative infrastructure, you will need to consider how your organization will put the actual collaboration technology it needs in place. Ernst & Young implemented Quickplace as part of our global Ernst & Young IT infrastructure, while the CBK maintains the responsibility for the use of the tool. This mitigates some of the direct cost of managing and maintaining our collaborative infrastructure, and account teams are charged a nominal fee (approximately US$2,000) to help offset the remaining direct costs.

The costs in your organization are likely to be different depending on the elements of collaborative infrastructure you already have in place. At a minimum and in addition to the IT administration roles, you will need a help desk analyst to provide Level 1 support and a knowledge manager to support promote, train, troubleshoot, and advise collaboration sponsors and managers. From the IT perspective, a number of vendors and Internet service providers offer hosted collaboration solutions (including Quickplace, but also, for example, Sitescape, eRoom). It is worthwhile to explore the cost, functionality, and service levels that each offers and to compare them with the cost of developing a complete collaborative infrastructure from scratch. After all, your focus should be on enabling inter-organizational collaboration and managing user-driven development.

Concluding Thoughts

Online collaboration is perhaps the most demanding e-business strategy to attempt, but it is also the strategy that is most likely to provide your organization with a competitive advantage. This is because the development of the capability to collaborate online takes more than just the right technology, and if you make the investment this is not something that can be easily replicated by your competitors. This is reflected in the experience of Ernst & Young where IBM's Quickplace software has provided Ernst & Young with the right tool, but our unique knowledge management capabilities enabled us to apply it in practice. The CBK and other support functions, in particular, have provided the business with the collaborative infrastructure that enables us to successfully team up with our clients using this technology.

References

Carlopio, J. (1998). *Implementation: Making Workplace Innovation and Technical Change Happen*. Sydney: McGraw-Hill.

Davenport T.H. (1998). Some Principles of Knowledge Management, February 01, 1998. http://www.bus.utexas.edu/kman/kmprin.htm.

Evaristo, R. and Munkvold, B.E. (2002). Collaborative Infrastructure Formation in Virtual Projects, *Journal of Global Information Technology Management*, 5(2), 29–47.

Levitt, M. and Mahowald, R.P. (2002). Worldwide Team Collaborative Applications Competitive Analysis, 2002: What You Need to Know to Make the Team. Framingham, Massachusetts: IDC.

Lipnack, J. and Stamps, J. (2000). *Virtual Teams: People Working Across Boundaries with Technology*. 2nd ed. New York: Wiley.

Nambisan, W., Agarwal, R., and Tanniru, M. (1999). Organizational Mechanisms for Enhancing User Innovation in Information Technology, *MIS Quarterly*, 23(3), 365–395.

Porter, M.E. (2001). Strategy and the Internet, *Harvard Business Review*, March 2001.

Standards Australia International (2003). *AS 5037 (Int)—Interim Australian Standard Knowledge Management*. Sydney: Standards Australia International.

Knowledge Management Processes and Tools at Ford Motor Company*

11

Stan Kwiecien

(in collaboration with Dar Wolford, Robyn Valade, and Sanjay Swarup)

> The object of education, as I see it, is not to fill a man's mind with facts; it is to teach him how to use his mind in thinking. One may fill his head with all the "facts" of all the ages—and his head may be just an overloaded fact-box when he is through. Great piles of knowledge in the head are not the same as mental activity.
>
> *Henry Ford Quoted in "The Power That Wins"*
> *by Ralph Waldo Trine, 1928, pp. 33–34*

Company Profile and Culture

The Ford Motor Company celebrated its 100th anniversary on June 16, 2003. Ford currently employs approximately 335,000 people and represents more than 200 distinct markets on 6 continents. Despite its size, Ford continues to be a unique place to work due to a strong sense of family. It is difficult to describe this family atmosphere, and I would find it difficult to work without it. It is this culture that simplifies the concepts of knowledge management (KM) and makes it somewhat seamless.

My formal involvement with KM began in 1995. Upon reflection, I now realize that it actually began in 1972 when I was first hired. Although there were no labels, no formal processes, and no fancy tools and technology, there was the essence of KM. This can be explained simply as an environment where it was okay not to know, but

---

* *Editor's Note:* This highly informative chapter, based on the extensive knowledge-sharing experience at Ford, highlights the importance of relying not just on technology for KM, but on integrating IT systematically with organizational culture, capacity, and processes. Ford has always had a knowledge-sharing culture, and formal processes along with Web-based technology have extended this culture to the company's global operating units. The processes and roles for KM initiatives like best practice replication and engineering CoPs are thoroughly dealt with in this chapter.

IT support for best practice replication evolved from early "dumb terminals" and fax transmissions to a portal and knowledge-based engineering. Key lessons learned on the KM tool front include the importance of documentation, professional usability design, adherence to content templates and taxonomy, optimization of infrastructure, automated alerting mechanisms ("nagware"!) to coordinate knowledge validation processes, and testing first via pilots.

not okay not to ask; where mistakes were viewed as a learning experience, but repeating mistakes had serious consequences; and where anyone would receive help when in trouble and criticism when not admitting they needed help. The reason for this preamble was to set the stage for a description of KM processes and tools that are based on our history and that are now recognized and designed to support our future.

The culture I described exists and thrives locally and regionally. Without some formal processes and communication tools, it could not exist globally. This supports the notion that KM is not about managing the knowledge of people, but rather enabling people to share their knowledge.

KM Processes

The KM process that I am personally most familiar with (since I was involved with its architecture and implementation) is called Best Practice Replication (BPR). Wish we had never labeled it that; people still experience angst when confronted with the phrase "best practice." How do I know it is best? Is there something better? Prove it to me! With some convincing, people accept a best practice as nothing more than a "proven" improvement to a business process that can be applied at more than one location and is expected to be further improved as it is copied (no, replicated) by others. We do not expect people to copy exactly; we expect them to take the knowledge of others and apply it to their own situation. Inevitably, the replication of a best practice results in an even better practice. Thus, I say that there is no such thing as a best practice. Best is merely a point in time.

BPR, although it may sound thin, is based upon a set of inviolable principles and a very distinct process with specific roles and responsibilities. It is based upon the concept of communities of practice (CoPs) that we simply define as "a bunch of folks who perform the same work and are geographically dispersed." For example, Paint is one of our CoPs. Every assembly plant has a paint shop, and they all paint vehicles and all follow similar base processes. Each of our 60 CoPs are similar in construct in that they cover a well-defined business segment and are a "natural" grouping of people who perform similar work and can share experiences.

The principles of BPR are as follows:

1. The process improvement must be proven. We do not want to replicate ideas. Ideas have no value until implemented, and ideas are loaded with flaws that will be uncovered during the implementation. Take the idea, implement it, uncover the flaws, identify the value, then share your success and experience.
2. The process improvement must contribute a well-defined business value.
   i. Unless a value is associated with an improvement, why would anyone want to replicate it? We are far too busy to waste time making changes that do not add value to our base business processes.
   ii. The value of the best practice must be expressed in terms understood unilaterally within the CoP. Rarely is the value expressed as money, but rather in terms of values by the CoP such as time, percentage improvement, and first time through capability.
   iii. Our 60+ CoPs have identified more than 200 ways to measure value; interestingly, fewer than 20 are expressed as hard U.S. dollars or any other currency.
   iv. Note that the inclusion of dollars is important, not to the CoP members, but to the executive sponsors. Since 1995, use of BPR has added more than US$1 billion in value and productivity.

3. The process improvement must be replicable. Unless others can benefit from change, there is no need to communicate. This differentiates between simply bragging and sharing knowledge.
4. There are specific roles and responsibilities.
   i. The focal point is the "conduit of knowledge."
      a. He/she represents the CoP at their location.
      b. He/she is the first filter to assure that the content meets the criteria set by the CoP and that their peers within the community would benefit.
      c. He/she is also responsible for disseminating new knowledge to the appropriate persons or teams for possible replication.
      d. Most importantly, they provide "feedback," thus verifying the value of the practice.
   ii. The gatekeeper acts as the glue for the CoP.
      a. He/she leads the CoP and is typically assigned to a staff support function, but is rarely management.
      b. He/she is typically a subject matter expert (SME) regarding the business process performed by the CoP.
      c. He/she has the responsibility of vetting the draft submissions that come from the focal points. The gatekeeper collaborates with other SMEs to assure that the submissions support the organization's standards and strategies.
      d. He/she has administrative responsibilities to maintain the communication tools used by the CoP.
   iii. The sponsor provides the energy of the CoP.
      a. He/she is an executive leader at the vice president or director level.
      b. His/her job is to support the activities of the CoP:
         • Attend any face-to-face meetings the CoP conducts.
         • Ask the question, "How is it going?"
         • Congratulate those who actively participate.
         • Encourage those who do not.
         • Do not get involved in the details.

Now that we have an understanding of the principles, we can deal with the process:

1. Identify and submit a new best practice:
   i. The focal point at a location within a CoP recognizes that a significant process improvement has been achieved by their organization. He/she submits details about the process improvement via a predefined template on the BPR Web-based computer application. This template includes some mandatory data fields designed to capture information about the process improvement, some taxonomies to categorize the submission, and costs to implement, as well as the achieved values from implementation. Most important are the fields that identify the true SME and any lessons learned during the transition from "idea" to "best practice."
   ii. The application allows only a registered focal point to initiate the best practice submission; however, anyone identified as an SME has full rights to edit the draft submission. This allows the SME to fill in the details without burdening the focal point with the task of relaying the details that the true SME has knowledge of.
   iii. Encouraging attachment of photos, streaming format video, or a link to any Web site or common personal computer (PC) file confirms proof of imple-

mentation. This "proof" adds credibility to the submission and allows the intended recipients to have a better understanding of the process improvement and allows them to clearly describe the change to their colleagues at the replicating sites.

2. Review of the submissions:
   i. The CoP gatekeeper is notified via notification profile e-mail and reviews the submission for completeness, clarity, and relevance to the processes relevant to the CoP. If the gatekeeper does not have the SME expertise regarding the topic, he/she will invoke the BPR collaboration tool to forward the submission to appropriate SMEs soliciting their opinions (see Figure 11.1). This is a time-based process with the default being 7 days to reply and an automatic reminder 3 days before the collaboration period expires.
   ii. Once assured that the submission supports the strategies and values of the organization or business unit, the gatekeeper changes the status from *draft* to *approved*.
   iii. An option is to flag the submission as *priority*, meaning that the submission is such a great process improvement that everyone should be encouraged to replicate.

3. Replication:
   i. The change of status triggers a chronology routine that begins at midnight each day. This routine configures and sends an e-mail notification to focal point members of the CoP (excluding the authoring location).
   ii. The fresh best practices are now in the queue for replication feedback.
   iii. The focal points at the replicating locations now have the responsibility to disseminate the knowledge contained within the best practice with the appropriate and affected people at their location. They are the ones who must decide if the process improvement can be adopted or adapted, when the replication is planned, and what the value of replication will be. The decision to adopt (or not) is signaled via the BPR feedback process. A decision to not replicate allows for comments as to why not; if *priority*, an explanation is mandatory.
   iv. An appropriate response may be "under investigation," in which case a clock starts. Sixty days after being placed under investigation, the focal point is reminded by "Nagware" that this has been under review long enough and a more definitive feedback response is required. If ignored, 30 days later, the feedback status reverts back to "Not Responded To" (more about this later).

4. Managing the process:
   i. Ford has a strong culture of process and metrics. We measure everything we do, so it is natural (and expected) that the activities of the CoPs are measured and reported.
   ii. The sponsor is also the stakeholder and has expectations that the community representing the line of business is effectively improving the processes and adding value. A series of reports summarizing real-time data quickly shows not only the activity of the CoP, but also the value derived. The value derived shown is not only from the original implementation, but more importantly the cumulative value of replication across all represented locations.
   iii. Other stakeholders are the business operations managers. These people are continually challenged with tasks to improve safety, quality, delivery, cost, morale, and the environment (corporate citizenship). This "SQDCME" is the basis of the balanced scorecard. A different series of reports is available

Figure 11.1

Typical structure of a BPR community of practice and how it functions and roles and responsibilities

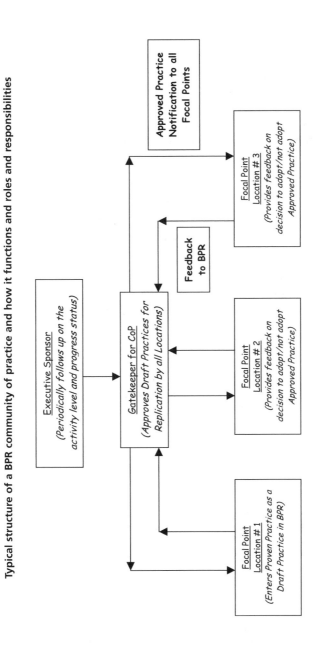

to allow operations to review the activity and results of all CoPs at their location.

iv. Ultimately, the stakeholders are the senior executive leadership, the stockholders, and most importantly the customers who benefit from improved quality and value of our products and services.

v. If the activities and results generated by the CoPs were not measured and monitored and did not have a business objective, then they would (and have) become stagnant and shut down.

KM Tools

Now it is appropriate to describe the tools and technology developed and used to support the principles and processes described above.

The BPR Web-based application was designed to support the existing manual process of sharing process improvements among vehicle assembly plants.

Phase 1

From the mid-1980s through 1995, Ford relied on a computer network based on mainframe applications accessed via Raytheon on "dumb terminals." The e-mail system used was IBM "PROFS." The BPR process as described was conducted "manually" at first, literally mailing the best practices and collecting the feedback via phone calls and fax. Three people worked mostly full time to administrate this process for the initial four communities. As the desire to share grew, this became an "administrater nightmare." The advent of products such as Word Perfect and Excel and the newly learned ability to transfer files via PROFS was a godsend.

Phase 2

The World Wide Web began to emerge as a viable business tool circa 1995. Ford had begun to seriously develop its intranet and was looking for good business applications. BPR was seen as a viable candidate, and an effort was made to automate the existing process via the Web. BPR became one of the first transactional database applications at Ford Motor Company. Since the process, templates, and reports were designed, it was a matter of a few weeks to exercise newly found Web development skills and build a successful fully electronic tool to support the BPR process.

Early releases of the Oracle database combined with a mix of JavaScript, HTML, and Perl code delivered by a Sun Operating System made up the BPR application. This was an opportunity to learn about these emerging technologies.

The delivery of PCs to plant and office locations was prioritized to those who had focal point and gatekeeper roles. This in itself incentivized people to participate.

Training was never an issue. We spent time up front ensuring that the users first understood the process. Since the application was developed to support a process, the various templates and workflow were quite intuitive. Starting slowly built up a base of knowledgeable users who could readily teach or help members of other CoPs as they were launched.

Good, clear, succinct documentation is vital. We provide an online detailed user manual and one page user guides. The greatest value of the manual is for the support staff. As we prepare the words and screenshots, we cannot help but touch every infinite detail. This helps usability.

Involving a professional usability group also ensures an intuitive product.

Phase 3

By 1999, the number of CoPs had grown to 18 and the existing architecture was straining at the seams. Two full-time developers were required to maintain the application and add functionality that the users were demanding.

A project was initiated to "rewrite" the BPR application. The investment of 2,100 development hours and 600 testing hours delivered a robust product that now included more than 60 data tables, 66 Perl Programs, and 13 Perl modules that drove 70 distinct input, feedback, and reports screens. The design also enabled one developer to maintain and enhance the application. Embedded documentation made for an easy transition as developers rotated through the application. Each brought fresh skills and ideas to further improve the application.

The current state is an application that requires literally no maintenance by a skilled developer. Tools have been developed for use by the end-user such that a new CoP can be built and customized with no input from a developer. Thus, the technical support requirements are minimal; our one Web developer spends his time enhancing, not supporting, applications. Hardware and technical cost are also minimized by sharing server space and by running "chrons" at non-peak hours.

Phase 4

Once the Y2K issue passed, our efforts focused on further enhancements to the BPR process and, of course, the supporting BPR application. We began to refer to the base process as "vanilla" and concentrated on applying the KM techniques we had mastered to further enhance the business by developing and applying derivatives of the BPR system.

1. Internal benchmarking process: An internal benchmarking process was derived that would unequivocally determine which of the 57 assembly plants were truly the "best" at specific assembly processes with the base measurement being time efficiency (productivity). Factored into this benchmark were quality, safety, and material cost considerations. Armed with this data and knowledge of WHY one particular location stood above the rest, the challenge was to develop plans to improves one's processes to be as good as—no, better than—the benchmark. It was very interesting to note that of the 160 discrete processes studied, no single location was best at everything and every location was best at something.

2. Stamping business unit: A similar effort was undertaken by the Stamping business unit and was instrumental in redeveloping Stamping Standards and Strategies.

3. Safety derivative: We are especially proud of a safety derivative, which became the most widely used CoP under the BPR umbrella. The context of the CoP was to use the BPR application to instantly notify the safety engineers and management of any significant accident, near miss, fire, or security situation. These preliminary incident reports go out "unfiltered" and are often followed up by an immediate corrective action, which requires feedback to indicate compliance. The activity of this particular CoP has greatly reduced not only the number of injuries to our employees, but also the incidence of near-miss situations. This can be attributed directly to enhanced communication of these situations and a willingness to share "bad news" with the understanding that doing so will help prevent reoccurrence.

4. Environmental reporting system: This is another derivative spurred by the success of the Health & Safety process. This CoP allows environmental engineers

to log and report environmental concerns. This information is then processed by the corporate environmental office and, if necessary, the Office of the General Council. The data collected generates a very specific report which is a governmental reporting requirement.

5. Policy deployment: Management has also recognized the ability of the BPR process and technology as a means of policy deployment. Specific instruction regarding a revised process and a need to verify that it has been understood and implemented is a natural application for BPR.

6. Nagware: Nagware is another powerful tool in the BPR arsenal. This development reminds people of scheduled tasks only if they are recalcitrant. Remember that BPR is a push process. People do not need to search for content—it is pushed to them. When they have not provided feedback in certain cases, they are politely reminded.

7. Collaboration tool: As the CoPs matured and the members developed increased trust of each other, they asked for a means to easily communicate not just best practices, but problems or issues. A collaboration derivative allows any member of a CoP to initiate a collaboration request rather than receiving potentially hundreds of individual e-mail responses in an unorganized manner. The suggestions and solutions come back to the originator attached to the original request. The initiator can set the time period for the collaboration and specify when those who have not responded be reminded. The initiator is automatically sent a link to the collaboration when the time has expired or everyone has added comments.

Phase 5

2003 was a year where we turned our attention to "consumption management." The adage was that "memory is cheap." This may be true, and the technical capability and costs of storage are increasingly improving. However, we must apply a mindset of achieving zero waste. Applying "Six Sigma" methodologies showed us where we were using excessive CPU and server time to store potentially thousands of pre-formatted reports that were infrequently used. We discovered that if we took a different approach and stored just the data and not the actual reports, then the CPU consumption dropped from approximately 8 hours per day to less than 1 hour and that the storage requirements were relatively miniscule. The identified savings were on the order of a few hundred thousand dollars when factoring in the avoidance of purchasing added hardware and storage media. A plus is that the users could access reports with real-time data rather than settle for day-old data provided by the previous batch method. BPR again established a methodology that could be applied to other applications.

We thus have a proven track record of quickly embracing and supporting new business initiatives. This will continue in the future.

Portals, Knowledge-Based Engineering, and More

Most of this chapter has focused on one aspect of KM, that being the identification, the codification, the distribution, and the replication of best practices. You should now understand that the concept of BPR has existed for some time. It began in the mid-1980s using paper and non-technical means of sharing knowledge. The burgeoning Internet and intranet propelled the process in the mid-1990s, and today it is considered a world-class KM effort, licensed by Shell Oil, Kraft Foods, Nabisco, and segments of the U.S. Navy. Although effective, this is not the only KM methodology used at Ford Motor Company. I will briefly describe some others.

Portals

When the intranet was launched at Ford, the Hub, as it was called, was basically a search engine for Web content and access to the corporate directory. As the intranet evolved, the Hub became more complex, and as content was added, the search engine began to provide more volume of results with less frequency of expected results.

The root cause of this consternation was a lack of governance regarding the documentation that was posted for search. The solution was EKB (Enterprise Knowledge Base), where strict governance and requirement for taxonomy (classification) was a requirement. Before posting, it is required to determine if a document supersedes another and that the appropriate taxonomy is applied. This has enabled a corporation the size of Ford Motor Company to maintain a document repository of approximately 1 million documents, while conversation with similar-sized organizations divulge with dismay that they deal with more than 50 million documents!

The Hub has evolved to a true portal, a gateway to knowledge. The pure intent of the portal is to be a source of information regarding the activities of the organization. Each division or organization can develop its own sub-portal or "community." Herein lie a collection of specific information, links, and tools that are used for everyday work. Examples are expertise locators, program or project details, and metrics and specific "gadgets."

Each user (more than 200,000 of the 345,000 Ford employees have intranet access) can customize the layout and appearance and functionality of their portal. Some communities allow the user to develop their own personal portal or "MyPage." Once a gadget is developed, it is up for grabs; anyone can borrow a gadget and apply it to their own means. Portals also have a governance procedure. This assures that a common approach is used.

Knowledge-Based Engineering (KBE)

An exciting advancement in Product Design and Development is a procedure and supporting technology that helps the engineers through the design process by relating a knowledge database containing known physical attributes as they relate to a specific component or system as well as the relationships to accompanying systems.

Without disclosing proprietary information, the interface with the CAD (computer-aided design) system and the knowledge base notifies the engineer in real-time if a proposed design violates known rules or may interfere with another system also being designed for the same product. Not only is the concern flagged, but as KBE matures and contains more knowledge, alternate suggestions are offered.

Innovation is still a requirement, however, and the designer can "override" the database. The design is flagged as having a potential issue, and more evaluation, testing, and review are required before implementing the design. When proven, this innovation can now be part of the rules base.

Conclusion and Recommendations for KM Practitioners

These are just a few examples of KM processes and technologies. I do not think it would be possible to uncover and classify them all. Indeed, any methodology that enables people to discover the experience and thoughts of others can be considered a KM activity.

KM continues to evolve. Once people understand that knowledge is not a commodity, but rather simply the way we think and that it is based on experience, then they can grasp the concept of KM. What works for me is that KM is no more than a process, actually multiple processes, that enables people to connect with people to share information and, more importantly, the way we think. It is all about relationships and trust. You must have a culture that allows people to do what we all normally want to do, share what we know and learn what we do not.

Let me end now with some additional words of wisdom from those who have "been there and done that."

1. You must have sincere support from leadership. They must understand the business value and expect results. Their expectations will help develop the KM process.
2. Identify the WIIIFM ("What is in it for me") at each level of participation. This is important, and the WIIIFMs are usually different for the various roles.
3. Process, process, process. Understand what you want and need to accomplish.
4. Try the process manually, run pilots, involve the potential end users, and listen to what they have to say—they are the ones who will be using it, not you.
5. Do not worry about the code. If you have a well-defined process and clear specifications, the technology will support it.
6. If you simply ask for an information technology solution, then worry.
7. Never, ever, try to force a CoP. CoPs are naturally occurring groups. Each thinks it is special. They are not really special, just different. Regardless, let them feel special and support their unique needs. Just do not let them wander away from the proven process.
8. Recognize that a CoP will eventually reach a plateau; they have identified solutions to most common problems and have picked the low-hanging fruit. Encourage them to climb the tree. It is more work, but the fruit is much sweeter.
9. Keep management out of the process; the roles must be filled by practitioners who perform everyday work. Drive it down to the lowest possible operating level. Let the managers set the expectations; let the practitioners share their knowledge. They are the ones who have it and need it.
10. Do not think you can manage knowledge, at best you can manage a process and let it happen.

The Knowledge Assessment Program for Visualizing the Knowledge Dynamics of Organizations*

12

Takahiko Nomura

What is in books is information; what is in the database is data. Knowledge exists only between two ears.

Peter Drucker

Abstract

This chapter describes the framework of the knowledge assessment that is a diagnostic methodology to assess various requirements for successful knowledge-based management. It is difficult for a corporation to identify important knowledge assets and to know how to shift them for the future. Although it is the individual knowledge worker who creates knowledge assets, it is very difficult for a corporation to under-

---

* *Editor's Note:* This fascinating chapter explores the frontiers of knowledge work, classifies knowledge workers based on the nature of their work, and identifies tools and environments ("ba") to enable greater knowledge sharing among different kinds of knowledge workers. It is important for companies to understand how knowledge workers actually create knowledge. This chapter illustrates these principles via a knowledge assessment study conducted in ten leading Japanese corporations. The growth of IT-based tools for KM is leading to a shift in thinking in these companies, whereby explicit knowledge bases are being perceived as increasingly important in the future. Leveraging external knowledge sources (universities, the Internet) and more internal forums for networking are strongly recommended in this chapter.

Two key types of knowledge workers are identified, nomad and analyst, who are the resources for creating innovation (other types are agents and keepers). Nomad-type workers are self-determined and have a lot of interactions. Analyst-type workers have high self-determination, but their interactions with others are fewer. They use IT most frequently and have a strong tendency to build new ideas through individual thinking; it is necessary for companies to increase their interactions, including via virtual space, in order to enhance the knowledge creating process. In conclusion, this chapter stresses the importance of the seamlessness between the physical workspace and the virtual one for knowledge workers.

stand actually how knowledge workers create knowledge. Knowledge assessment helps clarify knowledge strategies in corporations by visualizing the relationship between knowledge assets and knowledge workstyles. The results of the knowledge assessment, in which ten leading Japanese corporations participated, are also presented. The key findings of the research are knowledge strategy patterns for corporations as well as knowledge work patterns for employees. In this chapter, we further describe two typical cases of applying the Knowledge Assessment Program to the Japanese companies.

Introduction

In the 21st century, the economy will become much more software/service based. We have entered a new age where knowledge is the source of a company's competitive advantage. Corporations must continually create new values for their customers in the face of rapidly changing social and economic environments. Thus, we believe that the development and promotion of knowledge are more important than the management of conventional managerial resources such as people, material resources, and money, because knowledge adds new values to the conventional managerial resources.

Knowledge management, in a narrow sense, entails the enhancement of corporate competitiveness by identifying, sharing, and utilizing knowledge and best practices existing both inside and outside the corporation (American Productivity & Quality Center, 1996; Woods and Cortada, 1999). To gain new competitiveness to cope with drastic changes taking place in the 21st century, each corporation must focus not only on the effect of knowledge management in a narrow sense, but also on the value and significance of knowledge. Therefore, knowledge management must be understood in a broader sense as the encouragement and promotion of innovations, considering the potential of employees and customers for creating knowledge. In this sense, knowledge management is a new paradigm for managerial innovation that should be recognized as "Knowledge-based Management," not as "Managing Knowledge."

In the following sections, we first show the key findings of the first pilot research of the Knowledge Assessment Program with ten Japanese companies in 2000. Then, we introduce the concept and framework of the Knowledge Assessment Program. We also describe the results of the research according to the framework: Knowledge Assets Model, Knowledge Creation Model, and Knowledge Work Pattern Model. We further give two case studies for the adoption of the Knowledge Assessment Program. Finally, we form a conclusion on how knowledge assessment drives corporate knowledge management initiatives.

Key Findings of Knowledge Assessment

The key findings of the knowledge assessment research are knowledge strategy patterns for corporations, knowledge work patterns for employees, and further the interrelationship between the knowledge strategy and the knowledge workstyle. The findings imply that changing the workstyle directly drives knowledge management. In other words, the design of "ba" to create knowledge is necessary for managing corporations as knowledge-driven companies. Professor Ikujiro Nonaka defines "ba" as follows: "a shared space for emerging relationships, which could be physical, virtual and mental" (Nonaka and Konno, 1998). Dynamic ba provides opportunities for individuals to create new value and to leverage the quality of their knowledge work. We have uncovered that although the style of knowledge work is different, the design of ba for each department in a company is standardized and does not apply to the current situation. This is because a guide for strategic design of ba does not exist, even though the importance of ba for interactions that go beyond organization is increasing, which is necessary for business that creates value added.

Key Finding 1: Knowledge Strategy Patterns

As for knowledge that is the source of value currently, there is strong overall recognition that tacit knowledge is important. However, in the future, important knowledge assets will be divided into two kinds: "Maintain tacit knowledge" and "Change to mechanism." It interested us that out of the ten participating corporations, seven corporations' internal opinions split into two.

From a management viewpoint, it means that they need to specify knowledge assets to focus and enhance employees' shared recognition. On the other hand, from the worker's viewpoint, it means that both ba for sharing tacit knowledge face-to-face and ba for encouraging sharing explicit knowledge systematically are needed.

Key Finding 2: Knowledge Work Patterns

We discovered nomad-type workers and analyst-type workers who are the resources for creating innovation. Nomad-type workers are self-determined and have a lot of interactions. Both provide and absorb knowledge vigorously, spend a lot of time for the knowledge creating process, and utilize ba and communities effectively. The nomad-type worker has the most remarkable workstyle as human resources that create innovation.

On the other hand, analyst-type workers have high self-determination, but their interactions with others are far less. They use information technology (IT) most frequently and have a strong tendency to build new ideas through thinking by themselves. However, the pilot research revealed that the analyst-type workers' time division for the knowledge creating process is notably short, so it is necessary for them to increase their interactions, including virtual space, in order to enhance the knowledge creating process. It is a serious problem of overall ba that the interaction by analyst-type workers is insufficient, and not enough time is spent for the knowledge creating process.

Knowledge Assessment Program

Knowledge assessment is a diagnostic program for knowledge management. It makes knowledge assets and knowledge capabilities visible. In order to shift to knowledge-based management, corporations must first understand the current status of their knowledge management efforts. Knowledge assets and knowledge work become manageable only when they are visible.

Knowledge assessment comprises two surveys: Knowledge Executive Interviews and a questionnaire survey called Knowledge Scanning. At the heart of this assessment program is Knowledge Scanning, a questionnaire survey in which subjects (knowledge workers) are asked to answer 200 questions over a period of three days.

The survey helps corporations understand what points to focus on in their further pursuit of knowledge-based management by unveiling the characteristics of their organization, how individual workers work, interrelations between their knowledge workers and communities or ba, the gap between the top executives and knowledge workers in their awareness of the importance of knowledge assets, etc.

This program includes the "SECI Model" (Nonaka and Takeuchi, 1995) and knowledge audit of "Knowledge Assets" by KIRO (Knowledge Innovation Research Organization), which has experience in this area, and the Time Utilization Survey of DEGW. Through these methods, assessment by different perspectives becomes possible.

Results of Knowledge Assessment Research

In this section, we describe the framework of the Knowledge Assessment Program and present the results of the recent research according to the framework Knowledge Assets Model, Knowledge Management (KM) Architecture Model, Knowledge Creating Process (SECI) Model, and Knowledge Work Pattern Model.

The survey of knowledge assets and knowledge work patterns are especially important for guiding the design to a physical and virtual knowledge workspace, so we present the results in detail.

Knowledge Assets Model

The first conceptual framework is a model to classify knowledge assets, the source of corporate values, into 12 cells (Figure 12.1). The columns are divided into three sections by location of knowledge: (1) knowledge shared in relationships with customers such as customer knowledge/market knowledge, (2) knowledge of individuals and organizations existing inside the corporation, and (3) knowledge contained in products and services. The rows are divided into four sections by type of knowledge: (1) knowledge acquired through one's work experience such as knowledge possessed by sales representatives or service representatives; (2) knowledge recognized through perception such as brands and product designs; (3) knowledge stored in fixed forms such as documents, databases, and technology licenses; and (4) knowledge as systems (systems to be incorporated in organizations) such as internal training programs.

In the survey based on this model, we asked the subjects to show us which kinds of knowledge assets were contributing to the sources of their corporate values using ten coins (actually stickers). We also asked them to tell us to what degree of importance these assets were expected to change in the future.

Figure 12.1

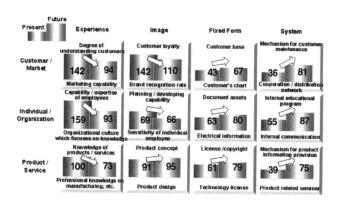

Direction of the important knowledge assets

Figure 12.1 shows the results of the Knowledge Assets survey. Two graphs, which are placed in each cell, mean the average number of 10 coins placed by 100 people for both the present (left bar) and the future (right bar) knowledge assets. The arrows of each cell indicate whether the knowledge asset's importance increases or decreases from the current to the future.

The majority of the subjects, 70% of them, thought that the source of their current corporate value resides in experience or images such as brands, namely, tacit knowledge. On the other hand, the answers to the second question, about knowledge assets expected to become important in the future, were split into two groups: 53.6% of the subjects believed that they would keep depending on experience and images (i.e., tacit knowledge), and 46.4% thought that they would shift their focus to knowledge in fixed forms and systems (i.e., explicit knowledge). The trend of the huge shift of importance from experiential knowledge to explicit knowledge and mechanisms seems to correspond to the sizzle of IT-based knowledge management.

Through the results of the Knowledge Assets survey, each company will be able to ascertain which knowledge assets are to its current advantage as well as which knowledge assets need to be newly created. It corresponds to the knowledge vision of a knowledge creating company to specify future knowledge assets for acquiring and encouraging necessary knowledge creation.

KM Architecture Model

We use our original KM Architecture Model as the second framework. The model was derived from the results of our studies on KM best practice corporations and practical experiences accumulated by the members of the Xerox Group (Figure 12.2). The survey based on these models was designed to unveil the characteristics of each company by questioning the subjects about 40 requirements for knowledge management.

Knowledge Creating Process Model

Professor Ikujiro Nonaka has taken the first letter of the Knowledge Creation Model and named it the SECI model. SECI stands for the four modes of the knowledge creating process, "Socialization (S)," "Externalization (E)," "Combination (C)," and "Internalization (I)." As you may understand, new knowledge is created from the

Figure 12.2

KM Architecture Model

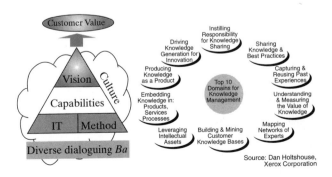

Source: Dan Holtshouse, Xerox Corporation

interactions between tacit knowledge and explicit knowledge. It is important to remember that the original source of knowledge lies mostly in tacit knowledge.

The survey based on this model was designed to reveal how intensely each subject company and its knowledge workers were committed to each mode of the SECI process. The subjects were questioned about the time they spent on the 12 most typical activities of each mode and asked how much time they spare and the degree of importance of such activities. Table 12.1 indicates the top ten knowledge creation activities whose gap between the degree of importance and the activity time is huge. These, in other words, are ten activities that "should be done but have not begun" concerning knowledge creation.

Table 12.1

SECI gap						
		SECI	Average gap	Sates	R&D	Staff
1	Contact client directly to elicit needs or problems	S	1.31	0.9	Rank 1 1.59	Rank 1 1.53
2	Sense new needs or perspectives through interactions with people from other companies	S	1.23	1.18	Rank 2 1.23	Rank 2 1.33
3	Get know-how or new perspectives through joint projects or other interactions with experts outside the company	S	1.16	Rank 1 1.29	0.96	1.11
4	Create new ideas with relevant departments by combining each other's information	C	1.1	Rank 2 1.27	0.85	1.19
5	Share different perspectives with different people in a cross-functional project team	S	1.05	Rank 3 1.19	1.81	1.03
6	Find a new market opportunity or a strategic direction by observing consumer trends	S	1.04	0.92	Rank 1 1.05	1.12
7	Visit worksite to collect useful, hands-on information and find problems	S	0.97	0.77	0.93	Rank 3 1.3
8	Sense new needs or perspectives by putting yourself in the customer's or user's shoes	S	0.96	0.92	0.84	1.09
9	Walking around the company to uncover problems which cannot be shown in documents	S	0.94	0.86	0.94	1.08
10	Systematically organize existing problems by utilizing any problem-solving or idea-conceiving method (such as the KJ method)	E	0.94	1.02	0.91	0.83

The most seriously insufficient activity of the knowledge creating process is socialization. Specifically, typical R&D people and corporate staffs are overwhelmingly lacking contact with customers and communication with other companies. On the other hand, sales reps greatly lack activities for designing a new concept through a dialog with experts, as well as other department staffs.

Knowledge Work Pattern Model

We used the TUS (Time Utilization Survey) Methodology developed by DEGW to uncover how knowledge workers use their work time.

In this survey, the subjects were questioned about their work time spent outside and inside their offices. They were also asked about how they split their time between routine work and creative work and between work on their own and interactive work with others. It revealed that one-third of the total work time of knowledge workers was spent outside their offices, and two-thirds was spent inside their offices (see Figure 12.3).

It also revealed that 15.9% of the total work time spent outside the offices was used for creative dialogues, while 14.3% of the total work time was spent for the same inside the offices. Though the results showed that 22.7% of the total work time was spent inside the offices for creative and individual work, it might include writing e-mails or making phone calls.

The results of the survey also show that half of the knowledge workers spent more than 50% of their work time at places other than their desks. On average, they spent approximately 40% of their work time in face-to-face communication with others. It implies the importance of the seamlessness between the physical workspace and the virtual one.

It is quite interesting that the most important activities for the creation of knowledge are spontaneous collaboration with others. It also suggests that informal interactions and environments or communities to support them are very important.

We also conducted a survey to classify knowledge workers by their workstyle, by asking the subjects about their motivation and their behavioral patterns (Figure 12.4). The key findings of this survey were the discovery of nomad-type workers, whose work was highly autonomous, focusing on interactions with others, and analyst-type

Figure 12.3

Results of the Time Utilization Survey

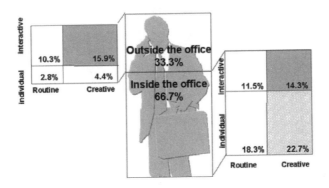

Figure 12.4

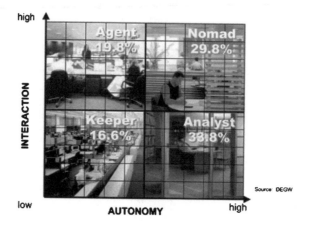

Knowledge Work Pattern Model

Source DEGW

workers, who did creative work mainly inside their offices. There were also "agent-type workers," who did routine work with frequent interactions with others, and "keeper-type workers," who did routine work with few interactions with others. To derive these four work patterns, we filtered them using two matrixes, for instance, the nomad-type workers are categorized in the "Creative" and "Working with others" area, as well as the "Autonomy" and "Interaction" areas in Figure 12.4.

The results of the survey revealed that nomad-type workers, who made up 29.8% of all the subjects, were making a considerable contribution to the distribution of knowledge by acquiring new knowledge outside their offices and offering it to their colleagues.

It is also notable that the behavioral patterns typical to the workstyle of nomad-type workers, such as "walking around," "having dialogues with others," and "communicating knowledge," were observed in any type of job site to a certain extent. Therefore, by intentionally introducing the workstyle of nomad-type workers to job sites dominated by other types, for example, research centers where many analyst-type workers work, corporations can improve the quality of knowledge interactions. How to foster quality nomad-type workers is one of the important challenges for us. Figure 12.5 shows how each workstyle corresponds to each job. It can be identified that the nomad-type worker's workstyle is not completely the same as a salesperson's workstyle.

Each company is able to identify what kind of ba is needed by visualizing four types of knowledge worker distribution in every department. The important issue of ba of organizations with a number of nomad-type workers is the possibility of reusing activities and dialogs at the physical workspace that were recorded. On the other hand, in an organization with a number of analyst-type workers, the method of activating dialogs in virtual space and nurturing cross-functional communities is important.

As a result, it is important to design ba according to the workstyle of every organization. When knowledge assessment is employed, this becomes possible. Moreover, after introducing ba, by applying knowledge assessment again, it is possible to measure the effect through the change in workstyle.

Figure 12.5

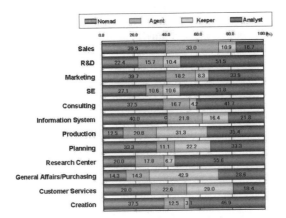

Ratio of knowledge work pattern for job

Examples: Two Typical Cases of Knowledge Assessment
===

We show two typical cases of applying knowledge assessment to the Japanese companies. The first pattern is a typical case of R&D departments. They prefer to be more innovative. The second pattern is a typical case of operation units. It is important for them to share their experimental knowledge among districts and functions. (These cases do not correspond to a specific company.)

Typical Case of R&D Department

The first case is the assessment of an R&D department. From the survey of the Knowledge Assets Model, we found that an R&D department tends to recognize that the most important capability to be leveraged in the future is to construct their own research concepts. Furthermore, they recognized that the following knowledge is very important: customer information and market trend, design proposal know-how, cutting-edge technology, etc. It implies that for promoting innovation, the social function of the technology should be considered, as well as technological advantages. However, under the present circumstances, only a few people can utilize the knowledge well.

Why can such important knowledge not be utilized? The main reason can be found from the research of the Knowledge Work Pattern Model. The results of the survey revealed that more than 70% of the respondents are analyst-type workers who work creatively, but have low interaction with others. Less than 10% of the respondents are nomad-type workers who work autonomously and have high interaction with others. By comparing with the Knowledge Creating Process (SECI) Model of analyst-type workers and nomad-type workers, we found that the socialization activities (i.e., sharing tacit knowledge by visiting various places inside and outside the company) of analyst-type workers are typically insufficient. By asking the place of acquiring important knowledge, it showed that the source of analyst-type workers' knowledge is truly limited, such as asking their own group members or investigating on the Web. On the contrary, nomad-type workers like to get knowledge from various sources, for instance, by asking other departments, participating in academic seminars, interviewing university professors, and hearing the customer's voice directly.

Since it is very common that R&D organizations have a high proportion of analyst-type workers, we further investigated why most R&D people tend to be analyst-type workers. From the KM Architecture Model survey, we found that the problem exists in organizational culture and the management style. First, from the question of corporate culture, the results showed that they have good customs for helping each other or motivating each other. However, it is hard to start new activities and it has less opportunity to contact the outside world, especially research staffs, compared with research managers, who recognized this problem strongly. Next, from the question of knowledge vision, the results showed that employees did not recognize that they have a clear vision and it is not reflected in the department's action plan and the movement of employees. The reason is that the vision of knowledge sharing is not embodied in the support system, such as a cross-functional team for knowledge sharing, and utilizing is not designed at all.

To solve the above problems, we consider the following points to be very important for the corporate research laboratory to be more innovative.

1. Share the research hypotheses among each other.
2. Increase external networking.
3. Involve staffs of other divisions in the early stage of research to get vital information.

As a conclusion, to raise organizational power, the current workstyle dependent on an individual needs to be changed. We recommend establishing new work practices based on these three ideas.

Typical Case of Operation Units

The second case is the assessment of typical operation units. They tend to have lots of branch offices and job sites in different areas.

The results of the Knowledge Assets survey show that the source of their current corporate value resides in the brand assets, but in the future the customer/market knowledge asset, especially the mechanism for customer maintenance, should be enhanced. At the same time, their planning capability should be enhanced as well.

By investigating the awareness of importance and utilization of each knowledge category, we found that the respondents recognized the importance of the experimental knowledge, such as operational know-how and customer contact know-how, etc. Moreover, in the survey of knowledge experts of each category, it had an unexpected result; that is, about 80% of the respondents did not know the expert who had important knowledge. From the answers of these experts, it became clear that most of them, especially those who have experimental knowledge, are located in each branch office or job site, rather than in the head office.

Why would the phenomenon occur? The main reason could be found from the Knowledge Work Pattern survey and KM Architecture Model Survey. The results of the Knowledge Work Pattern survey revealed that more than 50% of the respondents are analyst-type workers and more than 30% of the respondents are keeper-type workers who have the same features, such as lack of interaction with others. Less than 10% of the respondents are nomad-type workers. Above all, we saw numerous keeper-type workers as the biggest problem because they are mostly engaged in routine and individual work.

From the KM Architecture Model survey, we found that the strong control management style would become grit in the gears of organizational reformation. From the corporate culture survey, it was revealed that the employee's discretionary power is restricted and cross-organization movement cannot begin easily, although the top management has encouraged the employees to start new activities. This tendency is especially strong in branch offices and job sites, as compared to the head office.

We have come to the following impressions from the above-mentioned analysis.

- The sensitivity that draws up an environmental change and customer demand is scarce.
- The conservative organization control obstructs the change of action.
- Lack of interactions interrupts individual knowledge to be transformed into organizational properties.

To solve the problems above, we made recommendations as follows:

1. Make all employees aware of what knowledge is important for them in the future.
2. Practice a pilot project to share and solve their common problems.
3. Create an environment to support a pilot project, such as a workplace for increasing dialog and a specific system to recognize knowledge holders and admire their knowledge-sharing efforts.

The most important thing is to execute pilot projects to validate which systems and environments work for their initiatives.

Conclusion

Let us now conclude by summarizing the importance of knowledge assessment in knowledge management.

First of all, the type of knowledge that should be created for the future is revealed, and a company should be able to concentrate on measures to create its necessary knowledge. Furthermore, the assessment will allow the company to identify human networks that actualize such knowledge creation. This will further lead to recognition of what kinds of communities of practice are necessary for this creation. It is a key issue for knowledge management to succeed by focusing on human factors which create this new knowledge and information rather than the work processes which just use knowledge and information.

The second important aspect is the opportunity to understand the fundamental strength of knowledge companies such as leadership for taking the initiative of knowledge management, organizational culture for knowledge sharing, and whether each individual is spending enough time for knowledge creation. Even though a good system is introduced, when there is no trust among people, no one will be willing to provide information to this system. Therefore, it is important to focus on human factors, and, simultaneously, to actualize building communities of practice, maintaining them, and enhancing fundamental strength as a knowledge company.

Acknowledgment

I would like to thank all of the knowledge leaders of the companies in the Knowledge Dynamics Initiative (KDI) community. Furthermore, I want to thank Miss Liu Ming of Keio University and all members of the KDI at Fuji Xerox for their tremendous contributions.

References

American Productivity & Quality Center, Houston, Texas. (1996). Knowledge Management.

Cohen, D. and Prusak, L. (2001). *In Good Company—How Social Capital Makes Organizations Work*. Boston: HBS.

Duffy, F. (2000). The new office, Antique Collectors' Club.

Hayashi, K., Nomura, T., et al. (1998). Temporally-threaded Workspace: A Model for Providing Activity-based Perspectives on Document Spaces, Hypertext'98.

Hayashi, K., Hazama, T., Nomura, T., et al. (1999). *Activity Awareness: Framework for Sharing Knowledge of People, Projects, and Places, Proc of ECSCW99*. pp. 99–118.

Lave, J. and Wenger, E. (1991). *Situated Learning: Legitimate Peripheral Participation*. Cambridge, UK: Cambridge University Press.

Nomura, T., et al. (1998). *Interlocus: Workspace Configuration Mechanisms for Activity Awareness*. Proc of CSCW'98, New York: ACM Press, pp. 19–28.

Nonaka, I. and Takeuchi, H. (1995). *The Knowledge-Creating Company*. London: Oxford University Press.

Nonaka, I. and Konno, N. (1998). The Concept of "Ba": Building a Foundation for Knowledge Creation, *California Management Review*. 40(3), pp. 40–54.

Woods, J.A. and Cortada, J.W. (1999). The Knowledge Management Yearbook 1999–2000, Woburn, MA: Butterworth-Heinemann.

Hewlett-Packard: Making Sense of Knowledge Management*

13

Bipin Junnarkar and Joan Levers

> Computers need complete information to make partial sense. People can make sense out of incomplete information.
>
> *Professor Murray Gell-Mann*
> *Nobel Prize Laureate and Founder of Santa Fe Institute*

Context: KM in an M&A Environment

Hewlett-Packard Company's announcement on September 3, 2001, of their intentions to merge with Compaq Computer Corporation sent shock waves through the high-tech industry. Many doubted the feasibility of such a merger, but Carly Fiorina, HP's President and Chief Executive Officer, was firm in her resolve. The merger, she felt, would make HP stronger and dramatically improve our product offerings.

The merger of Compaq and HP was finalized in May 2002. As a result, HP now has 140,000 employees with capabilities in 178 countries. For the fiscal year that ended October 31, 2002, our combined revenues were $72 billion. We spend $4

---

* *Editor's Note:* This chapter covers the changing face of knowledge management in HP after its merger with Compaq; both companies had successful pre-merger KM programs. Collaboration is now seen as one of the key priorities for the company. A company-wide KM group has been formed to define the company KM strategy and robust processes for KM implementation. The KM team also participates in the definition of HP's enterprise architecture. The KM Tools and Technology Forum defines the standard tools and processes for KM within the company. The KM Leadership framework aims at modeling a positive KM culture and behaviors. KM technology building blocks include datamining, groupware, knowledge repositories, and expertise locator systems. The HP "Community of Practice Handbook," a collection of instructions, tools, and templates to help organizations form communities of practice, has been released. A "building block" approach is being used to devise KM solutions efficiently. Seminars about KM conducted by world-renowned experts are Webcast on the intranet. HP's education department is developing an online curriculum about KM.

Collaborative knowledge networking will be used to join the "power of many"—the knowledge of the employees—with the "power of now"—instant access to information—to speed up the decision-making process. Key learnings and recommendations include the importance of striking a good balance between tangible and intangible measures and sharing credit for KM successes.

Figure 13.1

Operating model of HP

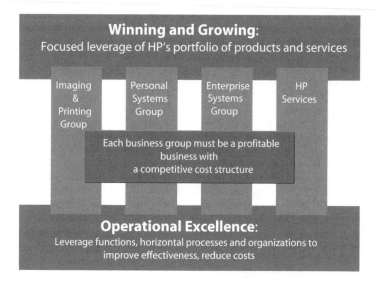

billion annually in research and development that fuels the invention of products, solutions, and new technologies.

The merger moved HP into leadership positions across the markets and product categories in which we compete. Already the leading player in the consumer market, the company became the #1 information technology (IT) solutions provider to the small to medium-business segment and was positioned to challenge competitors, such as IBM, in the enterprise business area. The merger gained HP market share—the company is #1 globally in Windows©, Linux, and Unix© servers; #1 globally in enterprise storage; #1 globally in imaging and printing; #1 globally in PC shipments; and #1 globally in management software.

The merger required HP to forge a new leadership framework and revise its corporate strategy. For the first time, collaboration was seen as one of the key priorities for the company.

HP's operating model consists of four business groups, developing their own products and solutions, and strong horizontal organizations and processes to ensure that the businesses work together and leverage all of the opportunities available (see Figure 13.1).

Company-wide KM Organization Is Born

To implement the merger, a core team made up of both pre-merger Compaq and pre-merger HP employees spent months planning. They used an "adopt and go" approach to quickly evaluate and select the processes and systems that would be used in the new combined company. In many cases, it was easy to evaluate and select the best process or system. Then, the company would "adopt" the best and obsolete the second choice. However, in the area of knowledge management (KM), there was no obvious choice.

Both pre-merger HP and pre-merger Compaq had KM programs. Compaq's sponsorship of communities of practice had resulted in savings of more than $15 million, and HP Consulting's knowledge master program has been recognized as an industry best practice. HP has received the global MAKE (Most Admired Knowledge Enterprise) award six years in a row. While both companies had KM programs, neither was a strong differentiator. So, the chief information officer decided that KM was an area that needed investment for the future. He formed the company-wide KM group. This organization, part of the corporate IT function, is chartered with taking the leadership role for KM in the company. This includes defining the company KM strategy, defining KM standards for tools and processes, and developing robust processes for KM implementation.

Under the leadership of Bipin Junnarkar, the organization consists of experts in KM, KM technology, content management, program and project management, and training development.

The group, though small, is clear on its charter: to define the company-wide strategy for KM and then to focus on specific "proof points" to make KM real in the company.

HP Leadership Framework Helps Position KM Activities

One of the outcomes of the HP/Compaq merger was the development of a leadership framework. This framework (see Figure 13.2) provides the context for how HP gets work done—giving equal attention to the company strategy; structure and processes; metrics, results, and rewards; and culture and behavior.

HP KM has taken the company's operational model to heart. We have leveraged the leadership framework to reflect the KM framework—and are using it to help define how we will work together as a group and with our partners throughout the company.

Figure 13.2

Leadership framework

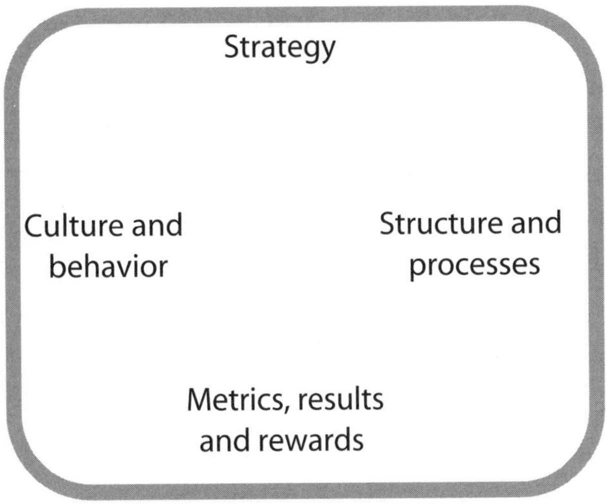

Figure 13.3

KM framework

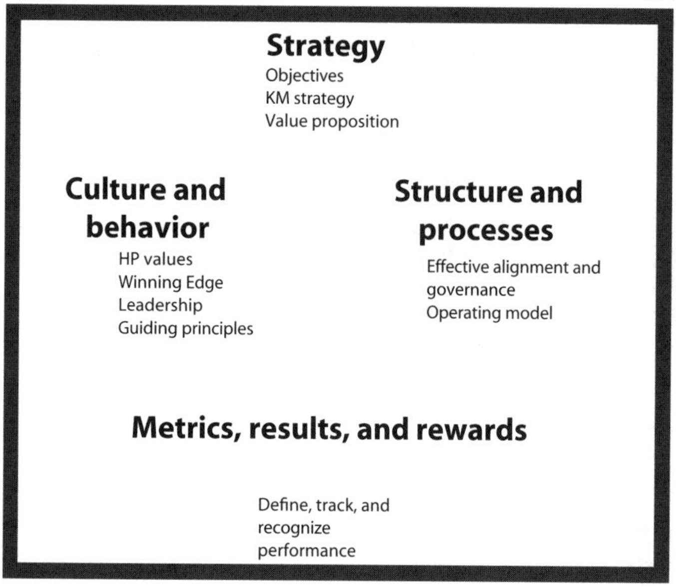

Using this KM framework, we are developing our KM strategy, our operating model, and our structures and processes. We hope to model positive KM culture and behaviors, so that other groups within the company can learn from us. And when we work with HP organizations in KM implementations, we will ensure that they address all four quadrants of the framework in their projects (see Figure 13.3).

Building Blocks Enhance KM Projects

One of the first activities of the KM organization was to define a set of building blocks—individual roles, processes, and technologies that can be combined in numerous ways to create unique KM solutions. We hope to have many robust building blocks that we can pick and choose from when designing and developing KM solutions. This approach will allow us to implement KM within the company more quickly and at less cost, while providing our "customer" with a custom-built solution. We have identified building blocks in four distinct areas (see Figure 13.4).

The first, People Roles, are definitions of roles that people must play when implementing a KM solution. Among the People Roles building blocks are facilitator, subject matter expert, cross pollinator, and change manager.

Some of the Processes building blocks are knowledge mapping, performance management, information mapping, skill assessment, and governance. Technology building blocks include datamining, groupware, knowledge repositories, and expert locator systems.

These three areas—people roles, processes, and technology—can be combined to form specific KM methodologies. Some typical methodologies include communities of practice, after-action reviews, and instructional design.

Figure 13.4

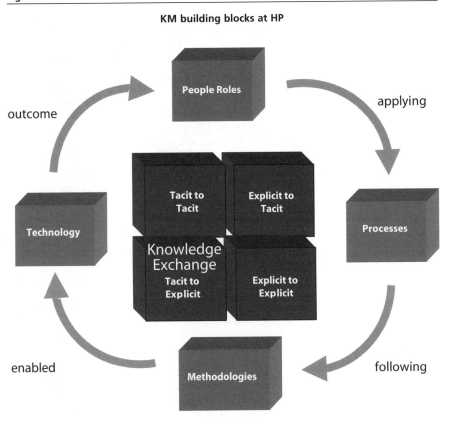

KM building blocks at HP

Together, these building blocks will lead to better systems of knowledge exchange, and we will be able to use these building blocks on specific proof points within the company. Our ultimate goal is to be able to use these building blocks, and the successful proof points, to develop HP's go-to-market capabilities in KM.

Providing KM Leadership

There are several KM activities going on within the company. However, there has never been a company-wide KM strategy or approach. One of the goals to support our charter of providing KM leadership is to bring these activities together under a strategic "umbrella" of standard processes, tools, methodologies, and behaviors. To do so, the KM group is organizing a cross-company task force to define the KM strategy and standards. We hope to develop a dense network of KM practitioners who can share and learn from each other and then take that expertise to their individual businesses and functions.

Many of the tools are already in place. Last year, we introduced the HP "Community of Practice Handbook," a collection of instructions, tools, and templates to help organizations form communities of practice. This year, that handbook was expanded to include communities of interest and more details on the training and skills required to form and maintain communities. The handbook is available to all employees within Hewlett-Packard and can be downloaded from the KM intranet Web site.

We are using standard KM tools, such as instant messaging, visualization, e-mail, virtual conferencing, and so on. Our emphasis on the building block approach (and having a variety of technologies, processes, and people roles ready to choose from) will allow us to develop KM solutions quickly.

The KM team also participates in the definition of HP's enterprise architecture. This architecture defines all of the business processes, and the underlying tools and technologies to support those processes, within the company. The KM group is responsible for the many areas that KM touches, including the KM domain, the content management domain, the portal framework domain, and the collaboration domain.

The KM group also heads up the KM Tools and Technology Forum, a forum made up of representatives from across the business that is focused on defining the standard tools and processes for KM within the company.

Another way that the KM group is educating HP employees about KM is through a series of knowledge seminars. These quarterly seminars, held in different locations around the world, feature internationally recognized experts in specific areas of KM. The seminars are Webcast to audiences around the world and are available for replay for those who are unable to attend the live broadcast.

The team is also working with HP's education department to develop a curriculum around KM. These courses would begin with a general introduction to KM and would be available both in physical and in virtual classroom formats.

Focusing on Collaborative Decision Making

A key focus area for the group is collaborative decision making. Historically, HP was known to follow consensus-based decision making and was slow in its decision-making processes. Compaq was known for its speedy decision making, but sometimes the decisions had to be changed because a thorough analysis was not done. Our focus on collaborative decision making takes the best of both worlds to help the company make quick, effective decisions with less risk.

Collaborative decision making is different from consensus decision making, in that the decision maker may still be a single person. The major difference, however, is that the decision maker has the ability to tap the power of his or her people—the depth and breadth of their knowledge—to make more informed decisions. By joining the "power of many"—the knowledge of the employees—with the "power of now"—instant access to information—the decision maker can speed up the decision-making process.

Collaborative decision making is very useful when complex decisions have to be made rapidly. It is applicable when the problem is not clearly defined, there are multiple solutions to the problem, there are multiple factors influencing the solution, the consequences of a wrong decision are severe, resources will need to be reconfigured to support the solution, or the time to decision is critical.

Establishing Proof Points to Model Success

Because our group is small, we are limited in what we can take on. So, we determined early on to develop two or three successful KM projects that we could use as proof points—examples of collaborative decision making and the results that are possible.

We use the approach outlined in Figure 13.5 to evaluate and implement a KM project.

Figure 13.5

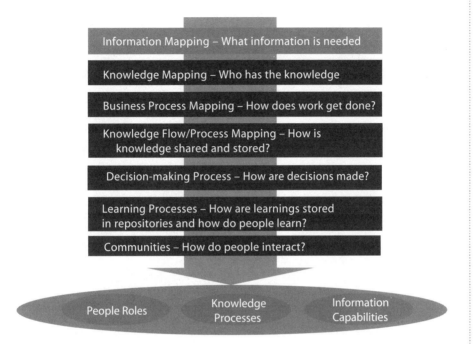

KM project components

Information Mapping – What information is needed

Knowledge Mapping – Who has the knowledge

Business Process Mapping – How does work get done?

Knowledge Flow/Process Mapping – How is knowledge shared and stored?

Decision-making Process – How are decisions made?

Learning Processes – How are learnings stored in repositories and how do people learn?

Communities – How do people interact?

People Roles   Knowledge Processes   Information Capabilities

Business leaders often want a KM project to jump straight from "What information is needed?" to the solution—information capabilities. We guide these leaders through the full process illustrated in seven steps in Figure 13.5, so we can ensure that all elements have been addressed. This illustration is useful to help leaders understand how a KM project needs to be implemented.

Our first project, which began in June 2003, is working with HP's enterprise software group in their customer support area. The manager of the support center wants to free up some of his support engineers to work in a new area of the business. He felt that by implementing better collaboration tools and processes, he could gain enough efficiencies that the number of employees could be reduced, and the freed-up employees could tackle a new area of need. Our first step was to conduct interviews with a cross-section of the organization. The purpose was to determine the "current state"—how were things working, what tools were used, how satisfied the employees were with their tools, and so on. We then developed the "future state"—how everything would be in an ideal work. This allowed us to identify the gaps and develop a plan of action to address those gaps. We are just finishing this analysis phase and will soon take on Phase 2—the implementation of the KM design.

Similar projects are now being discussed with other support areas in the company.

Challenges Facing the Industry

Over the past several years, IT has gone through several major changes. As can be seen from Figure 13.6, we have moved from the mainframe era, where limited data

Figure 13.6

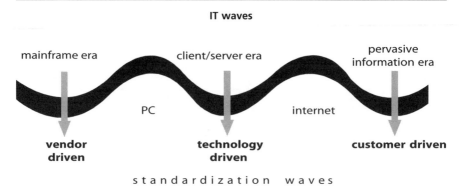

was available and often not until month end, to pervasive, instant information. We refer to this instant access to quality information as the power of now. The next challenge confronting business executives is how to use that instant information for rapid and effective decision making, and execution of those decisions, within the organization.

According to Paul Nutt, Professor of Management Science at Ohio State University's Fisher College of Business in Columbus, Ohio, business managers fail to make good decisions about half the time. This 50% failure rate, which Nutt believes is a conservative estimate, is alarming. Why do so many decisions go astray? According to Errol Wirasinghe, a Houston, Texas-based consultant, the two most significant problems facing decision makers are subjectivity and the mind's inability to process more than a handful of details at any moment. IT adds to the problem, as it continues to provide more and more data that is harder and harder to process into relevant knowledge that can be used and applied to effective decisions.

The ability to sense and respond quickly to rapidly changing market conditions can be the difference between a high-performance organization and a mediocre one. However, many companies do not effectively use the knowledge of their people—the power of many—to make effective decisions. Effective implementation of a comprehensive KM program can change that.

At HP, we are working to make sense out of this instant information, and share it broadly and effectively, so that we can make effective, rapid decisions.

Recommendations for KM Practitioners

Based on our experiences, here are some recommendations we offer to our fellow KM practitioners in the industry.

- **Align KM strategy with your business strategy**—To get management's attention, and to ensure your best chance of success, you must be adding real business value and solving real business problems. Your executive sponsor can help ensure that you are on the right track.
- **Couple your efforts with business metrics**—Show that you have real results. Do not track only KM-specific metrics, such as how many documents were stored and accessed, but show the outcomes, such as how the KM project produced results.

- **Engage business leaders**—Your KM efforts should involve the business leaders, not just IT or KM functional staff.
- **Strike a good balance between tangible and intangible outcomes**—As discussed above under business metrics, you will need to have real, tangible results, not just subjective outcomes.
- **Spread the credit across the participating organizations**—Once you have positive results, spread the credit around. If a business leader feels responsible, you are more likely to get strong support for your next effort.
- **Watch out for corporate hyenas**—There will always be naysayers. Do not let them derail your KM efforts.
- **Success could be your failure**—Make sure that your KM efforts are sustainable over the long run. Once you have proven successes, you will have plenty of people knocking at your door. Do not commit to more than you can handle.

References

Allee, Verna (2002). *The Future of Knowledge: Increasing Prosperity through Value Networks.* Boston: Butterworth-Heinemann.

Allee, Verna (1997). *The Knowledge Evolution, Building Organizational Intelligence.* Boston: Butterworth-Heinemann.

Davenport, Thomas H. and Prusak, Laurence (2000). *Working Knowledge.* Boston: Harvard Business School Press.

Dixon, Nancy M. (2000). *Common Knowledge: How Companies Thrive by Sharing What They Know.* Boston: Harvard Business School Press.

Fisher, Kimball; Fisher, Maureen Duncan; and Fisher, Mareen D. (1998). *The Distributed Mind: Achieving High Performance through the Collective Intelligence of Knowledge Work Teams.* New York: AMACOM.

Hamel, Gary and Prahalad, C.K. (1996). *Competing for the Future.* Boston: Harvard Business School Press.

Ghoshal, Sumantra and Bartlett, Christopher A. (1999). *The Individualized Corporation: A Fundamentally New Approach to Management.* New York: Harper Business.

Levy, Pierre and Bononno, Robert (2002). *Collective Intelligence: Mankind's Emerging World in Cyberspace.* Cambridge, MA: Perseus Books Group.

Nonaka, Ikujiro; Takeuchi, Hirotaka; and Takeuchi, Hiro (1995). *The Knowledge-Creating Company: How Japanese Companies Create the Dynamics of Innovation.* New York: Oxford University Press.

Nutt, Paul (2002). *Why Decisions Fail.* San Francisco: Berrett-Koehler.

Quinn, James (1992). *Intelligent Enterprise: A Knowledge and Service Based Paradigm for Industry.* Free Press, New York.

Saint-Onge, Hubert and Wallace, Debra (2002). *Leveraging Communities of Practice for Strategic Advantage.* Boston: Butterworth-Heinemann.

Wiig, Karl M. (1995). *Knowledge Management Methods: Practical Approaches to Managing Knowledge.* Schema Pr., Arlington, Texas.

Wiig, Karl M. (1994a). *Knowledge Management Foundations: Thinking About Thinking—How People and Organizations Represent, Create and Use Knowledge.* Schema Pr., Arlington, Texas.

Wiig, Karl M. (1994b). *Knowledge Management: The Central Focus for Intelligent-Acting Organizations.* Schema Pr., Arlington, Texas.

Wiig, Karl M. (1994c). *Knowledge Management Series (3 Vols.).* Schema Pr. Arlington, Texas.

Wirasinghe, Errol (2003). *The Art of Making Decisions: Expanding Common Sense and Experience.* Shanmar Pub., Houston, Texas.

Knowledge Networking on a National Scale: A New Zealand Case Study*

14

Paul Spence

Knowledge is action. Without action there is no value creation!

Karl Erik Sveiby

Speaking to a live Web forum about leveraging knowledge intangibles within business

The Context: KM and Entrepreneurship in New Zealand

- **Scenario 1**—The managing director of a niche e-learning software developer, based in Christchurch, New Zealand, realizes that the local market for her product is limited, but does not have the resources to mount an offshore research and marketing campaign. How can she quickly identify potential sales channels in distant markets and be mentored through the exporting process by others who have been down the same path before her?
- **Scenario 2**—One of her peers from the same city seeks a reliable data center in Singapore. The Innovators Online Network (ION) virtual network found him a service provider that would not only host his video and voice conferencing application, but that was able and willing to assist with his market development.

---

* *Editor's Note:* This chapter highlights the role that well-designed KM tools can play in inter-organizational knowledge networking on a national scale. Small- and medium-sized businesses in New Zealand have been successfully using the Web-based Innovators Online Network (ION) for offshore research and marketing campaigns, thus overcoming constraints of distance and inadequate individual resources. The use of smaller sub-groups and periodic face-to-face meetings helped foster trust, authority roles, and bonds between the practitioners. This case study also highlights some of the classic challenges in facilitating online communities of practice and the means of tackling them, such as drawing user attention to fresh content, tools for easy publishing, secure access to confidential information, maintaining overall focus, training moderators, evolving rules regarding veto power and anonymous posting, and strong involvement of the overall project manager. In sum, electronic forums can indeed be a catalyst for driving intellectual discussion as well as delivering tangible gains on projects, provided adequate attention is paid to issues of capacity and culture.

Most of New Zealand's small technology companies face challenges such as these when first embarking upon offshore market development. While the New Zealand business community has both an excellent reputation for ethical business practice as well as high levels of innovativeness, gaining the level of recognition that our little country deserves has always been problematical. Securing respect above the background noise of the global marketplace is no easy task. Geographically, New Zealand is about as far removed from major world markets as one can possibly get. Information communications technologies have improved the situation somewhat over the last decade or so, but there is no substitute for face-to-face meetings or personal introductions to build trust. However, it is also a difficult and expensive exercise to obtain market intelligence by remote means. Unfortunately, there is a dearth of assistance available for the many small, but aspiring businesses looking to take that next step toward being a global player.

Government-operated trade and economic development agencies are still predominantly focused on assisting the large agricultural commodity traders, upon whose backs the New Zealand economy was founded. Small technology companies in the sub-million-dollar per annum turnover bracket receive only a token amount of support from government agencies. Sadly, a great many worthy ventures are left to cope on their own. Often, these companies have existing sales records and already successful products and services, but they are left to battle on alone as they attempt to develop new market opportunities for themselves. Yet, most employment in New Zealand is within the small- and medium-sized (SME) business sector, and the key to economic growth is to stimulate these industries. How, then, could "tech-venture" SMEs be aided to take that step to identify and access new markets offshore, without repeating the same costly mistakes of their predecessors?

That was the question faced by a dedicated group of 20 or so academics and business people that began to debate the issue in mid-2002. Members of the group came from a variety of backgrounds and were dispersed all over New Zealand, as well as abroad. The "innovators group" was one of two formed as part of a Ph.D. research project on the theme of "virtual networking." The members communicated by a simple e-mail list server based at the University of Waikato in Hamilton, New Zealand. Plans were set in place to find a permanent virtual home for the group, which had become known as ION.

Basis for a National Knowledge Network

It had become clear that some form of knowledge networking solution was required on a national scale, a solution that would provide a roadmap for technology ventures to identify market intelligence and to receive guidance from others who had themselves already been involved in the development of high-value, high-technology export ventures. The author took on the role of project manager and a sub-group was formed to act as a steering committee. The original e-mail list server was maintained for use by the committee, and, after some discussion, it was decided to develop a public, Web-based forum to further the aims of ION. The University of Waikato Management School offered server space and a modicum of technical support, and the hard work of installing the appropriate software and cultivating a new virtual community began in earnest.

Wenger et al. (2002) identify distance, size, community affiliation, and culture as the four key issues faced when setting up virtual communities and knowledge networks. We knew that we could solve the problem of community size and geographical separation through the use of technology, but building the social capital that would provide a conduit for knowledge sharing was going to be the real challenge for the initiative. Furthermore, providing an incentive for ongoing engagement was essential if we were to grow membership and participation to a level at which the community would be self-sustaining.

Community Development and the Importance of Face-to-Face Meeting

To ensure a sense of affiliation within the ION community, we began by forming several sub-groups drawn from the most active members of the original mailing list. Those members that could attend an initial face-to-face meeting did so; there were three sub-group breakfast meetings in three separate cities around New Zealand. At each of these meetings, there was a brainstorming session about strategy to move the initiative forward. The results of all the meetings were shared through the e-mail list, and a number of participants agreed to take on moderator roles within the electronic forum (see Figure 14.1). At this point, several of the original dozen or so indicated they could not commit any further time to it and have remained as distant observers since. At this point, we began to plan for a mini-conference in a central location. That location was Taupo, a small town in the heart of New Zealand's volcanic, scenic wonderland and itself a poignant study of an economically flat (but resource rich) region that could benefit from the ION initiative.

I am convinced that without those early face-to-face meetings and facilitation by several key players, the venture would not have flown, so to speak. It allowed for an establishment of trust between the participants and conferred authority on those who needed to take action to move the project forward. Our host at the mini-conference was Rob McEwen, a recently returned expatriate, who had a decade of experience marketing software in the United States and, like others in the group, had a passion for championing small players who had innovative technology offerings to bring to market. He was also pivotal in driving the vision of ION as a knowledge network and enabler for regional economic development.

Developing a sense of affiliation and a culture of knowledge sharing were instrumental in carrying the ION venture forward initially, but it was the Web site and online discussion forum that swelled participation from 10 or so members to around 200, in the space of a few months. Not bad for a hitherto unknown project with no cash budget to speak of. Because the project manager was based 600 km from the Web developer, regular project meetings were not possible. However, the researcher who developed the initial concept, Annick Janson, was engaged to liase between the host university, the technical staff, and myself, the project manager. She also performed an important role, acting as opportunity scout and project champion in the wider community.

A Tailor-made Solution to Knowledge Networking

By October 2002, we had an installation that included a Web site homepage, an electronic discussion forum, and a content management system. The homepage received a stylistic makeover to ensure that it reflected the themes of innovation, creativity, and community. News items about online events and success stories are currently presented "front and center" on the homepage in order to capture the viewer and quickly inform about the value that is being delivered. This was seen as essential because of the high caliber of site visitor for many of whom time is a precious resource. It was also essential that the project manager and steering committee be able to publish content directly to the site.

Figure 14.1

Electronic forums at the Innovator Online Network

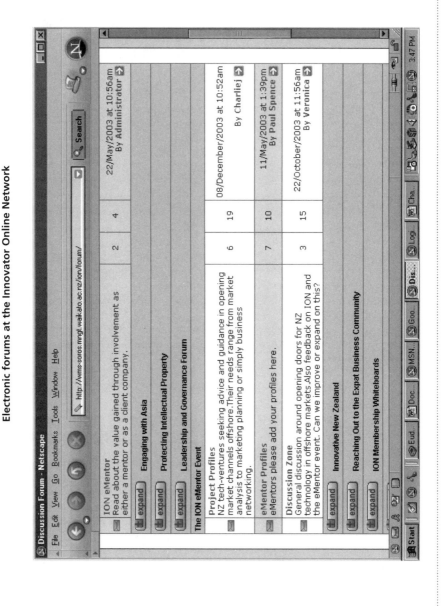

Microsoft's Content Management Server 2002 was deployed to support the growing need for remote publishing to the Web site. With secure password access via the homepage and fully customizable templates, the content management server (CMS) ensures that all content is published in a similar format and only by those approved to do so. The site administrator also has final right of veto, prior to publishing, over any submitted document. The CMS was seen as critical to delivering relevant and topical news and event information in order to retain the relevancy and freshness that would be necessary to cultivate the ION virtual community. The reality has been that content production has been left largely in the domain of the project manager and the electronic forum has served as the message board for site visitors who could only afford a few minutes to post news or project information. That development was not altogether unexpected and proved just as effective in aiding the organic growth of the community because, more often than not, contributors found it more economical to simply add comments of their own to the original forum topics.

Addressing Forum Security

So the electronic forum has proven to be a catalyst driving intellectual discussion, as well as an efficient venue to focus on actually getting project work done within the community. The Web forum was constructed using a freeware product called WebWiz, available at www.webwizforums.com. The software proved to be as advertised in that it was indeed an easily installed and completely scalable solution. The system can be database backed with either the structured query language or the Access server and provides 160-bit password encryption for users. The security features offered were essential because of the commercial nature of the forum content. The built-in administration manager allowed full tracking of forum membership and some gatekeeping in respect to which forum members are involved in the project areas.

The issue of gatekeeping proved controversial among the foundation members. On the one hand, it was argued that serendipity plays an important role in virtual networking, and this aspect could be undermined if too many restrictions were placed on forum access. On the other hand, there was a desire to eliminate "tire kickers" who might waste the time of genuine participants or worse become disruptive. A compromise was reached that allowed full public access to the discussion forum while limiting access to the project zone. The software allows for qualification of forum members as well as the ability to close off sections of the forum or make them read-only, as required.

What we have found is that the subject matter attracts a certain caliber of individual, and there has been little in the way of abuse of the concept or disharmony among participants. More of a concern is the issue of maintaining the privacy of forum members within the context of a live virtual environment. How this was addressed was by ensuring that the sign-on process gives the new member the option of displaying their e-mail contact details or not. The WebWiz forum has a completely self-contained internal messaging system. This means that it is possible to make an initial approach to another forum member without compromising confidentiality. Immediately upon logging in to the forum, the member is alerted to any new e-mail. Most importantly it means that e-mail addresses can be kept off the site and away from the prying eyes of Webcrawlers, spammers, and other less than savoury inhabitants of the virtual world.

Because some of the forum subject matter could potentially be commercially sensitive, it was important to offer password-protected discussion areas available upon request. However, the bottom line was the rule that participants should only post material that they would normally be happy to post on their own Web sites or in other media in the public domain. It was always made clear that ION was simply the electronic venue for meeting potential collaborators and that once the initial contact was formed then the conversation should go offsite. It was sometimes necessary to reassure participants that there was no requirement to publish any of their intellectual property directly within the forum.

Training and the Roles of Facilitator and Moderator

It was understood from the beginning that forum community moderators would be needed to bring life to the ION virtual community. The role of the moderator is to steward the direction of a given forum discussion and to provide fresh impetus when needed. Over time, a number of the foundation members as well as several other keen contributors volunteered to act as moderators. The facilitator role has fallen to the project manager and is twofold in that it involves directing and informing the moderators as well as acting as a go-between or knowledge broker. The latter role has become a pivotal one in the case of the ION virtual community. The facilitator is the one player with a grand view of who is involved and what is topical. Quite often the facilitator will step in and "match-make" an introduction where deemed appropriate.

The site facilitator also acts in a training capacity to forum members and moderators. Instructions about how to register on the Web forum are posted on the site homepage. Most of our target market is reasonably adept with technology, and it has been our experience that most registrants were able to complete this process without any further assistance. However, in a small number of cases, the site facilitator was contacted directly in order to help with registration. In fact, the administration area on the forum allows the facilitator the freedom to generate and activate a new login from scratch at any time. The forum members responding to verification e-mail that is sent to their nominated address normally conclude the registration process. However, one difficulty encountered was that some individuals were failing to complete this last step. It was later discovered that the forum server e-mail had been accidentally shut down and new signups were not receiving their validation e-mails. It is likely that quite a number of potential new participants were lost because of this problem. It underlines the importance of keeping a close eye on the day-to-day technical operation of any Web-enabled facility.

Posting to Web forum threads is a reasonably intuitive process, and little support has been required for users. However, the site facilitator trains new forum moderators on some simple rules of engagement in order to streamline forum discussion and debate. The forum has an anti-abuse filter that blocks postings or e-mail that contains abusive language, and aggressive or disrespectful behavior of any kind is not tolerated. This is especially important because of the global, collaborative nature of the project. It is pleasing to note that so far there has been no need to censure any forum participants. However, readers considering establishing virtual forum projects of their own should be mindful of the potential for abuse and establish firm protocols about what is acceptable.

Problems Implementing a Virtual Community Project

One of the early issues of concern was that the Web developer was not actually a foundation member of the ION group and he did not have the depth of understanding about the direction of the project. Initially, technical questions had to be forwarded on by the university liaison person. Frustrations emerged over time as site development was held up, technical failures of the Web server happened, and misunderstandings over style and structure occurred. The original developer departed for overseas travel and left his apprentice to carry on. From this point it was decided that the project manager would relate directly to the new Web developer by the use of e-mail and MSN chat sessions, ensuring that each had an immediate understanding of the other's needs at any time.

Although the Web forum was never the subject of abuse, there were always other human foibles and odd sociological phenomena to deal with. For example, it was known that a great deal more users visited and registered on the site than were ever actively posting on the Web forum. At times, it was hugely frustrating until we realized that having "lurkers" on the forum was quite acceptable, even desirable. The lurkers are those registered users that simply observe the proceedings without contributing to the forum discussion—much as in real life where people attend seminars and may simply take ideas away to be considered without adding substantially to the debate. The real value of the virtual community lay in how the participants acted on those ideas.

Another difficulty was that registration on the virtual forum required only minimal information to be input by the user. So it was sometimes difficult to ascertain the origin and background of the user, especially if they used a Webmail address. Over time, it became clearer which individuals were most enthusiastic about posting items to the forum, and it was these users who were singled out and invited to participate in other ways. The most active users often agreed to take up temporary roles as moderators or else participate in mentorship or governance of the ION venture itself and indeed of other ventures that had been profiled within the virtual community.

Building and Profiling a Community

The target audience for this online initiative is New Zealand's "growth phase" technology companies and the owners and management of such organizations. To capture the interest of this group, we drove media activity by running online events and announcing successes as they emerged. In the future we expect to increase the amount of activity, such as matching companies with mentors and potential clients. The other side of the equation is that we needed to attract experienced business people of sufficient caliber to be of benefit to the small companies in the network. At the time of writing, there were over 240 members signed up to the forum. The lack of a profiling facility on the Web site has made it difficult to track the exact nature of the community. However, anecdotal evidence suggests that about 25% of the users were technology business operators, another 25% were potential mentors, and 25% were interested parties from the government or investment sectors. The remainder were somewhat of a mystery. In any event, it did not matter because it was believed that those who saw value in the initiative and who had the capability to act would do so. In any given month we determined that only about 10% of users were monitoring the Web site for opportunities.

Ten percent does not seem like a great deal, but it is the nature of virtual communities and online engagement. If only 20 individuals sat around a table there would be 20 by 19 or 380 potential linkages, and almost certainly quite a number of common interests would emerge if everyone had a chance to tell their story. But it would take such a long time to tell those stories. A virtual round table allows that process to happen asynchronously and at the convenience of each participant. With a target of 500 forum members by the end of year two, that represents almost 250,000 potential knowledge links.

The Way Forward

The site was launched in mid-November 2002 in conjunction with media activity around the release of the Global Entrepreneurship Monitor (GEM) report. ION hosted the public online event discussing the findings of the report. Subsequently, forum membership has grown to over 240 members. For the initiative to gain real momentum, we believe that a minimum of 500–1,000 members will be necessary in the long term. It is evident that only about 20% of forum signups remain active and interested. To retain (and improve upon) that level of interest it is necessary to keep the content fresh and to continue to present new opportunities and ideas for discussion. Again, this is where the facilitator plays a critical role. Another one of the key technical challenges ahead is developing a secure area where members can profile themselves.

Plans are also afoot to add a multimedia collaboration center. A New Zealand software company called Optecs has agreed to install and support a video and voice conferencing facility that is based on Internet protocols. The service will be free to use for ION members and will provide a means by which online business relationships can be cemented through multi-user conferencing. The software includes image push and whiteboarding capabilities that enhance conversation and collaboration. This new facility may well become a centerpiece that provides a further point of difference to the ION initiative.

Key Learnings: Recommendations for KM Practitioners

— Include some face-to-face events to help develop the community.
— Ensure the project team shares the community vision from day one.
— Select a secure and customizable technology platform.
— Engage subject matter experts to moderate areas of the forum.
— Keep site content fresh and communicate frequently with participants.

It will also be necessary in the future to keep an ongoing dialog with other interested parties such as government, regional economic development authorities, and other networks. A bi-monthly e-letter and digest of key projects on the site is sent out to all forum signups and other stakeholders and supporters. This in turn catalyzes site activity. The collaborative fashion in which the project was quickly established is in itself a testament to the power of virtual networking. One of the early success stories involves the e-learning content developer mentioned in scenario 1 at the beginning of this chapter. Through an introduction on ION, she was able to identify a health sector consultant who opened doors into the health NGOs that might otherwise have remained shut. That collaboration led to real business value in terms of a substantial project. So the ultimate measure of the success of the knowledge network will not be numbers of hits on the Web site, but how many actual success stories emerge over time.

Reference

Wenger, E., McDermott, R., and Snyder, W.M. (2002). *Cultivating Communities of Practice.* Boston: Harvard University Press.

Technology Applications of Communities of Practice: The Nursing Leadership Academy on Palliative and End-of-life Care*

Cynda H. Rushton and Susan S. Hanley

> If you want to teach people a new way of thinking, don't bother trying to teach them. Instead, give them a tool, the use of which will lead to new ways of thinking.
>
> *Buckminster Fuller*

The Context: One Vision, One Voice

This story begins with a short history of palliative and end-of-life care to describe the knowledge domain and the evolution of the beliefs and practices of the field leading to the creation of an innovative community of practice.

While there have been efforts in many arenas to change the way health care professionals deal with patient death and dying, the most innovative and aggressive work

---

* *Editor's Note:* Moving beyond organizational boundaries, this chapter showcases the uses of online collaboration tools to enable knowledge sharing across geographically extended CoPs. The field of palliative and end-of-life care has pressing information needs but distributed communities of experts, thus making it an ideal candidate for Web-based collaboration tools as a way of knowledge networking and lifelong learning. The Nursing Leadership Academy for End of Life Care housed in the Institute for Johns Hopkins Nursing is leveraging KM methods and tools among nurses, physicians, medical specialists, and bereavement counsellors who are changing the culture of patient care.

Such online CoPs stay connected for problem solving, instant dissemination of best practices and lessons learned, conducting opinion surveys, providing member profile and patient support information, publishing photo galleries, and sustaining the momentum of face-to-face meetings. Close interaction between users and developers, ease of use, simple low-bandwidth design, minimum training needs, features for posting urgent queries, online discussions with experts, and indexing of Web content were other success factors in this platform for distributed CoPs.

is being done in the nursing community, especially through the Nursing Leadership Academy for End of Life Care housed in the Institute for Johns Hopkins Nursing at the School of Nursing of Johns Hopkins University.* The Nursing Leadership Academy is leveraging best-in-class knowledge management processes and technologies to enhance their critical mission.

A Short History of Palliative Care

In the late 1800s, health care professionals had little to offer the sick beyond palliative care—the easing of symptoms associated with disease. Most deaths occurred at home in the care of family members, and most died within days of the onset of the illness.

In the following centuries, advances in health care changed the trajectory of dying. Improved nutrition and sanitation, preventative medicine, widespread vaccination use, the development of wide spectrum antibiotics, uses of cardiopulmonary resuscitation, and an emphasis on early detection and treatment of disease have resulted in fewer deaths in infancy and fewer deaths from acute illness. Today, the majority of those who die are over the age of 65, and death occurs after a long, progressively debilitating chronic illness such as cancer, renal disease, lung dysfunction, heart disease, or acquired immuno-deficiency syndrome (AIDS).

These improvements and the resulting extension of life have led to both benefits and challenges for society and today's health care professional. Obviously, most people would like to have a longer, quality-filled life. However, our ability to medically intervene more effectively than in the past has created a culture that equates death with medical failure in the minds of some health care professionals, patients, and families. The problem arises when there is an emphasis of "cure" over "care" or the mindset that only considers palliative care when all hope of cure is extinguished. Ethical issues arise with regard to how much curative technology and procedure are appropriate at the expense of a patient's quality of life. For many patients, the diagnosis of a chronic or terminal disease means the instant end of a good life, that they must now just survive and submit to curative attempts, waiting to die. Palliative care, however, seeks to integrate the cure with the care to improve the quality of life and support the patient's view of a "good death"—one that is free from avoidable distress and suffering for patients, families, and caregivers; in general accord with patients' and families' wishes; and reasonably consistent with clinical, cultural, and ethical standards (Coyle, 2001, p. 3, cited in Ferrell and Coyle, 2001).

The Challenge of Integrating Palliative Care into Daily Practice

All health care professionals face the challenges of providing care to patients who are living longer, but it is traditionally the nursing profession that has responded to the challenge of patient care. The very essence of the nursing profession is a commitment

---

* The Institute for Johns Hopkins Nursing is a collaborative partnership between the Johns Hopkins University School of Nursing and the Johns Hopkins Hospital Department of Nursing, which is designed to foster communication and collaboration between nursing education and nursing practice. The institute was formed in 1995 by the university and the hospital (two separately incorporated entities). The Governing Board consists of the hospital vice-president for Patient Care Services and the dean of the School of Nursing. They delegate the operation of the institute and its programs to the director and a small staff. The overall mission of the institute is to share the innovations in practice, science, and scholarship of Johns Hopkins Nursing with other health care professionals locally, nationally, and worldwide.

to provide comprehensive, humane, and compassionate care and support to patients and their families during a patient's life span. Nurses actively seek ways to improve the quality of life for their patients throughout their life span, whether that life is just beginning or entering its twilight. It seemed appropriate, then, that nurses take the lead in advocating for quality palliative care and breaking the traditional "cure versus care" cultural mindset of the medical community. If nurses effectively emphasize the need for quality palliative care, they, in collaboration with other members of the medical community, can change the culture of health care through a team approach of nurses, physicians, bereavement counselors, and others who will integrate palliative care into all aspects of a patient's care plan.

First, however, they must educate themselves. In nursing curricula, palliative care has often been loosely integrated into a variety of courses, but the reality is that it is more often an invisible part of education. For example, for decades, pain assessment and management was given short shrift across the medical community. Health professionals thus lacked a thorough grounding in the technical aspects of pain assessment and management, as well as a belief that pain control is a vital part of medical care. Widespread educational, regulatory, and legal reforms have begun to increase clinician competencies and accountabilities for managing pain.

In addition to improving their knowledge, nurses also must unite, organize, and help build an infrastructure that will focus on patient- and family-centered care, pain and symptom management, and the art of humane caring. In other words, they must become effective agents to change the culture of patient care.

The Response: The National Nursing Leadership Academy on Palliative and End of Life Care

Starting in September 2000, leaders from 44 national nursing organizations representing more than 500,000 nurses gathered in Baltimore, Maryland, to attend the National Nursing Leadership Academy on Palliative and End of Life Care. The academy was designed to educate, train, and organize a network of nursing leaders prepared to galvanize the profession and transform end-of-life care. The academy, administered by the Institute for Johns Hopkins Nursing, was funded by a grant from the Open Society Institute's Project on Death in America. Academy members represent the majority of existing nursing specialty organizations across the United States. Each organization provided one or two delegates to the Nursing Leadership Academy. The delegates, in turn, provide a link back to their member organizations, who had committed to use their existing infrastructure and communication methods to raise awareness and educate nurses about palliative and end-of-life care.

Academy participants took action plans back to their respective organizations for implementation, which responded by committing time, money, and expertise to galvanizing their memberships and informing the public about the options for minimizing the symptoms that accompany chronic illness and maximizing opportunities to live the last phase of life with greater peace and independence. The results of the work of the first cohort, the group that met in September 2000, were apparent when they reconvened in Baltimore on March 14–16, 2002, to share their projects and products. The second cohort reported in September 2003. As a result of the efforts of these nurses, 18 new articles were published in nursing journals, six National Nursing Conferences included palliative and end-of-life care on their agendas, and two organizations are writing core curriculum on the end of life. Several participants are involved in writing end-of-life questions for certification exams, and at least five organizations have developed resource lists of experts and materials available. Since the first meeting in September 2000, palliative and end-of-life care initiatives locally and nationally have increased markedly as a result of the efforts of academy participants. A survey documenting the impact of the academy has recently been distributed to all participants.

The major concern voiced in the second meeting of the Nursing Leadership Academy was how to sustain their change efforts and their academy community. The concept of **communities of practice** was suggested as a vehicle to keep the members connected for problem solving and dissemination of best practices and lessons learned. The communities of practice model offers a way to nurture the synergy, enthusiasm, and wisdom of the participants using people-to-people interactions and technology solutions.

As the Nursing Leadership Academy explored the concepts of communities, they realized that given the geographic dispersion of their members, they needed to create a dynamic and meaningful electronic forum for continuing the interaction and sharing begun at the academy, a technology platform for the community of practice. The post-conference environment challenged the academy organizers to think about how they could create a solution to sustain their efforts beyond the beginning stages. The team needed to create an infrastructure that would help nurses leading change initiatives in palliative and end-of-life care be successful within their own nursing organizations and beyond. To achieve this goal, they had to address member needs to connect with each other and provide access to critical resources as they dealt with challenging issues of raising awareness, education, and strategy for integrating palliative and end-of-life care into all nursing specialties.

Ultimately, this forum could be extended to address the needs of not just the core Nursing Leadership Academy community, but the entire community of more than 500,000 nurses, other medical specialists, and the general public. Initially, however, the goal of this solution was to create a collaboration forum for the initial 100 or so participants in the Nursing Leadership Academy.

The Technology: Microsoft Windows SharePoint Services

Working with Dell Professional Services (DPS), the Johns Hopkins team chose to use a solution based on Microsoft® Windows® SharePoint™ Services, a component technology in Windows Server 2003, to create an online collaboration community that would increase the rapid exchange, accessibility, and impact of information that is available to palliative care practitioners. Windows SharePoint Services is a Web-based team collaboration environment built on the Windows Server 2003 platform. It gives any workspace member with a Web browser the ability to create and access virtual workspaces, in which they can develop and share best practices documents, engage in discussions, conduct opinion surveys, and provide member profile and patient support information. The back-end database for the Johns Hopkins project was the SQL Server. The entire project, from design to deployment, took five weeks. The solution environment itself requires very little information technology maintenance. There is only a limited part-time resource available (and necessary) for tech support for the operational solution.

The solution met a demanding set of criteria that supported three overarching objectives of the academy:

- **Knowledge**—Providing key information and resources for the nursing community regarding palliative and end-of-life care, leadership, and the change process

- **Self-awareness**—Helping users keep abreast of the experiences of other nurse leaders who were engaging in change initiatives focused on palliative and end-of-life care
- **Support**—Enabling users to reach out to one another for advice, best practices, and general support

"The mission of the School of Nursing, which in collaboration with the Johns Hopkins Hospital formed the Institute for Johns Hopkins Nursing in 1995, is to provide leadership within the nursing community," according to Claire Bogdanski, Associate Dean and Chief Financial Officer for the Johns Hopkins University School of Nursing. "We are using the new [Windows] SharePoint Services online community to leverage collaboration and communication between institutions and nurses around the country. Our early experience already demonstrates that this project will be a huge success."

The biggest advantage of this technology is that, with only minor customizations, the "out of the box" solution provided the basic features and functions needed for a collaborative community, including:

- Membership directories
- Threaded discussions
- Document repositories
- Photo galleries
- Online surveys
- Links to relevant external Web sites

The solution strategy was to deploy an online workspace that was designed around the specific needs of the palliative care community of practice, so that the health care professionals could collaborate to share best practices, sustain the momentum of their face-to-face meetings, and unite the nursing profession around common goals.

Collaboration solutions are more about people and process than they are about technology. By looking for platforms that are based on established technology and that provide a significant number of features and functions out of the box, more time can be spent in the design process, focusing on what users really need and how they can embed that technology into the way they work. The consulting team from Dell mapped the core requirements of the palliative care community directly into the core features and functions of Windows SharePoint Services, which enabled the project team to go from concept to implementation in less than four weeks.

Figure 15.1 shows the "homepage" for the palliative care community site. The highly customized user experience for the homepage was created by the DPS team. However, with the exception of the homepage user experience, very little custom application code needed to be written to develop the solution, making it an excellent platform for communities of practice such as the Nursing Leadership Academy.

The Results: Expected Outcomes

The palliative care portal for the Nursing Leadership Academy was launched to the leadership team in April 2003. The leadership team consisted of a small group of senior members of the Nursing Leadership Academy. Until the next full meeting of the academy in September 2003, new users are being added slowly. The system is straightforward and easy to use, requiring very little training. To help ensure the success of the full rollout, the leadership team used the time between launch and rollout to ensure

Figure 15.1

Nursing Leadership Academy palliative care portal

that meaningful, relevant content was populated on the site. In addition, since the portal software was not fully "production ready," the team elected to wait until the software was released to market before rolling out to the broader community. There were several important benefits expected from this solution. The primary benefit of the solution was to provide rapid and timely solutions to key problems in both the practice of palliative care and the adoption of palliative care principles to established nursing disciplines. Specifically, the collaborative workspace provides a real-time environment for members to:

- Find and make connections with one another by using the membership directory search features to find members with key expertise. This provides an avenue to significantly reduce the time it takes to solve specific problems related to patient care or palliative care practices.
- Share best practices in a comprehensive document library. This helps to reduce duplicative efforts across nursing organizations, ensuring that each member organization does not "reinvent the wheel."
- Solve problems by leveraging both the document library and the online discussion boards. The solution includes a monitored "urgent help" discussion area where the leadership team has committed to a 24-hour turnaround for all problems posted to the site. The discussion board leverages the automated alert

feature to send an e-mail to whoever is assigned to monitor the urgent questions discussion thread for that week or month.

- Find key resources within the site by using the comprehensive search capability or outside the site by clicking on one of the annotated links documented on the site. This feature provides a significant reduction in time to find relevant information, allowing community members to spend more time on their "day jobs."
- Learn from experts in a "guest discussion" area where members will have an opportunity to engage in asynchronous discussions with invited guests.
- Provide support for the caregiver in a unique "reflections" area of the site where community members can post stories about personal lessons they have learned, create a memorial statement about a patient, honor a colleague who has helped them, or just reflect on the importance or relevance of the work they do. Nursing is a profession of caring for others; the concept behind the reflections area is to provide an opportunity for the caregiver to get support and care for themselves.

Next Steps: The Road Ahead

Ultimately, the goal of the Institute for Johns Hopkins Nursing is to create a comprehensive Web-based portal for both information and collaboration about palliative and end-of-life care, extending beyond the original Nursing Leadership Academy and the members of each member organization to the broader nursing, medical, patient, and family population at large. To accomplish this goal, the plan for the technology platform is to extend the solution to incorporate Microsoft SharePoint Portal Server, which will provide the ability to index and search sites outside the existing community platform and enable the team to embed application software into the community framework, for example, to support e-learning modules.

By leveraging existing platform technology, the Johns Hopkins team, working closely with DPS and Microsoft, was able to build knowledge management technology that not only works, but adds value for end-users. This is because the solution designers could focus on the most critical areas for successful knowledge management solutions—people and process—rather than technology. This is an important lesson for other teams looking to leverage technology to support knowledge management initiatives.

The solutions partners include DPS experts who work with clients to develop a sound strategy for developing and promoting collaboration within their organization. Dell also develops metrics to measure value and implement advanced technologies for business improvement, such as knowledge management portals and expertise profiling systems. Its knowledge management offerings include productivity solutions, corporate portal servers, content management servers, and intranet solutions.

Lessons Learned and Recommendations for Knowledge Management Practitioners

1. Work closely with your users to define requirements. One of the reasons this project was able to be deployed in such a short time frame was the close cooperation of the user team with the development team.
2. If possible, leverage familiar frameworks and technologies, such as Microsoft Office and browsers, when you implement your knowledge management system to minimize the user adoption curve.

3. Design your user interface for the appropriate level of end user bandwidth—in other words, no pictures and flash for dial-up users.
4. Be sure to factor in additional development time when you are working with new technologies.
5. Spend time understanding end-user business objectives, goals, priorities, and work environment. Everyone says this, but it's worth repeating—no knowledge management solution is primarily about technology. People and their work processes will make or break your solution's success.

Reference

Ferrell, Betty R. and Coyle, Nessa (2001). *Textbook of Palliative Nursing*. New York: Oxford University Press.

KPMG: Leveraging KM Tools for Practice Areas and Clients*

16

Hemant Manohar

Knowledge rests not upon truth alone, but upon error also.

Carl G. Jung

Company Profile

KPMG is the global network of professional services firms whose aim is to turn understanding of information, industries, and business trends into value. With nearly 100,000 people worldwide, KPMG member firms provide services from more than 750 cities in 150 countries. Its revenues in 2002 were $10.7 billion.

KPMG member firms are a leading provider of assurance, tax, and financial advisory services. Fundamental to KPMG's approach is our focus on industry sectors. We believe that we can add value for our clients if we truly understand their industry. This is why we invest in continuously improving our knowledge of the industries we serve.

With a global approach to service delivery, we are also focused on helping our people to deliver our clients consistent methodologies and common tools across industry sectors and national boundaries.

---

* *Editor's Note:* This chapter highlights the issues facing global organizations that wish to balance a decentralized approach to KM along with a centralized effort to standardize and coordinate these disparate efforts. The challenge is not just technological, but involves content and culture as well. KPMG, one of the winners of the global Most Admired Knowledge Enterprises (MAKE) study, has KM tools that are both global and practice specific. Coordination of KM initiatives and tool design helps cut costs and also improves relevancy of the tools. A global CKO, regional CKOs, and KM practitioners develop knowledge centers of excellence. The Knowledge Management Steering Group advises the business units on what KM tools should be purchased or created and what processes should be developed to make knowledge available to employees.

Through the KWorld intranet, KPMG users can access KM tools like the KSource virtual library of knowledge, regional intranets, skills experience locator, and a universal search engine. The collaboration tool KClient provides client service teams a protected Web-based environment for sharing work in progress with clients. Extranet sites for clients and the kpmg.com Internet sites showcase the company's knowledge to larger audiences. Key lessons are that KM technology cannot work without communication, training, and basic customer service; third party KM tools can be more efficient than in-house tools; small-scale pilots are recommended for new initiatives; and templated Web sites are popular for creation on the intranet.

Brief History of Knowledge Management at KPMG

KPMG's mission has long been to turn knowledge into value for its clients by drawing upon the intellectual capital, skills, and experience of its staff. Until the mid-1990s, this knowledge resided almost exclusively in the human and technological networks rooted in the national member firms.

A changing business environment compelled KPMG's international leadership to reevaluate existing methods for capturing and sharing knowledge. In 1998, KPMG International kicked off an initiative to bring the knowledge systems of member firms together under the umbrella of a global system.

The technological challenge of uniting national firms with a diversity of technological systems was daunting. However, along with it came the challenge of establishing processes and supplying content that would be relevant to a variety of service delivery groups. The success of this project depended on the cooperation of diverse national and corporate cultures.

After some false starts, missteps, and major successes, KPMG today enjoys a strong global knowledge-sharing infrastructure, both technological and cultural. The KPMG knowledge management system and culture are sufficiently established to allow continued knowledge sharing despite significant and ongoing changes in the business environment.

Knowledge Strategy

As one of the winners of the 2002 global Most Admired Knowledge Enterprises (MAKE) study,* KPMG has been commended for its ability to deliver knowledge-based products and services to clients.

The mission of knowledge management at KPMG is to connect our people, clients, and knowledge in support of KPMG business objectives to increase growth, profitability, and quality of service.

Our strategies for achieving that mission are simple:

- Provide KPMG people a single gateway to knowledge resources whether they are inside or outside the KPMG network.
- Consistently expand the knowledge-sharing and collaboration tools and resources available to KPMG people in response to business needs.
- Showcase KPMG knowledge to prospective clients and employees.
- Leverage knowledge activities under way in the member firms to the greatest extent possible.

The core challenge for KPMG's knowledge management team is to promote and enable knowledge sharing between member firms existing in 150 countries, each with its own priorities and challenges, strengths, and limitations.

The two main elements in executing the strategy are people (an internal network of international knowledge management practitioners) and tools (both global and practice specific).

Knowledge Organization

KPMG is focused on making knowledge management tools relevant to KPMG people serving clients. To do so, the knowledge management organization developing

---

* See KNOW Network (©Teleos) Web site:
http://www.knowledgebusiness.com/make/index.asp.

the tools must gather, understand, and then meet the knowledge requirements of the business units throughout the member firms worldwide.

KPMG knowledge management groups within business units, marketing, technology, and other support groups collaborate to leverage all knowledge initiatives. Costs have been reduced, but, of equal importance, alignment improves the relevancy of both tools and content.

We have learned that the arrangement of people who deliver knowledge-sharing capabilities to KPMG must mirror the firm's structure. At KPMG this structure is a matrix of geographies, business units, industry professionals, and infrastructure groups delivering services to clients.

Rather than force a large centralized knowledge organization on this complex matrix, KPMG found it more effective to leave business decisions to the business. Most of the content and some of the process and people elements of knowledge management are managed by knowledge practitioners within the business units. Global and regional level groups drive strategy and coordinate the efforts of the end-user focused groups.

Each national member firm appoints a chief knowledge officer (CKO) and establishes a knowledge organization that best fits national needs and resources. Each works closely with local business units to gather and present content that is relevant to their people.

At the next level are small regional services groups comprised of knowledge management practitioners. Regional services supports national groups with deployment, training, and assistance in leveraging global knowledge management tools. Regional services also help to ensure that local business requirements are considered in global knowledge management project planning.

Knowledge centers of excellence located in different practice areas throughout the firm focus on knowledge innovation specific to their practice areas.

For instance, KPMG's global Assurance Advisory Services Center conducts research and creates knowledge tools exclusively for KPMG's assurance practices. Among other things, their tools provide staff-relevant knowledge at different phases of service delivery workflows and provide value-added content to clients and staff in the field. The scope of their mandate also includes sharing tacit knowledge through activities like sharing forums, which are regular facilitated conference calls focused on industry, service delivery, and other issues.

Coordinating all this activity is a small global knowledge management team led by a global CKO. The global CKO meets monthly with the CKOs of each geographic region and of the global business units, marketing, and technology units. The role of this Knowledge Management Steering Group is to promote alignment between planned knowledge activities and business priorities. Their ultimate goal is the creation of knowledge tools and services that support client service.

Knowledge practitioners in the global knowledge management group do more than just coordinate national practices. They also conduct their own research. They analyze information about business and knowledge trends and determine how to best deliver knowledge to KPMG people. They advise the business units on what tools should be purchased, what tools should be created, and what processes should be developed to make knowledge available to KPMG employees.

The KPMG knowledge organization is lean and focused on leveraging ongoing knowledge activities throughout the firm. We believe this is the model that should be followed in both lean and fat business cycles: it allows client service requirements to rise more quickly to the top of priority lists, while helping to ensure that access to content is a primary objective.

Knowledge Toolkit

This knowledge organization (local and global, service line, and industry) has created a rich selection of options for KPMG employees. At the topmost level is KWorld, KPMG's gateway to all the knowledge resources within KPMG.

Through the KWorld intranet, all KPMG users find:

- KSource is a virtual library of KPMG knowledge with multiple search options.
- A global homepage provides easy-to-find links to the tools and information available to all KPMG firm members, including news and research from external content providers.
- Homepages and intranets are created and managed by individual geographic and/or business communities. It is through these home sites that each practice presents its team members the knowledge tools and resources most relevant to their daily work. Employees can choose their practice community's home sites as their default browser homepage.
- The Skills & Experience system is where employees can enter resume information and skills. This information can be searched to find the right KPMG person with the right experience for specific projects.
- The Clients & Targets system provides employees news and information about specific companies and names of KPMG people working with that company.
- A variety of intranets help KPMG people do their work. These intranets are devoted to business development and proposal support, human resources, travel, marketing, regulatory compliance, security, and other important support functions.
- A Universal Search tool lets employees scan many of these sources concurrently.

Beyond the cross-border, cross-function internal knowledge sharing in KWorld, knowledge management at KPMG includes sharing information with clients. Our main collaboration tool, KClient, provides client service teams a protected Web-based environment for sharing work in progress with clients.

Our extranets provide clients valuable, timely, and self-selected information in an easily accessed password-protected environment. This has been particularly successful for our tax practice. Finally, our kpmg.com Internet sites showcase the knowledge created through the knowledge processes in KWorld and the different practice areas.

Looking forward, we plan to improve the internal knowledge-sharing capabilities already in place, while expanding the capability for collaborating both internally and with clients. We are also looking at ways to further leverage internal knowledge and tools in our Internet sites.

Best Practice Lessons and Recommendations

- Building KWorld was an exercise both in global technology deployment and in understanding the needs of customers in a knowledge-sharing environment. No matter how sophisticated the technological and theoretical underpinnings, the knowledge management initiative could not be successful without communication, training, and basic customer service.
- Following on the first lesson, no knowledge management initiative can be successful without a strong business value proposition and a commitment from the business to support usage of the tools, processes, and content.
- From a technology perspective, several core technologies were developed and integrated into a single Web-based interface. However, successes were also

achieved with off-the-shelf technologies used "as is" or tailored to KPMG. The efficiencies of using third party tools led KPMG to prefer off-the-shelf to homegrown.

- Without exception, KPMG's greatest knowledge management successes have come when it delivered simple, straightforward tools developed in response to specific business problems.
- Small-scale pilots expanded in response to positive take-up are more successful than large-scale "big bang" deliveries.
- The KWorld team launched its initial version with high-level sponsorship; cultivating and maintaining sponsorship at all levels is necessary and requires consistent communication and continuous successful project deliveries.
- The firm has included knowledge sharing in annual employee performance evaluations. Additional integration with human resources and training, marketing, and communications groups is critical to adoption efforts.
- Individual employees cannot be expected to contribute content in the early stages of a global knowledge management initiative. Content submission by knowledge managers designated within each line of business was more successful.
- The KWorld team rolled out a set of collaboration spaces, separate from the knowledge-sharing application, that stored submissions of internal content. These spaces could be shared with clients within a secure environment or used for internal collaboration.
- Some of knowledge management's most popular tools are templated Web sites that allow business units to establish an Internet and/or intranet presence quickly and inexpensively.
- Frequent communications in both traditional one-way messaging and monthly meetings with business representatives to update knowledge management leadership on the business and knowledge management issues they face were very successful in creating trust and buy-in. However, care had to be taken to ensure that the knowledge management organization was responsive to business needs without losing sight of its own guiding principles.
- Keep the solutions simple.
- Successful knowledge sharing and management is, in the final analysis, cultural.

Inter-organizational KM: The Experience of Australia's National Office of the Information Economy*

Luke Naismith

Policy tools will have to closely conform to the characteristics of the current technological revolution and its paradigm. The nature of the new economics and of the tools it provides for government action—and for redesigning its scope—will have enormous bearing on the direction given to the potential of this technological revolution.

*Carlota Perez***

---

* *Editor's Note:* Knowledge and networks have been identified as key inputs into the dynamics of public and private sector organizations, and government agencies like Australia's National Office of the Information Economy (NOIE) are implementing policies to assist in the generation of their knowledge economies. Formed in 1997, NOIE has developed the Government Online Strategy and has leveraged Internet infrastructure for e-government services, promotion of collaborative supply chains, and the development of rural Australia. NOIE uses KM tools not so much for achieving intra-organizational knowledge creation and sharing, but rather for promoting inter-organizational collaborative activities. NOIE considers KM to be a new socio-institutional framework and is represented on a Standards Australia committee that published an interim standard on knowledge management in early 2003.

One of the KM tools NOIE uses is similar to a best practices knowledge-base: a collection of case studies (storytelling) of effective and practical applications of information and communication technologies, e.g., e-commerce in small businesses. Key learnings from this experiment include the promise of increasing application of Web technologies to inter-organizational activities and the use of new media to spur further innovation.

** Perez, Carlota (2002). Technological Revolutions and Financial Capital: The Dynamics of Bubbles and Golden Ages. Cheltenham, UK: Edward Elgar.

Introduction

Many writers*** have noted changes in the key building blocks that generate wealth and development within society. Information, knowledge, and networks have been identified as these building blocks for the current technological revolution, acting as key inputs into the dynamics of public and private sector organizations. Governments at the national, state, and local levels are implementing policies to drive the development of key resources and infrastructure to assist in the generation of their information/knowledge/networked economies.

Australia is no exception in this regard. In 1997, the National Office for the Information Economy (NOIE) was formed as the federal government's lead agency for information economy issues. It has direct responsibility for the development and coordination of advice to the government and acts as a catalyst in generating collaborative activity in the information economy. Since its inception, it has coordinated various programs including the development and implementation of the Government Online Strategy, at the conclusion of which Commonwealth agencies provided more than 1,600 services online, targeted funding to improve telecommunications services and Internet access points, distributed funding for innovation and research excellence, and undertook measures to protect Australia's critical information infrastructure.

Importantly, this has resulted in Australia taking and maintaining a strong place in the leading group of countries across all major information economy indices. There is healthy take-up by businesses and consumers of many forms of digital technologies, including the Internet, e-government transactions, mobile phones, and software applications. In addition, Australia has been a consistent performer in economic growth over the past decade, despite the fluctuating performance of its major trading partners. While the measurement of productivity growth is problematic, the best information suggests that information and communication technologies (ICTs) have contributed up to one-half of the productivity growth over the past growth cycle.

The key mission for NOIE is to strengthen Australia's participation in the information economy for the benefit of all Australians. Participation for consumers and citizens includes improving the rates of Internet adoption in households; facilitating online transactions with government; and enabling social interaction between distant individuals, a situation particularly pertinent to rural Australia. Participation for businesses includes increased confidence in using a secure online transaction environment, collaborative ventures to streamline supply chains, and mechanisms to promote interoperability between organizations.

The technological view of delivering services online has been the principal entry point for engagement in the information economy, requiring existing channels of communication and transactions to be streamlined using the Internet to reduce costs and to promote collaboration and innovative service offerings. As the information economy matures, the above view is evolving to focus increasingly on the importance of intangibles, resulting in new interest in the non-technological components of skills, knowledge, and experience. The combination of these non-technological components alongside the corresponding use of information and communications technologies is the broad thrust of knowledge management. In turn then, knowledge management becomes another entry point for organizations to engage in the information economy and hence the reason why knowledge management is an important area for NOIE.

*** See the writings of Manual Castells, Peter Drucker, and Michel Porter to name but a few.

This chapter investigates the use of two knowledge management tools by NOIE. NOIE's knowledge management activities are unlike many other organizations. The primary intent of using knowledge management tools for NOIE is not for achieving intra-organizational knowledge creation and sharing, but rather for engaging and enacting inter-organizational collaborative activities. NOIE's role as a catalyst in engaging firms and public sector agencies in using technology requires it to heavily invest in collaborative activities.

NOIE's View of Knowledge Management

As a discipline, knowledge management has emerged over the past decade as a tool for organizations to broaden their focus on tangibles to incorporate intangibles. Instruments such as intellectual property rights, concepts such as innovation, and approaches using social and technological networks are all intangible aspects of the information economy. Mass production, economies of scale, and standardized products are steadily giving way to the segmentation of markets, proliferation of niches, and diversity of service offerings. Organizational structures are changing away from hierarchies toward those based on networks. What has caused such significant change over a relatively short period of time?

Perez* provides an interesting perspective on the causative factors associated with this change. She states that major technological revolutions occur at regular periods and that newly developed technologies attract financial capital, leading to the breaking out of new developments that disrupt existing industries. For the current technological revolution, she states that the important trigger was the development of microelectronics in the early 1970s that initiated a new age of information and telecommunications, initially in the United States and later spreading to the rest of the world. More recently, the rise of instant communications and globalized industries has resulted in increased forces of competition, sparking higher rates of productivity and spreading innovations further and faster than that of previous technological revolutions.

The rise of knowledge management can be considered as an early socio-institutional response to the technological revolution of microelectronics. That it has yet to be widely adopted and that its adoption has met with mixed success and relatively low rates of satisfaction* should not call into question the merits of knowledge management, but rather acknowledge the stage of the revolutionary process under way. Over the last 15 years, there has been a frenzy of activity, culminating in the late 1990s manic behavior of financial markets followed by the inevitable dot-com crash. In the view of Perez, it is during the synergy phase that follows the transition period after a financial crash that new institutional frameworks are established that allow financial capital to be recoupled with production and for a new techno-economic paradigm to emerge.

NOIE considers that knowledge management is one of these new socio-institutional frameworks. Paradigmatically, it makes sense when organizations understand that the old ways of working (hierarchies, horizontal integration, and mass markets) will not be as productive as the new ways (networks, specialization, and intangibles). This realization is slowly emerging. The length of the transition period, based on past tech-

---

* Perez, Carlota (2002). Technological Revolutions and Financial Capital: The Dynamics of Bubbles and Golden Ages. Cheltenham, UK: Edward Elgar.

* Rigby, D. K. (2002). *Management Tools 2003: An Executive's Guide*. Boston: Bain and Company.

All NOIE reports are available through our Web site at www.noie.gov.au.

nological revolutions, could be quite lengthy, but the benefits are high for national economies that resolve the socio-institutional situation earlier.

One of these new institutions could include the development of a standard in knowledge management. NOIE is represented on a Standards Australia committee that published an interim standard on knowledge management in early 2003, the first national standards body to achieve this milestone. The standard is not intended to act as a tool where organizations need to adjust their business practices and processes for compliance purposes. Instead, it is context sensitive and outlines a broad methodological approach for identifying and harnessing an organization's knowledge resources by the effective interaction of the enablers of technology, process, content, and people.

As an executive agency of the Federal Public Service, NOIE acts as a small strategy and policy organization. It has little ability to coerce or control the actions of industry or other government agencies. Instead, in order to achieve its aims, NOIE must influence other organizations to adopt knowledge management practices, embrace the information economy, and build and implement strategies and activities to meet their own business objectives.

Knowledge Management in NOIE

In describing NOIE's core processes, workflows, and internal management approaches, the term "knowledge management" is not used widely. Although NOIE does not possess a formal knowledge management strategy, we conduct various internal activities that others would routinely describe as knowledge management. Instead, we use terms such as project teams, briefings, publications, and reports, as well as standard business plans to describe our knowledge-based activities.

As a small policy-based organization, our role is to catalyze, facilitate, coordinate, and lead. Our internal processes, therefore, tend to be relatively fluid and our technological systems relatively basic in comparison with other public service agencies with highly sophisticated applications and databases for program delivery. We make strong use of collaborative office software including electronic mail and structured file sharing systems for the creation, distribution, and internal access of policy documents.

Externally, NOIE makes strong use of its Web site as the major channel for distributing information to the public. All of our reports, media releases, and project status updates are made available online. We have a strong tradition of open access to government information and are highly regarded as a trustworthy and credible source of key knowledge in relation to the Australian information economy. Our Web site, along with its electronic mailing update list, is the cornerstone of our external relationships.

As a small agency with a large and important role, stakeholder relationship management is also critically important. Our collaborative management team makes regular contact with executives from leading Australian businesses and government agencies. Our policy officers have regular contact with industry, government, and academic researchers to keep abreast of current events. Relationships with our stakeholders are highly leveraged to facilitate the communication of key messages of our work.

NOIE's Use of Knowledge Management Tools

Unlike many other organizations in the private sector, issues of beating the competition and improving internal profitability are not key motivational forces on the activities of NOIE. Instead, our motivation comes from generating innovation and boosting productivity in the Australian government and across the business sector. The imperative of this motivation lies in our wish to keep Australia at the forefront in the leading group of nations in the information economy.

Two knowledge management tools are extensively used by NOIE in its dealings with other organizations. The first involves taking a leadership position in embracing cooperative action when dealing with others. Working collaboratively, enabled but not driven by technology, provides a mechanism for allowing other organizations to reap the benefits from participating in the information economy. The second knowledge management tool is the effective use of case studies. These studies demonstrate that the use of technologies coupled with good governance and strategic alignment can provide significant quantifiable monetary benefit.

Leadership in Cooperative Action

As the information economy has the management of knowledge assets as one of its bases, the expansion of the field of knowledge management in business organizations and community groups is vitally important to boosting Australia's international competitiveness. Knowledge management is essentially a communal activity. It is primarily cooperative rather than competitive, favoring, for example, knowledge sharing over knowledge hoarding. Within NOIE, the development of formalized cooperative ventures with other organizations is well advanced. These range from high-level, government-wide strategy committees through issue-focused, inter-organizational communities of practice to lower level consortia who are provided small amounts of highly leveraged funds for the development of e-business joint ventures.

A major example of NOIE's leadership in cooperative action is the establishment of a two-tiered structure for ICT governance in the Commonwealth Government consisting of an Information Management Strategy Committee at the departmental head level, supported by a Chief Information Officer Council. Development of these governance bodies recognizes that government has moved beyond putting its services online to a wider use of technology that spans the whole of government, one that is more integrated, comprehensive, and responsive. Moving government services online has created an expectation from those in business and in the community for further advances in interacting with government.

These further advances require additional investment in technology, and extra funds could be difficult to source, particularly for smaller government agencies. The previous approach that funded technology on an agency-by-agency basis precluded funding for shared infrastructure such as for interoperability and secure communications. The new governance framework includes revised investment frameworks and the development of a model for architecture, governance, and investment for the secure business systems of the Commonwealth.

The whole of government approach to investment also covers new approaches to program and service delivery. The implementation of government services into the online environment in the three-year period from 1998 through to 2001 opened a streamlined pathway for citizens to gain access to government information and conduct transactions with government. More recently, the approach has turned toward e-government encapsulating the use of customer-focused portals and multiple channels for accessing government information and for enabling closer engagement with the Australian community.

NOIE's leadership role in catalyzing cooperative ventures has not been restricted to government service delivery. NOIE was originally established to focus on facilitating the emergence of the business-to-business and business-to-consumer e-commerce elements of the information economy. Once the regulatory impediments had been removed to legitimate electronic transactions, NOIE focused on establishing early success stories in collaborative engagement. Some of these include setting up e-business collaborative forums in a wide range of industries, including health, education, pharmaceuticals, insurance, finance and superannuation, construction, and logistics and transport. NOIE acts as a facilitator and catalyst of these collaborative communities, and we reduce our direct involvement if the community is collaborating effectively.

A small but popular program has been the direct funding provided under the Information Technology On-Line (ITOL) scheme. These grants epitomize the collaborative NOIE approach. A small amount of NOIE funding is provided to a consortia of organizations that have come together to develop a business-to-business e-commerce solution. The grants are provided on a competitive basis, which encourages industry groups and small businesses to identify opportunities that can support collaborative productivity and profitability.

These examples of collaborative communities have emphasized the importance of operating in an inter-organizational manner. In fact, interoperability issues are now central to the public policy objectives of NOIE. Not only is the underlying connectivity between different technology platforms essential for the exchange of structured information, but further advances are now shifting toward the interoperability of systems. NOIE has initiated a series of projects to build interoperability across systems in industry, including e-catalog management and developing supply chains. It has also produced a draft interoperability framework that describes a base set of policies and standards to allow electronic information and transactions to operate seamlessly across government agencies and jurisdictions.

More recently, NOIE has established both internal and external communities of practice. Using a standard electronic mail (Mailman) program and specific Web site pages, these communities of practice aim to share information regarding new developments in particular policy approaches or technological solutions. For example, one internally structured community focuses on the emergence of new technologies that could impact upon various NOIE projects and acts as a radar system to detect potential over-the-horizon issues. Another example is of an externally structured community that focuses on content management in various Australian government agencies and meets every two months with invited guest speakers.

NOIE's capability to adopt a leadership role in facilitating cooperative action is a critical knowledge management tool. Australia is a relatively small player in the global information economy, and we require a greater proportion of participation in order to reach critical mass. By adopting a catalytic role and outlining the benefits of collaborative action, NOIE is able to manage the various stakeholders and achieve win–win outcomes. Both developing formal cooperative action in establishing governance committees and facilitating informal networks of leading industry players are undertaken to improve productivity and commence the transformation of industry and government processes and structure.

Case Studies

The second major tool that NOIE has used to engage participation in the information economy are case studies. Case studies outline the practical application of information and communications technology in specific organizations to demonstrate success stories and help others understand how various issues may impact upon a particular context. In many cases, these case studies are further analyzed to provide additional information such as macroeconomic analyses on the wider economy. Major reports detailing these case studies are produced by NOIE and are available online and in printed format. These have covered e-government, e-business, and effective ICT investment.

In late 2002, NOIE organized a major e-government event in Australia's Parliament House. This event showcased the use of ICT by a variety of government agencies to Australia's ministers, parliamentarians, and senators and their advisors and office staff. The success of the event resulted in the production of a publication that outlines 20 case studies of particularly successful and innovative use of technologies in e-government. These case studies articulate how government service delivery is being transformed through the use of new technology, whether it is transforming transactions, transforming information provision, or transforming processes.

An earlier case study example was in 2001 when NOIE commissioned an analyst company to examine the business gains from introducing e-commerce in small businesses across a wide range of industries. The published report detailed 34 case studies from across Australia. It identified two essential financial benefits from introducing e-commerce: increased revenue from additional sales and savings generated by business efficiencies. The additional revenue came from new clients attracted to the Web site, but a greater proportion of the gross benefit of e-commerce came from efficiency savings including leveraging electronic communications, conducting financial transactions online, and using the Web site as a marketing tool. One of the key findings of the case studies was that fully maximizing the benefit of e-commerce was not possible until more suppliers and customers commenced using the Internet.

A recent set of case studies published by NOIE in 2003 is a report commissioned from Ovum Consulting entitled "Productivity and Organisational Transformation: Optimising Investment in ICT." This report outlined the experience of 18 Australian organizations as they sought to gain maximum benefit from their investments in ICT. The case studies demonstrate that productivity increases of 5% or more are achievable through effective implementation and use of ICT. However, the case studies also show that ICT is only an enabler, a necessary but not sufficient condition for process efficiency and innovation. Appropriate policies and supportive environments are also required, as well as ensuring that the business processes and strategy are right.

The use of case studies by NOIE is a highly effective knowledge-sharing technique. Rather than providing just the key facts or base analysis of a particular situation, case studies provide a storyline to engage readers in the context of a particular organization and in understanding the reasons for the specific approach undertaken. Readers can place themselves in similar situations and consider what they would have done or match the context of a particular case study with their own and assess whether the lessons learned are applicable or whether the storyline could become the future story of their own organization. Additional exercises in obtaining case studies are planned, including the publication of case studies on the effective application of knowledge management in various Commonwealth public sector agencies.

The Road Ahead for NOIE

NOIE's work in strengthening the participation of Australians in the information economy is incomplete. While some impressive productivity gains have been made through the implementation of ICT, these have yet to be fully diffused through businesses and the community. The existing economy is yet to have completed its transformation; new services and approaches have emerged, but we have yet to progress from the transition period between the frenzy of the Internet and telecommunications mania and Perez's Golden Age of the productive application of capital investment in new technologies.

NOIE has drafted its second "Strategic Framework for the Information Economy," updating its previous 1999 version. While our case studies have identified that productivity gains are taking place at the enterprise level through effective implementation of ICT, the next wave of innovative ICT systems cross organizational boundaries, allowing new service delivery arrangements to emerge. The result will require a mutual adjustment of technology, economy, society, and the regulatory framework.

The new strategic framework is currently under consideration by the government. It outlines the strategic intent of government, the policy principles that underpin it, and the policy priorities that inform future government strategies and actions. These priorities cover, among others, information infrastructure development; public sector productivity; the support of innovation and transformation; and the enhancement of capabilities, skills, and knowledge in Australian industry and communities.

Lessons and Recommendations for Other Knowledge Management Practitioners

The key lesson from this chapter for other knowledge management practitioners is to consider extending the established view of internal practices that have organizational benefit to include practices that encompass the activities of other organizations. The application of ICTs is increasingly being applied to inter-organizational activities, including customer relationship management, supply chain logistics, and cooperative inter-organizational standards setting. Knowledge management activities thus far have generally been applied to strategies and activities within an organization. Commencing collaborative ventures with participants from other organizations that have the potential to achieve win–win outcomes is an approach that should be considered by knowledge management practitioners.

An example of this lesson has recently occurred. Various government agencies have established communities of practice to focus their internal resources on common issues such as corporate governance, human resource practices, or content management. The next evolutionary step for these communities of practice is to extend their reach so that communities focusing on similar issues in different organizations can share their knowledge and findings. This does not replace the organizational communities of practice, but provides another level for knowledge sharing to occur and hence improve the potential for further innovation and transformation to develop.

Conclusion

Knowledge management is emerging as a multi-disciplinary framework for organizations to adapt to the demands of the current technological revolution that is disrupting existing industry structures and dynamics. Gaining productivity efficiencies, promoting opportunities for innovation, and transforming processes and structures are all important outcomes that need to be achieved for organizational success. As the business and government environment becomes increasingly networked and technologies are implemented that automate business processes, organizations need to shift their focus of knowledge management from exclusively within the organization to incorporate collaborative knowledge networks with other organizations.

NOIE's approach to inter-organizational knowledge management demonstrates that success can be achieved without coercion or dominance. Promoting the desire for win–win outcomes with potential collaborators and developing cooperative clusters where innovation can flourish are important elements to drive growth within a group of organizations. A broad focus on activating and maintaining knowledge flows between organizations is essential to harness the full potential of this current technological revolution in ICTs.

Knowledge Strategy in Small Organizations: The Office of Small Business, Australia*

18

Christena Singh

> If a little knowledge is dangerous, where is the man who has so much as to be out of danger?
>
> *T.H. Huxley, 1877*

The Office of Small Business is the Australian government's unit for small business policy advice located in the Commonwealth Department of Industry, Tourism, and Resources. It is a small group of approximately 30 staff. Prior to the commencement of the knowledge strategy, the Office of Small Business was organized into five groups structured around main policy advising areas, as depicted in Figure 18.1.

---

* *Editor's Note:* This chapter focuses on KM approaches and tools for small organizations. In most countries, over 90% of the business population consists of small businesses. For small organizations, knowledge flows in the external environment become particularly important (as compared to larger organizations where much KM activity takes place within). Australia's Office of Small Business turned to KM as a way of dealing with voluminous knowledge flows, retaining knowledge of retiring employees, and keeping up with rapidly changing information needs of small businesses in a globalized economy. A knowledge "SWOT" was used as a knowledge audit tool to identify knowledge gaps, and social network analysis (SNA) helped map knowledge sources and flows inside and outside the organization (see also Chapter 6 about SNA in Computer Services Corporation). It was discovered that some sections, such as Small Business Information and Markets, tended to operate as "knowledge seekers," whereas the Finance and Tax Policy and Regulation Reform sections tended to act as "knowledge donors." A correlation between the length of time that staff served with the organization and their use as a source of knowledge by other staff was observable.

A mix of codification and personalization strategies was incorporated in the KM practice, based on electronic file structure and the intranet. A new document management system was devised, with document names based not on organization structure or on staff names, but on key areas of work; this, along with the creation of virtual teams, helped systematize and spur knowledge exchange. Content was also shared via newsletters and forums. Lessons learned include the importance of conducting a knowledge audit before selecting KM tools and the significance of external knowledge flows for small organizations.

Figure 18.1

Structure of the Office of Small Business

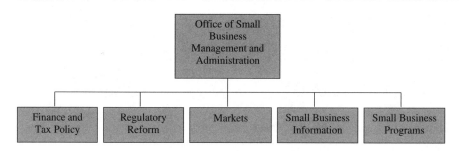

Although the Office of Small Business was organized into a section structure, this structure was relatively informal, with relatively soft boundaries between sections and tasks regularly spanning sections. At the outset of the process, the pervading culture was for staff to make linkages across sections as necessary to achieve their outcomes.

The Importance of KM to the Office of Small Business

As a federal government policy-advising unit, the products of the Office of Small Business are different from those generally encountered in the private sector. Key outputs are policy advice to the ministers responsible for small business. However, underlying this is a range of activities, from coordinating various small business consultative mechanisms to liaising with a wide range of government and private sector organizations to improve the operating environment for small businesses.

With over 1.1 million small businesses in Australia (ABS, 2002), the small business community is exceptionally diverse. Small businesses* make up in excess of 96% of the Australian business population; indeed, the only factor that unifies small business as a group is their size. Consequently, the needs of small businesses are disparate, and to effectively advise on small business policy, a large amount of knowledge on a vast range of topics collected from a large number of different sources is required. The enormous variety of knowledge required for successful operation cannot be emphasized strongly enough. Subject matters for this small group range from a wide array of compliance reduction and taxation issues, across fair trading and market issues, to issues as diverse as e-commerce and drought relief. With timeliness and quality being driving factors for the Office of Small Business, knowledge management will continue to grow in importance. Staff turnover, both inwards and outwards, caused by departmental restructuring, coupled with the high workload and voluminous knowledge flows, highlighted the need for a more strategic approach to knowledge management.

Within six months from conception, the Office of Small Business had developed a knowledge management strategy and had completed the first phases of implementation, with benefits already starting to accrue to the organization. Ongoing implementation and development of the strategy has continued from this point, with the commitment to the knowledge strategy now firmly embedded within the organization.

---

* In Australia, the most widely accepted definition for a small business is a business with fewer than 20 full-time employees, although different definitions are used from time to time.

While the development of the strategy described in this chapter was initiated and strongly supported by senior management, the need for a more strategic approach to knowledge management was also supported by staff. Overall, the level of support for the development and implementation of this strategy was high throughout the organization, with the strategy generally seen to be a useful exercise to assist staff in better handling high workloads.

The quotation from Huxley at the beginning of this chapter played an important part in communicating the need for a knowledge management strategy within the Office of Small Business. It resonated within the organization and served as a starting point for a shared strategy among staff. Since the development of the strategy, this quotation has been used to communicate the knowledge management experience of the Office of Small Business to other organizations. It encapsulates the feeling of not being able to harness enough knowledge in an era where we are flooded with information. It speaks of our quest to be able to bring together what knowledge we have and to use it to the best of our ability. It entices the reader to link the consequence of having too little knowledge with the real prospect of danger.

Tools for Analyzing the Knowledge Context

In developing the knowledge strategy, the Office of Small Business used the results of a knowledge audit process to determine the best options for the specific organizational context. Two key tools were used: a knowledge "SWOT" and social network analysis. These two tools complement each other in their usage. The knowledge SWOT is a useful tool to analyze how an organization deals with knowledge. Social network analysis techniques can analyze what knowledge sources the organization has access to, as well as what gaps exist. Used together, these two tools can provide a comprehensive understanding of the knowledge context of an organization.

Knowledge SWOT

Zack (1999, pp. 130–131) notes that a knowledge strategy should support the business strategy. To do this, Zack proposes four steps: (1) defining a business strategy, (2) determining what knowledge is needed to achieve the business strategy, (3) assessing what knowledge it has, and (4) comparing these two to find out what "knowledge gaps" there are. One method Zack proposes to achieve this is a "knowledge-based SWOT analysis."

The Office of Small Business has already outlined the key knowledge challenge it faces in its operating plan: "There are diverse requirements for skills and knowledge— we need knowledge and understanding of often complex subject matter, but have limited staff."

It is in this context that the senior management of the Office of Small Business decided that the development of a practical knowledge management strategy was to be an organizational priority. Figure 18.2 shows the knowledge-based SWOT analysis for the Office of Small Business at the commencement of the development of the knowledge strategy.

Social Network Analysis

The knowledge management strategy will need to address the weaknesses and threats identified above which form the knowledge gap. However, it is also important to audit the knowledge flows within the organization. Cross and Prusak (2002)

Figure 18.2

Knowledge-based SWOT for the Office of Small Business

STRENGTHS	WEAKNESSES
Culture of sharing information, not hoarding	Knowledge sharing compromised by lack of time/workload
Staff already have large number of sources, both internal and external, to obtain knowledge	Not good at organizing large volume of information – e.g., Chaotic IT drives
Small enough to be able to readily share information	Lack of "early warning system" for new issues – resulting in reactive responses to new situations
	No protocols for storing explicit knowledge
OPPORTUNITIES	THREATS
New knowledge opportunities through new staff	Staff turnover might result in lack of corporate knowledge
Opportunity to gain more knowledge links in new department	Increasing workload might further compromise ability to share knowledge
Opportunity to develop knowledge protocols and strategies before serious problems develop	Historically increasing size of organization will continue to make knowledge sharing more difficult.

contend that analysis of the social networks in an organization can show both where the concentrated flows of information are and, importantly, what flows may be missing. Lee (2002) describes a tool for analysis of knowledge flows used in BHP, using social network analysis. In this example, sources of knowledge were obtained from employees to try and gauge where the flows of tacit knowledge were occurring.

While Cross, Prusak, and Lee concentrate on flows within and between the informal networks that exist within an organization, for small organizations such as the Office of Small Business it is also necessary to focus on the flows of information to an organization from outside. In order to develop an understanding of where the knowledge flows were for the Office of Small Business, standard social network analysis tools were modified to analyze the knowledge flows both within and to the Office of Small Business.

In undertaking this analysis, staff in the Office of Small Business were asked to nominate "who they seek advice from in the area of their expertise," a question based on Lee (2002).

Figure 18.3 shows the internal knowledge flows. As the senior managers obtained knowledge from each person within the organization, the knowledge flows from these individuals have been removed so that other knowledge flows can be more easily identified. The internal analysis shows that some sections, such as Small Business Information and Markets, tended to operate as "knowledge seekers," whereas the Finance and Tax Policy and Regulation Reform sections tended to act as "knowledge donors."

Figure 18.3

The internal knowledge flows in the Office of Small Business

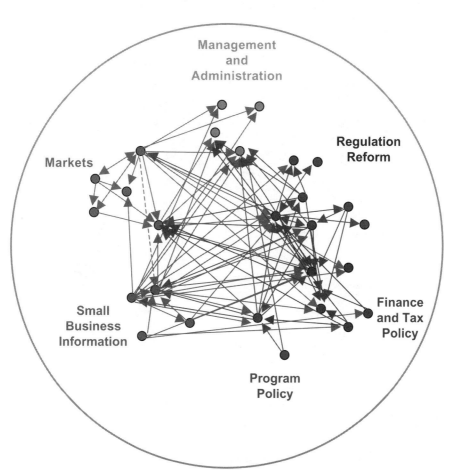

In general, a correlation between the length of time that staff have been with the organization and their use as a source of knowledge by other staff was observable. This is highlighted in the Programs section, a relatively new section created entirely with staff new to the organization, which can be seen to have relatively fewer internal knowledge flows.

Figure 18.4 shows the same analysis, with the inclusion of external knowledge flows. This diagram gives some idea of the richness of the potential knowledge base available to the Office of Small Business. In the diagram, each section within the Office

Figure 18.4

The complete knowledge flows of the Office of Small Business

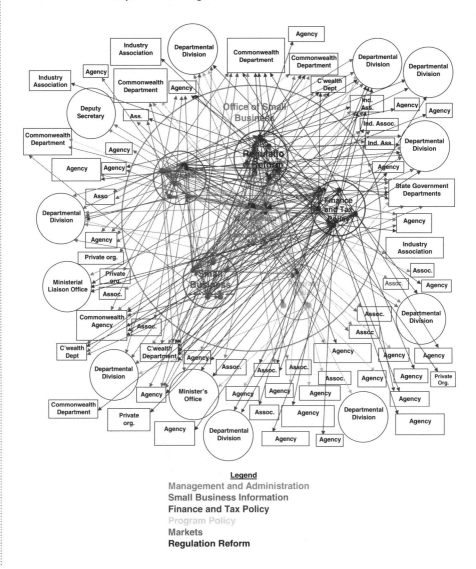

Legend
Management and Administration
Small Business Information
Finance and Tax Policy
Program Policy
Markets
Regulation Reform

of Small Business is represented by a different strength of line, as shown in the legend. External organizations are represented by circles (for other areas within the Department of Industry, Tourism and Resources) or boxes (for other departments or external organizations and industry associations).

Developing the Knowledge Strategy

After studying the results of the knowledge audit, the Office of Small Business developed a knowledge strategy which aimed to better utilize the large amount of knowledge that was available to it. The clear message coming from the social network analysis was that managing relationships with external organizations needed to be a key component of the strategy. Using available knowledge to be able to proactively address issues as early as possible was also a key need, as was organizing available information to be easily accessible. A further area requiring attention was the reduction of knowledge loss through staff movements.

As the Office of Small Business is heavily reliant on uncodified knowledge, the knowledge management strategy comprises a core personalization strategy to enhance the flows of uncodified knowledge and a supporting codification strategy enabled by information technology, as suggested by Hansen, Nohria, and Tierney (1999), to assist in the utilization of knowledge that is able to be codified. The personalization strategy for the Office of Small Business in part acknowledges many current activities that are not formally recognized as being knowledge management and builds upon them. The core elements of the personalization strategy are a relationship map, an emerging issues monitor, after-action reviews, interviews, and knowledge-sharing forums.

While it is important for the strategic emphasis for the Office of Small Business to be on personalization strategies, there is still potential to harness information technology to assist in managing knowledge flows. Two projects identified in this area were improving the electronic file structure and developing a simple intranet site, with improvement of paper file processes being added later as part of the evolution of the strategy.

To enable effective implementation, the knowledge strategy was broken down into a series of discrete projects, chosen to fit within the flexible nature of the organization. These projects are outlined in Table 18.1.

The resources for the implementation of the knowledge strategy were mainly absorbed in-house, with responsibility for the strategy being shared by all staff, although ultimate responsibility for driving the strategy was with the Finance and Tax Policy section. In-house implementation was an effective strategy for the Office of Small Business because of its small size and the importance for all staff to feel ownership of the strategy to be successful. The main resource implication was time of the staff. Despite the fact that actual financial outlays for the strategy were quite low, it would not be correct to say that the implementation of the strategy was done this way to save funds. In an organization of this size and with this level of workload, staff time was incredibly scarce and of high value, requiring a considerable level of commitment from management.

The commencement of the implementation of the strategy was the restructuring of the group drive. This project was started because it was an area that, as was generally agreed, required urgent attention and was capable of producing a quick win for the strategy. However, as the risks of this project were relatively high compared to the other projects, for example, the loss of electronic records, it was necessary for this project to be implemented in a low-stress environment. As implementation was the

Table 18.1

The Knowledge Strategy of the Office of Small Business	
Project	**Key actions**
Relationship management	Management of external relationships to be improved through: • The Office of Small Business Stakeholder Consultation program • Development of supporting IT, in conjunction with E-Business Division, to better track and share information on external contacts • Promotion of better knowledge-sharing practices both throughout the department and with external organizations as appropriate
Emerging issues monitor	Earlier notification of issues to be obtained through: • Monitoring of ministerial correspondence • Better relationship management
After-action reviews	Recommended target projects for after action reviews include: • National Small Business Forum • Small Business Newsletter • Drought and Bushfire Programs
Entry/exit interviews	Implementation of: • Entry interviews for staff joining the Office of Small Business • Exit interviews
Knowledge-sharing forums	Implementation of monthly knowledge-sharing forums providing staff with an opportunity to gain in-depth insights from a variety of staff
Restructured group drive	Analysis and restructuring of electronic file storage
Intranet site	The Office of Small Business will contribute to the department's Internet and intranet redevelopment projects, with the aim of development of an Office of Small Business intranet site
Paper file management	The Office of Small Business will develop processes for improving paper file management

responsibility of all staff, this project was scheduled for a strategic window during the Christmas/New Year holidays, when workloads were slightly lower, giving staff the opportunity to transfer files to the new structure in a less stressful environment. In practice, while the bulk of this project was completed relatively quickly, the project did stretch out due to a heavy, unanticipated workload caused by the bushfires in January 2003, which affected many small businesses, particularly in the Canberra region, and required the development of a new small business program.

Overall, however, this project was very successful and brought many unanticipated benefits. For example, the new file structure was developed to ensure that staff did not continue to save files under folders with names based on organization structure or on staff names; instead, the new structure was based on key areas of work. This meant that staff now had to look through other folders on the system and could see more easily what work was being done by other areas, resulting in the sharing of knowledge and creation of new linkages. While this project was initially considered to be IT based rather than culture based, in retrospect the sharing of knowledge through this project was much stronger than anticipated.

The New Structure of the Office of Small Business

A year into the knowledge management strategy, the Office of Small Business underwent a restructuring to better align itself with evolving business requirements. A key part of this was an attempt to describe the organizational structure in a more accurate way. The Office of Small Business worked in practice without the silos that can so often become an impediment to effective knowledge transfer in many organizations. A flexible, flat working environment such as the one that operated in the Office of Small Business does not easily sit well within the traditional organization charts that consist of interlinked hierarchical boxes, as seen in Figure 18.1. However, there is an additional problem with the traditional type of organizational structure chart, apart from not accurately describing an organization like the Office of Small Business; that is, having such a visual tool may make the organization psychologically try to confine itself within those boundaries. Having separate boxes for each organizational unit tends to make employees think within those boxes, rather than try to form the linkages that are so important to the effective sharing of knowledge.

As a result, the new organizational structure of the Office of Small Business tries to overcome these problems by moving to a structure illustrated by a series of interlinking circles, as seen in Figure 18.5. This structural paradigm more accurately reflects how the organization operates. It is a structure that lacks the silos of traditional models, with the physical interlinkages between sections being formally recognized and encouraged as an operating standard. It also formally recognizes the important role of virtual teams within the organization. In this model virtual teams are seen as temporary features brought together within the organization to address specific temporal issues. In this instance the model shows two virtual teams: one team looking at drought policy for small businesses—a feature of the Australian operating environment during 2002–2003—and the second team aiming to look at evaluation of various program and policy elements.

Lessons Learned

Overall, the key lesson learned from the development of the knowledge strategy for the Office of Small Business was the value of conducting a knowledge audit to have a firm foundation to construct a knowledge strategy on. When discussing the knowledge audit process there seems to be one question that consistently bothers those trying to develop knowledge management practices—namely, how do you develop the strategy from the audit?

In fact, the process of the knowledge audit made the development of the strategy relatively simple. The analysis of the knowledge SWOT and knowledge flows brought the key needs of the organization into sharp relief. From that point it was merely a matter of selecting tools from the literature that would address the knowledge needs and fit well within the organizational context. Without going through the process of a knowledge audit, one could easily be left wondering where to start or could just randomly select knowledge tools which happened to have some appeal, rather than those with a good strategic fit.

In addition, the importance of communication and shared vision for the strategy was crucial to its acceptance and implementation. Consultation sessions took place with staff throughout the process, and these engendered a high degree of ownership.

Figure 18.5

New structure of the Office of Small Business

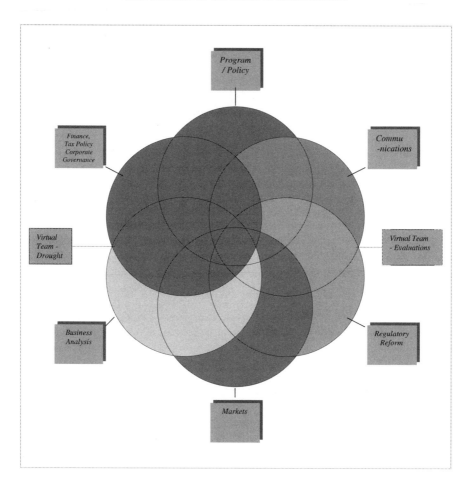

In addition to assisting with the acceptance of the process, constructive two-way communication sessions, combined with openness for continual feedback, led to many positive modifications to the strategy.

Concluding Remarks

In conclusion, there are two key messages that I would like to emphasize. The first is the importance of having a sound foundation to build a knowledge strategy. Not only does the analysis that takes place as part of a knowledge audit highlight the key knowledge challenges, it also points the way forward in tackling them. As always, the most difficult part of finding a solution is defining what the problem really is. Once the underlying nature of the problem is discovered, solutions become apparent.

Second, there are many small organizations for whom knowledge strategies are essential to be able to effectively leverage their core strengths—knowledge strategy is not solely the domain of large businesses. In most countries, over 90% of the business population consists of small businesses. Indeed, small organizations are becoming increasingly relevant in today's society, where e-globalization continues to shrink the world. In the future, there will be a greater range of opportunities for small organizations that are able to respond more easily to changing environments in innovative ways. The challenge for the knowledge practitioner, however, is that with small organizations the external environment becomes more important, and this adds complexity to the development of a knowledge strategy. For a large organization, the task of knowledge practitioners has been relatively confined within organizational boundaries. For the smaller organization there are no bounds—knowledge can come from anywhere—making the challenge far more complex. Dealing with these challenges and ambiguities is something knowledge practitioners will have to become increasingly more comfortable with in the future.

References

Australian Bureau of Statistics (ABS) (2002). *Small Business in Australia*. ABS Catalogue 1321.0, Commonwealth of Australia, Canberra.

Cross, R. and Prusak, L. (2002). The People Who Make Organizations Go—or Stop, *Harvard Business Review*, June 2002, 105–112.

Hansen, M., Nohria, N., and Tierney, T. (1999). What's Your Strategy for Managing Knowledge?, *Harvard Business Review*, March–April, 107–114.

Lee, Lawrence Lock. (2002). Knowledge Sharing Metrics for Large Organizations, in Morey, D., Maybury, M., and Thuraisingham, B., Eds., *Knowledge Management: Classic and Contemporary Works*. Cambridge: MIT Press, pp. 409–413.

Zack, M.H. (1999). Developing a Knowledge Strategy, *California Management Review*, 41(3) Spring, 125–145.

A Day in the Life of a Rolls-Royce Knowledge Manager*

19

Darius Baria

> My advice to anyone considering knowledge management is just **go and do it**. It pays off.
>
> *Mike Zdybel*
> *Head of Propulsion System Design, Defence Aerospace, Rolls-Royce*

Tuesday, Summer, 2003

It is a glorious warm and balmy morning. You could not have guessed we were in England!

Before I tell you about what is going on in the wonderful world of knowledge management (KM) here, I had better clear up one thing from the start: We are Rolls-Royce plc, not Rolls-Royce Motor Cars Limited.

---

* *Editor's Note:* Written in a delightfully witty "diary" style ("a day in the life of . . ."), this chapter shows how KM tools can be smoothly integrated into daily activities of knowledge workers—provided adequate attention is provided to design, discipline, and alignment with existing work patterns. Rolls-Royce launched its KM system in 1996. Project reviews, benchmarking, and knowledge communication behaviors are strongly promoted. Knowledge communication occurs not just via the intranet, but also by traditional methods like manuals, posters, training courses, guidelines, presentations, and checklists. Capacity building is enhanced via The Capability Intranet with single-point access to quality procedures and KM techniques. Structured Knowledge Auditing is used to provide visualization of key knowledge areas via group and individual interviews.

The KM Lessons Learned Log has detailed procedures for knowledge validation and peer review; dedicated staff help maintain the log. People Pages capture expertise profiles of company employees. Lessons Learned Reviews are conducted after events to enable replication of best practices and avoiding mistakes. The company also has a corporate Community of Practice Leader to strengthen CoP activity. All these activities are coordinated by a KM head who keeps a vigilant eye on company news to identify potential candidates for Lessons Learned and even sends promotional e-mails about KM tool usage. Key lessons to share include the importance of starting KM initiatives small and simple with proven tools that can ensure a successful pilot, promoting KM practices by word of mouth, and the use of surveys to assess and prioritize KM projects.

Rolls-Royce plc

Rolls-Royce plc is a global company providing power on land, sea, and air. The company has established leading positions in civil aerospace, defense, marine, and energy markets.

For more information, go to www.rolls-royce.com.

Let me introduce myself. I head the knowledge management activities in Defence Aerospace (DA) Engineering—part of the business that strives to deliver innovative solutions that meet customer requirements at ever-reducing costs—a ripe ground for KM and knowledge sharing. I have been leading the KM activities here in Bristol for two years and previously had a similar KM role in the airlines side of the business based in Derby.

8:00–8:30 AM—E-mails

One e-mail of interest in my inbox this morning was from a department that has just completed a KM benchmarking exercise. This department has yet to embark on a KM program, but a few people there are really keen to get started. As with most "new starts," I recommended to them a couple of weeks ago that they complete the benchmarking first to establish their knowledge-sharing strengths and weaknesses, as well as their knowledge needs and assets.

Benchmarking is a good way to see if your department:

- Has a knowledge-sharing environment
- Understands its knowledge needs and assets
- Shares experience between people
- Documents and structures its knowledge well

I will analyze their results later and then suggest a couple of simple suitable KM tools to get things kick-started. I have learned over the last few years to start small and simple with proven tools that can ensure a successful pilot.

8:30–10:00 AM—Knowledge Acquisition Project Reviews

This morning I had three half-hour review sessions. The first one was with three modern apprentices who are doing a knowledge acquisition project. They have their scoping review tomorrow—a critical process quality control gate to ensure that the customer, users, experts, and other key stakeholders understand what the deliverable will be, what the business benefits of the work are, and what "knowledge capture topics" it will and will not cover.

Knowledge acquisition (KA) is a great tool used for quickly and effectively eliciting tacit knowledge. It is a proven way of acquiring new knowledge quickly, getting to know a department, finding out who the right people to ask are, and being able to start being "useful" and productive in a short space of time.

KA in Rolls-Royce has gone from strength to strength since being continually improved by lessons learned and being strongly linked to business improvements. To date, approximately 220 people have completed 150 KA projects in the last 7 years and the demand for them is continuing to grow.

A typical KA project is 12 weeks long, but some can range from just a few days to a year. (Most projects are 12 weeks long because this is the length of a placement for a graduate trainee or modern apprentice.) In DA Engineering, all graduate trainees must complete a KA placement before going into a line job, following the success of previous projects.

Graduate trainees and apprentices, however, are not the only people who do KA projects. Other people that have completed successful projects include people (at all levels) moving into a new department, job relocation, re-skilling, secondments, industrial trainees, and people looking to move onto a new career path. The training is conducted in the form of face-to-face training sessions and workshops supplemented by online help. The training is delivered as and when the trainees need it, as opposed to a solid training schedule at the start of their project.

One of my responsibilities as the knowledge manager is not only to ensure the quality of the deliverable, but to make sure that it is a valuable learning experience for the person conducting the project and beneficial to the company.

Not many people have a clear understanding of what KM is and, importantly, what it is not. People on a KA project learn about a whole range of KM tools and techniques that could help them during their placement and in their work afterwards. We do get a lot of KM enthusiasts and champions coming out of a KA placement which helps to spread KM organically across the company.

They also learn of the origins of KM in Rolls-Royce. Although we have always been managing our knowledge over the years, we started formally calling it "knowledge management" in 1996 when the Capability Intranet was developed and introduced. It was in the same year that Rolls-Royce was involved with a business process reengineering project involving industry and academia. This developed a process for capturing knowledge and publicizing it in a user-friendly form, which has been continually adapted and improved into our KA process over the years.

Nevertheless, we do not randomly do KA on a whim. One way of prioritizing and focusing KA projects is with our expert prioritization process.

Expert prioritization is a straightforward method that identifies and prioritizes which expert's knowledge is most at risk and needs capturing. The priority list is reviewed at management meetings to discuss which KA projects are carried out first.

Expert prioritization was born out of a need to have a structured way to prioritize KA.

Following the pilot KA projects in DA Engineering, word of mouth spread the benefits and I was swamped with requests for projects. I adapted the knowledge auditing methodology to help.

A simple two-sheet questionnaire was sent to the director of engineering and his direct reporters and then cascaded throughout the organization to department heads, chiefs, managers, and team leaders. The questionnaire asks who are the top experts in the department and what do they know. It then asks them to score the knowledge areas with the same criteria as the knowledge audit.

These questionnaires' scores were then collated and put into a spreadsheet so that the scores could be summed. From the experts and knowledge areas with the highest scores, a "Top 40" list of experts and topics was produced in order of knowledge risk.

This Top 40 list was then used in a management meeting and discussed to agree which experts and topics should be considered for KA first. The list derived from the process is never definitive as the basic process is not scientific, but it does help to quantify priorities and give the management a good start.

Expert prioritization is carried out in DA Engineering every 6 months because experts retire or move to another department, people's circumstances can change as well, and therefore the Top 40 list changes. This updated list has enabled DA Engineering to have a current KA project plan for the next 12 months. Most of the topics of the KA project ongoing today are a result of the expert prioritization process that we have pioneered and adopted.

There is a lot of knowledge being captured and validated at the moment, but it is of little use unless we share and apply it effectively. In KA projects, the chair of the pre-project launch review gate asks the question, "What is the best way to share this knowledge so that people can easily access it and so that it delivers the most benefit?"

The answer is not always a Web site. It is far too easy these days to get blinkered into thinking that a pretty looking Web site is the answer. The outputs of KA projects now vary from manuals, posters, training courses, guidelines, presentations, and checklists. We use whatever is the best medium to share that knowledge depending on the type of knowledge and the users' needs.

If it has been agreed that a Web site is the better medium, we have a global Capability Intranet to locate the site.

The **Capability Intranet** is a useful information tool very similar to the Internet or World Wide Web. It is intended to provide quick and easy access to all the latest information about how to complete a task.

The Capability Intranet gives access via a single route to:

- The Company Quality Management System containing the corporate mandatory procedures
- All materials in support of the procedures; this includes:
  — Standards
  — Detailed working practices, technical methods, prompt lists, criteria, and best practice necessary to complete a high-quality job
- Technologies and capabilities
- Specific project reports, which provide examples of good practice

All of the information is held centrally, making it easier to keep it up to date and ensure that everyone uses the same reference material. The advantage of this is that tasks are completed consistently and individuals know that the information is complete and up to date. Making important information easier to maintain minimizes the errors that are made when using incomplete or out-of-date information.

10:00–11:00 AM—Structured Knowledge Auditing Meeting

This meeting was with a departmental management team that wanted to find out more about structured knowledge auditing and whether it could help them.

Structured Knowledge Auditing is a methodology to provide visualization of a knowledge area that is supported by descriptive data to help managers take direct control of a knowledge resource.

The technique is based upon group and individual interviews. The output is a "knowledge dependency map" of a knowledge resource area. It displays the structure of knowledge, not the knowledge itself. The technique also incorporates scoring each of these knowledge areas to identify which of these areas are most at risk. Knowledge auditing allows managers to make informed decisions about organizing, developing, and protecting their knowledge resource.

11:00–11:30 AM—Entry into KM Lessons Learned Log

Another e-mail I received this morning was from one of the KA project trainees saying how much they had benefited from a "KA Coffee Morning" we had last week. This was when all the people currently doing KA got together over some coffee and biscuits for an hour to share what has been happening in their projects, what has worked well, and what has not.

Actually, last week was the first time we did this, and it was a pilot to see how it would go. Judging by the feedback I have had, I would recommend this to my KM colleagues around the company. To share this experience of what worked well, I entered it into our corporate lessons learned log under the KM section.

Lessons Learned Log and Process

The corporate lessons learned log is an online holding place for all lessons on all topics. Anyone with access to the intranet can submit a lesson learnt to the log and allocate it to the most relevant subject area or business group. This log is also used to record new advances in the company's capability and changes to the technical content of the company's best practice.

New lessons are temporarily held in the "unapproved" folder of the group until they are "sentenced." New lessons are submitted to the capability owners for peer review. If accepted, the lesson will be entered in the "approved" lessons learned log for the appropriate topic web. If rejected, the topic capability owner contacts the original submitter of the lesson to explain why. Rejected lessons are also stored online.

The Rolls-Royce lessons learned process is controlled by a corporate procedure that defines the process by which new knowledge and experience, resulting from these lessons, are incorporated into the Rolls-Royce quality system—a framework within which working processes are recorded and mandated across the company. The quality system also comprises the Capability Intranet that contains best practice and guidelines to supplement the procedures.

When carrying out a task, people will learn how to perform the task better, find problems with completing the task, or discover new capability. It is essential that these new methods, hazards, or capabilities be recorded to ensure that the next person produces a better quality deliverable.

One of the departments here in DA Engineering has one of the most extensive and most used lessons learned logs within the corporate log. Keys to success here are:

- A dedicated person who maintains the lessons and logs and arranges lessons sentencing meetings
- Senior management support, insisting on the use of the lessons learned log for all work
- Popular use due to the log being easy to use, updated, and helpful in tasks

The person who maintains the local lessons learned log also structures and coordinates the relevant Capability Intranet Web sites and runs the department's people pages.

People Pages

Previous research has shown that engineers spend a large percentage of their time searching for the best source of both tacit and explicit knowledge. Despite a comprehensive telephone directory, many people in Rolls-Royce do not find it that easy to locate the right expert among 37,000 employees who knows what they need to know.

Several expert "people pages" have been set up across the company in different areas, and the most successful ones, like many other KM activities, are those that have someone with the time and resources to maintain these sites. Eventually, these separate people pages will be combined into one corporate system that can be accessed and searched by anyone. Several across-company meetings have been held to get a joint consensus of what format this system should take.

The local departmental people pages I mentioned above are proving to be very popular, even in their early pilot stage. It is a simple system that allows a user to search for experts by topics and sub-topics, by keywords, and also by geographical location. The keys to success here are ease of use, regular updates, management support, and word of mouth to communicate the benefits.

11:30 AM–12:30 PM—Promotional E-mail

I spent this hour putting together an e-mail to send out to people within a team in engineering to promote the usage of simple KM tools. I have already given some of the team a briefing on this, which was added to the agenda of one of their regular meetings. This e-mail was to follow up on that briefing and to provide further information.

As quite a few team members could not make it to the briefing, I ensured the e-mail was eye catching, easy to read, and tailored to help the reader, rather than just saying "look at these wonderful tools we have to offer." The e-mail then linked them to Web pages with further information as necessary.

12:30–1:00 PM—Lunch

While leafing through our company newspaper at lunchtime, I came across a story about a successful trial of an engine. I thought then about how other projects and teams could learn from successes, and a lot of triggers for these come from the newspaper, communications, or briefings.

I contacted the engine program director, congratulated her, and suggested that now was a good time for the team to carry out a lessons learned review.

Lessons Learned Reviews

A Lessons Learned Review (LLR) is a facilitated team meeting that has the objective of capturing lessons learnt during a project. A *lesson learned* is an action that should or should not be performed the next time a similar project is run. Rolls-Royce's LLRs are based on the U.S. Army's after-action reviews and BP's retrospects and have since been adapted to suit our company's needs.

I always recommend to people that an LLR should be held soon after a phase or gate of a project is completed and soon after deliverable has been produced. This is because:

- More team members are available.
- The project is still fresh.
- Issues are "unvarnished."
- Learning can be applied straight away.

The time required for an LLR is estimated by allowing between 20 and 30 minutes per team member. This gives ample time for all the team members to contribute and discuss the lessons.

The process is so simple that it only takes an hour or so to train a facilitator, as long as the trainee already possesses some proficiency in facilitating. The facilitator then guides the participants through a simple process that covers the original objectives, what actually happened, what could have gone better, and what went well.

The benefits of an LLR are obvious, and after attending such an event, participants quickly see how LLRs certainly help themselves, their colleagues, new starts, and the rest of the company. Other proven benefits include:

- Best practice is repeated
- Known mistakes are avoided
- Better understanding of project
- Improved performance
- Time saved
- Reduced costs
- Better customer satisfaction

An LLR can deliver a lot of lessons (for example, one 1-day review produced over 100 useful lessons). Initially, they will be technically unapproved lessons, which have been evaluated, sentenced, and signed off as approved lessons according to the corporate quality procedure as mentioned above. This validation of the lessons usually happens at a separate meeting. Then these lessons are entered into the corporate lessons learned log or into a Hazard Indication Prompt List (a type of checklist to use when doing a task), process documentation, best practices, or even a relevant topic web depending on where best this knowledge can be shared. These lessons should enable the next project team to perform even better by ensuring good practice is repeated and known mistakes are avoided.

In engineering, 21 LLRs have been held to date here with over 90% of the participants (on average) saying that they have "learned many valuable lessons which they can apply." Word of mouth alone has communicated the benefits of this simple technique—one of the keys to its success. It is important that LLRs are conducted throughout projects, for example, at formal stages of a gated process, and not just at the end. DA Engineering is ensuring that the reviews are embedded into its program management and is also training project managers in this technique.

An LLR is great for generating lots of lessons and for the participants to understand their teammates' objectives. However, there is an even more important step afterwards to make sure that the lessons are not only shared, but *learned*, i.e., people change their behavior the next time a similar project or activity is done. We do this with the aid of the lessons learned log and the process on how to deal with lessons as mentioned above.

1:00–2:30 PM—Video Knowledge Acquisition

This afternoon's session was fascinating as it was the first time we have tried the use of video for KA purposes. We had a pre-meeting a couple of weeks ago to first discuss how it was going to work, and we scoped out which topics we were going to cover using our knowledge auditing techniques.

Attending the session was the primary expert, the "customer" of the project (the team leader), another expert, a new start to the department, the cameraman, and myself. We felt that it was important for the primary expert to talk to an audience; the customer, the other expert, and the new start were there to ask questions from their different perspectives as potential future users of this knowledge.

After just a few minutes of recording, it was obvious just how rich the knowledge capture was using video. However, we were also aware not to overdo the use of video and to switch to audio recording and then other KA techniques as appropriate, depending on the type of knowledge being captured. I cannot wait to see the finished product!

2:30–3:00 PM—More Entries into the KM Lessons Learned Log

Just like at the end of any other KM activity, we did a "mini lessons learned review" at the end of the video KA session. Because this was our first time, there were certainly lots of lessons to share with my KM colleagues.

3:00–4:30 PM—KM Community of Practice Minutes

I set aside this time to write up the minutes, actions, and, at the risk of repeating myself, lessons learned from last week's KM community of practice (CoP) meeting, which this time was held here in Bristol. We have about 250 members, mostly based in the United Kingdom, and the community is steadily growing around the world.

Just like any other good community, we have a dedicated facilitator who updates the Web site, administers the discussion boards, and sets up face-to-face meetings. Even though we may be KM practitioners or enthusiasts, we still need prompting and the community reenergized every now and again by a passionate facilitator.

Last week's one-day meeting had presentations and discussion grouped into two themes: CoPs and measurement. We try to have people presenting from all over the company and at any level of KM implementation. We also have external guest speakers to help share and understand good practice from different organizations. Some of the speakers are from our KM research collaborations with universities, which are a vital part of our technology acquisition strategy as a knowledge intensive business.

This community is proving to be a good forum to share experiences, good practices, and lessons learned between people who are striving to get more value and business benefit from better KM.

Our community facilitator tried a basic **storytelling** technique at the start of the day, and this helped people meet each other, break the ice, and share stories of why they were here and what they wanted to get out of the day. Just before the end of the day—you can probably guess what is coming up—we did a mini LLR to find out how we could improve the community meetings even further the next time we met.

4:30–5:00 PM—E-mails

I did a final clearing up of my inbox before heading off home. There were a couple of postings from the CoPs I belong to.

For Rolls-Royce, a CoP is "a facilitated network of people sharing knowledge and experiences across organizational and geographical boundaries."

Communities already exist within Rolls-Royce, and they can be found in every type of environment. They consist of a number of people who, over the years, have developed a method of working which suits both themselves and their business aims.

There is a now a corporate CoP leader who is trying to expand on these communities and make them accessible to a wider audience. The hardware is becoming available to allow a wider group of people to communicate on a regular basis where more traditional face-to-face meetings are not possible. Web (Intranet)-based discussion groups, e-mail group folders, and videoconferencing are all being used to help people communicate in an effective manner with people all over the world who deal with the same problems.

CoPs have been proven to benefit both the business and the individual.

Recommendations for KM Practitioners Based on the Rolls-Royce Experience

- Start with simple techniques
- Pilot projects
- Use everyday language
- Utilize word of mouth
- Ensure business benefits
- Learn lessons
- Continually improve

- Problems can be aimed at specific groups, allowing both a real and a virtual resource to discuss issues.
- Best practices can be spread throughout a global community.
- New strategies can be implemented quickly and more efficiently.
- Individuals can increase their own knowledge of a specific subject by having greater access to peers both locally and globally.
- There is a greater chance to increase personal profiles by dealing with larger audiences.
- If individuals are given the opportunity to choose a level of involvement in subjects of particular interest, the amount of job satisfaction is increased.

Sixty communities have been set up in Rolls-Royce to date. The top five communities (in terms of posting activity and participation) were investigated to find out what has made them successful. The common threads to these successful communities are:

- Regular community meetings, at least once every 3 months
- Active facilitator to encourage people to use the community
- Support from management to use the community

5:00 PM

My inbox is clear and lessons have been shared (of course, I must continually ensure they are learned). It's time to go home and enjoy the rest of the sunshine!

Creativity, the Knowledge Connector*

20

Nel M. Mostert and Hilbert J. Bruins Slot

Creativity is destruction, tearing down old insights, notions, thoughts or feelings in order to create something new.

Pablo Picasso

Introduction

If knowledge fails, creativity is the key to solutions. Following Arthur Koestler's (1964) bisociation terminology, we define creativity as the process leading to a sudden problem-solving insight in the connection between two formerly independent separate knowledge domains. The issue is to facilitate connecting—unexpectedly—corporate knowledge. Does this build on to another chaos theory? No, it does not. Creativity can be managed successfully. If you would like to know how, read on.

Unilever is dedicated to meeting the everyday needs of people everywhere. The two divisions of Unilever, Home & Personal Care and Unilever Bestfoods, provide washing powder, shampoo, toothpaste, teas, ice cream, meal components, and oils and spreads for consumers all over the world. In 2002, Unilever's turnover was €52 billion, which generated an operating margin of 14.9% (Unilever, 2002a).

Unilever has a clear goal to drive the growth of their world-leading brands through fast, large-scale, exciting innovation. Research and development are at the heart of

---

* *Editor's Note:* This chapter situates the role of IT-enabled creativity tools within overall idea generation mechanisms in organizations. Creativity is a key knowledge connector and has been managed successfully in companies like Unilever as part of a formalized innovation process with a strict discipline and selection methodology. Projects are continuously fed into the innovation funnel, and the Creative Pathways Program and Creativity Awareness Program are used as social tools to enhance the use of creativity. A creative culture has the right mix of attitude, behavior, skills, structures, and environment.

Creativity sessions at Unilever are supported by various tools, ranging from basic flip-charts and Post-Its to advanced IT tools like MindJet's Mindmanager and Invention Machine's TechOptimizer. These tools help researchers state research and engineering problems correctly, manage technical knowledge, make predictions about product evolution, and resolve potential technological contradictions by analyzing over 2.5 million patents. However, use of these tools must be augmented by measures of the success of creativity sessions, as well as identification and removal of potential barriers to innovation.

this, combining world-class sciences with deep consumer insight to produce revolutionary new technology that delights consumers. In 2002, Unilever spent €1.2 billion on research and development (R&D).

The Unilever R&D programs are executed by some 8,000 people in product category dedicated Global Technology Centers, Regional Innovation Centers, and Unilever R&D organizations. World-class science and technology have driven an ever-increasing stream of innovations across the range of the famous brands of Unilever like Knorr, Lipton, Slim-Fast, Axe, Dove, Cif, and Andrélon. R&D professionals have recently delivered breakthrough innovations such as Becel/Flora Pro.Activ margarine that reduces blood cholesterol and Persil Revive for the treatment of "dry clean only" clothes in the home.

The authors of this chapter are based at Unilever R&D Vlaardingen, The Netherlands. The scientific research in Vlaardingen aims at the supply of innovative products and processes and can be subdivided into applied research, in cooperation with the Regional Innovation Centers spread throughout the world, and fundamental research, generally in cooperation with universities and scientific institutions.

Rationale

Innovation is seen as the major key to long-term profit of any organization. Underpinning this view, Unilever experiences increasingly shortened product life cycles combined with consumers that are more demanding and discerning and that require convenience plus, above all, quality and value for money. Next to that, being first to market is now more important than ever with products that become increasingly more science and technology sensitive. This means that Unilever needs to deliver new products that are superior to existing ones, meet consumer needs better in performance or ease of use, are more environment friendly, or are just cheaper.

Unilever recognizes that the key success factors to achieve this include a formalized innovation process with a strict discipline and methodology for selection of new projects. This process needs top-management commitment and cross-functional project teams with dedicated resources guided by professional project management. To show progress, measures for innovation are required, and creativity should be encouraged, combined with a passion to win.

> Well planned and managed innovation, inspired by top leadership, is the only way to gain share and margin ahead of competitors.

To achieve well-managed innovations, Unilever adopted in 1996 the Innovation Process Management (IPM) (Kahn, 2002), a way of working, as the key driver to both *"doing the right things"* and *"doing things right."*

For the former (*doing the right things*) each innovation project is mapped on a Consumer/Technology Matrix. In this matrix, one axis describes the consumer value perception, ranging from "new core product" to "no change." The other axis describes the enabling technology from "radical" to "base" technology. The position of each proposed project in this matrix is then used as a selection criterion for execution of that project and it enables strengthening of the portfolio management.

The latter (*doing things right*) is secured by the principle that all innovation activities, undertaken in the form of projects, are subjected to a structured review process, guarded by the business for which the innovation is relevant. This review process—the core of Unilever's IPM—is organized in the form of a number of phases and gates at critical stages in the project lifetime cycle. At each gate, a gatekeeper reviews the

Figure 20.1

The innovation funnel

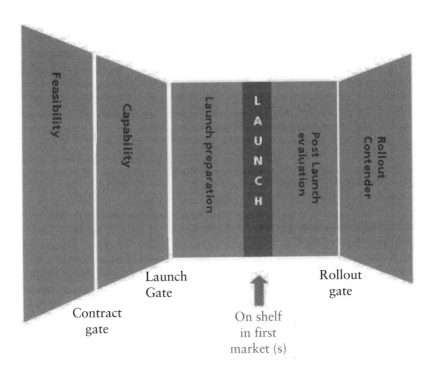

projects that have arrived and makes a go/no-go decision on the future of that project. Thus, the business case of each project is developed. Figure 20.1 illustrates this process as the so-called innovation funnel.

- *Criteria for passing the Charter gate—The idea has consumer merit. It is relevant to business strategy, there is some indication of how it might be done, and there are resources to explore its feasibility.*
- *Criteria for passing the Contract gate—The gatekeeper is confident that the proposed innovation is worthwhile and can be realized to a degree of confidence that justifies the allocation of material company resources and/or capital in order to bring it to market.*
- *Criteria for passing the Launch gate—The brand mix is complete in all essentials, it is robust, and it is ready for launch.*
- *Criterion for passing the Rollout gate—There is sufficiently robust evidence of success in the marketplace to declare the project a contender for roll out.*

In order to be sure that the innovation funnel is constantly filled with new projects, Unilever has suggested practical processes to address the challenge of "feeding the funnel." They are based upon the leading edge practices of a wide range of innovative companies and individuals from both inside and outside Unilever. The processes are focused on the three tasks involved in discovering and fostering new ideas (Unilever, 1977):

1. Building new understanding—A deep understanding of both consumers and technologies provides an essential foundation for successful innovation. Not only will the building of this understanding help stimulate specific innovation ideas, it will also provide a sound basis on management judgements and decisions to be made.

2. Finding new angles—Even in an environment of "understanding," there is always a need to find new angles that might stimulate unexpected insights and ideas. Marcel Proust once said, "The real art of discovery consists not in finding new lands, but in seeing with new eyes." To increase the chances of success, efforts must be made to discover new dimensions and view things from different perspectives.

3. Nurturing new ideas—The potential significance of new insights is easy to miss. New ideas are easy to kill. There are always good reasons for seeing them as unnecessary, costly, risky, or irrelevant. The problem is that the ideas which are obvious winners have probably been thought of already. If new ideas are to stand a chance, they must be nurtured with time, space, and encouragement.

In order to comply with the above three tasks, creativity is recognized as a key skill.

Chronology of Creativity Programs at Unilever

In late 1998, Unilever R&D started the Creative Pathways program in order to get a grip on the creative process. First, several facilitators are trained in the Synectics methodology (http://www.synecticsworld.com/home.htm). The Synectics Creative Problem Solving Method stimulates creative thinking by establishing connections between aspects of the problem at hand and contexts outside the problem area, allowing novel ideas to emerge. It tackles a number of questions. If creativity is the basis for new ideas, where do these come from? Where are they born? Which habitat is necessary? How to change into a culture in which employees feel free to come forward with ideas that might lead to innovations? Where to start? At Unilever R&D Vlaardingen, the Creativity Awareness Program (Mostert and Frijling, 2001) is internally designed to answer these questions and to build a creative culture.

Architecture of Creativity Practice

The Creativity Awareness Program (CAP)

The CAP comprises three elements:

1. Creativity Awareness Model
2. Creativity Climate Questionnaire
3. Creativity Awareness Training Modules

Individual members, teams, departments, or entire organizations looking for ways to enhance the use of creativity can use the CAP. Where creativity often seems to be a vaguely described concept, this program makes creativity tangible and concrete. It focuses on measuring and learning to use creativity. Participants are offered a set of tools to tap and use their own creativity and that of the team and to implement the results in the work and structures of the organization. The CAP leads to creative problem solving, which in turn leads to new projects, patents, products, and processes and the desired cultural changes as found, for example, in a new teamwork mentality.

The Creativity Awareness Model

The first element of the CAP is the Creativity Awareness Model. This model is derived from the barrier areas for creativity as defined by "?Whatif!" (2003). It defines five criteria for creativity: attitude, behavior, skills, structures, and environment. The model not only emphasizes an idea management structure, but also considers cultural aspects of the organization. The following is a summary of the five criteria for creativity and specific areas of attention within each criterion.

1. "Attitude" is the perception of employees of their own creativity. Employees learn to pay attention to their own flexibility, share their creativity, and learn the effects that mental models might have on creativity.
2. "Behavior" refers to the actions and interactions of the team with respect to creativity. Its areas of attention include team behavior, team composition, coaching style, and how the team deals with risk.
3. "Skills" comprise knowledge, learning, and the application method of creativity skills during work or problem-solving processes.
4. "Structures" refer to idea management structures and the organizational processes that stimulate creativity, like creativity measuring plans, rewards, and availability of time, money, and resources.
5. "Environment" includes top-management support, strategy definition, decision-making processes, communication, corporate culture, workplace layout, and maintenance of external contacts.

The Creativity Climate Questionnaire

As the need arose to make creativity measurable, the second element of the CAP, the Creativity Climate Questionnaire (CCQ), was developed. The CCQ can be used as a self-assessment tool. The employee fills in the CCQ, determines his/her score using a benchmark, and reads the "tips and hints" to improve on personal specific areas. The CCQ can also be used as a measuring tool for creativity within a team or organization where a facilitator draws conclusions from the total score.

In 1999, the Creativity Climate Questionnaire was published as a booklet, and it is currently listed as a Unilever Research publication (Frijling and Mostert, 2000).

The Creativity Awareness Training Modules

The outcome of the Creativity Climate Questionnaire may lead to the conclusion that creativity training is needed, which is the third element of the CAP. For each of the five criteria, a training module is designed, leading to customized 1–2 days training.

The training starts with an introduction into creativity, covering the definitions of creativity, the difference between creativity and innovation, and an insight into when a person is most creative. The modules for each criterion are described in Table 20.1.

Organizational Support

Organizational support—next to IPM and the CAP—is also embodied in Unilever Ventures and the Unilever R&D Vlaardingen Ideation processes.

In 2002, Unilever Ventures (for more details, see http://www.unileverventures.com/) was launched as a seed and early stage funding process to successfully identify and develop business opportunities for both within and outside Unilever. Employees

Table 20.1

Content of Creativity Awareness Training Modules	
Criterion	**Content examples**
Attitude	Mental blocks that prevent creativity Phases of resistance to change Maslow motivation theory (Norwood 2001, accessed October 2003)
Behavior	Selective perception Non-verbal behavior How a team can kill a good idea
Techniques	Creativity training possibilities Learning to use creativity techniques
Structures	Creativity helps to achieve the vision Idea management structures Leadership styles
Environment	Components of a creative organization Top-management support Innovations in the company

are encouraged to develop ideas for a new business or to leverage Unilever Intellectual Property. Unilever Ventures helps to turn these ideas into reality.

To create and to capture an even more continuous stream of new ideas for Unilever Bestfoods' leading brands, Unilever R&D Vlaardingen implemented the Ideation concept early in 2003. Central to this idea management system is a series of events in which research employees are triggered to produce a vast amount of ideas for a product or process proposition, triggered by experiencing a brand or opportunity. In these "Ideation sessions," the R&D community connects its knowledge and creativity to, for example, marketing or supply chain areas.

Having the structural aspects in place with IPM, the Consumer/Technology Matrix, the innovation funnel, the training of creativity facilitators, the Creativity Awareness Model, Unilever Ventures and Ideation, and the balance with the culture of the company—underpinned by the organic behavior of its employees—should allow for a continuous flow of ideas. Even this ideas flow can be managed.

Creativity Session in Action

Why Do Organizations Have Creativity Sessions?

With the start up of the Creativity Awareness Program, more and more creativity sessions took place in the organization, guided by the trained creativity facilitators.

Psychologist and engineer G. Wallis (Sengers and Smit, 2000; http://www.harpercollins.com.au/drstephenjuan/0211.news.htm, accessed October 2003) identifies the four phases of creativity:

1. The *preparation phase* is when a person becomes aware of a problem for which a solution is to be found. If this is not successful, the person might ignore the problem for a while.

"Sometimes you have to kiss a lot of frogs to find the Prince." (Anonymous)

2. The *incubation phase* is when a person is not consciously working on the problem, but the brains are. The unconscious mind works like an intuitive route that chooses paths and neglects others. Everyone organizes this incubation time in his/her own way; one person gets a cup of coffee or takes a shower, while someone else goes on vacation. No matter how, the aim is to find other contexts in the mind that remove the blocks for the possible solution to the problem. This phase might take some time. Sometimes problems linger on for many years. In organizations we do not have the time to stay long in the incubation phase. That is why creativity sessions are organized with the aim to mimic this naturally intuitive route by making use of creativity techniques.

3. In the *illumination phase* the idea is born, and it is up to the idea generators to share the idea or to keep it to themselves.

4. The *action phase* can also take a long time. For example, the idea of 3M's Post-Its was over 15 years old before it was brought to market.

As mentioned with respect to the incubation phase, the need for acceleration is also felt at Unilever R&D Vlaardingen. Therefore, many creativity sessions are organized throughout the company. They have the objective to look at problems (we prefer to call them opportunities) from a different angle and generate ideas that might lead to solutions. The creativity facilitator, together with the "problem owner," invites cross-domain colleagues to enter a creativity session, after a thorough intake interview about the problem at hand, context of the problem, expected outcome, venue of the session, and timing. If, for example, a creativity session is organized to solve a particular problem in detergent powder, people with expertise in food flavors and cereal solutions are also invited.

Information Technology (IT) Tools Supporting Creativity Sessions

The actual session is supported by various tools, as basic as flip-overs and Post-Its to advanced IT tools. One of the most frequently used e-Tools for capturing and structuring ideas in Unilever R&D Vlaardingen is MindJet's Mindmanager (http://www.mindjet.com/, accessed October 2003).

A much more advanced tool is Invention Machine's TechOptimizer (http://www.invention-machine.com/, accessed October 2003). TechOptimizer is a knowledge-based tool that helps researchers to state research and engineering problems correctly, create new concepts, and manage technical knowledge. TechOptimizer is designed to work with scientists in resolving research and engineering problems. The tool is used across different fields of research and engineering and offers a breakthrough process for strategic and guided thinking to create innovative, cost-conscious solutions.

It is divided in several modules. There is a module for stating the problem in a structured, analyzable way. There are problem solution modules that are based on known scientific and engineering effects, helping in solving contradictions. This help is based on the analysis of over 2.5 million patents and offers guidance in projecting the current problem on key trends in technology and future directions in innovation. As such, it builds on the seminal work of Genrich Altshuller on TRIZ, a Russian acronym for the Theory of Inventive Problem Solving (Althuller, 1996; Salamatov, 1999). This practical problem-solving paradigm is based on the discovery that technological systems evolve according to specific laws. For an overview of these laws and ongoing research in their applications, "The Laws of System Evolution" 2002 by Petrov (accessed October 2003) is recommended.

One of the possible applications of TechOptimizer starts with a functional analysis of the problem at hand and, subsequently, offers guidance to one of the solution

Figure 20.2

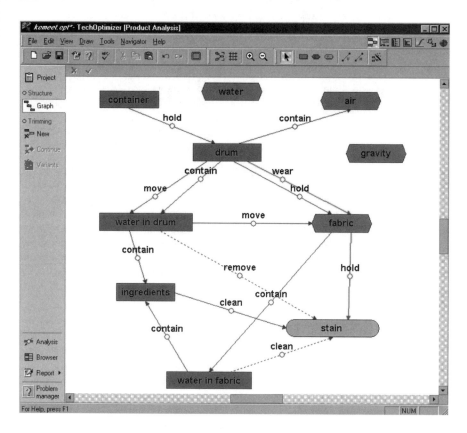

Functional analysis of a washing machine.
(Snapshot taken from TechOptimizer V4.0.)

modules. An example of such a "problem statement" and recommendation to use the Prediction module, exploring the trends of the technical evolution of systems, is illustrated by Figures 20.2 and 20.3. The example was taken from the Home & Personal Care discipline (*How to speed up the washing process to test the performance of new washing products?*).

How Successful Are Creativity Sessions?

In order to measure the success of creativity sessions, an internal investigation (Unilever, 2002b) was conducted to find out what was delivered from the 43 creativity sessions that took place in 2000/2001 at Unilever R&D Vlaardingen.

The conclusion is that creativity sessions play an important role in the innovation process, for two main reasons:

1. They result in project and product proposals, new projects, new products, patents, trademarks, innovations, new products on the market, and other opportunities.
2. They result in a more creative attitude of team members.

Figure 20.3

A snapshot from TechOptimizer's Problem Manager, which guides the user to specific problems in the system. It helps to select appropriate idea-creating modules, here the Prediction module, finding ways to improve an interaction by exploring the trends of technical systems' evolution

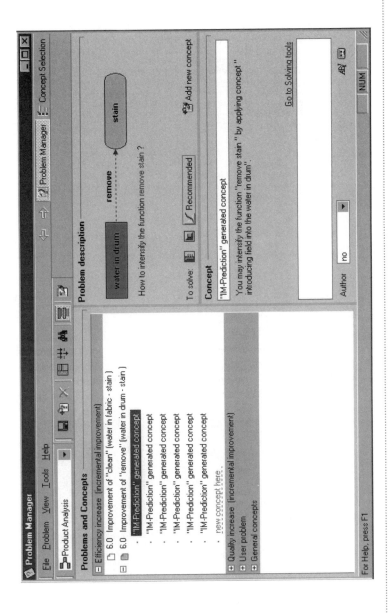

Table 20.2

Reasons to Organize a Creativity Session	
Reason	**% of sessions**

1. To solve technical problems
  • *How to reduce 50% production costs of product X?*
  • *How to improve dispensing of powder X?*
	42%

2. To start up a project/scan possibilities
  • *Think of new applications for ingredient X?*
  • *Think of new products for target group X?*
	28%

3. To generate ideas for new products or projects
  • *Think of a new project for department X?*
  • *What bothers you during your daily life that could be solved with expertise X?*
	13%

4. To think of consumer contact ideas
  • *Think of a campaign for the launch of product X?*
  • *How to identify signals that communicate benefit X in product and on package?*
	13%

5. To deal with culture and communication • *How to have more fun at work?*	4%
Note: An example problem statement is shown in italics.	

The investigation shows that there are five reasons for organizing a creativity session (see Table 20.2).

Assessing the results from the sessions, project leaders indicate that:

- 84% of the 43 sessions result in useful ideas. 35% of these useful ideas end up as product proposals, and 65% end up as project proposals.
- 56% of the 43 sessions have resulted in a solution, and 16% have not as yet.
- 22% of the sessions led to an innovation, and 40% of the sessions did not yet do so.
- 18% of the sessions led to an idea that can be tracked down in a product that is on the market, and 40% did not yet do so.
- On a scale from 1–10 (not/very useful) the project leaders give an average of 7.1 for the usefulness of the sessions.
  (*Note:* "not yet" means work in progress.)

In total, 922 participants from the different Unilever categories, science bases, and support groups participated in the 43 sessions. In some sessions we handed out an evaluation form. The participants (N = 281) replied as follows:

- On a scale of 1–5 they are positive about the success of the creativity session with a score of 4. They score the extent to which creativity applies to their work with a 3.9.
- 65% of the respondents are interested to (maybe) follow creativity training.

Next to product- and project-related results, it was shown that creativity sessions have a positive influence on the creative climate. Seventy percent of the problem owners of the 43 sessions stated that thanks to the creativity session, the team members obtain a more creative attitude in their daily work. The success of the creativity sessions is best reflected in the fact that 96% of the problem owners said they would make use of a creativity session again.

Operational Barriers Preventing Rollout of Ideas

Looking at the successes is great, but more important is to find out why not all creativity sessions have resulted in solutions or new products/projects. At the time of the investigation, 28% of the sessions generated ideas that were not pursued further for one of the reasons shown in Table 20.3.

These operational barriers show that creativity sessions can be successful only if the team has good insight in what will happen with the ideas after the session in the operational project context. The barriers have to be anticipated prior to the creativity session.

Organizational Enablers for Creativity

It is the tension between creativity and scepticism that has produced the stunning and unexpected findings of science.

Carl Sagan

In 2000, Mostert finalized her master's dissertation (Mostert, 2000) with a search for enablers for creativity in an R&D environment. Based on the five earlier mentioned criteria for creativity, she identified several key organizational enablers, specially applicable to an R&D environment, to provide a true creative culture.

Attitude

- The culture should really allow employees to show their emotions. If that is not the case, it leads to a "distant" atmosphere in which ideas cannot be totally free flowing.
- A remarkable finding is the fact that sharing knowledge between scientists is subject to the rule that there are only two reasons of living for true scientists: having patents and publications enlisted on their names. This, of course, does not help the free flow of ideas. If a scientist has to decide to either share a good idea or to keep it for her/his own scientific career, she/he has a difficult time.

Behavior

- Decision making is not a management-only affair. The creative input of employees must not be neglected. A "coaching" management style is popular, and it offers ample opportunities to take employees' opinions on board. Furthermore, a uniform management style is desirable, preventing confusion that might result from alternating coaching/directive management styles, especially with respect to taking risks. Creativity needs an environment where it is okay to take the risk to explore possibilities that might not lead to the desired solution.

Techniques

- The organization is to set aside time and budget for creativity training, so that employees can explore their creative power. People often go through a mental change during creativity training. They feel "relieved" and look at the world and their own lives in a different, creative, and more flexible way. At Unilever, various creativity training options are available, or aspects of creativity are integrated in training like Project Management, Leadership Courses, or Marketing Academy Courses.

Table 20.3

Reasons Why Ideas Were Not Pursued Further and Their Relative Abundance	
Operational barriers	**Percentage of sessions**
Support/ownership • *The idea did not have a real owner.* • *The idea has to be agreed upon by the person who is going to technically execute the idea.* • *It is important to maintain the positive and creative spirit of the session when evaluating the ideas later on.* • *The team liked and understood the idea, but was very disappointed by the response of the management.*	36%
Budgetary reasons • *Having to do the research on a lot smaller basis than was hoped for.* • *Resource limitations (recruitment stops).* • *One team had thought of several new subsidies projects, but then it turned out that no money was available.* • *The categories have a difficult time and tend to keep the money in their own pocket and not spend it on science bases working on new ideas.*	19%
Quality issues • *The idea is too new and does not fit in the strategy (yet?).* • *Food legislation issues.* • *Some ideas were perceived as too radical and therefore discarded, whereas I think that would make a real fresh innovation.*	14%
Change in scope • *The business is not interested anymore because of a changed strategy.* • *Changing priorities cause the ideas not to be pursued/ realized.*	12%
Technical issues • *Given the quality of an available solution, it was too much effort to go for something radically new, but possibly better.* • *We did not develop the specific expertise necessary for the suggested idea because that was outside our current scope.* • *The necessary raw materials to execute the idea are not available.*	10%
Lack of time • *There was not enough time to test and prepare the prototypes as we wanted to do.* • *The equipment that had to be developed would mean a too long time span.*	9%
Note: Quotes from the respondents are in italics.	

Structures

- A simple, accessible, and understandable idea management structure is to be in place. If not, employees do not know whom to turn to in case they have a good idea. Ideas do not live long, better catch them while they are young! At Unilever R&D Vlaardingen, the Ideation process is set up for that reason.
- "Having fun!" is also a key issue, which is not hard to organize. It is easy and very worthwhile to make public those real creative teams that are an example for the entire organization. Showing team results, how these were accomplished, and rewarding them (also in a non-monetary way) is fun and builds a creative attitude. To this end at Unilever R&D Vlaardingen, the URDV Team Awards has been called into existence.

Environment

- Employees at the senior management level serve as a model for the creative employee and should be trained and working accordingly. Only then can they truly show commitment and communicate the importance of creativity and give top-down directions on how to handle it. At Unilever, a senior manager is leading the Unilever Innovation Process Development and is responsible for gaining commitment for creativity and innovation.
- The working environment can support creativity as well, e.g., free use of colors, designated creativity areas, music, plans, anything supporting the unexpected to happen. At Unilever R&D Vlaardingen, some departments enjoy "open offices" and find a creative benefit from it.

Anecdotes

What is creativity? Is it artistic expressions like paintings, ballet, or books? According to Birch and Clegg (1995) there are three sorts of creativity:

1. Aaaahh! Creativity in arts as a combination of materials, music, and emotion, exploring a combination of senses, e.g., National Lampoon's Animal House.
2. Ha ha! Creativity in humor as an unexpected combination of events where "normal" relationships are abandoned. "What's brown and hairy and likes to ski? A Skiwi!"
3. Aha! This reflects creativity in science, like the combination of a mobile phone with a camera.

Project leaders who have done a creativity session within their project are often overwhelmed by the amount of useful ideas. To them, these ideas generate a lot of work because they are all worth checking—as opposed to being handed a single golden solution. Creativity sessions are not the holy grail for project teams. Ideas generated in a creativity session must be checked, thought through, combined, and investigated. During that process it often happens that two or three ideas from the session, combined with an unexpected external effect, offer the final solution.

Sometimes a creativity session is organized as a final escape. The conclusion of the session itself might be that indeed the team has tried everything and the solution is simply not to be found within the context of the project or with the expertise that is available. What could also happen is that ideas generated in the creativity session for one team are more applicable to another project, if such project teams can interconnect.

Strange, wacky ideas are all around during creativity sessions. How about using human hair as insulation material for ice cream cabinets? Why not change the culture in such a way that it is accepted to walk naked or body painted as a means of preventing to have to wash your clothes?

Future Considerations

At Unilever, as in many other companies, employees work in projects. Working in project teams might "blind" the team members to other projects and problems that are dealt with in the organization. According to the "garbage-can" theory of Cohen, March, and Olsen (1972), a free flow of problems, solutions, people, and decision points should be optimally available so that creativity can be used when the four items happen to meet each other in the garbage can. Finding an organization structure that allows the garbage-can theory and still seems well managed is a challenge.

Another object for further investigation is the way projects are led by project leaders. Every project has a life cycle that starts with an initiating phase, then flows into a definition phase, a design phase, a preparation phase, a realization phase, and finally a closure phase (Wijnen, Renes, and Storm, 1999). The first phase, the initiating phase, tends to be the most creative part of the project.

A project team has phases too. The Tuckman and Jensen model (1977) shows that each team goes through four team development phases: forming, storming, norming, and performing. According to Tuckman and Jensen, teams are most creative in the last phase: the performing phase. Team members might be selected based on roles that can be assessed by, for instance, a Belbin test (http://www.belbin.com/, accessed October 2003). Belbin gives the greatest creative skills to one of the nine character roles, "The Plant."

It is a challenge for each project leader to try to align the dynamics of the project and the team, both in attitude and in composition to the project's state of evolvement, thus allowing creativity to flourish all through the project. Maybe that investigation would show that the type of required leadership style, meaning the project leader him/herself, should also be aligned to the dynamics of the project and the team.

Integration with Other Tools

Creativity as a knowledge connector finds its way into or stands at the basis of many tools within Unilever R&D Vlaardingen.

Innovation Process Management

The IPM will benefit largely from creativity. The funnel needs to be fed by creative initiatives for Unilever new products or services.

Leadership for Growth Profile

Unilever is on its way to Path to Growth. This is a five-year strategic plan announced in February 2000 designed to accelerate top-line growth and further increase operating margins. The plan centers on a series of initiatives to focus on fewer, stronger brands to accelerate growth (http://www.unilever.com/news/finance/pathtogrowthsummaryupdate/, accessed October 2003). Creativity capabilities are recognized explicitly in one of the competencies: "Breakthrough thinking."

URDV Team Award

In 1999, Unilever R&D Vlaardingen introduced the URDV Team Awards, recognizing team commitment and team achievement. The awards are for teams that excel in Creativity, Alignment with business strategy, Entrepreneurship, Unileverage (meaning: are applications possible elsewhere in Unilever?), and Teamwork. Over the years, it appears that a substantial amount (20–45%) of the participating teams have been involved in facilitated creativity sessions.

Concluding Remarks

This chapter has given you insight on how Unilever R&D Vlaardingen ensures a structure and culture in which creativity can flourish. It also illustrates how ideas get a chance to be born and caught in an idea management structure while they are young and vital, along with facilitating support from IT tools.

The project and idea management structure of the organization offers opportunities to connect knowledge within the team, toward management, and among other projects and expertise areas, enabling germination of crucial, creative moments.

References

Althuller, G. (1996). *And Suddenly the Inventor Appeared*. Technical Innovation Center, Inc.: Auburn, USA.

Birch, P. and Clegg, B. (1995). *Business Creativity*. Biddles Ltd.: Guildford, UK.

Cohen, M.D., March, J.G., and Olsen, J.P. (1972). A garbage can model of Organizational Choice, *Administrative Science Quaterly*, 17, 1–25.

Frijling, L.H. and Mostert, N.M. (2000). *Creativity Climate Questionnaire*. Unilever Research: Vlaardingen, The Netherlands, ISBN 90 64 96 169 7.

Kahn, M. (December 2002). The global approach, in *Innovation: Making It Happen*, Russell, J., Ed., London: Caspian Publishing Ltd., and IBM UK Ltd., ISBN 1 901844 42 0, pp. 27–31.

Koestler, A. (1964). *The Act of Creation*. Baltimore: Penguin.

Mostert, N.M. (2000). "Eureka! In de Research. De plaats van creativiteit binnen Unilever Research Vlaardingen"; Master dissertation, 14 November 2000, Open Universiteit.

Mostert, N.M. and Frijling, L.H. (2001). Creativity in organizations can be measured and acquired, *Chemical Innovation*, Vol. 31, No. 11, pp. 50–53. Also available at http://pubs.acs.org/subscribe/journals/ci/31/i11/html/11manage.html (accessed October 2003).

Norwood, G., "Maslow's Hierarchy of Needs," in http://www.deepermind.com/20maslow.htm (accessed October 2003).

Petrov, V. (2002). "The Laws of System Evolution," http://www.triz-journal.com/archives/2002/03/b/index.htm (accessed October 2003).

Sengers, L. and Smit, A. (2000). "Denk Door, Iedereen is creatief." Intermediair, VNU, 13 Juli 2000.

Salamatov, Y. (1999). *TRIZ: The Right Solution at the Right Time*. Insytec BV: Hattem, NL.

Tuckman, B.W. and Jensen, M.A.C. (1977). Stages of small-group development revisited, *Group and Organizational Studies*, 2, 419–427.

Unilever (1974). Internal Research Report.

Unilever (1977). "Feeding the Funnel," Marketing Project Group, Unilever House, London.

Unilever (2002). Unilever Annual Review 2002 and Summary Financial Statement.

Unilever (2000). Unilever Internal Research Report.

?Whatif! Training Ltd. (2002), "Creating an Invention Culture," 1997, The Glassworks, 3–4 Ashlands Place, London W1M 3JH, UK. See also http://www.whatif.co.uk/ (accessed September 2003).

Wijnen, G., Renes, W., and Storm, P. (1999). "Projectmatig werken," Het Spectrum, Utrecht, ISBN 90 274 3328 3.

KM Tools in Human Resource Systems at the World Bank: Promoting Empowerment and Knowledge Sharing*

Michele Egan

> The theories back at the business school had mentioned labor, but there had been no talk of people. Yet the real world, the refinery, seemed to be full of them. And because the workplace was full of people, it looked suspiciously as if companies were not always rational, calculable, and controllable.
>
> *Arie de Geus (1997)*

Introduction

Arie de Geus' early revelation that knowledge had become today's critical production factor lends credence to the tired—and perhaps tiresome—expression "people are

---

* *Editor's Note:* This chapter provides an inside look at KM-supporting HR systems at the World Bank, in three focus areas: self-service; information publishing and delivery; and integration and communication. Some 10,000 development professionals from nearly every country in the world work for the World Bank. Integral to the mission statement of the Bank are the notions and practices of knowledge sharing and of building capacity. HR's website YourNet—was purposefully created as a "knowledgebase" by applying KM principles to an HR system. KM tools in HR nurture a sense of empowerment and ownership, and enable knowledge sharing by promoting a common set of "idioms" in the workplace.

Automated notifications are delivered to the KM team for new content created by HR staff, helping them to identify areas for possible collaboration with other HR content creators. Web-based tools are used for hiring professional associates, forming communities of practice, and supporting knowledge networking among alumni. Expertise directories are created via the People Pages tool, which captures everything from educational background to ongoing project experience. Fully 85% of surveyed respondents found the KM tool to be a credible source of information. Key lessons learned for sustaining an overall ecology of knowledge include the importance of harnessing the familiarity of known tools and mediums in new ways and creating consistent narratives.

our greatest assets." The fact is that the emergence of a new class of workers, the "knowledge workers," is fundamentally altering the nature of work. The ability of companies to acquire, nurture, and utilize knowledge, or as some call it "intellectual capital," will ultimately determine the success of a company.

Another truism is that information systems *are* the tools of the knowledge management (KM) trade in the 21st century. That is not to say that KM *is* about technology. That would be as false as saying that learning is about books. But just as books are a critical tool in the delivery of learning, information technology is the medium available to KM—integrating communication, collaboration, and transaction into an environment in which KM principles can be applied—by people and for people.

The trouble is that information technologies have grown up amid organizations for years prior to the introduction of KM practices. As such, today's knowledge manager and knowledge organization have to contend with a landscape strewn with disparate and sometimes incompatible applications built to meet specific business demands. Consider the multiple solutions proffered by numerous vendors with the promise of "providing knowledge" or "creating the knowledge organization." Integrating these solutions into an already established information infrastructure is invariably complicated at best. Introducing such solutions into an existing environment of information technologies—barring a complete house cleaning—only adds to the clutter.

The "hard work" for the knowledge manager is applying the lens of KM practice to that landscape. By taking the time to understand the impact of existing disparate systems on the common, day-to-day working language and customs of the organization, the knowledge enterprise can take full advantage of the technologies' accomplishments while correcting unintentional negative impacts to better achieve a knowledge-based result, potentially avoiding expensive and time-consuming systems integration efforts.

This chapter takes a look at human resource (HR) systems at the World Bank. It will target three specific areas of HR focus—self-service, information publishing and delivery, and integration and communication—to illustrate two notions:

1. That systems deployed to meet specific business needs without consideration of a KM agenda still can be utilized as foundations for movement toward establishing the knowledge enterprise
2. That with the application of KM practices, new applications can be introduced or old ones retasked that leverage unintentional outcomes and help sustain and enhance the knowledge enterprise as it moves forward

Organization Profile

The World Bank Group's mission is to fight poverty and improve the living standards of people in the developing world. It is a development bank which provides loans, policy advice, technical assistance, and knowledge-sharing services to low and middle income countries to reduce poverty. In 2003, the World Bank provided $18.5 billion and worked in more than 100 developing countries, bringing finance and/or technical expertise toward helping them reduce poverty. Some 10,000 development professionals from nearly every country in the world work in the World Bank's Washington D.C. headquarters or in its 109 country offices. Integral to the mission statement of the bank are the notions and practices of knowledge sharing and of building capacity—in our staff and with our clients.

HR is not usually thought of in conjunction with KM. However, HR looks after people—their skills, behavior, and potential—and, with 20/20 hindsight, it is only natural that we should be involved in enabling knowledge creation and sharing. So four years ago, we formalized that role by creating the first HR knowledge manager position—and the rest, as they say, is history.

Employee Self-service: Promoting a Common Language and a Sense of Accountability

The first-ever HR self-service application was christened the "HR Kiosk." Originally produced in the mid-1990s, it is a classic example of first generation self-service in which paper forms were replaced with electronic ones in order to consolidate requests for HR service and support and allow for simple edits to non-corporate data. This Web-accessible application is available through the World Bank Group's intranet and is used by every staff member in 109 offices worldwide. According to our Web statistics, an average of 11,000 individuals visit the site monthly to manage benefits and life events and to record personal and professional data, career progression, and learning events.

While the HR Kiosk was created to relieve HR of the overhead of dealing with paper requests, the application has been very successful in changing the face of HR transactions, from face-to-face and "brick and mortar" to virtual and desktop. Looking at it from a KM perspective, the unintended effects on our staff have been profound.

While "eliminating paper" and providing better service were the HR objectives, in this case both were essentially inward looking. Certainly, the workflows designed into the HR Kiosk are transactional, individual, and unidirectional, but the more important "outbound message" to staff has been of empowerment and ownership, coupled with personal responsibility.

Because the HR Kiosk is available 24 hours a day and 7 days a week, requests for HR's services are no longer bound by office hours; actions can be taken from any bank office in the world at any time. Since information such as address, phone number, number of dependents, educational achievements, and the like is editable through the kiosk, staff are subtly encouraged to "own" their information. Further, this type of automation offers a measure of control over processes, empowering an individual. With a direct system interface, the responsibility rests with the staff member, restoring personal accountability.

The HR Kiosk also evolved into a focal point, a "proto-portal," from which HR could provide a coherent and consistent "face" to its staff worldwide in terms of the information that is gathered; the data that is maintained; and the benefits, policies, and programs which the World Bank provides. This has been extended for each transaction by the use of hyperlinks to online HR information in order to provide reference, instruction, and guidance. In a fundamental manner, the HR Kiosk represents knowledge sharing in its simplest form by establishing and promoting a common set of "idioms" in the workplace.

HR's Knowledge-base: The Power of Integration

HR's current Web site, YourNet, was purposefully created as a "knowledge-base" and represents the first attempt at applying KM principles to an HR system (see Figure 21.1).

It was designed to meet two objectives. The first was to create an intranet for HR staff in the bank to share information and communicate about each HR business unit's

Figure 21.1

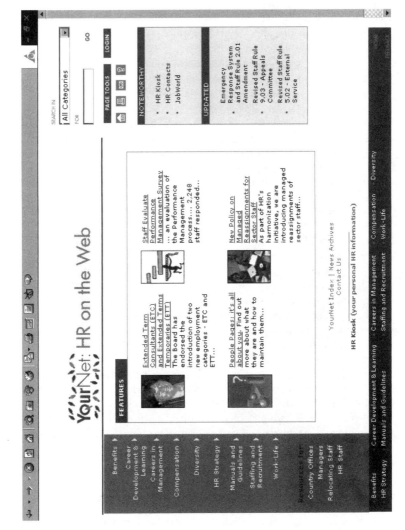

HR's intranet: YourNet homepage

roles and responsibilities, with the hope that such online information would lead to discoveries of efficiencies and new and unexpected synergies between different HR units around the world. For instance, HR staff routinely use YourNet to collaborate online on confidential information with a select audience before the information goes public, ensuring that everyone is, quite literally, on the same page.

The second equally important objective was to provide the bank at large with a view of the services and programs undertaken and supported by HR—presented within an integrated "space." This integrated approach would provide HR with the ability to demonstrate the relationships between seemingly disparate programs and policies in order to educate and communicate the intentions of HR and the institution transparently.

The key functionality of the application has been the ability for HR staff to publish Web pages without programming skills (including the capability to create entire Web sites online), effectively creating 300 HR Web masters on the spot. Designed to use the same interface employed by the bank's Lotus Notes e-mail system, the publishing interface uses a common template and allows a person to easily link Web pages created by them to Web pages created by others, generating a natural "web" of interlinkages that relate all the content created in the Web site to common themes. A three-tier categorization scheme provides meta-data and reference information for the visitor of the Web site. This three-tier categorization model is used in its internal search engine.

With content creation entirely decentralized to each HR expert, we put into place a system which delivers automated notifications to the KM team for each new page created by individual HR staff. This allows us to make interventions ranging from suggestions on style and formatting to identifying areas for possible collaboration with other HR content creators, helping to address the "left hand doesn't know what the right hand is doing" phenomenon. We deliberately chose an "ex-post" monitoring system rather than a controlling system of vetting content before publication with the assumption that the latter would be a deterrent to knowledge sharing. Statistics about the amount of information created have borne out that assumption, although we have at times overestimated the ability of some individuals to manage information in an online environment.

To date, HR's intranet has been successful in delivering integrated HR information to staff worldwide. Available both internally and externally, this Lotus Notes Domino-based application contains over 10 gigabytes (or close to 4,000 Web pages) of HR information, ranging from the bank's official staff policies to information on specialized programs for families and retirees. There is even information on bank clubs available online. On a monthly basis, an average of 10,000 individual staff access YourNet for a combined 384,000 pages viewed.

A basic analogy for the working model of YourNet is the Lego block. This translates into a dynamic set of objects-as-Web-pages that encompass both knowledge and information and that can be assembled and reassembled in unpredictable ways by the authors of Web pages. The HR intranet was the first HR application designed with KM principles clearly articulated. "You don't know what you know" was a continuous theme used to explain the importance of allowing authors to freely categorize and cross-reference their contributions and content using the tools built into the publishing interface. This web of linkages resulted in an immediate ten-fold increase in click-throughs when we replaced our previous, conventional Web site with YourNet.

YourNet offers a view of the HR function in the bank, not only as a comprehensive catalog of HR services available to staff, but also as a narrative that ties together the "story" of the bank as an employer and the way it sees, supports, and communicates with its staff. It has been twice included in bank-wide surveys on communication effectiveness, which indicated that fully 85% of the respondents found it a credible source of information—second only to face-to-face meetings with managers in the sharing and dissemination of HR-related information in the bank.

However, the importance in KM terms lies in the notion that people can have the information they need to formulate knowledge and use that knowledge in better ways. An old advertisement declares: "An educated consumer is our best customer." So an educated staff is a better staff. Our deliberate strategy is to always combine information with transaction—the "what" with the "how." For instance, when a staff member gets married, he or she can look up what changes will occur in the benefits area and, from the information pages, access the HR Kiosk, where he or she can register a new dependent, update a home address, change life insurance beneficiary information, and select a new family insurance plan. The integration of our systems appears to have been successful: staff talk about our Web site (YourNet) and our transactional system (HR Kiosk) as if they were one and the same.

Putting "everything on-line" allows people to make informed decisions, engage in educated discussion and debate rather than speculation, and, ultimately, contribute new and better ways of thinking—in this case toward HR policies and programs that impact their lives.

Hiring People without HR: Empower with the Right Tools

The big shift for HR has been to move away from electronic forms and transactions and toward disintermediation—the elimination of HR from transactional workflows. The first, tentative test of this notion came in 2001 with the introduction of a new employment program for young, entry-level professionals and a hiring interface for managers that allowed them to shop for and select applicants online without the assistance of HR professionals.

Called the JPA (Junior Professional Associates) System, the Lotus Notes Domino-based Web interface allows managers the ability to review candidates in the program, share the information, get input from colleagues, rate candidates in the system's database, and ultimately hire them at the click of a button from a single user interface (see Figure 21.2). Applicants apply online directly from the bank's employment Web site. The applications with CV attachments are passed through to the hiring system in minutes and available immediately. On a yearly basis, we receive approximately 17,000 applications toward that program (which represents 10% of the total number of applications for all our employment programs combined), out of which we hire about 200 individuals.

For HR to step away from direct involvement in the identification and selection of candidates has proven quite successful. The model has been popular enough to be applied to general employment and other specialized hiring programs as well.

In terms of knowledge, this notion of empowering people by giving them the tools to do what they need to do without the boundaries of time and place also allows people the flexibility to consider and chose at their own pace—to discover. The shift in the underlying message conveyed to staff by HR is a change from active intervention to active oversight, removing HR from the individual process of hiring while shifting accountability for actions directly to HR's clients.

This experience draws upon the successes of the HR Kiosk and YourNet in two important ways. First, it builds on the notion of ownership by allowing the hiring

Figure 21.2

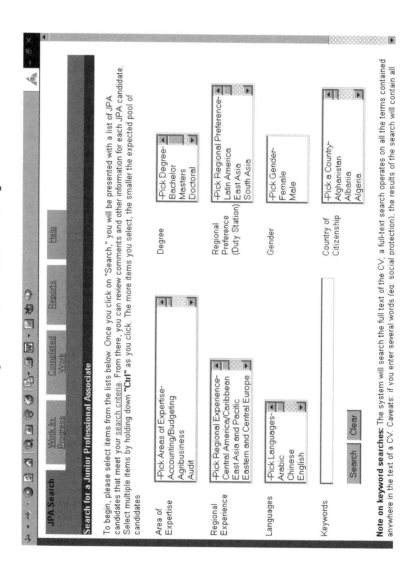

JPA Program—selection interface for managers

manager to control the hiring process from beginning to the end. Ownership of the process and outcomes equates to accountability by investing the responsibility of hiring with the manager and his or her staff and colleagues. By virtue of an already integrated HR knowledge-base on hiring programs and policies, the online JPA system communicates a common experience and set of tools and behaviors to all hiring managers, further reinforcing best practices throughout the organization and allowing HR to engage with clients in a different capacity—as advisors or "guides on the side" rather than as controllers.

As an interesting phenomenon, the JPA program hires have evolved into their own rather active community of practice, self-organizing around professional events (brown bag lunches, working committees, mentoring programs) as well as social events (volunteer activities, "happy hours," lunches), further promoting knowledge sharing and cross-fertilization within the bank. As the first JPAs graduate this year from their two-year employment program with the bank, we are forming partnerships with them through an alumni association meant to encourage continued ties with our organization and to promote "ambassadorship" elsewhere for the bank's mission and values—another form of knowledge sharing.

People Are Multifaceted: Capture the Nuances

In a large enterprise such as the World Bank, which neither manufactures nor sells, people and what they know and do become the essential strength of the organization—an irreplaceable foundation of the organization's effectiveness.

In the past, one's personal "golden rolodex" was the key to organizational effectiveness and pointed to the strength of individual knowledge, but it also underscored the liability of concentrating important knowledge in one person. In an environment of increasing decentralization of people and responsibilities, larger turnover of staff, emphasis on cross-organizational teams, and ever more rapid pace of work, how does one know who does what anymore?

In a relatively new experiment dubbed People Pages, we have just built and released a directory of expertise in which the attributes of a person become highly contextual (see Figure 21.3). Our reasoning was simple: people are multifaceted and cannot simply be defined by assigning them one (or even several) expertise descriptor(s). A person's profile best emerges when information is brought together about what they do (assignments—current and past), where they do it (sector-driven specializations, locations, project activities), with whom they do it (team member information, associative activities), what the foundation of their knowledge is (list of publications, educational background, languages), and so on. The result is much like assembling a puzzle: seemingly disparate pieces which together produce a coherent picture.

People Pages can be viewed as a "super-portal" of sorts, bringing together information from the full range of systems that currently capture data about people and work and allowing for insertion of self-entered data as well as providing for additional granularity, the "personal touch" if you will. The bank's environment may be somewhat unique because of its unique reliance on its staff as its principal value proposition in the market. However, the overall concept proposes that the integration of existing systems is possible through "front end" processing—human interfaces designed to take advantage of the KM principles that lead to knowledge creation and sharing.

This model would not have been as easily introduced without the foundations of the HR systems described earlier. Relying on ownership, accountability, and trans-

Figure 21.3

Sample of a People Page

parency, the bank's new People Pages not only tries to open the door to the multiple facets of each staff members' careers and contributions, but also gives back ownership of the data collected in the course of that work as attributes of their own personal profiles. Reactions have been multiple and varied, ranging from delight at the potential uses of the medium to anxiety about the wealth of information available, previously thought of as "personal." The common thread is that while most of that information was already available in other systems, its concatenation under a personal label has brought along with it a sense of ownership and responsibility for the quality of the information and a desire to improve on it. Statistics for the first 12 days since People Pages were released bear this out: the site saw just under 80,000 visits for 225,000 pages viewed.

Thus, this proxy of a directory of expertise is a means to reintegrate people into the data that has been collected about them, which in turn might prompt them to look at that data, provide additional context around it, correct it, and in some cases reassociate it to other work and data in unexpected and new ways. This could provide insight into new knowledge about the way in which the bank's work and people interrelate with one another.

Lessons Learned

From KM tool application and workflow alignment to narratives and collaboration, we have learned a number of lessons about supporting the knowledge organization.

- It is relatively easy to apply technologies to specific business needs. This "layering" of technological solutions, however, can lead to confusing the objectives of a knowledge organization. The role of KM can be to look at the knowledge organization from a "needs" perspective and discern from multiple points of view the noise that is generated by the application of systems and technologies to the overall ecology of knowledge and learning.
- By identifying complements and frictions in the system, there are opportunities for managing change without imposing massive social or idiomatic shifts in the culture. That is not to say that change is not by nature disturbing; it is. But within the knowledge organization, it is possible to mitigate that disturbance by harnessing the familiarity of known tools and mediums in new ways: there is no need to reinvent the whole wheel, perhaps tweaking a few spokes is enough.
- The "narrative" of the relationship between people and the organization is a continuous one. By virtue of old-timers and newcomers alike, that narrative is written every day, and the fabric of that narrative is increasingly reflected in the systems that are deployed to increase productivity, reduce costs, and improve the effectiveness of the organization and its people. Consistency of that narrative enhances the responses of the people to the organization, thus improving the quality of life within the workplace.
- Collaboration and facilitation (rather than control and vetting) are key drivers in the successful utilization of new and existing technologies, as well as in unleashing the willingness of people to contribute with their effort. The interdependence of systems to one another makes ownership by any one organizational entity an antiquated—and counterproductive—concept. Let a thousand flowers bloom does work, even if you have to pull a few weeds on occasion.

Acknowledgments

I acknowledge John Kim, Information Officer, for providing technical background information to this chapter.

Part II

"A Fool with a Tool Is Still a Fool . . ."*,**

22

Ritendra Banerjee

> It is well to remember from time to time that nothing that is worth knowing can be taught.
>
> *Oscar Wilde*

Introduction

"A fool with a tool is still a fool. . . ." Thus said an important industry friend to our head of research, while elaborating both on the potential as well as the limitation of technology. The interesting question that consultants like me are often faced with is this, "Do humans lead technology or is technology an important mentor (for lack of a more precise term) that contributes to the way humans evolve?" After all, someone did say that technology and software are nothing but programmable extensions of the human mind. Whatever it is, one thing is for sure: human beings and technology will continue to interface in myriad new ways to evolve unique combinations, which could find applications in doing business and in leading better lives.

---

* Inspired from multiple sources: Scott Ambler at http://www.evanetics.com/articles/essays/OO%20Training%20with%20Tool.htm; Prof. Narahari while talking to QAI's industry portal, www.softwaredioxide.com.

** *Editor's Note:* This chapter provides a comprehensive overview of the categories of KM tools and some of the notable vendors in each. More importantly, it details frameworks based on business logic to choosing and deploying KM technology. Based on first-hand research from QAI India, it also shares results on the nature of RoI realized from deployment of KM tools; KM tools have been successfully used in project management, brainstorming activities, and networking knowledge workers, but have been less successful in crisis management and large-scale organizational redesign.

Challenges have been observed in failure to control KM infrastructure costs, inability to integrate multiple IT tools, developing solutions without seeking external professional help, and not properly aligning KM tools and solutions with business needs. KM solutions best evolve out of an interplay of business requirements, the tool portfolio, and the human factor. Future trends include the use of systems thinking, pattern theories, and social network analysis.

The first part of this chapter, titled "Landscape," sets the context by covering the landscape of best-of-breed knowledge management (KM) technologies that we have seen in the last decade or so and elaborates on the key characteristics of these tools.

The next section, titled "Post Mortem" (in lighter vein . . . KM is not dead yet ☺), does a diagnosis of these tools and brings to the fore the immense possibilities that these tools would have had in developing themselves into more value adding propositions. It draws conclusions based on comparison and contrast within the universe of tools detailed in the Landscape section.

The third part of the chapter, titled "Business Scope," shares with the reader a few approaches in choice and deployment of KM technology based not so much on the attributes/characteristics of the tools (as is normally done in most instances), as much as the extent to which it is business compliant. In that sense, it details frameworks based on business logic for choosing and deploying KM technology.

The final section, "Techbuck Score Card," details the extent to which these technologies have paid off in return on investment (RoI) terms. It goes on to elaborate on the various components that have contributed to hiking the total cost of ownership of these technologies beyond control and imagination, thereby creating what I would call a "Messy Mess."

The chapter concludes with a wrap up of the key points and a projection on what the next generation of KM technologies could possibly be.

Landscape

Most tools that have been commonly in use have had typical features, which made them largely amenable to deployment in one phase or the other of what is commonly known as the Knowledge Management Cycle, i.e., Knowledge Generation–Codification–Retrieval–Transfer–Purging. Quite interestingly, toolmakers do seem to have focused enough on the purging bit. No wonder it has been remarked that "We live in a world where there is a flood of information, but famine of Knowledge" (quote from Auroville's Argo Diary 2003).

Use of a single tool operable across various phases of the cycle has also been rare. As per the author's last stock take, in India alone there have been close to 500 categories of Type 3 Tools (see below) that were in use, and sadly enough, many of these had failed to deliver on real RoI.

Tools for Knowledge Generation

The first category of tools in use are the ones that help support meetings and group decision support. These have enabled users to get into synchronic, collocated forms of cooperation and have been useful in structuring, visualizing contributions, polling, and assessment of decision making in group situations. The leading players include Think Tools, MIV's Group Vision, Aliah THINK, and Ventana Group Systems.

The other category of knowledge generation tools has been the ones which have provided sophisticated computational capabilities to analyze complex data along a more intuitive set of business rules and dimensions (e.g., profitability analysis by product, channel, geography, customer, repeat customer). These have been in the nature of datamining and OLAP (Online Analytical Processing) tools, with players like Brio Enterprise, Seagate's Holos, Oracle's Express Development Tools, and IBM's DB2 OLAP Server.

Tools for Knowledge Codification

This category of tools has "attempted to save knowledge in a structured way"* and represent them in the form of images, text files, database, real-time video, and sound clips. These have been the ones that have helped create knowledge repositories apart from aiding in document management; they include Documentum's Enterprise Document Management System; IBM's Lotus Notes; PC DOCS' DOCS Fusion, DOCS Open, and DOCS Fulcrum; and Open Text's Live Link. Apart from these, tools have also been used in automatic generation of knowledge directories and in taxonomy building. Text mining tools and taxonomy generators like SemioMap and Autonomy Knowledge Server have been widely used.

Tools for Knowledge Retrieval

Although this has probably been the category with the least available number of products to choose from, it has been, what I would call, action packed. This category has been characterized by powerful search algorithms meant to unearth knowledge from different sources. Retrieval systems, search engines, and navigators like Compassware's Infomagnet, Excalibur's Retrieval, and Verity Information Server figure here.

Tools for Knowledge Transfer

This has been the most crowded category in terms of the number of products available to choose from. Online collaboration tools and work coordination tools (for knowledge object sharing and exercises like electronic whiteboarding and workflow management) have been heavily deployed. While Microsoft's Net Meeting, Sony's Trinicom 500, and Intel's Team Station and Proshare have enabled dislocated and synchronic communication with audio and video channels, they have also offered remote views on collective objects on different desktops.

Lotus Notes and Rosetta Technologies' Preview have helped in the administration of remarks to a knowledge object, tracking of changes (such as those of authors of knowledge pieces, dates), and message services in case of changes in a knowledge object. Tools like Filenet's Visual Workflow have aided in synchronization, routing, and transport of knowledge objects, as well as modeling, manipulation, and administration of knowledge-driven business processes.

Post Mortem

The good news is that these tools have lived up to their features and potential in facilitating work and business. The bad news is that they have not delivered all the business results that they could have; KM tools have not upgraded continuously vis-à-vis tools in other areas of application, giving one a feeling that practitioners and developers did not really have a fix on "*What Next?*" No wonder some people even dare to call KM a fad which was meant to live for a day.

Based on insights from KM research and consulting at the QAI Organization Practice (for more information, see "Highlights" at www.qaiindia.com/international. com), I have attempted to detail the extent to which each of the tools has found usage (read: benefit and not necessarily effort) in Table 22.1. Importantly, an attempt has also been made to detail the *maximum potential usage* of the tool, if it were used in a

---

* A manager, while participating in the evolution of the QAI's Organization Practice's Model, called the Pentagon.

Table 22.1

KM Tool Capacity's Underutilization

Technology	Tool Type	Use	Maximum Potential[a]	Other Tool Type[b]
Knowledge Generation	Meeting support tools; Group Decision Support Software	Minimal	Moderate use	Data-mining tools
Knowledge Generation	Data-mining tools; Online Analytical Processing (OLAP)	Minimal	Ideal use	Group Decision Support Software
Knowledge Codification	Knowledge repositories; Document management systems	Minimal	Moderate use	Retrieval Systems
Knowledge Codification	Text mining tools; Taxonomy generators	Unacceptable	Ideal use	
Knowledge Retrieval	Retrieval systems; Search machines; Navigators	Unacceptable (in spite of extensive deployment)	Moderate use	
Knowledge Transfer	Online cooperative tools (video-conferencing, screen sharing)	Moderate	Ideal use	
Knowledge Transfer	Work coordination (knowledge of object sharing, electronic whiteboarding)	Unacceptable	Moderate use	
Knowledge Transfer	Work coordination (workflow management)	Unacceptable	Ideal use	

[a] Maximum potential for use, given existing features.
[b] Other tool type that this could have been used with so as to achieve maximum usage (given a specific business situation).

certain configuration with other tools, given a business situation. To that extent the matrix in Table 22.1 highlights a capacity underutilization of sorts as far as KM technology is concerned.

In sum, it is time we realized that there is nothing called an all-encompassing KM tool, as much as a portfolio of tools which could be effective given a business context.

Business Scope

I keep mentioning to knowledge managers, consultants, and evangelists that if one has to do KM successfully, the only way to do so is to understand that we are not so much in the business of knowledge as in the business of business. KM is an enabler/facilitator which helps us do business faster, cheaper, better, and right. Therefore, one must take a business scope perspective to evaluating and deploying KM technology, viz. use a business logic or business framework to do so.

The following subsections are three important frameworks which I have successfully used during my KM consulting journey.

The Spatio-temporal Framework

This is a way by which one can choose a certain set of tools by asking two fundamental questions.

1. How close or how distant (therefore *spatial*, as in space) are the givers of knowledge from the takers of knowledge?

So a one-location company aspiring to be a knowledge corporation would be required to access a different set of tools than, say, a multi-location company. As a one-location company grows into a multi-location outfit, the knowledge manager will be required to access, use, and institutionalize different KM technologies.

Similarly, knowledge sharing in a project team at one site would require a different set of tools to be used as compared to a project team at multiple sites.

2. What are the chances that the takers of knowledge would be required to access the givers of knowledge at the same time (therefore *temporal*, as in time)? In technical terms, what are the chances that knowledge needs to be managed and transferred synchronously and asynchronously?

So in a business like stockbroking, which is largely a real-time synchronous kind of environment, the set of tool requirements would be different from that of, say, management consulting, which is relatively an asynchronous business.

In light of this framework, a recent study of mine (Banerjee*) consisting of a sample of 100 leading software/software-enabled companies in Asia revealed that the percentage of users stacked up as shown in Figure 22.1. Needless to say, some of them did use a number of tools, but most of them failed to get the combination right.

The Multidimensional Matrix Approach

The KM situation in an organization is best represented through a set of three dimensions, namely, the organization's context (called the organization in the original model), the KM needs arising out of the organization context and needs, and the KM solution (note: it is called a solution and not a tool), as outlined in Table 22.2.

---

* Banerjee 2003. IEEE presentation, Bangalore, India.

Figure 22.1

Spatio-temporal Framework for KM tools (adapted from an original framework of Arthur D. Little, www.adlittle.com)

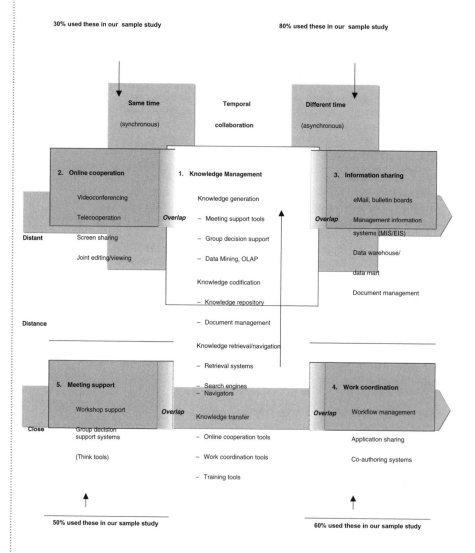

Table 22.2

Multidimensional Matrix Approach[a]		
Organization's context	Knowledge needs	Solutions derived out of organization's context and knowledge needs
• Type of organization • Market types serviced • Nature of business • Size of organization etc.	• Create • Capture • Organize • Access and • Use Related issues: location of knowledge, users of knowledge	Tool combinations could be a portfolio of: • IRS • DMS • Linguistic tools • Semantic search • Document analysis • Competency-driven tools

[a] Adapted from a concept by Fulvio Iavernaro, http://www.iwproductivity.org/research.htm.

Interestingly, this matrix goes further and looks at the possibility of implementing KM not necessarily from a tool-based technology perspective, but also the extent to which rollouts can happen through extensive leverage of the human element as well as of strategic initiatives. Specifically, the human factor (interpersonal interaction) becomes important not just for the fact that humans are great learners, but also for their ability to *reach out* and network with business communities beyond their own, which a vanilla tool just cannot do.

Organizations, therefore, take a final call on technology choice (and who said that the cheapest KM technology is a table and two chairs for two knowledge workers to talk!) based on their preferences that come out from the multidimensional analysis summarized in Figure 22.2.

Information Management Plus versus Ground Zero

Technology is like love. Managers tend to get into a *love at first sight* syndrome. However, what they forget is to take a second look at the first impression.

Quite often the best way to approach and choose a technology type is to look for one which builds on what one already has. This is what I call an *Information Management Plus* approach. While there are pitfalls here like limitations of choice, the biggest draw is that it helps in easy institutionalization of KM technology, as people would be comfortable with using something close to what they are well acquainted with. This is, of course, given the assumption that the information management systems have had delivered business benefits in the past.

On the other hand, there could be cases when information management systems have not been successfully deployed. In that case, it makes sense to embark on a clean slate approach *(Ground Zero)* and look around for newer KM technologies, provided the differential cost of ownership is not that significant.

In case the differential cost is significant, my experience has been to then try and get into shredding the existing technology, doing a *value analysis* and *engineering* of sorts, and looking at innovative ways of leveraging the human factor. A formal approach to managing change through people-based organization development becomes critical.

Figure 22.2

Multidimensional matrix in use: The business scope mapping corporate positions on KM technology (adapted from a concept by Fulvio Iavernaro, http://www.iwproductivity.org/research.htm)

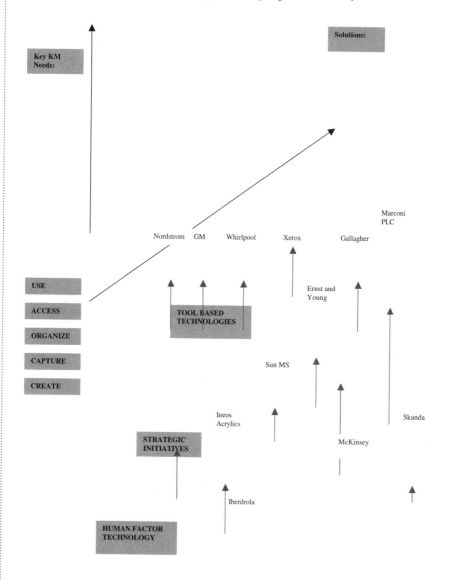

Techbuck Score Card

Noted underworld character Walter Salbury, when caught by the Chicago police while trying to rob a bank, was asked one simple question, "Why did you rob the bank?" He replied, "That is where the money is." If only we could say the same for KM tools and technology. My experience shows that KM technology has worked and not worked in the following ways and areas. This is purely a snapshot of what has happened and does *not* in any way reflect the potential of KM as a body of practice (see Table 22.3).

One of the key reasons for low RoI from KM, wherever so (apart from insignificant revenue growth due to lack of business alignment in the case of most initiatives), can be attributed to the abnormally high total cost of technology ownership. This is due to a number of factors:

- Failure on the part of KM tech managers to control infrastructure costs
- Extensive propensity to use in-house resources from the bench, thereby leading to innumerable trial and error situations (rather than seeking external professional help)
- Mess ups in platform integration
- Interruptions in connectivity

The following can be learned from these experiences:

1. The maximum potential of KM tools has not yet been realized.
2. Whatever potential of these tools had been realized, a large part of it had not paid off in terms of generating significant RoI, thanks to non-alignment to business needs and strategy.
3. The human factor/element is a critical moderator in analyzing, understanding, and deploying tools.
4. KM solutions best evolve out of an interplay of business requirements, the tool portfolio, and the human factor.

Looking ahead, one can identify a number of developments that could dramatically redefine the approach to KM technology. (One must confess that Predicting the future is notoriously difficult. Suppose 100 years ago someone suggested that every bedroom in the United States would soon have a bell that anyone in the world could

Table 22.3

The KM Techbuck Score Card	
KM Technology has successfully created RoI in • Managing efficiencies • Project management • Networking knowledge workers • Technology breakthroughs • Effective brainstorming • Problem analysis • Benchmarking • Process improvement programs • Vendor rationalization • Scaling up	KM Technology has been less successful in creating RoI in • Generating newer businesses • Facilitating change in work habits • Managing crisis • Helping cut information overload • Embedding knowledge processes into business processes • Large-scale business rehaul • Enterprise asset management

ring anytime, day or night. Would you have believed it? Nevertheless, the telephone caught on and has become a technology conspicuous only by its absence.) Developments worth watching on the KM tool front include:

- The shift from computational computing, such as reading e-mails, to non-computational computing, such as helping take baths and eating dinners (*the value of a computer would decrease with the square of your distance from its monitor*)
- The extent to which Systems Thinking gets applied to conceptualizing and implementing KM solutions
- Advances in the Theory of Patterns and Anti-patterns and its applicability to deciphering business context for doing KM
- Changes in the concept of Social Networks to isolated interdependent and connected individuals
- The extent to which technology starts adapting to human beings

How will these tools evolve and impact KM? Only time will tell. One thing is for sure: one thing which will probably not change is the fact the the trick in using technology will always be to know how not to get into trouble with it.

References

Banerjee, Ritendra "Knowledge Management: An Introduction," Coen, Michael (1999). The future of human-computer interaction, or how I learned to stop worrying and love my intelligent room. IEEE Intelligent System, Pages 8–10, March/April 1999. IEEE presentation. Also at http://www.qaiindia.com/Misc/thought_leadership/frameset.htm.

From "How I learned to stop worrying and love my Intelligent Room," Coen, Michael (1999). The future of human-computer interaction, or how I learned to stop worrying and love my intelligent room. IEEE Intelligent System, Pages 8–10, March/April 1999. http://www.ai.mit.edu/people/mhcoen/.

Collaboration Software: Evolution and Revolution*

Eric Woods

> Our knowledge can only be finite, while our ignorance must necessarily be infinite.
>
> *Karl Popper*

Introduction: The Networked Enterprise

What do the following have in common?

- A petrochemical company trying to improve the performance of its deep-sea drilling operations
- An advertising agency working on campaign collateral with a multinational client
- An aid agency trying to provide access to volunteers in Tanzania

The answer is that they are all looking to collaboration tools as a way to improve efficiency, reduce costs, and deliver a better service. Like so many organizations operating on a global basis, they are looking to make the network a shared space where people can work together and exchange ideas, independent of location and time.

The rising value being placed on effective collaboration—both within organizations and with partners, suppliers, and customers—is also being paralleled by a new wave

---

* *Editor's Note:* Collaboration is gaining increasing prominence both within organizations as part of knowledge work and among software vendors as a focus area for innovative product development. In addition to the Internet and intranet, the emergence of tools for peer-to-peer communication, mobile access, instant messaging, and Web services are all having an influence on collaborative platforms and methods. Collaborative behaviors in knowledge work underlie non-formal, bottom-up communities of practice as well as more formal team management and task execution. Collaborative tools can facilitate a practice (how people work together to get the job done) as well as a process (the explicit or formal definition of how work should be done). This chapter traces the growth of collaborative tools and activities (especially in large organizations), provides a model for companies to assess collaborative tool functionality, and covers communication channels ranging from e-mail to mobile messaging. Key observations include the proliferation of project-based collaboration tools in the market and the importance of a leadership role in encouraging collaborative solutions to knowledge work.

Figure 23.1

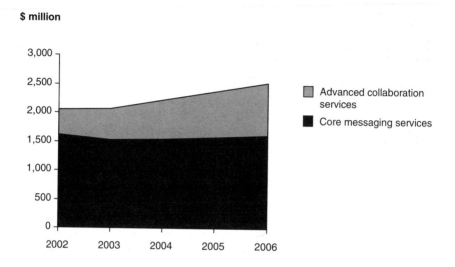

Collaboration software revenues

Source: Ovum

of innovation in collaboration technologies, driven by three interlinked but distinct developments:

- The requirement for new forms of networked environment that can support the extended and distributed enterprise—The pressure to realize the potential of all organizations is even greater today when budgets are tight and competition is fierce.
- New technical environments are changing the possibilities for collaboration—The Internet and the Web have made a huge impact, but developments such as peer-to-peer communication, mobile access, instant messaging, and Web services are all having an influence as well.
- Changes in the market ecology for collaborative software—For example, market leaders try to transform their offering to meet new requirements, new entrants emerge, and players from other sectors try to muscle in on a growth area.

Ovum (2002) estimates that the collaboration market was worth more than $2 billion in 2002. By 2006, the market will be worth more than $2.5 billion, but in that time the market for the new generation of advanced collaboration tools will more than double, growing from $435 million to $923 million (see Figure 23.1).

The Changing Forms of Collaboration

There is a dichotomy at the heart of organizational collaboration that has in the past hampered many projects and initiatives. How do you balance the different requirements of informal and formal collaboration? That is to say, how can you support flexible, pragmatic collaboration needs (both within and beyond the firewall), while ensuring the right level of managerial support and supervision? Our better under-standing of these requirements and improved flexibility in collaboration software are helping make effective collaboration a much more realistic goal for knowledge work in many organizations.

Informal Collaboration

Informal collaboration includes simple social tasks, such as arranging a team event or *ad hoc* discussions on specific project issues. These tasks generally require little more than some form of messaging. Informal collaboration also has an impor-tant role outside a project-based environment. Individuals may require support from others on an *ad hoc* basis, for example, the provision of online support through chat or voice/videoconferencing embedded in an application as an alternative to the traditional "hotline" telephone support. This may also include screen sharing within an organization, across organizations (for example, supplier to customer), and even within Internet-based transactions. The screen sharing may also be used to deliver presentations to potentially very large groups of people dispersed worldwide, within a single organization, or across multiple organizations. In this case, the "team" simply consists of the participants in the presentation and may only exist for less than an hour.

One of the most valuable forms of informal collaboration is that embodied in the concept of communities of practice. The knowledge management movement has long identified the importance of non-formal relationships among workers that support key business processes. We are now seeing these communities being given explicit approval and support within many organizations, as they realize the value of this type of intan-gible and strongly differentiating social capital that is hard to replicate. It is therefore important for collaboration software to support communities of practice and help the organization realize and (where relevant) capture the expertise embedded in these communities and their interactions.

Formal Collaboration

While informal collaboration is typically defined bottom-up by the requirements of the team or community supported, formal collaboration is more often defined top-down in accordance with the needs of the organization for process control.

At the intermediate level, most teams need to be managed. This includes task plan-ning and scheduling, task monitoring, scheduling of meetings, and passing work around the team for comment and approval. All team members need to be fully aware of what is expected of them and how their work fits with the rest of the team. The tracking of progress can be made substantially easier if all work in progress and com-pleted tasks are executed in a centrally managed location. This will ensure that every-one has access to consistent information and will provide an effective audit trail.

In its most developed form, formal collaboration becomes strongly process driven, with clear management of tasks and responsibilities.

The Changing Balance: Informal/Formal—Practice/Process

The need for balance between informal and formal collaboration can also be under-stood as a relationship between practice (how people work together to get the job done) and process (the explicit or formal definition of how work should be done). At best, there is a creative tension between these two aspects of work; however, too often,

Figure 23.2

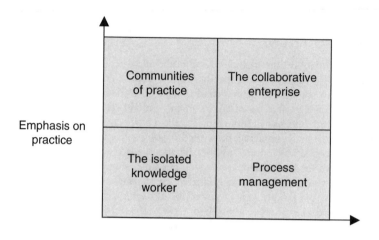

Effective collaboration is a balance between practice and process

Emphasis on practice

Communities of practice

The collaborative enterprise

The isolated knowledge worker

Process management

Emphasis on process

Source: Ovum

they are in conflict and thereby undermine the effectiveness of the organization. (For an insightful analysis of the relationship between practice and process, see Brown and Duguid, 2000.)

The goal for the collaborative enterprise is to combine the best of both aspects, as shown in Figure 23.2. In turn, this is setting the agenda for the development of collaborative software.

The Ovum Model for Collaboration Software

As with any rapidly growing area of software technology, there is a huge range of solutions claiming to provide effective collaboration facilities. Distinguishing between these solutions and selecting the most appropriate one for your organization is not a trivial task.

Ovum's model for collaboration software provides a basis for drawing up the functionality that you require from collaboration software and allows you to compare directly the functionality of the tools on the market. Ovum's model contains four major components: the workspace, communication, collaborative services, and management functions. This is shown in Figure 23.3.

Workspace

Workspaces provide areas where individuals and teams can carry out their individual and collaborative tasks. It also provides an environment that can be organized into multiple teams, projects, and topics. This creates the framework for the whole collaborative environment.

Figure 23.3

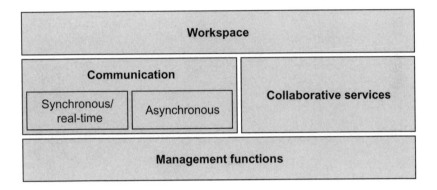

The Ovum model for collaboration software

The workspace provides the front end to the multiple functions provided in the collaborative environment—often through a portal-like user interface. This should be configurable at multiple levels:

- For a corporation to give it brand identity, which is particularly important when the collaboration tool is to be used outside the company
- For individual teams to deliver the necessary functionality and information access demanded by the team
- For the individual, for personal preferences

Within the generic workspace, it is necessary to set up multiple working areas; as a minimum, there will be one for each project team or topic. These need to be built "on the fly" as the need arises. It will also often be necessary to subdivide large teams into smaller teams, thus creating a hierarchy of work areas. Some of the bottom-level work areas may only be in existence for a period of hours or days. These individual areas are frequently referred to as work areas or meeting rooms. In addition, it will often be appropriate to create workspaces for each team member to provide a private workspace that is only accessible to that person.

Within each workspace, access to multiple individual functions is required. A component of this is the ability to create links to information outside the current collaboration. This may be to other areas of the collaboration tool, to material outside the collaboration tool but within the organization, or even to material outside the organization. The latter will typically either be to Web sites or to collaboration partners along the supply chain.

The workspace should be accessible through a range of devices, including the fixed-office personal computer, laptops being used from remote locations, and other mobile devices. Offline working will be essential for many mobile users, support for which requires functions to synchronize local and centralized collaboration and content repositories. The range of services available will be tailored to the type of device being used; small-screen devices such as mobile phones will not be appropriate for the more sophisticated project management tasks. It should be possible to send and receive alerts on mobile phones and carry out simple messaging through SMS.

Figure 23.4

Collaborative services (Source: Ovum)

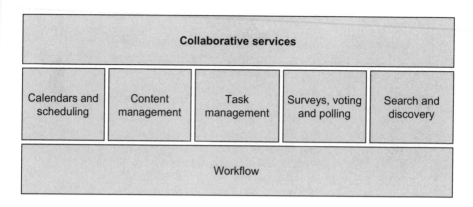

Collaborative Services

Collaborative services deliver major functions to the workspace. This includes access to authoring tools such as word processing, spreadsheets, and diagramming tools, together with basic content management and team-based functions such as calendaring and scheduling.

These functions provide facilities to make working together more efficient, such as group calendars and controls on content that is created within the workspace. The range of functions that need to be provided is shown in Figure 23.4.

Communication

Communication functions allow team members to communicate, both in real time, via synchronous communication, and through more traditional messaging approaches such as e-mail, which delivers asynchronous communication. Other typical functions include mark-up facilities, screen sharing, whiteboarding, and conferencing.

Synchronous communication covers all aspects of communication between team members and, potentially, individuals outside the team in real time. The major elements of synchronous communication are shown in Figure 23.5. One of the biggest benefits of synchronous communication is that all the content that passes through the collaboration system can be captured and stored for future use. This provides an effective audit trail of the collaborative tasks and may capture useful information for future use.

Asynchronous communication covers all aspects of communication between team members and, potentially, individuals outside the team on a non-real-time basis—the classic example being traditional e-mail. The major elements of asynchronous communication are shown in Figure 23.6.

Management Functions

Management functions deliver the facilities to create new team workspaces and manage the pages within any workspace, as well as manage the individual team members. Access needs to be carefully managed to ensure that the security and integrity of

Figure 23.5

Synchronous/real-time communication (Source: Ovum)

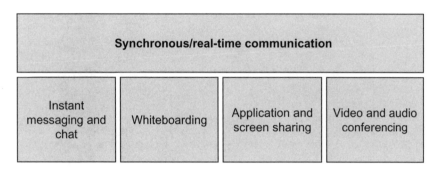

Figure 23.6

Asynchronous communication (Source: Ovum)

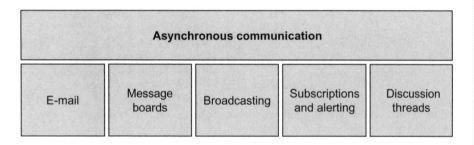

the content of the teams' collaborative activities are not compromised. This is particularly important where collaboration is being executed across corporate boundaries. The range of functions that are required is shown in Figure 23.7.

The Future for Collaboration Software

The roots of collaboration software can be traced back to the launch of Lotus Notes in 1989, which more or less kick-started the "groupware" market. However, the concept of collaboration has long been praised and less often implemented.

During the 1990s, actual deployments of Notes and its competitors grew slowly. The mid-1990s saw further expansion due to Microsoft's entry into the corporate e-mail market and the new impetus given to Lotus after its acquisition by IBM. In the late 1990s, it was given another push by the emergence of Internet e-mail, the growing interest in knowledge management, and by the development of corporate intranets. This period saw new entrants into the market, such as Open Text and Intraspect, which offered to fill the gaps in the offerings from IBM Lotus and Microsoft.

The extension of Internet technologies has provided further impetus to these developments in recent years and has offered new dimensions to collaboration in the form of Web-based environments, instant messaging, and peer-to-peer communication. Vendors such as eRoom (since acquired by Documentum), Groove Networks, WebEx,

Figure 23.7

Management functions (Source: Ovum)

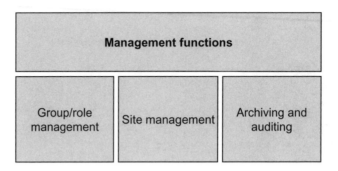

Figure 23.8

The evolution of the enterprise collaboration platform

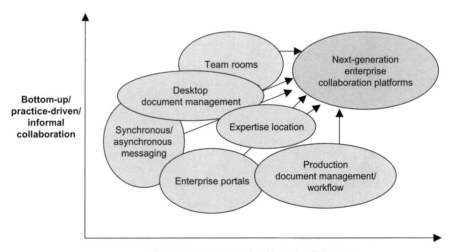

Source: Ovum

and Placeware (acquired by Microsoft) emerged to provide additional approaches to collaboration. Lotus has also developed its own offering in this area with QuickPlace and Sametime.

At one level, the collaboration market has gone through significant consolidation, with IBM Lotus and Microsoft battling between themselves for the dominance of the enterprise messaging market. At other levels, however, the market is more dynamic and fragmented than ever before, with not only a host of start-ups in the market, but also the entrance of bigger players such as Oracle and Documentum.

Over the next two years, we will continue to see much wider adoption of project-based collaboration tools, as well as an increased use of synchronous communications such as instant messaging. We will also see the integration of collaboration tools into a wider range of business applications and also more integrated collaboration services with enterprise portals.

However, larger organizations are already becoming concerned about the proliferation of project-based collaboration tools. As a result, they will look for a more cohesive strategy for supporting collaboration across the enterprise. Collaboration solutions need to be able to cover the many and varied contexts for collaboration. As a consequence, we are seeing the market evolve toward the provision of a new generation of enterprise collaboration platforms that can support the requirements for both informal and formal collaboration—both the bottom-up requirements of communities and teams and the top-down requirements for management and process control.

A new class of enterprise collaborative platforms will emerge over the next two or three years to support this requirement. Figure 23.8 shows how various technologies are evolving and being combined to deliver that enterprise platform.

Collaboration: A Leadership Issue

The modern organization inhabits a multidimensional space with fluid boundaries not limited by restrictions of geography, location, or time. Finding new and effective ways to work together in this environment is therefore an imperative for all businesses. This requirement is making collaboration one of the most exciting areas for software innovation. However, you should never forget that the technology is only a means for realizing a wider vision of how people can work together. The organizational challenges that have bedevilled attempts to develop a wide-scale and lasting collaborative solution have not gone away. In his thought-provoking 1995 book, Schrage wrote perceptively of the challenge to be faced:

> The single most important issue confronting the leadership of collaborative organisations, then, is how to pose problems and opportunities in forms that will elicit and inspire a collaborative response.

In other words, it is not enough to simply bemoan the cultural barriers to knowledge sharing or the failings of technology. We have to start creatively thinking of how we pose questions in a manner that encourages collaborative solutions. As Schrage says, it is, above all, a matter of leadership.

References

Ovum (2002). Collaboration Software: Evolution and Revolution—An Ovum Report. http://www.ovum.com/go/product/flyer/016117.htm.

Brown, John Seely and Duguid, Paul (2000). *The Social Life of Information*. Boston: Harvard Business School Press.

Schrage, Michael (1995). *No More Teams! Mastering the Dynamic of Creative Collaboration*. New York: Currency Doubleday.

Competitive Intelligence and Knowledge Management: Complementary Partners, Reinforcing Tools*

24

Arik R. Johnson

> Carefully compare the opposing army with your own, so that you may know where strength is superabundant and where it is deficient.
>
> *Sun Tzu*
> *The Art of War*

CI and KM: Natural Allies

Competitive intelligence, or CI as it is known to practitioners, has risen to prominence in the past several years as a mission-critical, systemized function that every business must employ to succeed tactically and strategically in its various markets.

As the coordinated and ongoing monitoring of the external business environment in order to mitigate risks, CI is an undertaking that every business has always performed and always will. It also involves seeking out opportunities for growth and market dominance. The degree of sophistication and formalization of the intelligence

---

* *Editor's Note:* This chapter draws out the connection between competitive intelligence (CI) and knowledge management (KM), natural allies in the drive for organizational competitive advantage. There are numerous CI software applications, content aggregators, and service providers who can both provide market intelligence to a company's knowledge inputs and use KM themselves for better managing their own services. KM methods and tools such as communities of practice and subject matter expert networks lend themselves well to the CI function.

This chapter provides a useful landscape of CI's contributions to minimizing risks and maximizing opportunities via competitor monitoring, performance benchmarking, intellectual property exploitation, regulation tracking, and M&A activity. Of late, the CI function has embraced Web-based tools like collaborative technologies and even blogging (Weblogging). Blogs are emerging as a key low-cost component of building *ad hoc* communities of practice, while also creating a platform for delivery of market monitoring by the intelligence team to its customers. Other useful content tools for CI include periodic newsletters. The increasing use of XML and RSS are emerging developments to keep an eye on as well.

process and the various resources devoted to it are the foremost characteristics that differentiate success from failure in any CI initiative. That said, a sizeable percentage of the U.S. Fortune 1000 group of companies have no such formal CI function, and many more operate on shoestring budgets that restrict their ability to succeed.

The differentiable factors between world-class intelligence and *ad hoc* efforts chiefly involve levels of sophistication in techniques for collection and analysis, the extent of infrastructure support for storage and processing, the availability of delivery mechanisms to and from the intelligence constituency, and the degree to which every person in the firm's employ is integrated into the intelligence mission.

CI and knowledge management (KM) have become natural allies in the drive toward organizational competitive advantage. It has been said that some 80% of what a firm needs to know about its external marketplace is already present within the boundaries of the firm; accessing that information has been the barrier. Indeed, KM materialized as a countervailing force to much of the Business Process Reengineering (BPO) trends of the late 1980s and early 1990s, replacing the social networks previously enabled by newly "right-sized" middle-management with communications and storage-retrieval infrastructure largely brought about by the advent of Web-based technologies.

Certainly, while KM's applications are much broader than simply that of enabling the efficient and effective use of internally housed intelligence about the marketplace, competitors, customers, vendors, and other forces affecting risks and opportunities, KM technologies and methods can contribute a great deal to CI's overall strategic effectiveness and tactical efficiency of mission. Likewise, CI has proven itself as a sort of "beachhead" or business case for a KM initiative to wrap its arms around—in a sense, providing a clear-cut example of how KM can profit the firm through its alignment with the intelligence needs of the organization.

Communities of Practice and Subject Matter Expert Networks

The two highest impact application methods to cross over from KM to CI in the past decade have been communities of practice and subject matter expert networks.

Communities of practice as *de facto* interest groups with a shared set of characteristics that can be identified and queried, often anonymously, have contributed as research and opinion sources in CI decision-support applications (i.e., wherever specific questions exist in the mind of the CI analyst about whatever subject he or she is interested in). Likewise, subject matter expert networks, often based on a historical profile of enterprise users that also accounts for their captured (and therefore searchable) work history, communications among colleagues, and document authorship, can provide similar infrastructure to the CI analyst seeking to leverage tacit human expertise about external conditions.

However, it is relatively rare for both CI and KM functions to cooperate in this way. CI has always had its own internal rivals—usually the market research and strategic planning groups—and, in many organizations, KM has become just another competitor for resources and mission. For this reason, CI infrastructure has often ignored existing KM tools in favor of building its own or force-fitting third party tools specific to CI's primary mission.

There are dozens of CI software applications designed to tie the function together between corporate and business unit activities, while also acting as a central repository for storage and delivery of finished, actionable intelligence. Many more provide analytical frameworks for a fledgling CI organization to begin turnkey delivery of intelligence to its customers. Likewise, newsfeed and secondary source data vendors sell their products to many different constituencies within the same organization, often redundantly. It is perhaps too obvious to say that KM and CI are natural partners and *should* work together, just as market research, strategic planning, and other "competitors" have learned to work with CI on a different level.

However, to understand how this is possible, we must first understand exactly what the scope of CI's mission can and should be at different points in its evolution and life cycle.

Application Priorities of CI

If one asks any business managers how they define CI, we would hear responses ranging from "corporate spying" and "industrial espionage" to more traditional definitions as described above. However, CI has priorities that range much more broadly than understanding competitor behavior, although that is a key part. In the pharmaceuticals business, for example, CI plays a role at almost every level of the organization's external information collection, both at the corporate level and at the business unit—from regulation and legislation to intellectual property protection and exploitation.

While CI remains primarily concerned with tracking and monitoring direct competitor behavior to support the firm's strategic and tactical decision making, never before has CI played such an important part in so many diverse areas of the enterprise. It has expanded from its still-noble beginnings of helping the company to win the zero-sum game of "we-win-and-they-lose," often more than a little sinister in its ends (and the reason for its association with "spying"). Today it includes supporting, through external information collection, analysis, and formulation of strategic recommendations, virtually all of the sundry short- and long-term market objectives of the firm, or at least those related to the organization's competitiveness in key market domains.

Despite this evolution in mission toward a more entrepreneurial and opportunistic cash-flow driver, the fact remains that CI is still largely perceived by its internal customers as a cost center: an overhead expense that can be scaled back when macroeconomic tides change. Belt-tightening in the face of slowdowns in economic growth have forced firms to concentrate more broadly on operational *efficiency* instead of comparative *effectiveness* of those operations enterprise wide.

The mistake that is usually made by these kinds of CI teams is a myopia of scope and scale as regards to their original mission—a definition of their own value proposition to the firm as primarily related to competitor tracking and risk aversion in the near-term businesses in which the firm competes today—with little concentration or effort directed toward helping the firm to grow most profitably or take advantage of opportunities presented by these same contractionary economic circumstances.

Competitive strategy is still critical to the firm during economic downturns; it is just different in nature from that which we pursue during expansionary business cycles. For example, rather than expansion through marketing or production partnerships, M&A, and licensing intellectual property for new products, competitive strategy might concentrate on capitalizing on the pain of one's smaller, cash-starved rivals, especially those with market capital invested in faster growing markets that hold the future of the firm's diversification strategy.

Minimizing Risks

CI has always concentrated its attention on minimizing threats to current business activities. This focus has allowed many firms to build very effective CI operations with the mission of remaining aware and responsive to competition. This rather reactionary perspective remains CI's primary objective, but it can be argued that this is the *minimum* that must be done to craft an effective competitive strategy in the short term.

Maximizing Opportunities

The most common area in which new CI functions disappoint their internal customers is that of maximizing new business opportunities for the firm. While many managers fail to accept CI's role in helping the company to select new markets for existing offerings (a.k.a. "low-hanging fruit"), fresh revenue streams, or other opportunities for the firm to grow value for shareholders, this is a vital lesson for CI teams to understand. CI's value will best be judged on the basis of contributing to the net *income* of the enterprise at large, or their net cost to the enterprise in defending or recommending abandonment of some market segments. It is far more important in this respect for the CI function to help the firm find new markets for existing or adapted products and services, even if those products and services have very little to do with what the company does today.

Key Intelligence Topics and Entrepreneurial Intelligence

KITs, or Key Intelligence Topics, have traditionally dominated CI as the preeminent list of priorities by which all intelligence activities will be judged. Within this set of questions, most firms will deal with three subject protocols: Strategic Decisions and Issues, Early-Warning Topics, and Key Players in the Marketplace. These areas further divide into such diverse competitor and environmental variables as Financials, Products/Services, Sales/Marketing, Value-Chain, Personnel, and the competitor's Customers.

The list below describes these priorities in rough order of levels of sophistication and relative importance to the average organization. This approach also adopts a mindset of "intrapreneurship," where the CI team becomes a sort of business within a business, thus focusing intelligence personnel on growing its "business" with internal customers through continuous expansion of their products and services. Similarly, such a diversification strategy would, much like any other business, build out its own product, service, and market offerings to deliver value to a broader customer base.

1. **Current competitor activities and behavior monitoring**—This is the standard and most fundamental deliverable of the CI program. It is important to remember that, above all, customers expect the CI team to be aware of and helpful in understanding competitors' current activities and plans. The preeminent goal herein is to understand how to successfully transfer marketshare from the competitor's company to one's own company.
2. **Customer and vendor monitoring**—Threats of backwards and forwards integration by customers and vendors is a possibility most often realized by firms every day—even described as two of the drivers of competitive strategy within the classic Porter Five Forces Model. These threats are known as "latent competitors," or those which could relatively easily move back and forth in the value chain to exclude the firm. As customers and vendors move up and down the value-added ladder, healthy profits at different stages create opportunities for such traditional allies to move quickly into a "cannibalization" mode against the firm. Likewise, an understanding of customer-share, or "wallet," can be revealing in showing up-selling and cross-selling opportunities.

3. **Operational/performance benchmarking**—Benchmarking initiatives can prove beneficial in studying latent competitors, "parallel competitors" (or substitutes for your products/services), as well as best-in-class or best-in-world firms that can easily move into diversified businesses. Benchmarking studies often begin by isolating the operational deficiencies present in the firm, identifying practices at firms that excel in those areas, and then conducting research to determine why they excel in order to transfer that knowledge to the firm to increase tactical efficiency. This is tied to an understanding of Gary Hamel and C.K. Prahalad's "core competence."

4. **Strategic probabilities and possible futures**—"Scenario planning" has been a tool used by many competitive strategists to understand the sum total of possible futures and assign a probabilistic likelihood to each of those possibilities. Closely tied to war gaming, the most common method of scenario planning is characterized by "decision-trees" or the "implications-wheel" models that have been used to comprehensively and statistically weigh ideally *all* possible outcomes and then craft decisions based on the least harmful or most helpful series of outcomes predicted.

5. **Product/service sales and marketing support**—As one of the highest impact areas that the intelligence team can assist in, a solid understanding of strengths and weaknesses (not only of competitors, but of the firm's own customer and market perceptions) can be the make-or-break metric of tactical success or failure. While the ability to contribute recommendations to salesforces for ensuring "FUD-Factor" (fear, uncertainty, and doubt) in the minds of customers about competitors' products and services is important, it is also critical to understand the marketing messages relayed to this customer base by competitors. This is closely related to value chain, channel, and customer intelligence, but usually conducted anonymously, in order to ensure truthful discussion by customers and distributors of the relative perceptions of their sourcing alternatives.

6. **Intellectual property exploitation/protection**—As what might often prove to be the cornerstone of a firm's core competence and competitive differentia, intellectual property (IP) can determine who ultimately wins and loses the competitive battle in the hearts and minds of customers. In many markets, IP is the single greatest influencer of competitive advantage.

7. **M&A-alliance-investment support**—Buying, investing in, and allying with companies that have something to offer can provide a company with the engine of growth for future expansion plans. Many deals fail to produce the often overestimated *shareholder value* they hope to deliver. This is most often due to a lack of due diligence in the qualification process—and a source of tremendous validation value for the CI team. Recent efforts to include pre-deal due diligence by intelligence teams have had substantial effects on post-deal success, beginning with selection of candidates and ending with final consummation of the deal and integration of enterprises together.

8. **Long-term market prospects**—Are we in the right business today? Tomorrow? Every business is locked into the iron-clad business law of the "product life cycle" that includes not only the most profitable periods of product/service lifespan, but also innovation and eventual decline and death. While most commonly directed toward understanding which markets will be fastest growing (a traditional market research activity) and then making recommendations to decision makers on the means by which the firm can come to dominate those markets, a solid understanding of core competence is important here.

9. **Counterintelligence and information security**—One *must* assume that each organization is under the scrutiny of its rivals, and methods will be used to extract sensitive information from the firm to enable the competitor to win in the marketplace. While most often deployed against industrial espionage activities, counterintelligence is often a very highly developed process—sometimes even designed specifically to *dis*-inform one's competitors as to the firm's future plans. The legal and security teams are most often considered the liaisons to counterattack these specific initiatives, despite the fact that legal and security tend to be better at minimizing the impact of intelligence breaches *after* they have occurred rather than preventing against such actions beforehand. Former employees, contractors, and other individuals privy to the nature of the firm's proprietary information can be significant sources of CI for competitors.

10. **Legislative/regulatory impact on business issues**—In certain industries, more than others, government activities, in both legislative and regulatory realms, can be disproportionately influential in enabling or hobbling a firm's competitive strategy. Typically most influential in industries for the public interest such as telecom, finance, energy, health care, and transportation, this is also important in understanding the implications of strategic initiatives such as merger and acquisition approval. If a government denies approval for a certain merger, as we saw happen in Europe with MCI and Sprint as well as GE and Honeywell, the competitive benefits of the deal will certainly be compromised.

Web-based Intelligence: CI's Holy Grail

Since the World Wide Web began deconstructing and rebuilding the information industry in the mid-1990s, intelligence practitioners have been trying to decipher how the Web and its technologies would affect CI as an undertaking. At first, the movement of traditional database content from CD-ROM and BBS to HTML-based retrieval and display meant simply that the common platform for delivery made content available to anyone with an IP address, a great unifier in terms of moving toward ubiquity of access. Still, collaboration between and among knowledgeable internal human sources has remained elusive, even as the volume of intranet and portal content has exploded beyond anyone's early estimates or, for that matter, utility of purpose.

Indeed, the "infoglut" is the greatest problem afflicting intelligence systems' effective and efficient operation and application in business today, and collaborative technologies have only recently become a part of CI systems in the past couple of years with the advent of knowledge management technologies and eventual extension of consumer tools such as Weblogs or "blogs" into the enterprise toolkit. While I believe Weblogging as a function will almost certainly be absorbed into the broader software marketplace for collaboration—and therefore probably lose the Weblog moniker—there is room in the near-term to discuss Weblogs as a discrete and important new evolution in low-cost, comprehensive KM enablers for CI.

Weblogs, Market Monitoring, and Optimizing Intelligence Systems

Weblogging has become a hobbyist pastime of many Web surfers on the consumer Internet and has also penetrated the corporate sphere for many different purposes. One of the biggest trends being observed between CI and KM recently has been the use of Weblogs as a key low-cost component of building *ad hoc* communities of practice, while also creating a platform for delivery of market monitoring by the intelligence team to its customers.

Within the diverse list of mission priorities discussed above, one of the most visible deliverables of any CI function is the production and distribution of a market or competitor intelligence monitoring product—a.k.a. the "newsletter"—usually produced weekly or monthly and broadcast throughout the organization to anyone interested in reading about competitors, industry events, and thoughts and ideas related to the company's ability to compete in the marketplace.

Since such deliverables are often the most highly visible product the intelligence team might deliver, getting it right has never been more important to a CI team's future success and survival.

The Process

First, it is important to understand what this sort of intelligence product is and is not. Monitoring deliverables like these are not intended to answer such specific questions as those sure to arise by consumers in the course of day-to-day market competition. Rather, monitoring applications are designed to produce a level of "current awareness" for the organization about its environment and, ideally, an "early warning" of risks and opportunities to come, based on the analysis of weak signals received from the marketplace, also known as "pattern recognition." We can see from our list of application priorities above that this crosses many of the domains CI can evolve to support.

Once consumers understand its purpose, a market monitoring function can take many forms, but the most common and useful approach is to produce a periodic briefing directed at a comparatively broad audience with broadly defined topical coverage. Then, through multi-versioning of each deliverable, those parameters must be differentiated by which certain subconstituents might receive various levels of intelligence granularity (depending upon their need to know those variables about the marketplace).

For example, in the beginning of a CI team's typical product life cycle, when keeping track of competitors is most often defined as its primary mission, most CI teams will focus on building the infrastructure required to satisfy that mission so that more sophisticated and value-added application priorities, ranging from helping the salesforce win bids to making merger and acquisition recommendations, can be satisfied later on. A monitoring product therefore must be based on the broadest possible understanding of the organization's particular market priorities from both its risk and its opportunity perspective.

Most companies have a list of top-tier competitors and other key players and then another list of secondary companies that, while they might not find themselves consistently losing business to rivals in this group with any regularity, the company believes *could* become a serious threat to the status quo at some point and are, therefore, worthy of watching.

For the CI team then, it is important to focus on all such key players in the marketplace as described in the KIT discussion above, and this is sometimes a list that can grow very long indeed. There exist monitoring applications among some large companies with a few dozen competitors listed as top tier and sometimes *hundreds* more listed as secondary in importance, depending on market niche, positioning strategy, and geography. The same goes for the other peripheral organizations that need to be scanned periodically—customers, vendors, regulators, etc. Sometimes, it is even necessary to monitor firms that have nothing to do with your current marketplace, but who might be a future threat should they decide to enter it. Finally, geography is also important if the scope will cover just the United States and Canada, but will there be individual components that look at Europe, Asia, and Latin America as well?

The CI team then needs to define those topics that, within this subject set, will rank high enough to be reported. This is very much a "human filter" activity, a task that software alone will be ill-equipped to do with any level of sophistication due to the highly situational context relative to the importance of events to a particular interest group. Topics such as M&A activity, product launches, partnerships and alliances, key executive changes, and even intellectual property activity all rank high on the list for most firms. The final, and often most difficult, component is deciding which conditions will cause the periodic format of the monitoring product to break out of schedule. In other words, events will often occur that are so important that to wait until next week to report them would be anathema to the very mission the CI function has been chartered to accomplish.

One key point must be made when considering the means and method of using a Weblog to distribute current awareness and early warning to the firm: intelligence does not focus on the business of alerting decision and policy makers to every change in administration a competitor might decide is of "strategic interest" to their shareholders and, as such, worthy of a press release. The real value provided by a CI team in this respect is in the implications analysis and situational recommendations that can be produced within the context of such events for one's intelligence consumers.

The Tools

The first component in the monitoring process must, of course, be some form of newsfeed to alert the intelligence team to events and changes in the marketplace. Most readers of this discussion are hopefully already knowledgeable about and aware enough of the litany of newsfeed and document retrieval services that exist to support business today. That said, there are myriad providers available ranging from very expensive to free, in terms of price. Additionally, the feature sets of such products are so sophisticated today that a CI team could effectively pre-assign search-and-retrieve specifications based on keyword includes and excludes to ensure they will not miss anything they need, while avoiding those subjects that will prove less useful.

In terms of selection criteria for such a vendor, it is unwise to select a provider with a pricing scheme linked to pay-by-the-item or pay-by-the-seat costing. It may turn out to be difficult to link back to original sources if one has to deal with per-seat and per-item copyright hassles at the raw collection and delivery level when real value added is in the form of interpretive analysis of those items.

Now, the analyst staff will perform traditional impact and situational analysis on each event deemed of high enough value to report before publishing the posting to the Weblog. Finally, the delivery of the output is published to a Web server where the Weblog is hosted, as well as broadcast via e-mail. However, one key advantage of Weblogging technology lies in its ability to use RSS (or "Rich Site Summary," an application of XML) to push intelligence to the field. In this way, an RSS reader can be used to sort and index incoming intelligence in whichever application it is enabled on, for example, a wireless telephone handset or PDA or even a public-access computer.

The real power of Weblogging begins to materialize when the users of the intelligence Weblog start delivering back to the CI staff the "rumor and innuendo" they are alerted to in the marketplace. The salesforce, for example, is a key customer of the CI staff, but the salesforce can also become a key supplier of information about the marketplace for obvious reasons.

Adding Strategic Value

In the end, one of the greatest benefits a monitoring deliverable can provide is harnessing and leveraging human-source intelligence as an additional component to add clarity and satisfy demand-related requests from intelligence consumers. Collecting human intelligence means talking to people in the marketplace, primarily customer and competitor staff, and eliciting the information required to fill in the gaps not provided by public domain sources. Although it is usually too tall an order to expect or call for human intelligence collection as a component of a fledgling monitoring system, it is worthwhile to think ahead about the ultimate evolution of the monitoring system to include knowledgeable, external human sources to augment the secondary (document) sources and impact analysis being produced day to day.

Likewise, as mentioned above, the real key to adding value and fulfilling the mission of track-and-scan intelligence is not in publishing everything there is to be known about a key player in the market. In fact, one of the major roles an intelligence function fulfills is its ability to purify news clutter and focus organizational attention span on just those factors which truly matter to the organization's present and future ability to achieve success.

Evolution of Knowledge Portals*

25

Heidi Collins

> Enterprise Portals enable companies to *unlock* internally stored information, and provide users with a single gateway to *personalized* information and knowledge to make informed business *decisions*.
>
> *Shilakes and Tyleman*
> *Merrill Lynch, Inc.*

Introduction

I have always found it difficult to begin a discussion on portals. The problem is that we have to agree on a common definition of the term to begin a meaningful conversation. Even now, the enterprise portal continues to evolve and the definition expands. This is why we always see a new term between the words "enterprise" and "portal." You often hear about enterprise information portals, enterprise process portals, and enterprise knowledge portals. The enterprise portal aspect of the conversation is focused on a solution that presents the user access to applications, information, and work processes that are presented as Web pages or other personal electronic devices. They personalize and interact with these Web pages. The purpose of the

---

* *Editor's Note:* This chapter covers trends in the evolution of enterprise portals, which now appear in various forms like enterprise information portals, enterprise process portals, and enterprise knowledge portals. Work environments need to be able to handle the growing diversity of content and applications, as well as increasing demands for flexibility by knowledge workers. Knowledge workers need to be able to access relevant documents, understand processes, and collaborate with colleagues. Challenges can arise in user-friendly design, employee training, application integration, security, and consistency.

Horizontal and vertical portals are emerging to support business intelligence, communities of practice, content management, e-learning, and even e-business and m-commerce. Companies implementing portals need to understand how the various vendors and products design, architect, and support all of this functionality. To provide the complete range of functionality users will need, it may be necessary to settle on a set of overlapping or complementary product offerings. Change will be the most notable constant for the future in vendor space and throughout the design and implementation of the enterprise portal. Ultimately, the enterprise knowledge portal must be organized around work processes, maintain a knowledge-creating organization, promote innovations, and support business objectives.

interaction is where the middle term is derived from. These terms that include information, process, and knowledge begin to describe some of the exciting changes that have occurred over time with the enterprise portal.

Knowledge is increasingly being recognized as the most important asset of organizations today. Your organization might already be approaching knowledge management as a set of principles, practices, and technologies focused on innovation and optimization of work processes, supply chains, and customer relationships. This clarification and identification of specific knowledge management opportunities in vertical markets like supply chain management and customer relationship management is making organizations consider browser solutions like enterprise portals to provide an entry point or desktop to functionality for collaboration, content supply chains, search and retrieval, taxonomy or category construction and management, analytics, application integration, personalization, and performance-based metrics.

The need for this hybrid of functionality, content, and applications that gives each individual using the enterprise portal a unique perspective and view of the organization is in demand by knowledge workers at every level in your company. With more access and control of information and knowledge, and with a work environment that provides flexibility for each knowledge worker, individuals are better able to create, execute, and be accountable for the underlying business processes that they are responsible for. Since lesser skilled and repetitive activities are being automated, your organization requires highly skilled employees who can manage complex processes while participating in and creating constant improvement or change.

The enterprise portal is an information technology enabling platform to implement your knowledge management initiatives. If you design the enterprise portal around your knowledge management strategy, you will have built an enterprise knowledge portal. To begin to envision a knowledge management solution that can be implemented to deliver the type of features and services that you want to have available for the enterprise, you have to establish an appropriate knowledge and information-sharing strategy. Your organization, like many organizations, wants a knowledge management solution that lets employees know what information is available to them and allows them to interact seamlessly with the multiple sources of data and applications they need to use while performing their daily tasks any time day or night. Knowledge workers need to be able to get documents and understand processes. They want to see their e-mail, projects, customer updates, and any other critical information in a single intranet or extranet window. They need to be able to collaborate with the appropriate people in your organization if they have questions or knowledge to share with each other, get answers, or provide insight.

Why Portals?

Employees throughout your organization are responsible for making operational and strategic decisions every day. In many situations there are several data sources, systems, and applications that need to be combined. For example, to place an order for a customer an employee might be working in two or three applications. There might be an Enterprise Resource Planning (ERP) system used to check inventory status of a particular part. The employee will have to review or interact with several screens to complete a single part of the process. To review the purchase order, a Web-based application that the customer will see might have to be launched to enter or review the purchase order. If any issues are encountered, a Customer Relationship Management (CRM) system will need to be opened and additional activities completed to finish the task. You can think of dozens of situations in your organization where employees spend a lot of time traversing disconnected applications and systems to find an answer to a question, make a decision, or take some action.

The difficulty employees have navigating to information is only part of the knowledge management problem. Enterprise systems are complex and designed for a specific purpose and function. An incredible amount of training and coaching is needed for a single employee to learn how to effectively complete all of the processes and steps involved to accomplish his or her assigned responsibilities. In reality, only a small fraction of your knowledge workers know how to use all of the functions of one system, and no single person understands all of the systems, databases, and applications that affect his or her job. Understanding these issues and adjusting for them in your organization will allow you to recognize and categorize your knowledge management problems so that you can build an enterprise knowledge portal solution to improve information access, knowledge sharing, and decision making.

The enterprise portal will help. For example, gathering and distributing document information, indexing and text search, and categorization can be identified as critical knowledge management objectives for your organization and prioritized as critical features to be integrated into the enterprise portal. Some of the defining characteristics that have made their way into the enterprise portal over time will continue to create new classes of enterprise portal capability. To understand more of what the portal is today, we need to spend some time and look at how the enterprise portal came into existence, how it has evolved through history, and what the future holds.

The Internet Revolution

There were several amazing changes that happened throughout the world in the 1980s and 1990s. The most publicized was the Internet revolution and the surge of information and services that became available over the course of just a few years. You could publish information whether you were an individual with an idea, a company with a product to sell, or a broker trying to bring supply and demand together. At the same time, there was an intranet revolution inside organizations. Business units and departments realized that they could publish information that needed to be shared with many people. They could post information and establish communication in a standard format that provided a much better solution than e-mail had been able to deliver. These departmental and functional Web pages and Web sites began to grow in popularity and reach across teams and departments in the organization.

The challenges became for both the Internet and the intranet to organize and find information more efficiently and to ensure that the information was accurate. These self-service objectives of the Internet and the intranet were different. So at this juncture you begin to see separate solutions emerge to resolve the problems, with one exception, the need for the portal or doorway to quickly locate whatever you were looking for.

The enterprise portal is a personalized browser-based application that allows you to gain access to information, collaborate with each other, make decisions in every aspect of your work or life, and take action on all relevant information regardless of the users' virtual affiliations, the location of the information, or the form in which the information is stored. The portal concept and technology are rapidly emerging and changing, making it important to focus on the types of portals available and their appropriate role and application. An enterprise portal implementation focused on knowledge management objectives will be comprised of multiple types of enterprise portals interfaced together as a single integrated solution. The four categories that evolved include enterprise information portals, e-business and e-commerce portals, mobile commerce portals, and Internet portals:

Enterprise Information Portals

This portal solution is designed for work processes, activities, and user communities to improve the access, workflow, and sharing of content within and across the organization. The enterprise information portal incorporates roles, work processes, workflow, collaboration, content management, data warehouses, learning, enterprise applications, and business intelligence. Additional complications are associated with large scopes, new technology, lack of resources, untrained staff, nonparticipation of users, and few standards or common methods. To encompass all your knowledge management objectives, a complex cross-organizational focus will be required. The federated enterprise information portal is developed and managed as an integrated and reconciled set of technologies, content, and work processes. The enterprise knowledge portal was created to replace the collection of stand-alone workgroup or department enterprise information portals. Examples of enterprise information portals becoming available in organizations include:

• *Horizontal portals—These portal solutions are generic in nature and cut across the organization. They provide personalized information for employees, as well as employee self-service. They are designed to support information flow, business activities, and processes across your corporation, suppliers, partners, and supply chain. The horizontal portal will support the following:*

1. Business intelligence—This is the functionality required for specific business objectives supporting data warehouses, routine data analysis, standard report writing, *ad hoc* querying, analytical processing, and datamining
2. Collaboration and communities—The ability to facilitate group collaboration, the creation of communities of interest, and best practices. These technologies enable virtual workspaces and workrooms that allow employees, vendors, partners, suppliers, and customers to share documents, e-mails, schedules, and collaborative document creation
3. Content management—This is the ability to organize, manage, and search across all available structured (databases) and unstructured (documents, records, e-mails, video, and audio files) information sources. This is a seminal enabling technology that facilitates discovery of internal, intranet, and Internet information and data sources
4. E-learning—The ability to bring electronic training, mentoring, performance improvement, wizards, and help assistance for the content and work processes available in the enterprise portal

• *Vertical portals—These portal solutions are designed to support specific functions, processes, and applications within the enterprise. They can be considered a subcategory of the horizontal portal and are designed using the same enterprise portal architecture and features. The vertical enterprise portal allows your organization to group individual users into specific roles with objectives that target screens, transactions, and other elements of a work process to be the focus of the enterprise portal user interface. Vertical portals are usually associated with packaged applications for ERP, CRM, sales force automation (SFA), or supply chain management (SCM). For example, if the vertical portal solution includes various participants in the supply chain, then marketing, retailers, suppliers, designers, buyers, and merchandisers will all be able to track materials and products through the work process focusing on the content and information that is relevant to their role in the work process.*

E-Business and E-Commerce Portals

The e-business and e-commerce portal can also be referenced as extranet portals. They are enterprise portal solutions that are designed to extend the organization to the people outside the company by including customers, suppliers, and partners in the ordering, billing, customer service, and business-to-business self-service work processes. Another example of an e-commerce portal is a company that provides commerce-related services to its community of customers, sellers, and vendors. Many companies are extending their e-business opportunities by connecting buyers and suppliers to industry-specific news and related product and service information. Buyers can find the information they need to quickly locate, source, and purchase products and services online using your organization's enterprise portal as the entry point. Suppliers are able to generate leads and showcase their products and services across multiple marketplaces to find qualified buyers.

Mobile Commerce Portals

Portals that are used for mobile commerce are enterprise portal solutions delivered through Web phones, cellular phones, wireless personal data assistants (PDA), pagers, and other handheld devices. Personal or mobile commerce portals are very important and continue to gain popularity with consumers and employees that need product and service information, prices, discounts, availability, order status, payment status, shipping status, scheduling and installation information, and other critical information from any location. The same content that is delivered to the enterprise information portal can be delivered to the mobile commerce portal. The user presentation that makes the same amount of information available for a wireless device will span several screens or menu options. Icons and drop-down menus are used to save screen space and might require that additional help assistance be made available from each mobile commerce portal screen.

Internet Portals

Internet portals are focused on building large online audiences that span across several demographics and professional orientations. There are two categories of Internet portals: the entire Internet community and specific communities of interest. Yahoo, Google, AOL, MSN, and Excite are examples of Internet portals designed to provide services to a broad demographic audience. Internet portals have become widely accepted media sources for online information, services, and products.

It is astonishing how many people insist that they do not like self-service, but removing time as a dimension so that we can bank, plan a vacation, or sign up for the company's annual benefits renewal online has become a new lifestyle for many of us. With some self-discipline to go along with the availability of self-service, we can do many activities and tasks at any time day or night. Although there are times we all miss the personal assistance of another human being, many are not willing to give up the convenience of self-service or enterprise portals when they work.

Find the Right Enterprise Portal Solution for You

The enterprise portal market grew out of the need to mainstream information on the Internet. Users became confused and frustrated trying to navigate through the vast number of Web pages and information available on Internet sites. Companies like Yahoo and AOL became popular search sites that also had the ability to guide users to specific Internet destinations. The next generation of these Internet solutions provided personalization to users by allowing them to configure hyperlinks to their favorite news sites, stock market information, sports teams, weather, and local content sites. Additional functionality like instant messaging, community groups, family picture galleries, and free e-mail have created virtual homepages for users to organize their personal electronic lives.

Your organization is looking to the enterprise portal to deliver the same type of organization and centralization of company resources and information launched from an employee homepage. The current enterprise portal software vendors offer a collection of several features and functions that work together to provide the benefits your organization is expecting in the enterprise knowledge portal solution. There are a number of products and vendors in the business intelligence, ERP, document management, search engine, and other markets that partially fill our definition of an enterprise knowledge portal.

A review of the enterprise portal market segment identifies at least nine different types of Web-based applications that have labeled themselves enterprise portal solutions. A collection of these enterprise portal market segments must be combined to match our definition of a complete enterprise knowledge portal solution. Your organization will want to consider an enterprise portal software solution to facilitate the implementation of a scalable enterprise knowledge portal. The relationship of these portal market segments outlined to match our enterprise portal definition is diagrammed in Figure 25.1.

Understanding the overlap of technologies available in the enterprise portal market with technologies in the business intelligence, content management, collaboration, knowledge management, learning, and many other markets is useful. How these vendors and products design, architect, and support all of this functionality is often unique and very different. In most cases, you want to minimize or standardize on the number of products that are providing the same functionality to users in your organization. At the same time, it is true that business objectives may be unique enough that two or three different software solutions in the same category of technologies can be required. For example, there are personal and workgroup document management requirements as well as sophisticated ISO9000 document management requirements that must be addressed.

Using the same document management solution for these very different user requirements might be difficult, complicated, and expensive. A high-functionality document management solution will be more expensive to deploy and support and will require training for features that are not needed by workgroups to meet their document management requirements. In this case, providing two document management solutions in the organization might be the best solution. Your enterprise knowledge portal infrastructure will want to standardize on as few duplicate technologies as necessary to provide the complete range of functionality users will need.

Determining the right vendor and products to get started on your enterprise knowledge portal is complicated. The most effective approach is to consider the enterprise knowledge portal features and functions separate from the vendors and products, to map the functionality needed to your knowledge management objectives, and to

Figure 25.1

Enterprise portal market segments

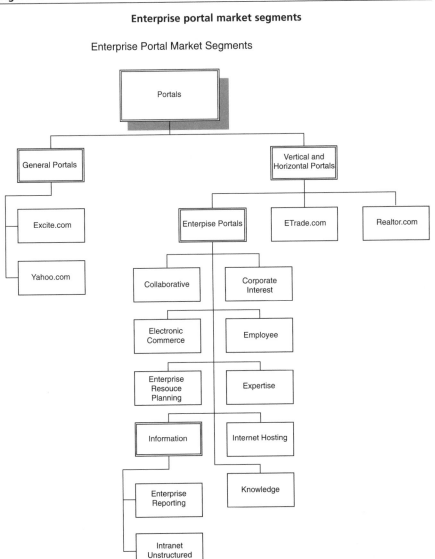

Enterprise Portal Market Segments

create a request for proposals to enterprise portal vendors. Vendors will be able to demonstrate their proposed enterprise portal design and architecture that will be able to deliver the enterprise knowledge portal functionality you need, taking full advantage of the technologies that currently exist in your organization.

Position for the Future

At the time that enterprise portals emerged as a solution to support employees, the first implementations tried to apply the basic concepts that made Internet consumer portals successful. There are several specific differences that have been identified, such as the processes available to an individual, the activities and assets available to support a user for a specified process, and how the information is personalized and presented within the enterprise portal. It is exciting to see the definition of the enterprise portal expand to include published content, navigation, mapping of how people and processes work, and improved standards and categorization to bring workflow and content to users. Security and a consistent look and feel continue to be very challenging, although there are several best practices and governance practices that are being implemented to improve the situation.

Change will be the most notable constant for the future and throughout the design and implementation of the enterprise portal. Everyone has a definite and adjusting perception of what should be available in the enterprise portal. We are all trying to figure out the best strategy to evolve our corporate intranet into an enterprise portal solution. We are all beginning to understand and appreciate the value of enterprise portal solutions that incorporate a complete landscape of technologies to support self-service and making decisions, not just information access. Our knowledge management objective is the ability to locate and bring together people and deliver relevant information to individuals who need it so that they can take effective action when doing their jobs. We need our enterprise portal solution to support a complete collection of business objectives that include:

- Be organized around work processes—These knowledge management objectives will concentrate on improving work processes for the general knowledge and performance of the organization. The objectives will specifically focus on employees and their individual roles, skills, and knowledge-base.
- Maintain knowledge and facilitate communication—There are two areas of focus associated with these knowledge management objectives. One collection of knowledge management objectives relates to management standards, guidelines, priorities, and best practices; the second collection is the audit and quality of these management standards.
- Focus on the future—These knowledge management objectives are associated with strategy and vision. They include market knowledge, process innovation, and recruitment, as well as planning and forecasting objectives to maintain viability and implement new initiatives.
- Support your organization's business objectives—These are the knowledge management objectives to meet the organization's mission and corporate objectives. They focus on setting context within the current culture of the organization and driving the change required to modify individual behaviors to ultimately modify the culture.
- Promote innovations—The relationships your employees have with your organization, teams, one another, and within the community are encapsulated in these work, life, and human resource-related knowledge management objectives.
- Maintain a knowledge-creating organization—These knowledge management objectives concentrate on how to bring continuous learning and improvement into work processes, management best practices, strategy, planning, vision, and change management activities.

There are hundreds of enterprise knowledge portal success stories beginning to emerge. As an example, a natural resource and manufacturing corporation that employs more than 100,000 people in over 50 countries wanted to increase operational efficiency. The goal was to transform the human resource services to a shared services delivery model that could easily be scaled to support more and increasingly complex business processes. The key components of the solution were:

- To provide employee self-service (ESS) and manager self-service (MSS) business processes
- To deploy an activity-based navigation and content management solution that integrates targeted business processes with ERP transactions, workflows, documents, and Web content
- To leverage as much of the ERP functionality and business logic as possible while improving the usability of transactions
- To align the human resource transactions with documents and other existing content whenever possible
- To integrate and optimize service delivery channels whether they exist within the organization or as outsourced solutions
- To utilize a common technology platform

The implemented solution is an enterprise knowledge portal that has been well received by employees and managers. The solution demonstrates how several key components of an organization's enterprise strategy can be integrated together. By using a collection of design templates, industry best practices, established frameworks, and strategies for enterprise portals, content management, business intelligence, collaboration, and e-learning, the first implementation was available within nine months. This enterprise knowledge portal continues to support an expanding number of business processes and users with every new release.

Merging knowledge management objectives with enterprise portal technologies creates the enterprise knowledge portal. Creating this partnership requires effective leadership. The enterprise knowledge portal effort requires leaders with a clear vision, a sense of direction, and a willingness to be the first to model desired behaviors. Your enterprise knowledge portal will provide a solution for you to engage directly in the change process, surfacing work processes for clarification and improvement and allowing you to exercise communication skills and personal influence to add momentum to your change management plan.

References

Andrews, Whit (2001). "Portals and E-Commerce: Different Goals, Parallel Projects." *Gartner Research Note*.

Delphi Group, Inc. (2001). "Business Portals: The New Media for E-Business Interchange." Boston, MA: The Delphi Group, Inc.

Collins, Heidi (2001). *Corporate Portals: Revolutionizing Information Access to Increase Productivity and Drive the Bottom Line*. New York: AMACOM.

Collins, Heidi (2003). *Enterprise Knowledge Portals: Next-Generation Portal Solutions for Dynamic Information Access, Better Decision Making, and Maximum Results*. New York: AMACOM.

American Productivity and Quality Center (2001). "Embedding KM: Creating a Value Proposition." Houston, TX: American Productivity and Quality Center.

Fritz, Ph.D., Roger (1994). *Think Like a Manager: Everything They Didn't Tell You When They Promoted You*. Shawnee Mission, KS: National Seminars Publications, Inc.

Phifer, Gene (2000). "Best Practices in Deploying Enterprise Portals." *Gartner Research Note*.

Phifer, Gene (2001). "How Portals Will Help Slow the 'Infoflood'." *Gartner Research Note*.

Rao, Madanmohan (2003). *Leading with Knowledge: Knowledge Management Practices in Global Infotech Companies*. New Delhi: Tata McGraw Hill.

From e-Learning to e-Knowledge*

2 6

Jon Mason

A manager is responsible for the application and performance of knowledge.

Peter Drucker

Abstract

There are numerous discourses associated with knowledge management, but it is only in recent times that e-learning has been identified as a strategic resource that can be utilized in an increasing diversity of venues (home, workplace, cultural, and entertainment venues, as well as traditional institutions of learning, education, and training). This chapter is concerned with three key ideas: the growing importance of e-learning as knowledge scaffolding; the emerging significance of knowledge management practice in informing strategic directions for the development of e-learning systems; and a conceptual framework that brings together these first two ideas, while also accommodating the proliferation and diversification of computational and communications environments.

---

* *Editor's Note:* This thought-provoking chapter focuses on yet another emerging frontier: the growing synergies between knowledge management and e-learning and the convergence of work and learning. E-learning is gaining importance as knowledge scaffolding in the 21st century, where home, work, and entertainment environments are becoming increasingly Internet enabled and seamlessly mobile. Content management and workflow management tools are infrastructural commonalities between e-learning and KM. Despite early growing pains, standards will play a pivotal role in shaping the Internet-enabled future of teaching and learning, thanks to organizations like IMS Global Learning Consortium, the IEEE Learning Technology Standards Committee, and CEN/ISSS WS-LT (the committee leading learning technology standardization in Europe).

Learning, especially on-the-job learning, has now become a key competency in knowledge-based economies. Such learning in KM-driven organizations can take place via mentoring in face-to-face CoPs, e-learning in digital environments, or blended learning. Further on down the road, Web services and next generation Internet technologies will further enmesh knowledge and learning processes. Standardization is proceeding on other fronts as well, thanks to consortia like the Workflow Management Coalition, the HR-XML Consortium, OASIS (Organization for the Advancement of Structured Information Standards), and GKEC (the Global Knowledge Economics Council).

Introduction

Stories that describe the evolution of e-learning could commence at any number of times and places, and they do. The story that is told here is one that ties together technical innovation, transformational practice, and the emergence of an "interoperability standards agenda." It is a story that can be told with a background context consisting of only a decade or so and a story of the emergence of a new industry. The central argument that follows is that much of the infrastructure development that supports e-learning can be seen to be convergent with systems developed to support knowledge management. The more obvious examples include content management and workflow management. However, observing convergent trends is only the beginning. From a service perspective, there are compelling grounds for *facilitating* this convergence.

But first, it is important to reveal some underlying assumptions. The first is that e-learning is no passing fad. Instead, it is positioned to thrive in a multiplicity of settings (from formal to informal). Second, e-learning will continue to drive the transformation of traditional institutions of learning and help shape a number of futures, not just for the education and training sectors but across most industry sectors. Third, it is argued that standards will play a pivotal role in shaping the Internet-enabled future of teaching and learning. This last key assumption is based upon the observation that the emergence of standards typically coincides with the early phases of new marketplaces, generally signalling consensus concerning key aspects of a new industry and maturity in innovation. In this sense, standardization of technical components enabling e-learning is no different from standardization of technical components that make aircraft fly. In addressing these issues, this chapter profiles some key standardization groups and discusses the standards life cycle.

So why is knowledge management important in this context? Put in its most basic form, the answer is simple: learning and knowledge have a symbiotic relationship; they depend upon each other. From a slightly more complex perspective, the creation, acquisition, transfer, and exchange of knowledge are all activities that are helping define the character of information—and knowledge-based economies—in which the primary assets of data, information, and knowledge all manifest digitally. The technological tools facilitating much of these interactions are information and communication technologies (ICT). It is through engaging with ICT that learning defines itself as e-learning.

However, while knowledge is inextricably linked to data and information, there is no simple, linear hierarchy and progression from data to information to knowledge. There is a complex intermeshing and continuous transformation of digital bits in combination with a churning of insight, where meaning changes according to context and through conversations with different participants. In this sense, knowledge is organic and cannot be completely rendered in digital form. This has warranted the use of a new term with broader reach: *e-knowledge* (Norris, Mason, and Lefrere, 2003; Norris et al., 2003; Mason and Lefrere, 2003).

Stories of Convergence

Convergence of work and learning has been a hot topic for at least a decade. As a major trend and driver of change, this convergence is taking place in the context of the ongoing digital revolution, a revolution that has enabled innovation and transformation in most settings associated with learning, education, training, and research, as well as their administrative and support services.

However, convergence has also been a buzzword of the digital revolution itself, where telecommunications and computing capabilities have been integrated into the daily devices through which we engage with the world.

Over the last three to five years, convergence can be seen to be taking place in the delivery of services. One of the clearest examples of this is in the development of e-government, where integrated service delivery has become paramount. Billions of dollars have already been spent worldwide on this effort.

In a similar way and more recently, services within the education and training sectors have been heavily influenced by the trends toward integrated service delivery as well as by portalization and personalization of information and services enabled through the Web. Moreover, the profoundly networked character of these new environments suggests that frameworks for service delivery will need to become increasingly flexible in their design.

There are, of course, many other stories of convergence, most notably in the publishing industry, where the creator and the consumer are becoming increasingly "dis-intermediated," and in the standardization world, where an increasing number of efforts are focused on similar challenges. However, in terms of the main argument running through this chapter, it is *all* these stories of convergence that together are facilitating the meshing of e-learning with knowledge management.

e-Learning: From Cottage Industry to Maturing Marketplace

Despite the fledgling e-learning industry having been swept along by the boom and bust of the late 20th century's dot-com attempt at redefining economics, there is now ample evidence to indicate that this new industry is maturing. With the enthusiastic adoption of e-learning by many human resource (HR) departments within the corporate sector, e-learning is being commonly described as moving beyond its cottage industry phase (McLean, 2003). Moreover, it can be argued that the requisite infrastructure for this is only now being assembled.

The early investments in e-learning capability can be seen as primarily motivated by capturing market share—even by the most prestigious of institutions and consortia (e.g., Fathom). With hindsight, it can be understood as preemptive and hype driven. Fathom's membership (Columbia University, The London School of Economics and Political Science, Cambridge University Press, The British Library, The New York Public Library, The University of Chicago, University of Michigan, American Film Institute, RAND, Woods Hole Oceanographic Institution, Victoria and Albert Museum, Science Museum, The Natural History Museum, and The British Museum) also reveals that their shared endeavor was heavily *content driven.*

It is now becoming increasingly clear that "content is king" can be seen as just another slogan from the late 20th century that no longer has the same appeal or applicability. After all, content only describes the "I" of ICT, while the "C" is more about connectedness, community, communications, context, processes, interactions, and engagement. Content may have been king at the peak of the dot-com boom—epitomized by the merger of AOL and Time Warner—but this slogan has obscured the fact that *context* will always shape its usage. The failure of Fathom indicates its business model was designed with little understanding of sustaining online culture or appreciation that "e" also stands for *engagement.*

As is well known, Fathom was not the only failure of e-learning's early promise. There is plenty of other prestige wreckage out there, as is well documented in an Australian government report, the "Business of Borderless Education" (Ryan and

Stedman, 2001). While the gap between the early expectations of marketplace activity and actual reality is now obvious, it is also true that investment in e-learning is entering another growth phase, characterized by strong activity in the corporate training market. For the university sector, however, this next phase is not without continued challenges as it tries to transform itself in order to remain viable and competitive. A good example is the time involved in launching U21 Global, the "virtual university" spin-off of Universitas 21, which blew out to well over 12 months behind its anticipated launch.

However, one of the key lessons to be learned from the early heady days of the dot-com boom is that failed or unproven business models do not necessarily equate with any failure of e-learning as a driver of change. On the contrary, when John Chambers, CEO of Cisco Systems, claimed at the 1999 COMDEX conference that education on the Internet was set to become the "next killer app" and that it would make "email usage look like a rounding error," he was not just being provocative. Hype, yes, but there is a fair chance he was being visionary and that this may yet come to pass. Among the reasons why—to underscore the earlier argument—is that knowledge-based economies are driven by a free flow and intermeshing of data, information, and knowledge, where value is created from an ever-increasing reservoir of abundance.

In such circumstances where resources are themselves not scarce, *value* must be created in novel ways. Thus, key competencies in exploring the frontiers will most likely leverage learning and knowledge sharing. It therefore stands to reason that Web applications supporting these activities will themselves be driven by new innovations. Getting an edge in a knowledge-based economy will bring a whole new meaning to the gathering of "market intelligence." As knowledge-based economies begin to develop depth, the principle of value creation will consolidate as a fundamental metric of success.

Among the many factors contributing to the development of the e-learning marketplace is the standards movement, a movement involving many stakeholders from industries other than education and training. However, before telling the standards story in more detail, it is worth setting the scene with a historical look at the depth of the foundations for the e-learning industry. What's in a name? It would seem there is quite a lot. One of the indicators of maturation can be seen in the stickiness of the term "e-learning."

In the decade prior to this new lingo, there had been a profusion of terminology associated with educational technology and technology-based training, such as computer-based training (CBT), computer-managed instruction (CMI), computer-managed learning (CML), computer-mediated communication (CMC), interactive multimedia, hypermedia, online learning, online learning environments, learning technologies, virtual learning environments, virtual education, and the often misused "distance education" and "distance learning." This is not to argue that e-learning will continue to stick (as other terminology such as "blended learning" gain acceptance), but what is clear is that the corporate world now owns this terminology as much as the traditional education and training sectors. There is probably a range of reasons for this, but Stan Davis and Jim Botkin (1994) articulated some useful perspective nearly a decade ago:

> If you are not being educated in your job today, you may be out of a job tomorrow. . . . Employee education is not growing 100 percent faster than academia, but 100 times—or 10,000 percent—faster. . . . Over the next few decades the private sector will eclipse the public sector and become the major institution responsible for learning.

Supporting such grand predictions are ample statistics to indicate that e-learning is indeed set to thrive in corporate settings at a pace that will not be matched in traditional educational settings (Obstfeld, 2002). The corporate sector can see this change unfold. E-learning is therefore developing as crucial scaffolding for knowledge-based economies.

Standards Develop as Markets Mature

The growth of e-learning now underway gains further significance when considering the role and outputs of the various standardization groups. There are, in fact, a large number of these groups engaged in standardization, all of which are helping forge a vibrant and sustainable e-learning infrastructure. These groups are not just associated directly with the mainstream e-learning industry; they are also associated with e-business, knowledge management, and organizational development. It is not the intention here to elaborate in any detail about these groups, as there are numerous accounts that already deal with this theme (Hodgins, 2003; Collier and Robson, 2002; Norris, Mason, and Lefrere, 2003, pp. 84–85). However, there are three key points that are worth making that provide further context in the emergence of e-knowledge.

First, while the early years (1997–2000) of the "learning technology" standardization effort seem to have been met with only lukewarm or spasmodic responses by many "natural" stakeholders (such as e-learning practitioners within traditional institutions of education and training), the fact remains that standards (that apply to any industry) generally develop in the early growth phases of those industries. This lukewarm response was often motivated by a distrust of the big information technology (IT) corporations and by a perception that standards lead to regulation and thwart innovation. Over the past few years, such views have been giving way to enthusiastic engagement, much of which is being supported by government-funded "interoperability standards" initiatives (prominent examples include Curriculum Online in the United Kingdom and The Learning Federation in Australia).

The growing internationalization of the e-learning standardization movement is also indicative of the industry maturing, facilitated largely through the efforts of groups such as the IMS Global Learning Consortium, the IEEE Learning Technology Standards Committee, and CEN/ISSS WS-LT (the committee leading learning technology standardization in Europe).

Second, innovation is being stimulated by the development of these standards. Once the basic specifications are in place and can be referenced as stable documents, then innovations typically flourish. In the case of e-learning, the first area of development has been focused on modular content development (through "learning objects") and content description, packaging, and exchange formats. Such developments have facilitated the seamless communication between digital content repositories and managed e-learning environments, providing end-users with the experience of working within an integrated environment.

Third, the Internet revolution would have been impossible without standards such as TCP/IP, HTTP, HTML, and, more recently, XML. Where the ongoing evolution of Internet infrastructure is concerned, three key areas of standards development can be identified as providing the foundations for the emerging e-knowledge industry:

- Web Services and service-oriented architectures to facilitate development of common services that support a broad range of industry sectors

- Next generation Internet technologies such as high-bandwidth Internet2 applications, the Semantic Web, and Grid computing
- Standards facilitating e-learning and knowledge management

Finally, standardization efforts in fields of e-business, HR development, and knowledge management have also been underway for a number of years. Groups such as the Workflow Management Coalition, the HR-XML Consortium, OASIS (Organization for the Advancement of Structured Information Standards), and GKEC (the Global Knowledge Economics Council) are all contributing to developing robust infrastructures and processes. These developments all describe yet another story of convergence. They also underscore the widening scope of knowledge and processes that can be meshed with the aid of ICT-enabled infrastructures.

Pervasive ICT

Whether it is "ubiquitous computing," "pervasive computing," "intelligent environments," "ambient technology," or some other descriptor, there is a range of terminology that now describes the ever-increasing presence of ICT-enabled environments and innovations in mobile communications. "Any time," "any where," and "any how" become the everyday descriptors for e-interactions whether they are wired or wireless. The proliferation of mobile computing and communications devices and the development of networks connecting new objects such as home appliances and security systems, transport, workplace, entertainment venues, and even the nursing home all point to the stimulation of all our modalities in making sense of the world and in developing effective skill sets in dealing with it.

Learning, then, is not only a lifelong requirement, its scope and character are also changing. "Digital literacy" is changing the basics of the so-called "three r's" and is itself a term that will demand ongoing reassessment, particularly in learning contexts. The ubiquitous nature of digital technology is also shaping game-based learning and defining the primary learning mode for "digital natives"—as Prensky has been arguing for some years (Prensky, 2001). The saturation of our environment with digital technology and networked connections therefore also extends the tools through which we create, acquire, share, and manage our knowledge.

Reflections on the Dimensions of Knowledge

Reflecting on the nature of knowledge is not just a philosophical pursuit. It can be integral to the way we make sense of the world (Dervin, 1998). It will increasingly become a routine competency of professionals sustained by knowledge-based economies. For anyone whose career is associated with professional education or training, it becomes a first principle in organizing information.

"Knowledge" is a word that has rich semantics despite its linguistic status as a noun. It is common sense that knowledge is much more than a "thing" and subject to continual change, in the same way as consciousness changes from moment to moment. In the highly networked digital domain this is no different. "Content" is both a static resource and something that can flow through networks manifesting itself in endless ways—as documents, audio, video, animations, communications, financial data, and transactional data. Just like knowledge and beauty, content is in the eye of the beholder; or, in other words, one person's knowledge is another person's data. Most certainly, though, digital content finds expression as data, information, and knowledge.

In an attempt to develop a framework in which the above discussion can be made more coherent, the model presented in Figure 26.1 and described in Table 26.1 portrays key facets or dimensions of knowing. Thus, *know who*, for example, has a very different quality from *know what* or *know how*. Unless one *knows why*, in some circumstances, the effectiveness of accomplishing an act dependent upon rationale for doing so is likely to be questionable. Likewise, without a sense of *know where* (from and to) or *know when*, there is not much strategy in any planning. Also, the practice of developing contingency plans through foresight planning rests largely upon a capacity to *know if*.

Most importantly, as we develop better models to support future e-learning and knowledge management systems, we will need to better leverage something that is

Figure 26.1

Facets of knowledge model

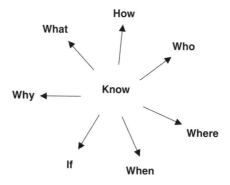

Table 26.1

Facets of Knowledge	
Knowledge facet	**Description**
Know what	The object of knowledge, e.g., knowledge management, the Internet, information systems, marine science, economics, . . .
Know who	Relationships, networks, connections, authorities, institutions, individuals, collaboration, associations, clubs
Know how	Skill, networking, consulting, collaborating, sharing, researching, reflecting, developing, testing, maintaining, doing, innovating, managing
Know why	Rationale, context, business planning, strategy, reasons, explanations
Know where	Location, where to, where from, strategic positioning, planning, reflecting, navigating
Know when	Just in time, timing, pacing, planning, scheduling, context, the past, the future
Know if	Just in case, scenarios, scenario development, foresight, futures, contingency

core to the way we learn and develop knowledge: our own experience. For, as one educationist argues,

> A crucial but often unrecognised dimension of learning is the capacity to make use of prior experience as well as emerging experience in new situations. With traditional methods of evaluating learning, we cannot discover just how a learner's prior experience might be brought to bear to help scaffold new understandings, or how ongoing experience shapes the content knowledge or skills and strategies the learner is developing (Syrverson, 2003).

Such perspective is only present in very rudimentary ways in the e-learning and performance support systems that are currently available. This will no doubt change, for as Norris has recently argued the very nature of our "experience of knowledge" is changing in much the same way as the scope and character of learning are being extended (Norris, 2002). "E-knowledge" is one attempt to describe this richer experience.

In Practical Terms

With a view to the practical implications of the foregoing discussion, the following prompts may be useful in determining appropriate action:

1. **Know what**—It is important to know not just your field of expertise, but also how it relates to the world of "e," where "e-anything" now signifies engagement with technologies that are transforming most industry sectors, from business process to learning, training, and knowledge management. What skills are needed?
2. **Know who**—We live within a profoundly networked world. Questions such as "who do you know who . . . ?" are important keys to unlocking connections and building networks.
3. **Know how**—As knowledge-based economies grow, key skill sets associated with knowledge sharing will shape business process and help identify the sources of value. Do you know how to harness the "e-tools" effectively? Know how is also about translating and applying knowledge into effective action. Do you participate in organizational storytelling as a means of knowledge transfer and organizational learning?
4. **Know when**—This perennial concern is both a strategic and an operational consideration, but not just for management.
5. **Know why**—Understanding *why* provides clarity and direction. Without such clarity company mission statements and strategic goals become meaningless.
6. **Know where**—Do you know where to find the information, tools, or expertise you need? Where within your organization and where beyond it? Questions of where are also to do with trajectory (where from and where to). Strategic planning is shaky without clarity on this.
7. **Know if**—Once upon a time. . . . Through storytelling and scenario development new dimensions to environmental scanning can be discovered, and the impact of the unexpected can be diminished.

Summing Up

The title for this chapter indicates a progression from e-learning to e-knowledge. However, this relationship is not a simple or linear history. The preceding discussion has focused on the development of e-learning as knowledge scaffolding, while also indicating a convergence of knowledge-based systems with e-learning systems. These trends are only just beginning. They are based on observations and practice and are not offered as fixed predictions. The world we live in and the worlds we share are always conditioned by uncertainties. Knowledge is conditional as is learning—both can be said to be complex adaptive systems. On this last point, John Seely Brown asks a key question: "What do we know that we didn't know ten years ago? That learning and knowledge are the result of multiple, intertwining forces: *content, context, and community*" (Seely Brown, in Ruggles and Holtshouse, 1999, p. ix).

References

Collier, G. and Robson, R. (2002). "eLearning Interoperability Standards," USA: Sun Microsystems White Paper Santa Clara, California.

Davis, S. and Botkin, J. (1994). *The Monster Under the Bed*. New York: Simon & Schuster.

Dervin, B. (1998). Sense-making theory and practice: An overview of user interests in knowledge seeking and use, *Journal of Knowledge Management*, 2(2), 36–46.

Hodgins, W. (2003). Information about All the Learning Standards Being Developed, www.learnativity.com/standards.html.

Mason, J. and Lefrere, P. (2003). Trust, collaboration, and organisational transformation, Proceedings, E-learn International 2003, International Journal of Training and Development, Edinburgh.

McLean, N. (2003). Towards global e-learning standards for interoperability, Initiatives 2003: Academics and Standardization, Versailles, France March 2003, www.initiatives.refer.org/Initiatives-2003/_notes/_notes/resumneil.htm.

Norris, D. (2002). Changing How We Experience Knowledge, www.strategicinitiatives.com.

Norris, D., Mason, J., and Lefrere, P. (2003). *Transforming E-Knowledge*. Ann Arbor: Society for College and University Planning.

Norris, D., Mason, J., Robson, R., Lefrere, P., and Collier, G. (2003). A revolution in knowledge sharing, *EduCause Review*, 38(5), 14–26; www.educause.edu/ir/library/pdf/erm0350.pdf.

Obstfeld, M. (2002). E-Learning Is where the Money Is at—new reports, EuropeMedia www.europemedia.net/shownews.asp?ArticleID=13031.

Prensky, M. (2001). *Digital Game-Based Learning*. New York: McGraw–Hill.

Robson, R., Norris, D., Lefrere, P., Collier, G., and Mason, J. (2003). Share and Share Alike: The E-Knowledge Transformation Comes to Campus, *EduCause Review Online*, www.educause.edu/ir/library/pdf/erm0351.pdf.

Ruggles, R. and Holtshouse, D. (Eds.) (1999). *The Knowledge Advantage: 14 Visionaries Speak on Leveraging Knowledge for Marketplace Success*. Dover, USA: Capstone Publishing, New Hampshire.

Ryan, Y. and Stedman, L. (2001). The Business of Borderless Education—2001 Update, Canberra: Department of Education, Science, and Training, www.dest.gov.au/highered/eippubs/eip02_1/eip02_1.pdf.

Rylatt, A. (2003). *Winning the Knowledge Game—A Smarter Strategy for Better Business in Australia and New Zealand*. Sydney: McGraw–Hill.

Syrverson, P. (2003). The Five Dimensions, www.cwrl.utexas.edu/~syverson/olr/dimensions.html.

Social Network Analysis in the KM Toolkit*

27

Patti Anklam

Relationships are the main activity of business and work.

Theodore Zeldin
Work futurist

Introduction

New tools and techniques developed for research in the social sciences, with new insights and tools from physicists and mathematicians, provide knowledge management practitioners with a new way to look at knowledge creation and transfer, to understand the nature of connections, to visualize them, and to analyze them for both tactical and strategic change. Figure 27.1 illustrates a set of networks, each from very different contexts and each the focus of research and application in very different knowledge domains, but similar enough to demonstrate the similarities of networks and the opportunity to apply learnings from one domain into the practice of another.

Each type of network has the same basic components: individual units (nodes) and links between them (ties). They also exhibit similar properties with respect to the strength of the ties and the patterns among connections. Some nodes (hubs) have many links to them, whereas other nodes have a more modest number or none at all. Network analysis is being applied to many problem types, for example, Internet and

---

* *Editor's Note:* Social network analysis (SNA), especially in its digital incarnation in large organizations, is emerging as a very useful tool for identifying social capital and improving knowledge flows (see Chapters 6 and 18 on SNA in Computer Services Corporation as well as in Australia's Office of Small Business). An International Network for Social Network Analysis (www.sfu.ca/~insna/) has also been formed. This chapter provides very useful tips on how KM practitioners may build capacity in SNA theory and methods.

This tool of sociologists and anthropologists can be used in the KM context to map teamwork, identify isolated individuals, balance workloads, devise better leadership schemes, and plan interventions for promoting knowledge networking. Automated data gathering and mapping tools can be supplemented with consultative interviews to get a better understanding of knowledge environments. Key learnings and recommendations based on the informative examples of SNA in action in this chapter include the importance of having top-level management sponsorship and using SNA for identifying potential CoPs.

Figure 27.1

Networks

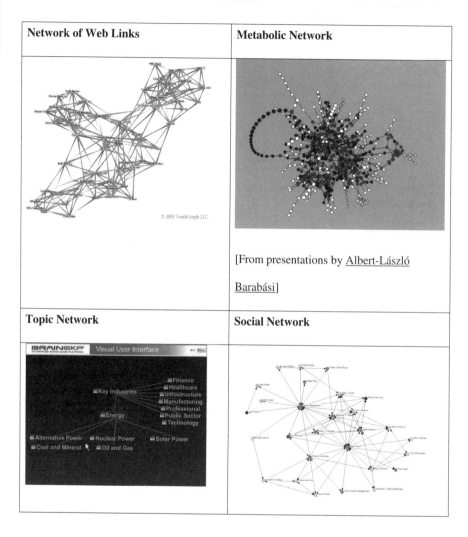

Network of Web Links	Metabolic Network
	[From presentations by Albert-László Barabási]
Topic Network	Social Network

Web typology, the energy grid, and the structure of cells. Social network analysis is a primary tool of sociologists and anthropologists; recent global events have demonstrated network analysis in action in epidemiology (think of AIDS, SARS) and in counterterrorism.

Uses of Social Network Analysis in Knowledge Management

In a human (social) network, a node is a person, and a tie indicates that a relationship exists. The relationship can be one of information giving, problem solving, advice for decision making, or any of a number of dimensions. Some of the particular goals and uses of analyzing the connections among people in a group or organization are to:

- Identify teams and individuals playing different roles in the organization—thought leaders, bottlenecks, boundary spanners, and so on
- Identify isolated teams or individuals
- Spot opportunities for connecting subgroups
- Target opportunities where increased or improved knowledge flow will have the most impact
- Raise awareness of the importance of informal networks

The premise of using social network analysis for knowledge management (KM) is that, quite simply, knowledge flows along the existing pathways in organizations. People talk to the people they already know and work with. The extent to which they share information, knowledge, insights, or ideas with these other people is based on the degree of trust that exists among them and the degree to which the organization supports these types of exchanges. The sum of the relationships among people, including their shared norms and values, is often called *social capital*. I like to relate social capital to the other forms of capital addressed in KM strategy as an element of glue, as shown in Figure 27.2.

Note that these four forms of capital do not lend themselves as easily to quantification as the methods for counting traditional capital—material assets, inventory, cash—but do, in most respects, represent what companies are actually valued for today (Stewart, 2001). Often, social capital is something that you can sense in the physical atmosphere of a company or on its intranet bulletin boards. You see smiles and cartoons on the walls; hear jokes; observe informal knowledge exchange through gossip, stories, and anecdotes; and hear engaged, purposeful dialog in meetings.

Leaders may instinctively know that organizational stovepipes ("silos") are not healthy, but they may not see stovepipes as a KM problem, nor think that KM approaches can improve collaboration. Most importantly, leaders may not be able to create a sense of urgency about the need for increasing communications across their organizations. Here is where social network analysis comes in: it creates an explicit, measurable view of the relationships that contribute to the company's stock of social capital.

Social Network Analysis

I have been asked whether a social network analysis (SNA) provides a numeric benchmark of "goodness" for an organization, as if there are social capital ratings for organizations or groups. When I queried a colleague who is an SNA expert about the availability of formulas to derive this metric, he said, "Oh, that's the holy grail of social network analysis!" The most important fact about SNA is that it does not provide absolute values. The intent of an analysis is not to pass judgment on groups or individuals; the intent is to understand the *patterns* of relationships, using both quantitative and qualitative views, in order to decide how to make improvements.

In a KM setting, it is the role of the KM/SNA practitioner to:

- Perform an analysis
- Facilitate the discussion of these patterns

Figure 27.2

<hr>

Forms of capital

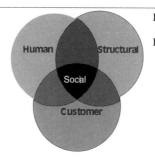

Forms of Capital of Interest to KM Practitioners

◆ Human Capital - the capabilities of the individuals required to provide solutions to customers; for example, its core competency

◆ Structural capital - capabilities of the organization to meet market requirements; for example its processes

◆ Customer capital - the value of an organization's relationships with the people with whom it does business; for example, its brand

◆ Social capital – the sum of relationships, norms, values, and trust in the organization

[Adapted from Edvinsson, St. Onge, and others]

<hr>

• Suggest knowledge management initiatives or interventions to improve knowledge flow in the network—in support of business goals

Consider the example in Figure 27.3 of a small group that is two months old, formed from other groups through reorganization. Paul (right center) is the group manager. There are three subgroups within the organization. The directional arrows indicate responses to the assertion, "I frequently or very frequently receive information from *[this other person]* that I need to do my job." (Thus, Ashok indicates that he gets information frequently from Jennifer, but this *frequency* of flow is not reciprocated.) The software is designed to arrange nodes in the network with those people who are most central (that is, who have the most direct connections to other people) near the center. Nodes representing people with fewer connections appear on the periphery.

Network Terms

Cohesion (also called **density**). The relative strength of the network, based on the percentage of connections

Centrality. The extent to which a network is organized around a single person, and therefore the potential risk to the organization at the loss of that person

Distance (also called **closeness**). The number of nodes between two individuals in a network (also called degrees of separation)

Betweenness. The extent to which a person is "between" other nodes in the network and can therefore control the flow of information

---

Using a Network Map for Diagnosis and Intervention

Notice that the network map in Figure 27.3 clearly shows that there is cohesion among the individual groups, but that ties across groups are sparser. For Paul, a key motivation for bringing these diverse groups of people together was to integrate the skills and perspectives of each of these groups. The point of analyzing the network is to determine whether making any changes in the network will improve knowledge flow and, therefore, the capability of the group as a whole.

The first view of a network map often confirms the conventional wisdom about the connections among people in a group. Figure 27.3 shows Paul to be very central, as would be expected, but it raises the question as to whether the ease of access to him deters individuals from seeking information from others in the group to either get or disperse information. The quantitative data from this analysis showed that this network was perhaps too highly centralized around Paul. (Networks that are too highly centralized tend to be inefficient and dependent on one or more people.)

Maps almost always contain surprises. For example, Brenda is part of one team, but communicates only with her group leader Wendy. What is going on with that? It

Figure 27.3

Information Flow Network

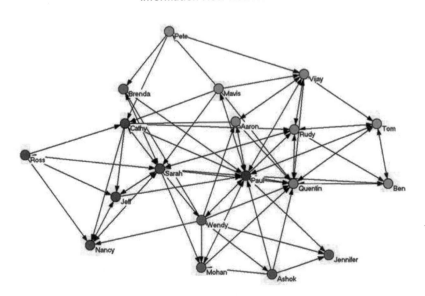

turns out that her unique skill set appeared to be related to that of the others on her team, but her practice area and experience was really unique; none of the projects she worked on were related to the goals of her teammates.

Look at Ross and Jennifer. They are well enough connected within their own teams, but do not appear to have any connections to the other groups. It is possible to put a number of interpretations on this pattern:

- They are not as important to the whole group and perform only peripheral roles.
- The work that they do is not relevant on a day-to-day basis to those in other groups.
- Others in the group are not aware of their expertise and experience.
- They are geographically isolated.
- They are new to the organization.

Note that this review of the network map only suggests *questions to ask* about the interactions. The data will provide insights, but must not prompt judgments. An SNA project is effective only when brought into focus in the context of an organization. You derive the context from interviews that take place before and after the actual mapping. From an understanding of context, you find out that Ross, Jennifer, Brenda, Pete, and Nancy are all geographically isolated and have not had a chance to work with other group members on projects. Simply, the other group members did not know what skills, knowledge, and experience each of these people has, nor were they aware of how they can leverage the work that these people do to become effective in their own work.

So, what do you do? In this case, a number of very simple KM practices were instituted that started the group toward greater cohesiveness.

- Reserve a part of every group meeting for someone to describe in detail what his or her work involves, what tools he or she uses, and how he or she could contribute to the work of others.
- Rotate responsibility among the group for collecting monthly summaries of work, distributing among the group, and editing for distribution to the rest of the organization.
- Set up a group space in the KM repository and structure it for ease of sharing documents across the three groups.

Given the size of the group, these were the appropriate interventions. In a very large group in which many people do not know one another, more technology-oriented approaches might be more appropriate, for example, expertise locators, homepages, knowledge fairs, and so on.

The Steps in an SNA Project

A typical SNA project consists of the following steps:

1. Determine the business goal for the SNA.
2. Collect data about the knowledge and information flow patterns in an organization.
3. Use computer tools to create a network map and statistical measures from the data.
4. Scan the results to look for gaps, or junctures, between individuals or groups.
5. Use consultative interviews to understand the context that is behind the data and the diagnostics.
6. Present the results to the managers/sponsors and to the group that has been surveyed.

7. Target areas where insufficient knowledge flow has a serious impact on the business.
8. Design organizational interventions to create the environment that will enable social capital to grow.

An SNA project is successful when it is tied directly to a business objective and when the participation rate for data collection (participation in a survey) is close to 100%. Therefore, the most important part of starting the project is to ensure that the project sponsor is a senior leader who has credibility with the group and who is trusted by the group to use the data responsibly. (You can only imagine what the participation rate would be if an SNA project were positioned in the context of a downsizing or series of layoffs.)

The second most important aspect is to ensure that there is business value to performing the analysis. There is negative value in performing an SNA without being able to present a business case.

Business Goals

There are many business and organizational effectiveness applications for SNA. Some KM-related examples include:

- Improving collaboration by making networks more cohesive—Leaders who understand that knowledge flow across organizations is important for responsiveness, innovation, and effective reuse and access to existing knowledge will want to expend effort on organizational changes and programs that will have the biggest impact. SNA can provide data that will focus that effort.
- Work load balancing—SNA can identify the people who may be carrying excessive loads in communicating across group boundaries and people who may be underutilized. The understanding created by an SNA can result in the redefinition of roles, the allocation of specific KM roles, or project reassignments.
- Assessing interactivity among groups following a merger, acquisition, or reorganization—Often, a reorganization is planned with assumptions about the "synergy" that will occur by bringing groups together, but there is often no way to validate that relationships are, in fact, established and working.

When the goal is clear, the communication to employees to participate in a survey can motivate participation. One manager headed the e-mail that distributed the survey with the heading, "Help Us Help Ourselves."

Collecting Data

Data for an analysis can be collected in several ways; these are summarized in Table 27.1. The examples from this chapter are all based on data collected from surveys.

In the survey method, the goal that is identified will lead to the identification of the group or groups who are to participate in the survey and the questions that will be asked. For example, if the goal were to build a more cohesive knowledge network, then the questions would be related to some dimensions of knowledge:

- "How often do you receive information from these others that you need to do your job?"
- "How well do you know and understand the skills and experiences of others?"
- "Is the type of knowledge held by this other person important to the work that you do?"

Table 27.1

Collection method	Comments
Collecting Data for Social Network Analysis	
Surveys	Each member of a network fills out a form that indicates the strength of his or her relationship in a particular dimension with each other member. This method is not practical for groups larger than 150 to 200, but the results within this range provide broad coverage and actionable results within groups up to this size.
Ethnographic interviews	Practitioners observe and interview individual members of a network, engaging them in questions about their interactions, and use the data collected to develop the data. This method is not practical for large groups, but can be very effective when used in conjunction with the development of a knowledge map of an organization (that is, you would map knowledge repositories and Web sites as nodes along with key individuals or groups).
Electronic activity mapping	Software tracks and analyzes the flow of e-mails among individuals in an organization, on an e-mail distribution list (listserv), or who access and use specific documents in a repository. This method cannot help you determine the context of the activity, and it is also difficult to use without addressing privacy concerns. However, this method is very useful in identifying patterns of interaction and the leaders of large networks.

- "Do you find it easy to access this other person when you need help?"
- "How much more effective could you be if you could communicate more with this other person?"

The SNA practitioner uses different types of questions for different situations and business goals; the questions listed here are, however, very typical and useful in many settings.

Surveys can be administered by distributing simple spreadsheet documents or by forms-based Web programs. The people being surveyed mark their response to the question with respect to every other person in the survey, rating the answers on a scale from 0 to 5 or 6. For example, shown here is a sample survey.

Please indicate the extent to which the people listed below provide you with information you use to accomplish your work.									
Pete		Response Scale:							
Mohan		0 = I Do Not Know This Person/I Have Never Met this Person							
Sarah		1 = Very Infrequently							
Quentin		2 = Infrequently							
Rudy		3 = Somewhat Infrequently							
Ben		4 = Somewhat Frequently							
Ashok		5 = Frequently							
Aaron		6 = Very Frequently							

Figure 27.4

Data for an SNA

	Pete	Mohan	Sarah	Quentin	Rudy	Ben	Ashok	Aaron	Tom	Nancy	Wendy	Paul	Mavis	Vijay	Jeff	Brenda	Cathy	Jennifer	Ross
Pete	0	3	1	2	3	2	1	4	2	1	1	4	4	5	4	5	5	3	0
Mohan	4	0	2	5	4	2	4	2	3	1	4	6	4	4	2	1	2	1	1
Sarah	1	5	0	5	5	3	4	2	4	6	5	6	4	4	6	6	6	3	6
Quentin	1	4	3	0	6	5	3	3	5	1	4	6	3	4	2	2	2	1	0
Rudy	3	4	6	5	0	5	2	3	5	2	4	4	3	5	2	3	6	1	3
Ben	3	2	4	5	6	0	3	3	6	2	2	4	3	4	2	2	2	1	0
Ashok	2	6	3	5	3	4	0	2	4	2	5	5	2	4	2	2	2	6	2
Aaron	4	3	1	5	4	3	1	0	4	1	4	5	3	6	2	2	5	0	0
Tom	1	4	2	5	6	6	1	3	0	0	2	5	2	5	2	2	2	0	0
Nancy	1	3	6	4	3	2	1	0	2	0	3	4	1	3	6	4	4	1	2
Wendy	1	5	4	5	3	2	5	6	3	5	0	6	4	3	4	5	4	6	4
Paul	3	6	6	6	5	5	4	5	5	2	5	0	5	6	4	5	5	5	3
Mavis	5	4	5	5	4	3	1	2	4	2	4	6	0	5	4	4	6	1	4
Vijay	4	4	3	5	5	4	1	6	5	1	3	5	4	0	2	2	2	1	2
Jeff	3	2	5	4	3	2	1	0	2	5	3	5	2	4	0	3	4	1	3
Brenda	2	2	5	4	3	1	1	0	2	4	4	5	2	3	4	0	2	0	4
Cathy	2	4	6	4	5	2	1	2	3	6	3	4	3	4	6	2	0	3	4
Jennifer	2	1	3	4	3	1	1	0	2	3	2	4	2	3	2	2	1	0	1
Ross	1	2	6	4	4	1	1	0	3	5	3	4	3	4	6	4	6	3	0

The resulting survey needs to be collated into a matrix format, similar to that shown in Figure 27.4.

When the surveys are returned and the data collated, the analysis begins.

Analyzing the Data

Software programs are available to manipulate matrix data, draw the network maps, and generate statistics. Because social networks are the subjects of so much research, there is a wide variety of tools designed to perform specific kinds of analysis. Commercial software applications for SNA are rare. Most researchers and consultants have developed their own software, which they make available via the Internet. Some of the software tools most widely used by KM practitioners are listed in Table 27.2.

Scan the Results

As we generate maps and data, we notice patterns that indicate central people, subgroups, and the intensity of connections. Figure 27.5 shows the analysis of a group that was dispersed in three geographical areas. The European group (on the left) showed up as two distinct subgroups, with one that is completely isolated. Within the larger organization in the United States, the group was highly connected except for a few individuals. The two nodes at the bottom also appear to be isolated.

Interviews to Obtain Context

The questions that arise from looking at the patterns provide the basis for interviews with the sponsoring manager and one or more of the individuals surveyed. The interviews ensure that the data can be presented in context. In the case of the group in Figure 27.5, a number of interesting points came out in the interviews. The small disconnected group of three consisted of people in an organizational group that was

Table 27.2

Social Network Analysis Software	
Software	**Comments**
UCINET	Combines spreadsheet editor (for data), statistical analyses using a variety of selectable algorithms, and integration of the NetDraw program for diagramming. Available as Shareware from the Web site of Analytitech (http://www.analytitech.com/).
InFlow™	Packaged solution for SNA diagramming and interactive "what-if" analysis. Provides a predefined set of statistics. Purchase includes training and follow-on consulting for practitioners. (Described in more detail on http://www.orgnet.com/.)
IKNOW (Inquiring Knowledge Networks on the Web)	Web-based software designed for organizations to collect data, map, visualize, and measure the patterns of knowledge and information flow. IKNOW is software copyrighted by the University of Illinois at Urbana-Champaign and is available for use by practitioners as part of its research program. (See http://www.spcomm.uiuc.edu/Projects/TECLAB/IKNOW/index.html)
Cyram NetMiner	Commercial software application that integrates SNA methodology with network visualization. (Available via http://www.netminer.com)
RepTools	A representational tool for the collection, analysis, and presentation of data. It was designed to make it easy for social scientists to graphically represent their field data. May provide useful maps and views of relationships to accompany SNA diagrams. (See http://www.practicalgatherings.com)
antology™	A general-purpose tool set for defining and exploring networks of information. Designed for applications from data architecture to business analysis, it includes the capabilities for SNA (http://www.cakehouse.co.uk).
NetVis Krackplot Mage Pajek (others)	Drawing packages used by social network experts. These tools, and other unique software developed by researchers, are cataloged on the INSNA (International Network for Social Network Analysis) Web site. Some are free, open source software, and others may require small license fees (http://www.sfu.ca/~insna/).

destined to be spun out of the larger organization; pending this spinout, almost all communication and sharing with the other groups had ceased. The manager of the group (GL, in the middle) was puzzled that besides the European group manager, the rest of the team in Europe was not getting information from him. He thought himself a good communicator, until he realized that he did not have these people on his e-mail distribution list.

Present the Results

SNA can be valuable to executives in gauging the work required to ensure successful collaboration across business units. Given a focused business case for doing an

Figure 27.5

Network analysis showing an isolated group

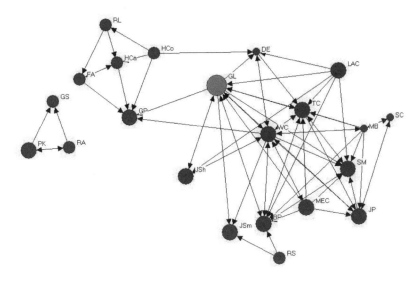

SNA, the presentation of the results can generate key strategic and tactical actions—the pictures generate many more than 1,000 words!

Consider the example of an executive team (president and vice presidents) that met to agree on common business goals and strategies. Prior to the meeting, the president, the vice presidents, and the managers (a total of 54 people) participated in an SNA survey. The survey group included:

- Three product lines (A, B, and C)
- Two customer business units, one for large accounts and one for small accounts
- Operations, human resources, and finance staff vice presidents

Although the organization was structured into three product lines, it was important for increased revenue and market share that the customer business units who sold solutions integrate products from the three product lines; it was important for teams in each of the product lines to cross-sell. The executive team assumed that the necessary levels of interaction were occurring among their teams. (One of the six myths about informal networking is, "I already know what is going on in my network." In this case, the group president himself was pretty sure what was happening, but the managers reporting to him did not. He turned out to be right. They were in for a big surprise.)

Figure 27.6 shows the result, with individual groups, main business units, and staff groups. The largest node is the group president himself, and the vice presidents are the next largest nodes. The network shows that most communication between groups goes through ("is brokered by") the president and the staff. Direct connections between business units are less numerous.

> **"Six Myths About Informal Networks and How to Overcome Them"**
>
> 1. To build better networks, communicate more.
> 2. Everyone should be connected to everyone else.
> 3. We cannot do much to aid informal networks.
> 4. How people fit into networks is a matter of personality, which cannot be changed.
> 5. Central people who have become bottlenecks should make themselves more accessible.
> 6. I already know what is going on in my network.
>
> *Source:* Cross, Nohria, and Parker, 2002.

In scanning the network results, we realized that the survey included administrative assistants for the executives (who, in almost all organizations, play pretty central roles in brokering and gatekeeping). Therefore, we decided to redraw the network without any of the administrators and without the operations, HR, and finance staff members. Figure 27.7 shows the resulting network map.

When they looked at this version of the network, the president and the vice presidents became very engaged in excited discussion as they drew inferences and reflected on what they saw:

Figure 27.6

Management group

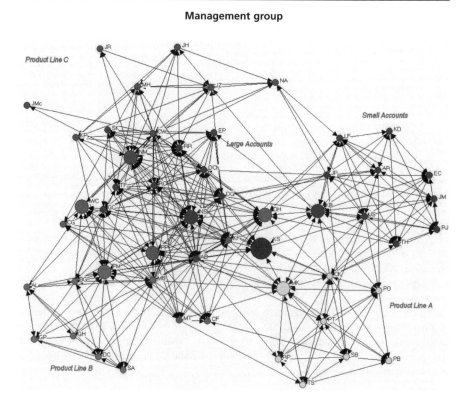

Figure 27.7

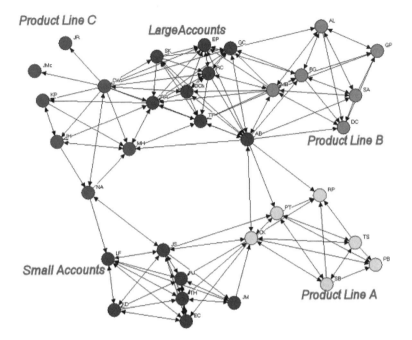

A focused view into groups in the network

- Product lines (A, B, and C) appear to have no frequent direct connections.
- Some of the cross-group connecting nodes are individuals who had been designated to be the "single point of contact" for a group. One vice president wondered whether establishing this role had sent a signal that stopped people from engaging directly.
- The customer business units for large accounts and small accounts were clearly not leveraging learning from one set of accounts to another.
- Two of the nodes in product line C (upper left) have connections only to one other person in their group—a person (CW) who turned out to be in a role that required him to collect status information from everyone on a frequent basis.

The network diagrams are based on the data in the matrices, from which the software tools can create a number of metrics for analysis. The quantitative view of the data provides additional insights. In this case, we found it interesting to look at the *density* of the network interactions. Density represents a percentage: the number of ties (links between people) that actually exist out of the total possible that could exist. The density statistics for this network are shown in Figure 27.8.

The shaded numbers on the diagonal indicate the density within a group. Scanning this line often shows anomalies. Here, a disparity between Product Line C (54%) and the other groups (ranging from 72 to 77%) becomes noticeable (look back at the two isolated nodes in the network diagram in Figure 27.7).

Figure 27.8

Comparative view of density of interactions

	SmA	PL A	PL B	PL C	LgA
	10	8	8	9	10
Small Accounts	72%	11%	0%	2%	5%
Product Line A	8%	77%	0%	1%	4%
Product Line B	0%	2%	73%	0%	17%
Product Line C	2%	1%	3%	54%	17%
Large Accounts	2%	5%	16%	12%	73%

Target Interventions for Business Results

As the executive team discussed these results further, they realized that the patterns in this density matrix correlated with their sales performance. The Small Accounts unit was not selling solutions from Product Line B. The expected cross-selling synergy between Product Lines A and C was not occurring. The SNA data reflected what was actually happening in the business.* The next step was to use the matrix to target interventions that coincided with the lower density numbers.

The executive team selected six junctures—points of connection—and requested managers to take action and report back on what they were doing to improve communications. The team also requested that each manager have the SNA results presented to each of his or her groups. During these presentations, additional requests for SNA work came up.

Interventions

The last step in an SNA project is to recommend and implement interventions. The goal is to change the patterns in the knowledge and information flow: to increase the connections, to alter the behavior of bottlenecks, and sometimes to cut down on redundant paths. There are typically three operational domains for designing and implementing interventions:

- Structural/organizational
- KM/process and practice
- Individual/leadership

Some examples of each of these follow. Notice that only one of these really taps into the KM practitioner's toolkit. For the others, it is almost always necessary to work with an organizational development consultant or human resource person.

Structural/organizational—An analysis may indicate the need to modify the organization or to introduce people into new, specific roles to assist the knowledge transfer. For example, the vice president of the Large Accounts group (Figure 27.7) hired a senior manager to be accountable for business development in Product Line A. Brenda, the

---

* It is important when looking at this data to recall that the analysis has been tuned to reveal only high-frequency patterns of information sharing. Zero percent does not mean that there is no knowledge transfer, but only that it is not frequent. The analysis is more meaningful when viewed in the context of the percentages among related groups (the *patterns*) and in the context of the business impact itself. Moreover, note that there is no absolute goal and that a density of 100% in a very large group is very inefficient, not to say chaotic!

"outlier" from the team in the Innovation Group, informally joined another team following the network analysis, as it became clear that her work was more closely aligned with this other team than with the original team to which she had been assigned.

KM/process and practice—Creating and maintaining the social networks in the organization is a leadership responsibility that can be supported by good KM practices and often the introduction of KM technologies. For example, if it becomes clear that people just do not know what the skills and expertise of others are, an organization may accelerate its adoption of technologies to support expertise location, communities of practice, virtual meetings, instant messaging, and so on. Face-to-face or other real-time programs that bring people together to share their individual experience and expertise start to break down the "don't know" barriers. One of the most powerful interventions to develop network cohesiveness is to put people together on teams—working toward a shared goal is a great way to develop or strengthen relationships. Here is where the full toolkit of a KM practitioner comes into play—selecting the appropriate KM practice to address each need for improving knowledge transfer.

Individual/leadership—The presentation of the results of the SNA should always allow as much time as possible for dialog and interaction. Everyone looks first to see his or her own position on a network map. Most individuals, but particularly leaders, will rapidly correlate the map to their own perceptions and intuitions about the context behind the map. They almost always decide on and take personal actions, either publicly or privately. For example, in one analysis of a large organization (72 people), a chief technologist realized that she had been very much a gatekeeper, though quite unintentionally. She began to sign her e-mails as "Kerberus" (in Greek mythology, the gatekeeper of Hades) to remind people that she was aware that she was often a bottleneck and that she wanted knowledge to flow around her and not always through her. Privately, she began to work with individuals who were on the outside of the network to bring them into projects, to introduce them to teams, to make their work visible to others, and to improve the overall cohesiveness of the group.

SNA as "Organizational Reflex"

You can use SNA to establish baseline metrics (density, distance, centrality measures, and so on) in an organization and then repeat an analysis following an intervention or over time. There is no set period "to wait" between analyses. You need to provide enough time to let an intervention work, which can be anywhere between two and six months, depending on the scale and scope of the interventions.

Over time, the organization that adopts SNA will naturally see occasions for conducting a survey and analysis—before and after reorganizations, in identifying key people for strategic roles and in succession planning, mapping networks of relationships with other companies, and so on. As one client put it, "tools should become an organizational reflex."

SNA for KM Practitioners: Developing the Skills

Tools for SNA are best learned through formal training or some form of apprenticeship or mentoring. The tools are not designed for novices; they assume some sort of prior training in the sociological and mathematical aspects of networks. Generally, the tools are taught in the context of a university course: either a graduate program (there are over a dozen universities, worldwide, that offer graduate courses in social networks) or (increasingly) in organizational development courses or in business schools. For the KM practitioner, the best approaches are to:

- Look for a conference that offers an SNA tutorial or workshop.
- Find a practitioner who is willing to serve as a mentor and teacher.
- Join one or more mailing lists frequented by both practitioners and researchers and look for opportunities to participate in research studies, courses, and so on.*

A number of the current practitioners (myself included) learned from working as part of an industry consortium, the Institute for Knowledge Management (IKM) at IBM. KM practitioners were able to participate in the research by Rob Cross and Andrew Parker at the institute and to learn how to use the tools and methods during the course of projects conducted at their companies. This is how I started in SNA, during my tenure as the Director of Knowledge Management for Nortel Networks' Global Professional Services. After working with Rob and Andrew on a project, I began doing projects myself, during which time they were available to mentor me through the learning process.

Many of the current practitioners of SNA learned from this work at IKM and continue to use it in their organizations today. These companies include Aventis, the Bank of Montreal, and Novartis. However, it is important to note that pioneers in using SNA in organizations, Valdis Krebs and Karen Stephenson, have been working for quite some time on what they have called Organizational Network Analysis (ONA).

Roles People Play in Networks

Central connector (hub). Someone who is highly connected to many others in the network, who may be either a key facilitator or a "gatekeeper"
Broker. Someone who communicates across subgroups
Boundary spanner. A person who connects a department with other departments
Peripheral specialist (or "isolate"). Someone less connected or not connected at all
Pulsetaker. Someone who uses his or her connections to monitor the health of an organization

---

If you are interested in adding SNA to your toolkit and want to purchase software, you should plan on spending between $3,000 and $5,000 to acquire and learn how to use the tools. There is variance in the quality and availability of documentation and training in each of the tools. You can download and try evaluation versions of some of the software products. In some cases, individualized training and mentoring are included in the price of the software. Conferences or workshops based on freeware or shareware tools (Pajek or UCINET) would cost an equivalent amount.

It is very important, if you are bringing SNA into an organization, that you have top-level management sponsorship. The process of a project and the results are an organizational intervention in and of themselves, so it is particularly important that, if you do not have organizational development experience, you partner with an organizational development specialist. The current trend toward popularization of SNA is exciting in many respects, but also is opening the door to the kind of thinking that derailed many early KM efforts: the myth that the answer is technology.

---

* You can find instructions for joining the SOCNET mailing list at http://www2.heinz. cmu.edu/project/INSNA/socnet.html. Be warned, however, that this is a list for serious academic research. It often has interesting insights and links to knowledge management activities, but most of the mailings are very technical.

Trends in Social Software

Beginning in 2002, software and methods for SNA started finding their way into a variety of applications. Some of these new applications are being developed within research communities in large corporations, and some are in development by Internet startups. Essentially, the term "social software" is being applied to any software that either generates data for SNA or assists in helping individuals extend their social networks by making new connections. Some examples are:

- The use of SNA techniques to identify emergent communities of interest that may be candidates for communities of practice
- The discovery of potential connections through corporate search and expertise location ("discovery") software
- Social networking software that enables individuals to manage and leverage their personal networks

All of these provide opportunities for SNA practitioners to collect data in different contexts.

Identifying communities—A number of recent experiments have tracked e-mail messages and participation in e-mail user groups to identify the structures of informal communities; that is, people who have developed or are developing a knowledge network around a specific topic and using e-mail to communicate news, information, events, and so on. The data collected during the tracking provides input to SNA software and produces network maps. These can be refined and iterated to show discrete communities and the patterns of interactions among members of the communities and the leaders.

This type of analysis can be extremely useful for companies who want to identify emerging communities of practice, particularly those that show promise in advancing the development of new capability or innovative business ideas. Similar software is already in use to map the network of links among Web sites, Weblogs, and other types of documents.

Discovery software—Expertise location software products, such as Kamoon and Tacit, and search and retrieval software, such as Lotus Discovery Server, Verity, and Autonomy, collect data on the specific searches and requests for information that individuals make. Because they have this information, the software itself can play the role of introduction broker. For example, if two people unknown to each other each begin searching a corporate intranet on similar topics, the software will inform the two people that there are related searches in progress and promote the collaboration between the two people.

Social networking software—Fueled by the interest in "six degrees of separation," the social software startups are hoping to aid individuals by automating the process of getting connected to new people. The applications all have slightly different operational models, but most work on the principle that an individual person submits his or her own profile and a list of his or her "connections." Depending on the software, the connections are intended to be personal or business or both. When a member searches the database, for example, to find someone who works at a particular company, the software will search all the profiles stored in the database and return matches along with the distance from the requestor (that is, the number of links between the requestor and each match). If requested, it initiates a chain of requests through those connections. The most promising corporate (KM) application for this type of software is currently in the area of sales force productivity—assisting sales people in finding contacts within potential client companies.

Summary

SNA is a powerful diagnostic method to support strategic and tactical KM. The recent explosion of interest and research in the properties of networks is providing insights into the dynamics of social networks, and new insights, ideas, and applications are showing up in the public press almost daily. KM practitioners can look to leverage social network data in their organizations to apply to KM initiatives where those precious KM program dollars will have the greatest impact.

Acknowledgment

My work with SNA was bootstrapped through working on projects led by Drs. Robert Cross and Andrew Parker while they were at the Institute for Knowledge-Enabled Organizations (IKO); I am indebted to them for their coaching and mentoring. Their book, *The Hidden Power of Social Networks: How Work Really Gets Done in Organizations*, will be published by Harvard Business School Press in 2004. Many members of INSNA (the International Network for Social Network Analysis) responded promptly and usefully to my question about SNA software. SNA practitioners also network relentlessly, and there are few experts out there who are more generous in providing connections, news tidbits, and examples than Valdis Krebs.

References

Stewart, Thomas, A. (2001). "Intellectual Capital and the Twenty-first Century Organization," in *The Wealth of Knowledge*. Currency Doubleday, New York.

Cross, Rob; Nohria, Nitin; and Parker, Andrew. (2002). *Sloan Management Review*, http://smr.mit.edu/past/2002/smr4337.html.

Self-organization: Taking a Personal Approach to KM*

28

Steve Barth

> The maintenance of organization in nature is not—and can not be—achieved by central management; order can only be maintained by self-organization.
>
> *Christof Karl Biebracher, Gregoire Nicolis, and Peter Schuster*
> *Address to the European Communities*

> An empowered organization is one in which individuals have the knowledge, skill, desire, and opportunity to personally succeed in a way that leads to collective organizational success.
>
> *Stephen R. Covey (1992)*

Rise of the Knowledge Worker

Long before most people had heard of a new economy, Peter Drucker defined the knowledge age and the new principles of knowledge work. He understood two fundamental things about the transition from the Industrial Age to the Information Age: first, that the changing nature of work puts more emphasis on intangibles such as knowledge than on tangible resources, and second, that performing and managing knowledge work required new personal and organizational skills. As early as 1959,

---

* *Editor's Note:* This thought-provoking chapter raises tough questions about the direction of many KM initiatives today: are they designed for knowledge managers or knowledge workers? Knowledge appears in multiple forms: explicit (e.g., work documents), tacit (e.g., individual experience), and implicit (e.g., in community values). Personal knowledge management (PKM) was a phrase barely whispered during the 1990s, but is now assuming more importance in collaborative knowledge work. Leading academics and market research firms are identifying PKM as key in training knowledge workers to become more effective and efficient in their development and use of knowledge. Personal information productivity has an important place in KM.

There are hundreds of available tools for PKM, ranging from local search to person-to-person collaboration. PKM also includes values, skills, and processes that cannot be simply replaced by these tools due to the social and even anthropological connections that personal information has to relationship contexts. In the PKM realm (e.g., the Millikin framework), tools that facilitate information and social skills at an individual level play a vital role. These range from information access and evaluation tools to idea organization and collaboration tools. Issues like security and trust should not be overlooked in this context.

again long before there was anything called "knowledge management," Drucker recognized that an emerging class of knowledge workers, who perform their labors with a valuable combination of skill and learning, would eclipse the industrial workers who then dominated the economies of developed countries.

"This is far more than a social change. It is a change in the human condition," Drucker explained in a 1994 *Atlantic Monthly* essay called "The Age of Social Transformation."

In truth, there have always been knowledge workers. Acquired skills passed from generation to generation or from master to apprentice were an essential part of any occupation before the Industrial Revolution and many since. On the one hand, they were skills that only had to be learned once by any worker because they generally changed little over the lifetime of a worker. On the other hand, knowledge has become increasingly important in the value of more types of work today, and the skills of today's knowledge worker require constant renewal. In the age of the knowledge worker, Drucker predicted, competitive advantage would be all about the management of knowledge resources.

"How well an individual, an organization, an industry, a country, does in acquiring and applying knowledge will become the key competitive factor. The knowledge society will inevitably become far more competitive than any society we have yet known—for the simple reason that with knowledge being universally accessible, there will be no excuses for non-performance" (Drucker, 1994).

Managing Knowledge as a Resource

From this notion of a knowledge economy eventually emerged the idea of managing knowledge and intellectual capital. There has been as little consensus about how to define knowledge management (KM) as there is about defining knowledge itself. In general, however, the phrase refers to strategies and structures for maximizing the return on intellectual and information resources.

Because knowledge occurs in *explicit* form (documents and data), *tacit* form (human education, experience, and expertise), and also *implicit* form (in cultures and communities), KM depends on both sociological and technological processes of creation, collection, sharing, recombination, and reuse.

Knowledge is not the same thing as a knowledge worker. There is a difference between the knowledge that exists in a KM system and knowledge that exists in the mind of the knowledge worker. There is also a difference between the kind of knowledge that exists in the mind of the knowledge worker and that which exists within a community of knowledge workers.*

The differences between tacit, implicit, and explicit knowledge are more than academic. By and large, the distinction determines who owns the knowledge. Explicit knowledge is most likely the property of the firm. One way or another it is either a data or work product. However, since tacit knowledge cannot be codified, it effectively remains the property of the knowledge worker. The knowledge that is implicit in communities and relationships is often accessible only in a social context. Companies have certainly tried to own or control all three types of knowledge. Employees may be ethically or contractually prohibited from sharing their knowledge

---

* Of course, not all knowledge is equally valuable. Accuracy, relevancy, and trust are highly variable and context dependent.

Table 28.1

Knowledge Types and Properties			
Key info and intellectual assets	What is their value?	How to leverage?	Who owns the asset?
Explicit • Transaction data • Work products (docs) • Research notes, etc. • E-mail and correspondence • Patents and intellectual property	Valuable	Collect	Organization
Tacit • Experience • Expertise • Relationships • Reputation	Invaluable	Connect	Individual
Implicit • Conversations • Trust • Values	Intangible	Cultivate	Community

Source: Steve Barth.

with competitors, but if a knowledge worker leaves the firm, he or she takes much of that knowledge and its inherent value with him or her (Barth, 2000b).

Because the knowledge-as-resource metaphor is imperfect, it highlights similarities as well as differences with other resource types under organizational management. A knowledge worker is an asset that appreciates over time. Knowledge itself is more often a depreciating asset. Patents quickly lose their value if not productized or licensed. A sales lead becomes worthless if the contact chooses a competitor's product or leaves the customer's company for another job.

Unlike other resources, knowledge is not depleted through use. However, the value of knowledge often increases with scarcity, and it is certainly subject to the law of diminishing returns: too much information quickly becomes a liability.

Table 28.1 suggests how different types of knowledge, information, and data need to be treated differently.

Managing Knowledge: Dubious Progress

Today, more and more studies indicate that the world's biggest companies are pursuing KM in some way. "Practices associated with knowledge management and organizational learning have begun to make substantial contributions to companies' financial statements—more than $600 million at both BP Amoco and Ford Motor Company," explains Brian Hackett (2000). "Results like that have spurred 80 percent of companies to launch KM efforts, including the creation of a chief knowledge officer or chief learning officer in 25 percent of companies."

The Most Admired Knowledge Enterprises studies conducted by Teleos (2003) have demonstrated that companies pursuing shareholder value through KM and innovation are out-performing the pack more than three to one.

However KM experts admit that, too often, KM initiatives still fail to be completely deployed, fail to ease information overload, fail to create knowledge-sharing communities, or fail to increase the efficiency of knowledge work. "Companies waste billions on knowledge management because they fail to figure out what knowledge they need, or how to manage it," says Thomas A. Stewart, editor of the *Harvard Business Review* (2002).

KM failures mirror the fates of other implementation and transformation efforts. "Less than 16 percent of the change efforts in business organizations achieve the results hoped for by management and more than 68 percent of these efforts encounter significant problems," according to Jeffrey A. Martin and Paul Carlile (2000).

The problem is that implementing an enterprise KM system is such a lengthy, expensive, and contentious process that initiatives often run out of time, money, or political support before they can contribute real value.

"Unfortunately, this is knowledge management (KM) today—a good idea gone awry," complains a report in *Darwin* magazine. "KM has fallen victim to a mixture of bad implementation practices and software vendors eager to turn a complex process into a pure technology play. The result: like many a business concept, KM has evolved from a hot buzzword to a phrase that now evokes more skepticism than enthusiasm" (Berkman, 2001).

One of the persistent failings of enterprise-wide KM projects, whether based on technological or sociological principles, has been that overemphasizing economies of scale of organizational knowledge often yields a solution that is useless to individual members of the organization. Too many KM applications are designed for managers rather than workers. Looking at KM from the perspective of the knowledge worker rather than the knowledge manager makes it clear that the productivity of knowledge is more important than the amount of knowledge stored in the repository. Whenever a corporation tries to maximize the value it extracts from its knowledge workers, it seems to end up discouraging those workers from maximizing their individual contributions.

Prospects for Personal KM

Personal knowledge management (PKM) was a phrase barely whispered during the 1990s. Now more and more KM practitioners are seeing how issues addressing individual knowledge work support the critical challenges of collaborative knowledge work (Barth, 2000d). Buckman Laboratories knowledge architect Melissie Rumizen (2001) even included a chapter on PKM in the *Complete Idiot's Guide to Knowledge Management*.

PKM rated a breakout session at TFPL's annual CKO summit in 2002. The group found that, "There is a premise that most organizations are capable of only poorly exploiting personal knowledge management with estimates of 30% or less of personal knowledge being used. To achieve a higher percentage, there needs to be an alignment of personal and corporate objectives—as well as the right values, policies, skills, behaviors and tools available" (TFPL, 2002).

An educational agenda has emerged which looks beyond basic literacy in information and communication technologies. At Millikin University's Tabor School of Business in Decatur, Illinois, Paul Dorsey, Associate Professor of Management Information Systems, leads a group of Millikin faculty investigating the concept of PKM in terms of training knowledge workers to become more effective and efficient in their development and use of knowledge (Dorsey, 2001).

At the University of California, Los Angeles, incoming MBA students were required to take a course designed by Jason Frand, Assistant Dean of the Anderson Graduate School of Management. According to Frand, "PKM, as conceived at the Anderson School, is a conceptual framework to organize and integrate information that we, as individuals, feel is important so that it becomes part of our personal knowledge-base. It provides a strategy for transforming what might be random pieces of information into something that can be systematically applied and that expands our personal knowledge" (Frand and Hixon, 1999).

Gartner KM specialist French Caldwell places PKM squarely on the adoption curve, predicting: "By 2004, more than 90 percent of knowledge workers will use personal knowledge management and consumer technologies to close the gaps in enterprise support for their information and knowledge needs" (Caldwell, 2002).

Companies are also starting to see reasons to incorporate the PKM perspective into their KM strategies. For example, global public relations firm Hill & Knowlton made "enlightened self-interest" a design principle of their hK.net knowledge portal. Hill & Knowlton has about 1,300 employees in 66 offices in 35 countries. Looking to tap the knowledge reserves of this global workforce, the company constructed hK.net in 1999. Based on corporate memory technology from Intraspect, hK.net is a multilingual, multimedia portal with libraries, tools, and collaboration spaces that let the company's PR professionals work with each other and with clients. The key to achieving critical mass is that employees are expected to participate in knowledge sharing for their own reasons first and the company's reasons second. Although there are traditional incentives for posting and accessing enterprise knowledge such as bonuses and micropayments, Hill & Knowlton employees are expected to participate out of enlightened self-interest: to do their jobs more efficiently and effectively and to be recognized by their peers and by the company for their expertise so that they will be in demand for the best assignments (Barth, 2001b).

Personal Knowledge in Collaborative Work

The "gap" that French Caldwell mentioned above is the difference between what the organization provides to knowledge workers and what knowledge workers themselves feel they need to get their jobs done. In many ways, this gap can be traced to two prevailing assumptions about KM. One has to do with social networks, and the other has to do with information and communication technologies—but neither in the way that people usually mean.

The first of these misperceptions is about the role of technology. Disenchantment with top-down KM technologies is well known. For example, a 2001 Bain & Company poll ranked knowledge management only 19th out of 25 categories of management tools (Barth, 2000c).

One problem might be that, in the context of knowledge work, people tend to use the words "tools" and "technologies" interchangeably. Technology is a very general label. Tools is more specific. Technology is provided by the company. Tools are personal. Workers have no sense of ownership or stewardship for the technology. If a tool is useful, it is "my tool." Otherwise workers think of them as "the system" imposed by management.

The effort to distinguish knowledge work from manual labor may serve to disconnect knowledge workers from the tools of their trade—and in doing so disrupt their sense of identity. Carpenters and auto mechanics take pride in using their tools skillfully, becoming craftsmen (and craftswomen) in the process. Their tools become symbols of their professional identities as individuals and as communities. How many knowledge workers think of information and communication tools this way? How many think of themselves as craftsmen in terms of how they use e-mail or search engines?

The second major misperception is about the implications of collaborative knowledge work. The evolution of KM from a field based largely on information technologies to one based on communities of practice as well represents genuine progress. However, this emphasis on community will fail if everyone neglects the needs of the individual knowledge worker.

If work today is more collaborative, it is natural that the focus has been on collective efforts. The problem here is the degree to which human networks—teams, communities, or societies—are ultimately only the consequence of individual actions and behaviors. The characteristics of the group cannot be designed as one would design a business process or product. They can only emerge from the complex interaction of those individuals.

At the same time, focusing on the increasingly collaborative nature of work often misses the difference between the collaboration and the work. People do work differently, teaming and collaborating more than ever before, and companies have accelerated rates of innovation to show for it. However, knowledge workers almost never actually produce their deliverables collectively. Instead, they cooperate by dividing tasks and then everyone goes back to his or her cubicle to research the subject, write up the report, analyze the problem, communicate with others outside of the group, and so on.

Thus, both the "knowledge" nature of work and the "network" nature of work put more responsibility on every individual, not less. Collaborative work requires more of the individual, not less. Therefore, we are left with a whole generation of knowledge workers ill-equipped to handle those obligations and responsibilities.

In other words, to be effective in today's jobs, knowledge workers need to manage three kinds of knowledge (Figure 28.1): their own tacit knowledge, their interaction with the information available in explicit form, and their interactions with other knowledge workers to tap the knowledge implicit in conversations and communities. The skills to do this efficiently and effectively more or less break down into two general categories: information skills and social skills.

Figure 28.1

Knowledge typology (Source: Steve Barth)

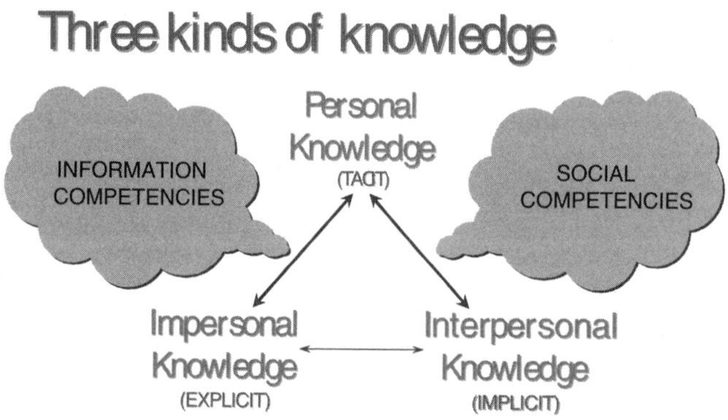

Three kinds of knowledge

Personal Knowledge (TACIT)

INFORMATION COMPETENCIES

SOCIAL COMPETENCIES

Impersonal Knowledge (EXPLICIT)

Interpersonal Knowledge (IMPLICIT)

Emotional Intelligence in the Workplace

Although we claim to understand the social imperative of knowledge work, workplace behaviors reflect little of that understanding.

In the old days of rigid hierarchies, employees needed little motivation to guide their interactions besides fear and greed. In today's workplace—characterized more by distributed decision making, ad hoc teams and networks, and multiple modes of interaction throughout the day—social, political, and emotional competencies are critical. These factors have a huge impact on the ways in which managers and workers communicate.

Social network analysis has demonstrated the degree to which dynamic, informal networks create value in modern knowledge organizations. According to Bonnie Nardi, Steve Whittaker, and Heinrich Schwarz, "Social networks are key sources of labor and information in a rapidly transforming economy characterized by less institutional stability and fewer reliable corporate resources. The personal social network is fast becoming the only sensible alternative to the traditional 'org chart' for many everyday transactions in today's economy" (Nardi et al., 2000).

Nevertheless, talented, ambitious individuals are still hired, promoted, and rewarded on the basis of their individual skills and accomplishments, even when their behaviors subtract from the value and productivity of the group. Rob Cross, Wayne Baker, and Andrew Parker recently demonstrated how much energy a single employee can add to—or subtract from—the workplace. "Energy in organizations matters for performance, morale, innovation and learning," they explain (Cross et al., 2003).

Many executives ignore the hard-dollar benefits of "soft" skills such as emotional intelligence. Although there are several somewhat conflicting definitions of emotional intelligence, they are all based on the idea of awareness of control over one's own

Table 28.2

Perspectives on Personal Development Skills			
	Peter Senge **Five principles**	**Stephen Covey** **Seven habits**	**Daniel Goleman** **Emotional intelligence**
Independence	Personal mastery[a] Understanding Mental models	Be proactive Begin with the end in mind Put first things first	Self-awareness Self-regulation Motivation
Interdependence	Shared vision Team learning	Think win–win Seek first to understand, then be understood Synergize	Empathy Social skills
E	Systems thinking	Sharpen the saw	

[a] This includes "systemic view, core principles, mission/vision, commitment to seek truth/knowledge, integrate yourself with the whole, creative tension."
Source: Steve Barth.

Table 28.3

Information Process, Skills, and Tools

Principles	Processes	Values	Skills	Tools
Accessing information and ideas	• Browse, buy, subscribe • Search (local, network, Web) • Research • Asking and listening • Learning	• Transparency • Concentricity (spiral out) • Learning and unlearning • Mobility • Persistence	• Question formation • Search techniques • Research strategies • Inquiry • "Know the map"	• Push/pull services • Desktop search • Web MetaCrawlers • Contact database • Wireless e-mail, phones, Web
Evaluating information and ideas	• Attribute info and ideas • Vet sources • Confirmation • Testing • Question motives	• Objectivity • Quality and relevance • Message literacy	• Source identification, qualification, and cultivation • Validation • Judgment • Intuition, feeling	• Collaborative filtering • Rating services • Trusted recommendations and references
Organizing information and ideas	• Capture, convert text and data • File, archive • Search automation • Map, categorize, index • Internalize and integrate	• Availability and flexibility • Version control • Personal Area Networks • Narrative*	• E-mail filtering • Discard (carefully) • Outlining • Networking	• Voice, character recognition • Journals, diaries, calendars • Indexers, links and bookmarks • Personal and enterprise portals • Databases

Table 28.3 continued

Analyzing information and ideas	• Sense-making • Hypothesis and Synthesis • Identify Trends	• Critical thinking • Systems thinking • Empathy • Narrative*	• Analytical techniques • Testing hypothesis	• Summarizers • Spreadsheets • Visualization tools
Conveying information and Ideas	• Answering • Explaining • Presenting • Publishing • Teaching	• Clarity • Articulation • Context • Language • Narrative*	• *This category is very practice-specific* • Written word • Spoken word • What's left unspoken	• Office suites: word processing, spreadsheets, presentations, databases, HTML editors, etc.
Collaborating with information and ideas	• Messaging • Sharing docs • Workflow • Brainstorming • Meetings and conversations	• Trust • Teamwork, compromise • Network ethics • Just-in-time collaboration • Gratitude, generosity	• Emotional intelligence • Facilitation • Relationship management • Play • Leadership	• Messaging • Collaboration apps • Mobile communications • Whiteboards, etc • Water Coolers
Securing information and ideas	• Backup • Inoculation • Insulation • Encryption	• Confidentiality • Privacy • Need-to-know • Responsibility • Integrity and confidentiality	• Self-discipline • Threat awareness	• Access controls • Passwords and encryption • Virus filters and firewalls • IP agreements

Source: Steve Barth.

emotions, combined with a sensitivity to and consideration for the emotions of others. By any of these definitions, there is plenty of evidence that the individual level of emotional intelligence in the workplace creates an organization of more effective individuals. Kate Cannon's pioneering work at American Express beginning in 1991 demonstrated a direct link between "soft skills" and the bottom line. By 1998 a retrospective study of business results for regions where sales managers had received "emotional competence" training found sales results were 11% greater than for those regions that had not. The company projected the bottom-line impact could be worth as much as $200 million in additional sales annually if all sales managers participated.

Adding these competencies to a knowledge worker's portfolio does not mean learning new skills from scratch. In fact, many popular personal development programs encourage similar skills that enhance both independence and interdependence. Three such approaches are compared in Table 28.2.

Framework for PKM

Based on the drivers above, an agenda for PKM involves a range of relatively simple skills and tools that workers use to acquire, create, and share knowledge; extend personal networks; and collaborate with colleagues. Knowledge workers should be encouraged to take initiative and responsibility for individual efficiency and individual effectiveness, as well as take initiative and responsibility for *who* and *what* he or she knows, does not know, and needs to know.

PKM should automate, accelerate, or augment human processes of individual knowledge work. Ideally, such a system would work anytime and anywhere. Such skills and tools would be available to individual knowledge workers without their having to always rely on the technical or financial resources of a corporation.

One way to maintain this focus on individual efficiency and effectiveness is to evaluate PKM principles, processes, values, skills, and tools in a framework originally developed by Prof. Paul Dorsey to help students at Millikin University in Decatur, Illinois. Dorsey and his colleagues are looking to bridge the skills gaps between information literacy and critical thinking, both of which are needed by students making the transition from academic studies to professional practice. The Millikin framework is interesting precisely because it does not confuse the raw material with the final products of knowledge work: decisions, recommendations, and actions.

Table 28.3 represents a modified Millikin framework, with the matrix populated for competitive intelligence professionals. The principles are explored further below.

Accessing Information and Ideas

For most people, a cycle of knowledge work begins with a question at the heart of a problem to be solved or a decision to be made. Answering that question is a process of research and learning. Accessing information is about locating, identifying, retrieving, and viewing documents and data to discover the knowledge contained therein. Accessing ideas is about learning, inquiring, and seeking out experts and other colleagues in the network who can help. Asking becomes a key skill, as does the ability to map and navigate vast landscapes of explicit knowledge.

Evaluating Information and Ideas

Information technologies such as document management and the Internet have led to a triumph of quantity over quality. However, after retrieving information and ideas, both quality and relevance to the question at hand must be evaluated. Evaluation depends more on skills than on tools, although trust in the tools we use is one of the most important factors. These skills include identifying and validating authoritative sources in terms of bodies of information or individuals.

Organizing Information and Ideas

Once the material is in hand, information and ideas become actionable knowledge by being internalized and integrated with what people already know and believe, sometimes even dislodging obsolete assumptions. Organizing is vital, but finding patterns, trends, and relationships is often a very personal process: some write in journals or diaries or dictate to a voice recorder. Increasingly, those notes can be digitized and indexed to be clustered and displayed with other captured data and information. Making sense of information and ideas is greatly facilitated by search, categorization, and indexing technologies that are increasingly available to individual users, reducing the time wasted relocating pertinent items.

Analyzing Information and Ideas

Calling this category "analysis" misses the point of all of our new ways of looking at both knowledge and work. Because sense-making equally depends on synthesis and hypothesis, it is deeply linked to the integrating processes of the organization category above. (http//www.intel.com/business/bss/swapps/knowledge/compass.htm) As Paul Dorsey noted in his original framework—and others have concurred—this is the most practice-specific category of knowledge work. So the professional skills and tools of one community are largely useless to another.

Collaborating Around Information and Ideas

Nothing about PKM should be taken to imply that knowledge work is solitary, only that the individual needs both skills and tools to bring to the table. So the key collaboration tools by now should be familiar to any KM practitioner: messaging, shared workspaces, discussion and chat applications, expertise locators, and the like. Some community-of-practice aids build in functions to maintain the social fabric of the group. However, more than any other, this category emphasizes how much tools must be subordinated to skills and values. Social, emotional, and political competencies cannot be automated, and they have much more to do with the success of teams, networks, and communities than do the tools.

Sidebar
A Personal PKM System

There are hundreds of available tools for PKM. Most of them can even be purchased, installed, and used by the average knowledge worker without having to rely on the financial or technical resources of his or her employer. These include metasearch tools for more effectively finding explicit knowledge on the Internet and local hard drives. There are capture tools to digitize spontaneous ideas and conversations for later retrieval. There are all kinds of communication and collaboration tools that make it easier to work together.

I have personal favorites, of course, and the choices will be personal for everyone. Here are some examples:

Continued

- I walk around with 16 years' worth of work on a 3-lb **IBM ThinkPad** laptop.
- I can not live without **Enfish Find** to instantly and intelligently retrieve the documents, data, and contacts I need during the day.
- I also love **Intelliseek BullsEye** for simultaneously searching dozens of Internet sources and consolidating the results (unfortunately, this product is no longer sold, but **Copernic Agent** is also very good).
- I use an **Olympus digital recorder** to capture conversations and interviews for easy transcription using a foot pedal, but I can also dictate to it for machine transcription by speech recognition programs such as **IBM ViaVoice**.
- Although there are lots of collaboration functions built into **Microsoft Office** and **Outlook, Groove** is a great peer-to-peer collaboration platform that anyone can set up in less than an hour.

Having these tools is one matter; effectively using them to capture ideas and information in a manner easy for future recall and use is another matter.

Being prepared, in advance, to capture spontaneous ideas and information is an important part of building an infrastructure for managing personal knowledge. It is a way to make sure that what you know is ready, available, and accessible (that is, organized) when you need it to create new knowledge.

How many ideas are lost forever before we can record them in any form? Even at our desks, ideas can evaporate faster than we can type them. We are rarely at the keyboard when the best ideas come, anyway. Some end up scratched out by hand if there is paper handy, or at least a napkin, or they can be quickly chatted into tape recorders. But even if they do get captured on paper or on tape, they rarely get transferred to digital files. In my case, the scraps tend to pile up in drifts at the corner of my desk or in spiral notebooks on the shelf.

Figure 28.2 describes the components of my personal PKM infrastructure, and how they fit together. These are the tools I use to perform many of the tasks detailed in the framework mentioned in this chapter. However, they should not be misunderstood as

Figure 28.2

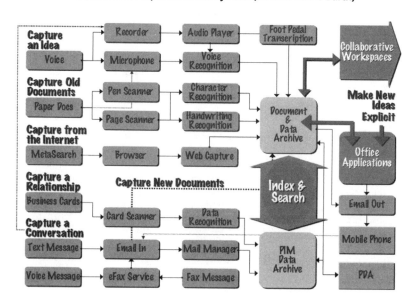

Components of a personal KM system (Source: Steve Barth)

a PKM system, which more importantly includes values, skills, and processes that cannot be simply replaced by these tools.

Consider, for example, a day in the life of a simple business card. I frequently return from a conference, trade show, or even an evening's reception with hundreds of cards representing potential opportunities.

In the old days, you would bring your stack of cards back to the office and hand them to a secretary who would staple them to Rolodex cards or slip them into plastic pages and then—this is important—compose a personal follow-up letter that started building a relationship. You could gauge someone's success by the size of his or her business card collection.

Now the business card follows another route. Think of the card as an artifact of social capital, a talisman that can set off a chain of events, both technological and anthropological, to build and maintain the relationships that hold your network together. First, drop a card for John Smith from Acme Ltd. into a business card scanner, such as the **Corex Technologies CardScan**, where the text is recognized and filed into the proper data fields of a contact entry, retaining an image of the original card as a memory aid. Synchronization software copies the contact to your desktop PIM, perhaps **Outlook**, as well as to your PDA and cell phone. Connections are just a button away.

More importantly, the new contact is picked up by an indexing tool such as **Enfish Professional**. Now when you open John Smith from Acme Ltd., you have a whole portal into everything there is to know about Smith and Acme, with relevant news delivered from the Web and relevant files and messages listed from local drives. Sending links and referrals to begin building a relationship is just a click away, and holding all of this together are a few drops of ink on paper or a few bits in a database.

Do not let anyone tell you that information productivity does not have a place in KM. When someone asks, "Who do you know at the World Bank who understands Pakistan?", you send him or her a name, phone number, and e-mail address. However, behind those few bits of information is a complicated transaction of social capital. Your reputation is on the line for making the introduction. If the people you are introducing build their own mutually beneficial relationship, it will reflect doubly well on you.

We have all heard the proposition that KM is about whom you know more than what you know. But how do you keep track of whom you know? In the old days, finding a World Bank Pakistan contact might have required an hour or two of going through the business card file or a weekend afternoon drilling through old conference notes. The time required limited the number of such favors you could provide. Now however, a few keystrokes in a personal search tool yields names in a matter of seconds. In this case, as it turns out, I do not have any World Bank Pakistan experts in my Outlook database. However, on several occasions I wrote or edited stories using such individuals as sources and that is enough of a relationship for a phone call to solicit their cooperation.

It is all information until you put it into context and into action by making introductions, suggestions, recommendations, or decisions. PKM tools help an individual knowledge worker to automate, accelerate, augment, articulate, and activate the information and the ideas that he or she works with every day to perform his or her job.

Conveying Information and Ideas

Distinguished from the collaboration category in terms of an intentional one-to-one or one-to-many transfer, communicating our knowledge to others is how we establish our value in a knowledge economy, by answering, articulating, and even advertising what we know. This is where most of us live, using the most familiar tools in Microsoft Office and other "productivity" suites that include word processing, spreadsheets, presentations, databases, and HTML editors to explain, present, publish, convince, and teach with written words, spoken words, and with what is left unspoken.

Securing Information and Ideas

Finally, if knowledge has value, then that value is worth protecting (Barth, 2001a). There are certainly enough tools to control access to digital systems, but today's emphasis on security overemphasizes inoculation from viruses, insulation from hackers, and encryption of sensitive communications. More valuable information is given away through lazy disregard for common-sense principles and practices. Likewise, we rely too much on contractual safeguards to preserve the value of intellectual capital. For individuals, there are ways to share their knowledge without losing credit for it or control over it.

Conclusion

In sum, the PKM argument goes like this. In a knowledge economy, the value of an organization derives from the intellectual capital of its knowledge workers. Unfortunately, few KM projects go far enough to understand or address individual priorities and processes. Even when everyone agrees about the potential value of enterprise-wide knowledge sharing, implementing an enterprise KM system is such a lengthy, expensive, and contentious process that initiatives often run out of time, money, or political support before KM can achieve critical mass.

At the same time, fewer and fewer of us rely on our corporations for identity or security. Organizations get too big, too impersonal, and too political, and our relationships to them are more transient; the companies themselves are more transient. So the basic organizational unit is only one.

KM cannot succeed unless every knowledge worker takes personal responsibility for what he or she knows and does not know. Management has to take responsibility for cultivating an atmosphere in which everyone has a reason to share, while building an infrastructure that makes it easy to share.

The most valuable intellectual assets, such as tacit knowledge, trust, and innovation, can be encouraged and exploited by the corporation, but never owned. Enterprise KM strategies should be designed to leverage rather than attempt to overcome individual motivations and behaviors. As an investment strategy for personal intellectual capital, PKM helps knowledge workers demonstrate their value to their organizations and in the job market, while they improve the aggregate value of intellectual capital for the organization. At the same time, it builds momentum to overcome the technological and sociological barriers to top-down, enterprise-wide KM initiatives.

Peter Drucker points out how much all of this comes down to personal responsibility for competence, integrity, and continuous learning—all aspects of managing oneself. Knowledge workers, as Drucker frequently points out, cannot be managed as if they were part of industrial structures or processes. Neither knowledge nor knowledge workers can really be managed at all. For one thing, knowledge workers frequently have expertise that their supervisors do not have and can take their expertise elsewhere. That is one reason knowledge workers should be managed as volunteers to maintain their loyalty. Also, knowledge workers tend to spend too much time on tasks they were not hired for (Barth, 2000a).

Maximizing human capital (in terms of experience and expertise), structural capital (practices and systems), and social capital (networks and relationships) on a personal level can meet the needs of both individuals and organizations. If organizational productivity depends on the efficiency and effectiveness of individuals, KM systems must be designed with PKM needs in mind, giving each worker the content, context, and connections he or she needs to acquire and create knowledge, share learning, collaborate with colleagues, and extend his or her networks. Taking a PKM approach also gives workers and managers more time for value-creating processes that can never be automated, such as reflection and innovation.

References

Barth, Steve. (2000a). "Heeding the Sage of the Knowledge Age," *CRM* Magazine, May 2000; http://www.destinationcrm.com/cr/dcrm_cr_article.asp?id=302&ed=5/1/00.

Barth, Steve. (2000b). "ID Check," *CRM* Magazine, June 2000; http://www.destinationcrm.com/cr/dcrm_cr_article.asp?id=287.

Barth, Steve. (2000c). "KM Horror Stories," *Knowledge Management*, October 2000; http://www.destinationkm.com/articles/default.asp?ArticleID=923.

Barth, Steve. (2000d). "The Power of One," *Knowledge Management*, December 2000; http://www.destinationkm.com/articles/default.asp?ArticleID=615.

Barth, Steve. (2001a). "Open Yet Guarded: Protecting the Knowledge Enterprise," *Knowledge Management*, March 2001.

Barth, Steve. (2001b). "Paul Taaffe: Hill & Knowiton's President Talks about the Role of Self-interest to Motivate Knowledge Sharing," *Knowledge Management*, November 2001.

Berkman, Eric. (2001). "When Bad Things Happen to Good Ideas," *Darwin*, April 2001; http://www.darwinmag.com/read/040101/badthings.html.

Caldwell, French. (2002). "Personal Knowledge Networks Emerge with Grassroots KM," Gartner Research Strategic Planning Research Note, November 2002.

Covey, Stephen R. (1992). *Principle-Centered Leadership*. New York: Simon & Schuster.

Cross, Rob; Baker, Wayne; and Parker, Andrew. (2003). "What Creates Energy in Organizations," *MIT Sloan Management Review*, Summer 2003.

Dorsey, Paul A. (2001). "Personal Knowledge Management: Educational Framework for Global Business." Decatur, IL: Tabor School of Business, Millikin University; http://www.millikin.edu/pkm/pkm_istanbul.html.

Drucker, Peter F. (1994). "The Age of Social Transformation," *The Atlantic Monthly*, November 1994; http://www.theatlantic.com/politics/ecbig/Soctrans.htm.

Frand, Jason and Hixon, Carol. (1999). "Personal Knowledge Management: Who, What, Why, When, Where, How?" Working paper of previous PKM presentations, December 1999; http://www.anderson.ucla.edu/faculty/jason.frand/researcher/speeches/PKM.htm.

Hackett, Brian. (2000). "Beyond Knowledge Management: New Ways to Work." The Conference Board Research Report 1262-00-BR, 2000; www.conference-board.org.

Martin, Jeffrey A. and Carlile, Paul. (2000). "Designing Agile Organizations: Organizational Learning at the Boundaries." Quinn, R.E., O'Neill, R.M., and Clair, L.S. (Eds.), *Pressing Problems in Modern Organizations: Transforming the Agenda for Research and Practice*. AMACOM; http://www.amanet.org/books/catalog/0814470521.htm.

Nardi, Bonnie; Whittaker, Steve; and Schwarz, Heinrich. (2000). "It's Not What You Know, It's Who You Know: Work in the Information Age," *First Monday*, May 2000; http://www.firstmonday.org/issues/issue5_5/nardi/index.html.

Rumizen, Melissie Clemmons. (2001). *The Complete Idiot's Guide to Knowledge Management*. Alpha Books.

Stewart, Thomas A. (2002). "The Case Against Knowledge Management," *Business 2.0*, February 2002.

Teleos. (2003). Global MAKE Report, October 2003; http://www.knowledgebusiness.com.

TFPL. (2002). "New Directions for Knowledge Strategies," Executive report from TFPL's Fifth International CKO Summit, October 2002, Dublin, Ireland; http://www.tfpl.com/thought_leadership/cko_summits.cfm.

Part III

Tools for Tapping Expertise in Large Organizations*

29

Lynn Qu and Stephen Pao

> The beginning of knowledge is the discovery of something we do not understand.
>
> *Frank Herber*

The Context: Expertise Location and Retention in Global Organizations

As different as the two may seem at first glance, the young engineering consulting firm Intec Engineering has something in common with the consumer products giant Procter & Gamble (P&G): both grew from small partnerships to become global businesses. P&G was started by William Procter and James Gamble in 1837 with just two products: soap and candles. Today, it markets over 300 brand names in more than 160 countries. Intec, on the other hand, was founded by W. J. Timmermans, J. Gillespie, A. R. Schultz, and D. S. McKeehan in Houston in 1984. It now services the exploration and production, construction, and transportation sectors of the energy industry worldwide.

As each company grows in size and complexity, its most valuable assets—the employees—gradually spread out. Whereas all its research scientists used to sit in one

---

* *Editor's Note:* Globally distributed organizations face a key KM challenge in locating expertise at the right time for the right answers. Simple communication channels like e-mail do not work too well if there is an overload of such queries, especially repetitive ones. These issues are further complicated by employee relocation and retirement. What is needed is a user-friendly KM tool which builds profiles of employee expertise, systematically channels Q&A activities, manages escalation mechanisms for urgent queries, provides rating and validation support, ensures authenticated and secure access, integrates with other workplace tools like document management systems, and routes and archives Q&A interactions for further reuse.

This chapter profiles one such KM tool, AskMe's Employee Knowledge Network (EKN). Case studies are provided of EKNs supporting expertise discovery and communities of practice in companies like Intel, Procter & Gamble, Intec Engineering, Honeywell, Boeing, and CNA Insurance. Key learnings include the importance of phased deployment with a pilot project for the right target group, devising the right reward and recognition schemes to spur knowledge contributions, designing appropriate business rules for handling critical queries, aligning taxonomies with work activities, making rating systems flexible or moving them to the background, and populating the EKN with content prior to launch so as to make it useful from the onset.

building and have lunch with each other, P&G's R&D group currently has 7,500 scientists working in 22 research centers in 12 countries. Intec, although relatively smaller in size, is almost nearly as dispersed with regional offices in Kuala Lumpur, Delft, Buenos Aires, Santiago, Perth, and London, and its engineering consultants could be at client sites anywhere in the world.

Employees at P&G and Intec face the same challenge: finding out who has the right expertise to solve critical business problems is harder than ever. The experiential knowledge that people carry around in their heads is scattered across the company (i.e., all over the world), and it is nearly impossible to find the right people directly unless they are already part of the employee's personal network. When employees cannot find the right expertise or solution, they must either spend time and effort to recreate that solution or settle for something sub-optimal.

This problem is not unique to the two companies: according to KPMG (now BearingPoint), 6 out of 10 employees say difficulty in accessing undocumented knowledge is a major problem. In fact, analyst firm IDC estimates that the average Fortune 500 company would have spent $64 million on redundant efforts in 2003.

The way many companies operate today exacerbates the problem: cross-functional teams that work together on a project, but then separate before moving onto subsequent projects; frequent organizational realignments; and mergers and acquisitions. Furthermore, as the baby-boom generation ages and starts thinking about retirement, companies have a good reason to worry that the current supply of highly trained workers is running out. This is especially true for the oil and gas industry, where the median age of geoscientists is near 50 years old. Employees that leave take vital knowledge with them; that knowledge may be lost forever if there is not a process in place to capture and transfer it to their successors. As a result, those who follow them in the job take a longer time to ramp up, important insights disappear, and the company's ability to act with intelligence and agility can be significantly handicapped.

Solution: An Employee Knowledge Network

Companies have undertaken various initiatives to address the knowledge management (KM) challenge that comes with the increased geographic and departmental dispersion. E-mail and file systems are no longer sufficient by themselves. KM-savvy companies have deployed software solutions such as corporate portals to make accessing unstructured data much easier, document management systems to optimize the use of documents within an organization independent of the publishing medium, and real-time collaboration applications to bring together colleagues from different corners of the world.

These tools operate with the assumption that the content or document already exists (portals and document management systems) or that the right group of people has already been identified (collaboration systems). They do not address the issue of expertise location and management—a critical component of any organization's overall KM strategy. For this specific area, companies have turned to a software system called Employee Knowledge Networks (EKNs).

EKNs focus on employees' expertise that has not been documented—the experiential knowledge that resides in their heads. This type of knowledge is an unstructured conglomeration of years of professional experience: insights from successful projects as well as failed ones, expertise from a prior job function, or intelligence from chatting with someone at a conference. Experiential knowledge is seldom documented (simply because no one wants to take the extra time to report on all his or her experiences and learning), and the only natural way to access that knowledge is to ask questions. As identified earlier, however, in many organizations it has become an overwhelming challenge to know *whom* to ask.

This is where the EKN comes in. It profiles the expertise of employees, assists people in finding others with the appropriate knowledge, and then facilitates the exchange of knowledge, often in the form of a Q&A. Through the Q&A process on the EKN, the employee's know-how is associated with a specific context (i.e., the question being asked) to form a solution to a business problem. That solution is digitized and stored on the system and can then be leveraged by other applications such as document management systems or portals. Even if employees should later change job function or leave the company, some of their knowledge stays in the system via these recorded interactions. In this way, the EKN enables companies to tap into organizational expertise and retain that expertise for reuse.

Furthermore, by identifying employees with common business interests, the EKN helps to drive the growth of communities of practice. As we will discuss later in this chapter, having thriving communities of practice is vital to reinforcing a knowledge-sharing culture. By using an EKN, a company can better leverage its most important asset: the global body of employees whose varied experience, knowledge, and perspective constitute the company's core competency. The result is faster and more informed decisions, reduced cycle times, and lowered costs associated with redundancies and reinvention.

EKN in Action

An increasing number of leading companies have implemented EKNs in recent years. Many are seeing impressive results and are sharing their experience in order to learn from each other. **Intel**, for example, has published a white paper on their system, named "Knowledge Compass," within the company. In the paper, Intel describes their motivation to launch the initiative, various stages of the project, and results to date.

Intel has the knowledge-sharing challenges typical of Fortune 100 companies. In late 2000, multiple groups in the company reported that it was very difficult to identify and access globally dispersed expertise, meet the shrinking "time to result" requirements, and assist employees to meet productivity demands. Intel decided that they needed to reduce the time and cost for employees to find the expertise required to solve business problems and make timely decisions.

Proceeding with diligence and caution, Intel first piloted the solution to 500 users and gradually grew that number to over 1,000 users. Pilot results showed an annual saving of $1 million through reduced training time, product cycle time, and business processing time. Furthermore, the Materials group that joined the pilot later expects to save as much as $2.2 million per year. After evaluating the pilot results and success factors, Intel made the solution available enterprise wide.

The staged approach Intel took is typical of EKN implementations in large companies. **Honeywell** also started with a small initial implementation, engaging 1,000 users in its Six Sigma and Digitization group. Honeywell has a very extensive, well-known Six Sigma program that has made significant impact on the company's bottom line. Those that are experienced with Six Sigma projects, however, are limited in number and scattered throughout the company. The EKN enables them to easily share project learning and broadcast best practices and, in the words of Knowledge Lead Drew Grimm, "reduce the six degrees of separation at Honeywell down to one." Results of the initial implementation showed an average of 40 hours saved per person per year, which means for every 50 employees to which the system is deployed, they effectively gain a new head count. As the pilot was moving forward, Honeywell mapped out the progressive steps to broaden the scope of its EKN. Currently, the EKN is available to the entire global Six Sigma organization, with plans for further expansion to other areas of the company.

Aerospace and defense companies such as Honeywell have another urgent reason to need a system to capture and retain employee expertise: just like oil and gas, this industry has a rapidly aging workforce. The percentage of employees under 35 years of age reduced by 50% in the last decade, and it has become common for companies to woo former employees out of retirement, offering them consulting engagements in the hope of leveraging some of the valuable expertise that could not be replaced once gone. This is one of the reasons why **Boeing Canoga Park** implemented their EKN.

As the maker of the most well-known and highly tested large rocket engine ever built (in 1981), Boeing Canoga Park has many veteran engineers who have worked in the program for over two decades. Their combined experience is an invaluable asset to the company and the aerospace industry as a whole; thus their impending retirement in the next 5–10 years has become a concerning event for the company. In anticipation of this, Boeing is doing its best to tap into that pool of knowledge before its owners depart.

Boeing Canoga Park also started with a relatively smaller implementation, initially rolling out the EKN to about 500 employees in the legacy rocket engine program. The feedback received was overwhelmingly positive—90% of the users liked the solution and believed that it should be made available to the rest of the organization. The more junior employees were especially enthusiastic, as many of them felt more comfortable browsing solutions and asking questions through the system than in person. The EKN is now deployed to all of Boeing Canoga Park with plans for further expansion to other areas in Boeing.

P&G is yet another example of a company that started with a pilot and expanded their deployment after seeing significant productivity savings. Already cognizant of the need to connect its scientists across business units and around the world, P&G had formally established research-focused communities and deployed several KM tools such as intranets and e-mail discussion forums. They soon realized, however, that while the intranet provided much improved accessibility to documents, it did not help scientists find the right colleague to collaborate with. The e-mail tool was also less than ideal: it would send one scientist's question indiscriminately to the rest of the community, and scientists gradually became weary of the constant broadcasts and disregarded the requests for help. P&G turned to EKN to fill the void.

P&G piloted an EKN with users from three research communities and involved senior scientists to evaluate how well the solution met their requirements. Pilot results showed that the EKN helped to advance research projects by an average of 1–4 weeks, and senior scientists determined that the top 50–60 captured answers alone would justify the investment. P&G proceeded to deploy the EKN into more than 30 communities of practice in their global R&D group.

In addition to ongoing quantitative analysis of their RoI (return on investment), P&G also looks for anecdotal accounts of how the system has impacted the end-users day to day. An example is what happened with a researcher in Kobe, Japan. The researcher was considering purchasing an analytical instrument for a chemical compound, but he needed to know how well it would work before investing in the costly instrument. Using the EKN he was able to quickly find someone in Cincinnati, Ohio, who had just purchased one a year ago with good results. The knowledge about how well an instrument works is typically not documented anywhere, and it would have been very difficult for the researcher in Japan to track down someone who could share the experience; the EKN enabled him to do this easily. Thus, regardless of whether the employee chose to put a dollar value on the answer, it undoubtedly helped him solve a business problem in the most efficient way.

An example of where a company did things a little differently is **CNA Insurance**. In 2000, this large insurance company was in the process of streamlining its businesses to focus on underwriting, and it sought technology and tools to help with this effort. The company's vision was to create a portfolio of underwriting expertise across the company, and to that end, the executive management team knew that the EKN would provide significant value. Under mandate from then-CEO Bernard Hengesbaugh, the EKN was rolled out to the entire organization within six months.

CNA's bold step paid off. Soon after the system was set up, an underwriter in the Commercial Insurance claims office in Syracuse, New York, received a claim from Alberta, Canada. The claim involved a lawsuit where numerous plaintiffs were alleging physical, emotional, and mental abuse from residence Indian schools that were run by an organization that was a client of a member company of Continental Insurance Co. (CIC), with which CNA had merged. Potentially any claims would now be the responsibility of CNA.

The underwriter talked with his co-workers, some of whom were former employees of CIC, and they seemed to remember that the Canadian book of business was sold when the merger happened. But they did not know specifically if the policy was one of those sold and, if so, to whom. Since no one in his personal network had the answer, the underwriter went on the EKN with his question. Sure enough, someone elsewhere in the company responded and directed him to Lombard of Canada, and after checking their records Lombard agreed that the policy belonged to them. This had the potential to be a very expensive claim, and the EKN played a critical role in helping the underwriter identify the business that should handle the claim, saving CNA time and money.

How an EKN Works

EKNs are software systems designed to fit into a company's existing business processes. Therefore, each company's implementation of the solution may be different. In most cases, however, the basic usage flow, based on the solution's core capabilities, is the same.

It starts with an employee that has a business problem. She describes the problem in a question and submits the question to the EKN via a Web browser, e-mail client, or even a portable digital assistant (PDA). The EKN then uses advanced search capabilities to find content related to the question. That content can exist in either the EKN knowledge-base or external repositories, such as document management, collaboration, or file systems. If the content retrieved does not answer the employee's question, the EKN then searches through user profiles to find someone with relevant expertise, presenting her with the list of people who are most likely to be able to help (see Figure 29.1). The employee sends her question to the expert(s) of her choice. The EKN provides an interface for the expert to answer the question. The user and expert can continue the conversation on the system until the issue has been satisfactorily resolved.

If necessary, the system routes the answer through a custom-defined approval loop before it is captured in the system's knowledge-base and sent to the employee. Because the answer is captured and reusable, others with similar questions can make

Figure 29.1

List of relevant experts found by the EKN

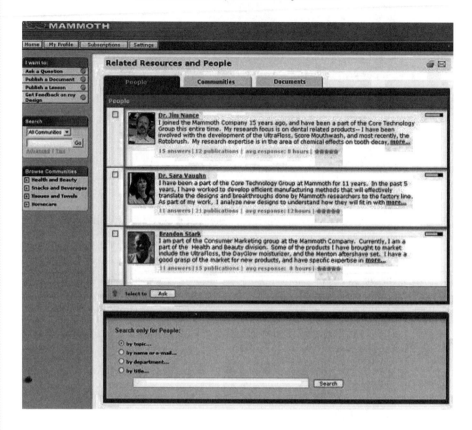

immediate use of it and the expert will not have to spend time answering the same question repeatedly.

In addition, the EKN automatically dispatches newly captured knowledge articles to interested subscribers (i.e., employees who may not necessarily have a pressing business problem, but are interested in obtaining expertise in specific areas). Thus, an EKN not only delivers value to the person who asks the question and the one who answers, but also to the community of users that can benefit from the rapid spread of best practices and lessons learned.

Although the concept of enabling knowledge exchange across an organization may seem straightforward, the specific capabilities that make the EKN truly practical and powerful are much more sophisticated. For example, it is critical to ensure that experts provide high-quality answers and that response times are appropriate to the context and urgency of the questions. If users are disappointed by the reliability of the answer or the turnaround time, they are not likely to use the EKN again.

There are a number of ways to control answer quality and enforce response times, and each of these falls under one of two approaches. The first approach appeals to the experts' sense of professional pride: users **rate** the answers received, other members of the community can **comment** on the answers, and the system **tracks** the

Figure 29.2

Example of an individual expertise profile

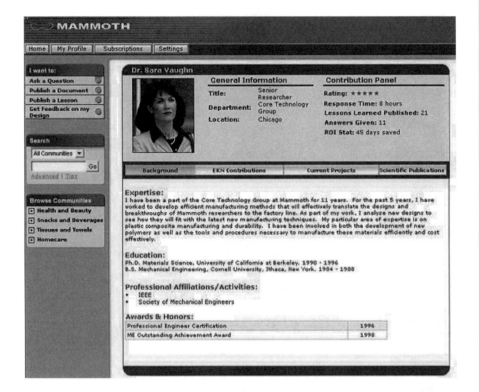

experts' overall rating and **response times** for all the users to see (see Figure 29.2). These capabilities create a self-policing environment that also facilitates the experts' goodwill, builds up their reputation, and fosters reciprocity.

Some companies even build incentive programs on top of these capabilities, recognizing those who have the highest rated answers and/or the quickest response times. For example, at an infant care company, such an employee is selected periodically and rewarded with an extra day of vacation. Regardless of whether there is a concrete reward program, the EKN provides employees valuable opportunities to gain recognition from their colleagues (as well as management) by providing the best answer in the quickest time.

It should be noted, however, that not all companies want to use these capabilities. In some cases, publishing information such as expertise rating may not fit within the **company culture** and thus these features need to be turned on or off as needed. For example, to comply with corporate policy, a European financial firm disabled the ability for all users to see expert ratings and answer times. However, the system administrators kept the behind-the-scenes tracking of this information in order to generate a report on the value of the system.

The second approach is to apply automated supervision by creating a set of *business rules*, which trigger actions based on the content and context of the questions and answers (see Figure 29.3). The EKN can monitor the state of the question and alert

Figure 29.3

Question and answers by various experts on the EKN

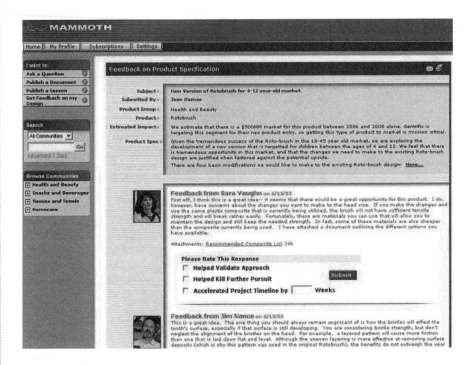

the right person to be involved if needed. For example, for questions about urgent customer issues that could impact company revenue, a business rule can be set up to escalate the question to the vice president of sales if it is not adequately addressed within 24 hours.

Similarly, other types of business rules, commonly called *approval loops*, are essential if the content of the answer is so critical that additional validation is required before it can be used. When a company is involved in litigation with one of its competitors, for example, it may require that any answer that mentions the competitor be reviewed by a corporate attorney. With the appropriate approval loops in place, the EKN monitors answers provided by experts and automatically forwards those that reference competitors to the legal department. If the answer is authorized, then the system routes it to the user.

The combination of the two approaches ensures that experts provide high-quality content in a timely fashion. While cultivating self-policing communities is generally desirable across an organization, different communities may well have distinct requirements for escalation and approval (e.g., human resources versus strategic sales, the former may not need as strict a turnaround time). Therefore, one of the most valuable capabilities of the EKN is the flexibility to support business rules and approval loops at various levels, whether it be community based or organization wide.

An EKN's *taxonomy* is the framework on which business rules can be configured granularly. It is a systematic way of organizing knowledge, similar to a file system hierarchy used to organize documents or an e-mail folder system used to group mail messages. A taxonomy organizes knowledge into topics or categories, and each category can have its own unique set of rules that enforces business rules. For example, the 24-hour escalation rule that is associated with the strategic sales category is independent from the 72-hour escalation rule of the human resource category.

A taxonomy also provides a simple and scalable model to enforce *security* or compliance policies. This is useful in areas such as the defense industry, where companies such as Boeing Canoga Park often have the customer requirement that information in certain programs be kept classified from other programs and that only users who have passed security screening be allowed to access certain content. With an explicit taxonomy in place, this requirement is easily satisfied by placing the secured content in a category that is only accessible to users who have the required attributes.

Many companies take the practical approach of mirroring the taxonomy to the communities of practice that exist in the organization. At P&G, for instance, the EKN taxonomy for its 18,000 R&D employees is designed around the existing 30-plus communities of practice. Each broad top-level topic and related sub-topics on the EKN, such as "Wipes and Substrates" and "Packaging and Delivery Systems," corresponds to the community of users that discuss these topics formally or informally. In this way, the taxonomy provides a Web-based common space to facilitate and capture conversations, helping to foster lively communities.

A lively community often has a *"community champion"* that is responsible for its health and vibrancy. This person is usually not an information technology (IT) staff, but a community member that is close to the expertise being shared. The EKN provides community champions with the right software tools to manage the people and content in the community. Typical tasks include ensuring that community members frequently share knowledge on the EKN, that the content retained is current and relevant, and that best practices are being reviewed and broadcasted.

Driving the certification and distribution of *best practices* is one of the most important tasks performed by a community champion (although in some companies, this is done by another designated personnel). As the EKN becomes widely used and the knowledge-base grows, the ability to pull the most important "knowledge gems," or best practices, out of thousands or more knowledge articles becomes very important.

There are several ways to promote a best practice within an EKN. The most common way is for a user to nominate an answer that has proven to be so valuable and broadly applicable that it should be made into a standard or be widely distributed. Alternately, an employee can also publish a knowledge article and **nominate** it him/herself. In this case, the article typically answers a question that is frequently asked of the employee. The ability to proactively **self-publish** would save him/her from spending a lot of time answering the same question repeatedly, and rendering it a best practice would give the solution even higher visibility.

In either case, after the user provides justification for the nomination, the EKN routes the article to the designated approver (who may be the community champion or someone else that is qualified). If approved, the article is automatically elevated to a prominent spot within the community common space on the EKN. Some companies allow users with the right privileges to directly create best practices and bypass the nomination process.

There are several ways to *distribute* newly minted best practices. In addition to posting to the Web-based community space on the EKN, another practical and effective approach is to *dispatch* it over e-mail. Most companies have integrated the EKN with their e-mail system, so that employees can use their most-used application—the e-mail client—to browse knowledge articles or search for expertise on the EKN.

E-mail integration also enables users with the appropriate privileges to *subscribe* to topics on the EKN that interest them (e.g., a customer service agent may subscribe to the customer service as well as the product development-related topics; a sales representative may subscribe to the strategic sales as well as marketing and public relations topics) and automatically receive updates, such as new best practices, via e-mail.

Integration

E-mail systems are just one of the integration points for the EKN. Companies who have successful EKNs (i.e., those that experience very high usage) often have numerous points of integration with their existing IT infrastructure. Some of the toughest challenges in deploying any new software stem from the fact that employees are wary of having to rely on yet another application, with a different user interface (UI) metaphor, authentication scheme, and separate data storage. In addition to e-mail, they already have to work with numerous other applications to get the content they need, e.g., networked file system, document management, team or project software, and the intranet or enterprise portal. Indeed, there would be little justification for deploying an EKN if the overhead of using the additional application actually decreases productivity.

At the front end, the EKN can take on the familiar look and feel of existing Web applications (e.g., enterprise portals). Additionally, many companies also integrate individual components of the EKN into other Web applications. For example, the expertise search interface can become part of the portal page, such that users can submit queries and see the EKN search results right from their own personalized portal homepage.

At the back end, it is also common to integrate with the company's current authentication scheme, leveraging the existing directory system and security protocols. The result, often called "single sign-on," enables users to access EKN content without having to reenter their usernames and passwords. This means the EKN automatically authenticates the user as needed (e.g., to obtain secured information or use special features) with the credentials already in the system, thus providing a seamless navigation experience for the user.

Another important point of integration happens at the database level. Integrating the EKN with various other content repositories ensures that the user needs to only look at one place to retrieve all the relevant information that exists in the organization. The benefit of this approach is twofold. First, the user saves time and effort with a more efficient search process—just one search query and interface. Second, the EKN becomes more powerful because it not only provides content from its own knowledgebase, but also those from other useful databases. For example, when a pharmaceutics researcher needs to know more about a compound, a search on the EKN not only returns the subject matter experts in the company and relevant existing answers from the knowledge-base, but also researches reports from the document management system, white papers from the online library, and the latest details on related current projects from the project software database.

These are just some of the most popular integration tactics many companies have taken to implement EKNs that are well adopted and highly used by employees. Other types of integration include directory information, taxonomy, administration, and permission models. Furthermore, the multitiered architecture and standard-based platform on which the EKN is designed enables custom integrations with various software solutions such as project management, collaboration, and e-learning, among others.

Integration not only renders the EKN more useful, but allows companies to derive more value of other IT investments as well.

Best Practices in Deploying an EKN

Although innovative technology and clever product capabilities always appeal, companies have learned that, ultimately, snazzy technology alone does not take them very far toward a successful EKN. In fact, there are no shortages of cases where stellar technologies fail because the team responsible for rolling it out to the company did not have the right approach to address people and process issues. These components, while less glamorous, are even more critical than technology to the success of an EKN deployment.

People and Culture

The participation of employees correlates directly to the perceived value of the EKN. If the solution is launched without having planned for the range of expected reactions from users, it will fail under all but the most fortunate of circumstances. The user's reaction to an EKN is dependent on the culture of the organization. If the culture is traditionally open and sharing, then the EKN is likely to be adopted without much resistance as it provides a new way of facilitating the kind of knowledge sharing employees are already used to. If the culture is traditionally cliquish and tight-lipped, then the EKN is likely to be met with resistance. In all cases, if the EKN does not bring direct or immediate benefits to a user's daily work, it will likely fail due to rapidly declining usage.

In general, most medium-to-large organizations take a phased approach to deployment, starting with a relatively small pilot as Honeywell and Boeing Canoga Park did. Once the solution has proven success and business value, then organizations proceed to a larger scale deployment. One of the most important work items prior to launching the pilot is to determine which group within the organization should be the pilot audience. This group's demographic should enable a good estimate of the business value that the EKN would deliver when the deployment is larger scale. For an organization like Boeing Canoga Park, for example, the 500 engineers in one of the rocket engine programs are an appropriate representation of the entire organization. Pilot results would certainly not have been nearly as useful if Boeing had selected its legal group as the target audience, as that group does not demonstrate the same requirements and behaviors of the overall engineering-focused organization.

To select the right pilot group, consider factors such as the type of common business problems employees face, their general attitude toward sharing knowledge and collaborating, and their overall professional goals and specific motivators, as well as the technologies they currently use. There should be a significant overlap between those of the pilot group with those of the organization as a whole.

Almost all companies that deploy an EKN pre-populate the system with existing frequently used documents in order to ensure that users derive value from the solution the first time they use it. For example, Intec Engineering imported their mini-resume database into the EKN and enabled the system to return detailed expert information without any additional effort from the experts. At a government agency that specializes in helping U.S. companies export overseas, the marketing research library was integrated into the EKN. Since its employees access this library daily, the EKN immediately becomes a useful tool as it not only returns the research report, but other relevant knowledge articles or expert profiles as well. In general, the value of pre-populating the EKN depends heavily on the extent of the technology's integration capabilities.

When the EKN is live, frequent communication helps to keep it at the top of mind for users. The means of communication include face-to-face rollout sessions, newsletters, e-mails, promotion on corporate Web sites, posters, and even giveaways. Some companies also implement incentive programs to encourage participation. Incentive programs are based on success metrics, which typically revolve around application usage (e.g., answers delivered, profiles accessed), knowledge-base creation (e.g., number of best practices or self-published answers), and perceived RoI (e.g., time or money saved as a result of knowledge exchange). The need for communication and incentive programs, as well as the programs themselves, can vary greatly depending on company culture.

Heeding company culture is fundamental in planning the deployment of an EKN. Not only does the company culture drive communication and incentive programs, in many cases it also dictates the customization of the EKN. A good example of this is Honeywell; its acquisition of AlliedSignal in late 1999 gave rise to employee concerns about job security, and the layoffs that occurred soon after due to the economic downturn exacerbated those concerns. As a result, Honeywell's employees tended to guard their expertise with caution. When Honeywell decided to launch the EKN, it evaluated the culture challenges that must be overcome and decided to bring in an external consultancy that specializes in merging technology with culture. The consultant discovered that it was not that employees stopped helping each other, but rather they only helped those within their trusted circles. Since employees' trusted business circles were typically small and isolated, Honeywell needed to help them expand these circles before a true knowledge network could be established.

To accomplish this, Honeywell tweaked its EKN to include elements that were outside of business. The system, called MyHoneywell, features information about the employee's family, hobbies, and activities outside of work, as well as a wealth of general lifestyle resources. Honeywell also decided to disable the rating feature for answers in order to ease off the pressure on experts. Honeywell's approach enables its employees to network with each other not just when they are faced with business problems, but also in a relaxed and casual manner that eventually cultivates trust and camaraderie.

Processes

Simply put, the deployment of an EKN should not require new processes or procedures to be created. A properly implemented EKN supports usage flow that is consistent with the way with which the company conducts business. This not only eliminates additional overhead associated with management changes to handle the new functionality, but also optimizes usage and adoption rates by allowing users to continue with their current business behavior.

Consider the example of an EKN that is deployed within a support organization. Employees that use it to help solve customer issues of various levels of urgency critically need the solution to enforce the established service level agreements (SLAs). If that enforcement is not automatic, employees will not use it lest they put their own jobs at risk. Another good example is the need to maintain secured content in organizations such as defense agencies. These companies absolutely will not deploy a solution that does not support the level of access control that is demanded by their clients.

Mapping the EKN to relevant existing business process requires thorough analysis of how knowledge and information flows within the organization. The analysis is often based on a set of data that includes the type of business problems that employees face, the urgency of solving these problems, the range of sensitivity of information being shared, and the kind of people or groups that usually need to be involved in decisions. Once the information flow is clear, then the EKN can be implemented with the appropriate taxonomy, business rules, and workflow, as well as permission model. Thus, it is the results of a thorough and correct analysis of the knowledge flow that enables the powerful capabilities that elevate the EKN from a technology to a practical business solution.

Conclusion

EKNs uniquely address a set of challenges commonly faced by medium-to-large organizations: those that stem from the inability to quickly find undocumented experiential knowledge among employees. Companies such as P&G, Honeywell, and Boeing Canoga Park have been using an EKN to locate employee expertise and identify best practices, raising the quality of work and reducing project cycle times. They also use the EKN to foster communities of practice, bringing together employees with common professional interests across geographic and organizational boundaries. By capturing the know-how of former and current employees into an ever-growing knowledge-base, and delivering that content to applications such as portals or document management systems, these companies are realizing more value than other KM or IT investments.

Deploying a successful EKN requires an overall strategy around the organization's people, culture, and processes, as well as technology. Companies need to adopt a holistic methodology that uses the technology's capabilities to integrate the solution into existing culture and business requirements. This ensures ease of use and immediate delivery of value to the users, as well as low total cost of ownership in the longer term. A phased approach allows companies to prove the business value and viability of the solution, while minimizing the cost and risk. Also, EKN vendors and consultants that have extensive customer experience can also serve as excellent resources for companies who are deploying the EKN for the first time.

Integrated KM Solutions: The Experience of Entopia*

30

Peter Katz and Manfred Lugmayr

The secret of business is to know something that nobody else knows.

Aristotle Onassis

The Context

Retaining, finding, and reusing business-critical content in the growing information technology (IT)-enabled network is more difficult than ever, especially with increasing information overload and competitive pressures. Entopia provides a wide array of KM tools for search, expertise identification (from profiles and online activity), content management, taxonomy, social network analysis, collaboration, and knowledge visualization. The tools reflect Entopia's "3 Cs" philosophy of KM: collect, collaborate, and capitalize.

With rapid flux in communication and publication activities, the enterprise is better regarded as a living entity. Accordingly, search engines also need to take into account the context and life cycle of enterprise content and incorporate results from dynamic activities rather than just static documents. Social network analysis (SNA) tools should be able to map communities of practices' (CoPs) community leaders, subject matter experts, peers, and sets of linked and disjoint communities (see Figure 30.1). These

* *Editor's Note:* An estimated 80% of KM solutions fail due to lack of company adoption, which in turn is the result of poor design, inadequate integration with workflow, and no quick wins. This chapter reflects KM vendor Entopia's "3 Cs" philosophy of KM: collect, collaborate, and capitalize. Its offerings include content management, social network analysis, and dynamic search.

Three case studies are covered: Gate5, Evesham Technology, and the U.S. Space and Naval Warfare Systems Center. The KM tools deployed were easy to use even for remote users with browser access, one-stop access solutions were provided for information assets, and dynamic profiles of experts were created. The solutions facilitated better knowledge sharing, which in turn improved customer service, avoided increasing head counts, and led to better decision making. Key KM learnings include the importance of making knowledge sharing a strong part of organizational culture, focusing on metrics, and starting in a phased manner. Trends to watch include the growing use of XML in content management, better understanding of the human component of networking activities (e.g., via SNA), and the importance of personal KM.

Figure 30.1

Entopia Knowledge Locator uses different techniques to return documents, people, and information sources

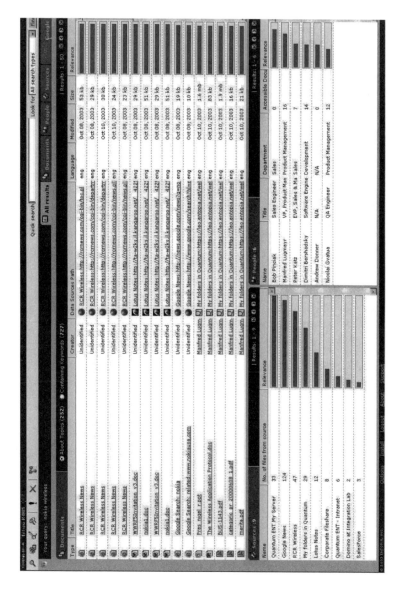

maps should be viewed over time to provide continuous change feedback to managers as they fine-tune their social network.

Case Studies

Entopia's award-winning knowledge management (KM) tools provide many of the desired features above, as shown in the following case studies.

Gate5: Using KM to Deal with Global Reach, Rapid Market Changes, and Information Overload

Gate5, a software company specializing in the development of software for next-generation, location-based mobile Internet services, was feeling the pressure of information overload. The company needed a way to gather and capitalize on enormous amounts of unstructured and disparate market data such as Microsoft Word files, e-mails, PDFs, and Web pages. The business of mobile Internet services, with its fast-changing market dynamics, necessitated a solution that allowed Gate5 to aggregate all their various forms of information into one location. In addition, having customers and partners around the world and with the fast-paced nature of the mobile Internet services market, the solution needed to be accessible by employees across the globe, yet flexible enough to encourage company-wide adoption.

Entopia's Quantum solution was deployed for one-stop content access across the organization within a year. The solution was designed to work with our employees' individual working styles, with a minimum amount of extra training. Dynamic profiling using semantic and artificial intelligence technologies helped tackle the problems of "a sea of server files" and employees scattered across the globe.

Evesham Technology Improves Help Desk Support through Knowledge Sharing

Evesham Technology, a computer manufacturing company, was suffering from a lack of knowledge sharing at its customer help desk. They needed a comprehensive customer support knowledge-base to manage the ever-increasing documents, information sources, and even the knowledge inside people's heads. Evesham needed to aggregate all the various forms of content into one location that all their support professionals could access.

Entopia's Quantum tool was picked due to its bottom-up KM approach and ease of use. The Evesham research and technical support teams were the first users of the KM solution; they were able to access it remotely thanks to the availability of a Web-based client as well as a local client. After a week of training on features like dynamic profiling, most other employees began to use the KM solution to access customer and product intelligence.

Within six months of usage, Evesham began to see the return on their investment. The company has been able to shorten call and resolution times by providing its customer representatives fast and easy access to the company's knowledge-base. The customer support team has been able to avoid increasing head count; this has saved the company from employing extra people in these departments with a return on investment (ROI) of approximately 110%.

Space and Naval Warfare Systems Center, San Diego, Improves Decision Making in the U.S. Navy Fleet

The Space and Naval Warfare Systems Center (SSC), San Diego, is responsible for the information management component of the U.S. Navy's initiative to develop and deploy an information/knowledge management system called VICTOR II to improve decision making in the fleet. Ship- and shore-based intelligence analysts needed a solution that would allow them to quickly gather intelligence concerning potential threats to the fleet into a centralized and Web-based repository. In the longer term, team leaders needed to identify expertise in the analyst pool to build teams with relevant experience.

SSC San Diego chose Entopia to build VICTOR II for integration to the Navy Enterprise portal. A workflow engine was built to manage intelligence gathering and analysis. The browser interface enabled access from shared personal computers on remote battleships. Dynamic profiles built according to the activity of the analysts enabled team leaders to dynamically find the right analyst for the topic based on his or her previous activity in the knowledge-base.

Learnings and Recommendations

Based on its experiences with client KM solutions, Entopia offers the following recommendations for KM practitioners, in increasing order of importance.

10. Do not ask or expect the end user to do too much for the benefit of others.
9. Consider technology as an important part, but not all of the KM solution.
8. Incorporate process and technology to leverage tacit knowledge/experience.
7. Incorporate process and technology that leverages existing legacy assets.
6. Knowledge sharing should become a strong part of the culture.
5. Knowledge services should become part of the application infrastructure.
4. KM is not a business outcome, just a way to help to achieve one.
3. Measure the impact on business outcome.
2. Never forget that the end user is your true customer.
1. Get started. Even if you have to start small.

The Road Ahead: Trends in KM

1. The biggest trend that Entopia foresees is that KM will become an intrinsic part of any business process. The capture and codification of knowledge will simply become an automatic function of all business software. The acceptance of XML as the standard to describe and store information is helping this trend and allows for universal manipulation of information, thus minimizing the cost of codification.

2. Organizations will grow toward a homogenous information infrastructure that will make all information actionable for employees and business processes.

3. Another trend we see is the optimization and better understanding of the human element of the workforce in the organization with regards to the flow of information and knowledge exchange. Tools that automatically capture the social activity and context surrounding information will better facilitate and allow for the analysis and improvement of information flow between employees. Maturing SNA systems will automatically connect employees and the content they are working on to avoid work duplication and spot

Figure 30.2

By combining Entopia's dynamic expertise location with its visualization techniques,
Entopia Enterprise Social Networks Analysis identifies the information flows or bottlenecks
within the enterprise

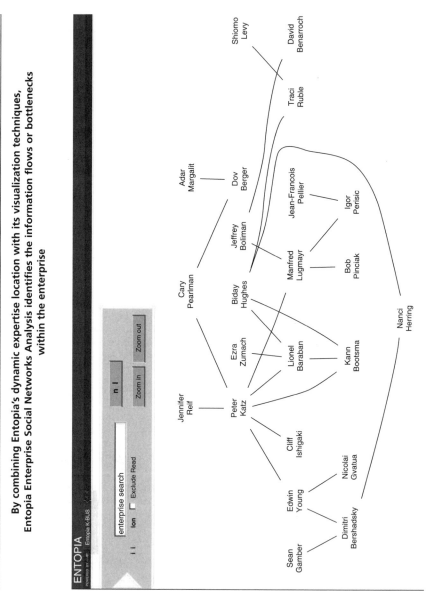

communication bottlenecks. Entopia is also enhancing its own real-time social networking analysis tool to automatically prescribe changes to the corporate social network to optimize it (see Figure 30.2).

4. Finally, we predict that personal KM will be a big trend driven by the availability of critical information from more and more information sources and devices. People will need to capture and track information across those different systems in the office, at home, and on the road. For example, new consumers' devices will bring real-time information to wrist watches and even kitchen magnets. Users need to be able to capture important information from whichever source and organize it for reuse or sharing. On the enterprise side, they can leverage those new channels to bring important information to employees more efficiently.

Effective Knowledge Management for Professional Services*

31

Dan Carmel

> Knowledge is the fundamental factor—the major enabler—of enterprise performance.
>
> *Karl M. Wiig*

Knowledge: The Lifeblood of Professional Services Firms

While knowledge management (KM) has value for every type of organization, it plays an especially crucial role in professional services firms, where knowledge is a primary driver of competitive advantage and content is the main deliverable. Implemented effectively, KM helps these organizations put their full institutional resources to work for their clients and ensures that the information gathered and lessons learned in each engagement are retained and made available for efficient future reuse.

In most cases, a professional services engagement is a process rather than a specific event, involving different personnel, resources, and skills each step of the way. Accordingly, KM for professional services requires a holistic approach that applies a

---

* *Editor's Note:* KM is the way of life in cutting-edge professional services firms, where knowledge is a primary driver of competitive advantage and content is a key deliverable. This chapter sketches the role of KM tools in four key process areas of professional services firms: pre-engagement, engagement execution, engagement close, and post-engagement. Reuse of lessons learned is critical to productivity at every stage of the engagement in a professional services firm. Integrated KM tools for content management and collaboration constitute the starting point for effective KM infrastructure in such firms, along with knowledge repositories, expertise locators, content templates, unified search, threaded discussion, collaborative extranets, and taxonomy generation.

Usability with existing tools, user-initiated knowledge activities, and security of content are key requirements for such KM tools. Three case studies are provided in this chapter, based on professional services firms which use iManage's collaborative content management products (as this book was going to press, iManage was acquired by Interwoven). Key learnings include the difficulty of getting users to make a wholesale switch to a new way of working (hence the need for integration with existing tools), balancing open access with security, the necessity of support from top management, the rise of near-real-time KM, and the pressing need of professional services firms to deal with new regulations governing records management.

variety of disciplines and technologies to support each stage of the engagement cycle:

- **Pre-engagement**—Bringing the collective expertise of the firm to bear in winning new business
- **Engagement execution**—Enabling efficient execution, an especially important consideration as many engagements move to flat-rate pricing
- **Engagement close**—Identifying and extracting valuable knowledge and records from the rest of the content generated over the course of the engagement
- **Post-engagement**—Ensuring that the knowledge generated in each engagement is retained and made available for reuse

At its most fundamental, the implementation of KM involves three key challenges. First, the firm must define its knowledge resources by identifying the documents, outside research, e-mails, scanned documents, images, voice mail, instant messages, and other content with potential value for its work and use a centralized repository to make them readily available throughout the organization. Second, employees must be provided with the right KM tools for each aspect of their jobs, including document management, research, collaboration, and content generation. Flexibility is essential to conform to different individual work styles, different stages of the engagement cycle, and different practice and industry groups. Third, the firm must have a way to measure KM usage, using metrics and user feedback in order to improve on the existing process, and demonstrate the value of KM to ensure that the initiative is funded.

In addition to these functional considerations, KM poses several technical requirements. To ensure adoption and usability, KM tools should be integrated with each other and with the knowledge authoring tools these workers already use, such as word processing, spreadsheets, presentation software, and e-mail. To minimize the complexity and cost of the implementation, this integration should be available out of the box, rather than accomplished through painstaking custom development. Similarly, the solution should be tailored specifically to the firm's market or services, rather than adapted from a non-professional services context. Security is paramount and must be both strict enough to enable secure online collaboration and flexible enough to accommodate ad hoc rules and policies. Finally, the system should be easy to use with minimal or no formal training; otherwise, it may not be adopted and will remain a well-intentioned but underutilized tool.

The Role of KM in the Professional Services Engagement Cycle

Although they do different work, professional services organizations such as law firms, accounting firms, consulting groups, and financial services institutions share certain common characteristics. Unlike companies that produce or trade material goods, the deliverables produced by these firms are driven entirely by content and knowledge—legal documents, court filings, accounting reports, consulting findings, and so forth. Knowledge is thus a primary source of competitive advantage; customers in these fields make their selection based largely on a firm's track record, the expertise of its professionals, and its ability to bring specialized knowledge and information resources to bear. Project work is often performed collaboratively, rather than by isolated individuals; project teams include members with specialized expertise from throughout the organization, often in multiple locations, and may mirror practice groups, industry groups, and other firm-wide structures. Because past work is highly relevant to future projects, the efficient reuse of information—successful client pitches, strategies that

Figure 31.1

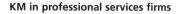

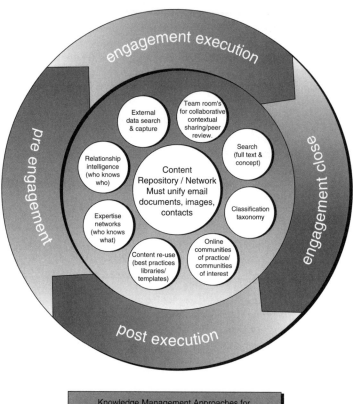

KM in professional services firms

engagement execution

pre engagement

engagement close

post execution

Team room's for collaborative contextual sharing/peer review.

External data search & capture

Search (full text & concept)

Relationship intelligence (who knows who)

Content Repository / Network Must unify email documents, images, contacts

Classification taxonomy

Expertise networks (who knows what)

Content re-use (best practices libraries/ templates)

Online communities of practice/ communities of interest

Knowledge Management Approaches for
Each Stage of the Professional Services life Cycle

have proven effective, specialized industry knowledge gained, similar precedents and situations—is critical to productivity at every stage of the engagement.

Given these characteristics, the link between professional services and KM is clear (see Figure 31.1). At every stage of the engagement cycle, KM tools and capabilities enable these firms to put their most vital asset—professional knowledge—to the most effective possible use.

Pre-engagement

To win new assignments, a client pitch must demonstrate the firm's qualifications in terms of both its professional resources and its ability to put them to work. KM streamlines this process by making it simple and intuitive to find all the resources relevant to the prospective client, to put together the best proposal, and, ultimately, to win the business. An easily searchable firm-wide repository makes it possible to mine past proposals for relevant information, as well as to identify specialized professional knowledge and content that can be highlighted in the pitch.

Relationship knowledge also comes into play, such as discovering professional or educational ties between firm members and client contacts that can be used to build rapport and identifying internal expertise to assemble the team best able to win the client's confidence. KM technologies designed to uncover and make available this kind of relationship intelligence include specialized customer relationship management tools; expertise identification systems that monitor e-mail to identify individual expertise on designated topics; and communities of practice and interest, in which self-nominating, ad hoc groups gather online to share relevant information. Such groups are especially valuable in geographically distributed organizations, serving in effect as an electronic water cooler.

When the time comes to prepare the final pitch, templates that embody firm best practices and knowledge can be used to speed delivery and ensure consistent quality of proposals across the enterprise.

Engagement Execution

Once the engagement begins, the firm mobilizes the project team and provides them with the tools and resources they need to meet the client's requirements. To help professionals distributed across multiple locations and time zones work together seamlessly, the firm must provide a robust infrastructure that includes content management, a centralized repository for all content and research materials, e-mail management, and the ability for any team member to check the current status of any aspect of the project.

Because of the collaborative nature of professional services work, collaboration, though not traditionally thought of as an explicit element of KM, plays an essential role in realizing full value from the firm's knowledge assets. Among other things, collaboration here includes the collaborative review and editing of documents within a collaborative environment that makes this process efficient (as opposed to e-mail round robin routing, which is prone to version control and workflow problems), discussion threads, issue tracking, group calendaring, and milestone modeling. For greatest efficiency and ease of use, this functionality is grouped in a single collaborative workspace, which also acts as a project library for content as well as an online space for both meetings and asynchronous discussions. By facilitating and documenting the flow of information and processes among team members, the collaborative workspace increases the team's aggregate knowledge and captures expertise that can be reused in later engagements.

As the research process begun in the pre-engagement stage continues, team members review a library of best practices that presents content from past engagements in its original context, alongside background information, discussion notes, and outcome details, to retain its full value for future reuse. A single, comprehensive repository for the entire firm eliminates the need for repetitive searching across multiple repositories. To make sure users find what they need easily and reliably, the repository should be searchable by multiple methods: full text, taxonomy, or concept. Best practice workspace templates serve a similar purpose, enabling the lessons of past engagements to be leveraged for present work. Codifying specific types of engagements, these templates can be used to set up a framework that automatically generates milestones, time lines, document templates, and even workflows for new projects.

The generation of new content evolves through a collaborative process that includes meetings and discussion threads around the project's requirements and the best way to address them. New documents, presentations, and other deliverables are drafted, based on best practice templates where available, and then edited online prior to delivery to the client.

An increasing number of clients are requiring the firms they do business with to provide dedicated extranet access. These extranets expose the internal collaboration and KM environment directly to the client, who can then participate equally in document review, calendaring, online discussions, and other project activities and enter into the communities of interest and practice described above. As an additional benefit to the firm, client extranets are also a valuable means of marketing the firm's expertise by showcasing its internal processes in action. As new deliverables are finalized, the extranet can be used to make these documents available on demand. At this point, KM is essentially extended to the client: the content generated for them is made available in context for their ongoing reference and use.

Sidebar
Case Study 1: Eisner LLP smoothes information work and boosts knowledge sharing

Eisner LLP provides certified public accounting and advisory services to clients ranging from individuals to publicly held corporations. In the 1990s, it faced challenges in complying with new regulations for records management and retention, and its existing hardcopy-based workflow was leading to out-of-control storage costs, classification problems, and productivity bottlenecks caused when physical files were in use elsewhere.

After conducting a proper audit trail and redesigning workflow in 1999, iManage's WorkSite tool was rolled out across the firm and integrated with Microsoft Word, PowerPoint, Excel, and Outlook. A move to new offices provided the ideal opportunity to clean house both physically and strategically, with an automation initiative designed to accomplish several goals including moving to a paperless office.

In addition to streamling internal content, the firm has now imported immense quantities of research materials, client tax returns, and financial records into an easily searchable centralized repository. Eisner's professionals can now draw upon KM capabilities that include a library of best practices, past engagements, and industry-specific checklists numbering in the thousands of pages.

Accountants in Eisner's Litigation Support group use WorkSite to share knowledge and make client documents readily available in court. In the past, these professionals would spend extensive time indexing 50 boxes or more of paper files for each case; it could easily take three days to find a given document. Now documents are scanned using optical character recognition and imported alongside electronic documents.

WorkSite also provided for a strong security model, which made the firm and its clients comfortable using the system. Full payback on the firm's investment in WorkSite was realized through savings in physical storage costs alone.

Engagement Close

Once an engagement is completed, the knowledge it has generated is captured, cataloged, and fed back into the organization for reuse, thus continuing the KM cycle. The robust content management infrastructure at the heart of the KM system takes care of the first step: all documents are retained in their final form, alongside the background materials and collaborative processes that went into their development, documentation of the project's outcome, and a critical evaluation of the strategies employed. Project workspaces can simply be frozen in their final state as a permanent reference point for similar future engagements.

There are two technologies in common use for categorizing knowledge into a taxonomic hierarchy. In the United States, firms generally use auto-classification based on meta-data or other automated inputs. Because this method is not highly accurate, it is typically complemented with search capabilities. A second method, used primarily in Europe but also by some U.S. firms, relies on human-based classification, in which a practitioner adds value and accuracy by reviewing the content before assigning it to a category. While more expensive, this method makes the resulting asset more readily actionable. An ideal method would combine the low cost and ease of the former method with the accuracy of the latter.

Post-Engagement

For the knowledge captured in past engagements to remain useful and valuable, it must be managed effectively. Integrated records management allows firms to establish policies for content retention and deletion, as well as to meet regulatory requirements regarding the storage and searchability of past work.

The system itself also requires continued care to retain its full effectiveness. By measuring usage and monitoring system access, the firm can gain an understanding of how employees are working—whether they are making the best use of the available resources or avoiding vital parts of the system due to usability barriers or other issues. A feedback mechanism such as an automated post-engagement survey can provide guidance for ongoing system iteration and enhancement and can keep the KM system a central part of the firm's work life rather than a neglected past initiative.

Meeting the Requirements for Effective KM

As this discussion makes clear, it is unrealistic to invent KM out of thin air; the benefits of KM can be realized only through the deployment of a solid foundation of integrated functionality for managing and collaborating around content. Leading-edge professional services firms are addressing this need by providing all the key functionality and capabilities needed for effective KM in a single suite, including:

- Firm-wide content repositories that include all forms of content—final documents, working drafts, spreadsheets, e-mails, discussion threads, memos—and make it available to users in any location
- Online workspaces specific to each matter, case, or project that hold every form of relevant content, including background materials, works in progress, meeting notes, discussion threads, etc., and also provide an online meeting space for distributed teams
- Powerful search tools based on rich meta-data that is assigned automatically as content is generated to ensure that every piece of knowledge finds its way to the relevant libraries
- Collaborative editing and review, including workflow and version control, to ensure forward direction, and a simple way for team members to bring their own insights and comments to works in progress
- Streamlined extranet deployment, so that firms can make knowledge and content readily available to their clients and can also provide a gateway for clients to contribute their own knowledge to the project.

Sidebar
Case Study 2: Rothschild bankers improve deal making and expertise sharing via KM

Rothschild Inc. is a leading international investment bank with offices in over 30 countries, providing a broad range of financial services to governments, corporations, and individuals worldwide. The competitive financial services arena placed a premium on the effective use of information, but the company's disparate filing systems and slow coordination among scattered locations were coming in the way of building competitive advantage, particularly in terms of sharing financial models, reports, and market data.

A solution based on iManage WorkSite now lets bankers build collaborative deal and department-specific pages by using standard templates; product groups market their resources and expertise to others in the firm; and administrative departments deliver information to specific groups or broadcast more general news to the entire company.

The document and collaboration solution was rolled out in the investment banking division at the end of 2001 and then to the realty and asset management groups in 2002. Extranet sites are being developed to share information with clients, partner companies, and investors. Rothschild is now adding new capabilities tailored specifically to the firm's financial services business and is using tools like WorkKnowledge to move into KM.

By providing a full range of KM capabilities and functionality to support the entire engagement cycle in a single, integrated solution, firms that invest in this infrastructure can make KM an intuitive part of their professionals' work process. The return on investment can be dramatic: increased deal wins, more efficient operations and reduced costs, higher quality work product, and greater client satisfaction.

No discussion of KM would be complete without a word on adoption; after all, no solution can make an impact if no one uses it. The keys to full adoption are simple but absolute:

- Users will resist any system that asks them to make a wholesale switch to a new way of working. Therefore, the KM system must be fully integrated with the tools already in use, such as e-mail, word processing, spreadsheet, and presentation software, to make for a more natural and productive adoption process.
- Similarly, the new KM tools must be easy and intuitive to use with little or no training.
- Strict security is essential to foster secure online collaboration; at the same time, the security model must be flexible enough for non-technical users to be able to bring in new team members as needed within a pre-established framework of roles and privileges.
- The KM implementation must be backed by a fully committed management—not just lip service, but genuine buy-in, including non-monetary incentives to encourage contribution and participation by users throughout the firm.
- Integrated functionality must be more than skin deep. The full range of KM functionality must be available through a single consistent user interface to minimize training and ease adoption. To prevent the KM initiative from bogging down in code and consultants' fees, this integration should be available out of the box rather than requiring extensive in-house development.

Trends in KM Adoption

As we look ahead, market forces and advances in technology are reshaping the KM landscape in profound ways. Three key emerging trends that bear consideration include:

1. The introduction of KM suites from content management, collaboration, and traditional KM providers: As the previous paragraphs make clear, effective KM relies upon providing professional service professionals with a comprehensive and integrated set of tools with which to work. Until now, the lack of functionally complete, readily implemented solutions has made KM initiatives more complex than many customers were willing to take on. Even if multiple point solutions could be successfully integrated, the resulting inconsistent interfaces or cut-and-paste functionality made the systems cost prohibitive, intimidating, and difficult to use while keeping information technology (IT) staff members busy with back-end support, maintenance, and administration issues. Now, as the KM market evolves, the preference of customers for doing business with fewer vendors is helping drive consolidation among KM software providers and leading to the introduction of comprehensive, end-to-end solutions that provide a broad spectrum of tools for KM and collaboration. Often, these solutions will be positioned not as KM tools, but rather as content management, collaboration, and portal solutions. By making the full scope of KM more easily attainable, these highly integrated systems will, in turn, help overcome the reservations of nervous customers, further broadening the adoption of KM among professional services firms and increasing the return on these initiatives.

Sidebar
Case Study 3: Fraser Milner Casgrain LLP leverages collaborative content management tools to achieve national integration

Fraser Milner Casgrain LLP is a full-service Canadian law firm with offices in Vancouver, Calgary, Edmonton, Toronto, Ottawa, and Montreal. It has approximately 1,400 employees, including 500+ attorneys. A key challenge was to function as one firm rather than six separate entities, since each was lacking efficient access to documents, resources, and expertise in the other five locations.

Work on a solution based on iManage WorkSite helped the company migrate its existing systems to an integrated platform, grow new business, and accommodate possible future mergers and acquisitions.

Fraser Milner Casgrain can now provide clients, internal work teams, and third parties with a secure, Web-based view of current projects. Matter-centric collaboration around shared documents, transactions, calendar information, and links to external resources helps distributed teams discuss projects with clients and each other to enable better, faster, and more accurate customer service. Similar sites enable internal collaboration firm-wide among committees, practice groups, and administrators.

---

2. E-mail and compliance initiatives as driving forces in KM adoption: A second driver of KM adoption is even more immediate: the pressing need of professional services firms to deal with the new regulatory requirements governing records management and retention. Many firms are currently undertaking projects dealing with e-mail retention, management, and productivity, as well as initiatives to support compliance with new regulatory requirements such as the Sarbanes-Oxley Act, which requires a holistic approach to firm-wide content centralization and retention/destruction. Although complementary to the effective KM approach outlined above, these projects may be implemented first, due either to business or regulatory pressure or to the compelling payback they promise. By addressing these issues in the context of a holistic approach to KM,

smart firms can extend these point initiatives to provide the kinds of KM benefits outlined earlier, with minimal additional cost. However, a poorly chosen or shortsighted approach to e-mail management or compliance can make future leverage of that effort into KM more difficult, not less so.

3. The move to real-time KM: As the market for KM continues its growth, improvements in technology and the wireless Internet will bring new real-time capabilities that further expand its value for professional services firms. Users will access powerful enterprise search functionality and other KM resources directly from cell phones and other Web-enabled devices, further empowering professional services providers at the client site and elsewhere. The KM infrastructure firms put in place today will provide platform functionality and support for subsequent initiatives as the theory and practice of KM continues to evolve.

Conclusion

In closing, for professional services organizations, KM is both a critical driver of competitive advantage and a key enabler of firm productivity. To realize its benefits, firms must get their content under control, including e-mail management, document management, and the creation of a centralized repository, and then provide a comprehensive suite of capabilities, including collaboration, to enable employees to put these resources to work. Successful deployments have already proven the potential impact of KM on a firm's success; for other firms that have not yet embraced it, the question is not if, but when.

Leveraging Content in Enterprise Knowledge Processes*

32

Ramana Rao

> A wealth of information creates a poverty of attention.
>
> *Herb Simon*

Introduction

Knowledge work heavily depends on the use of information and data. Large amounts of information reside in the form of so-called "unstructured data" available in large organizations. Thus, leveraging available content in the knowledge processes in large organizations has been identified as an important opportunity. Many see content as a strategic element in the processes of capturing, sharing, and reusing knowledge. Yet, current approaches toward content access and use show great limitations even after huge investments over the years.

In fact, content may be the most underutilized asset in large organizations today. Organizations typically buy and create large amounts of content at great costs, yet they often fail to truly leverage it. Content refers to collections of electronic textual documents including research reports, product collaterals, development specifications,

---

* *Editor's Note:* This chapter focuses on content not as unstructured data or part of well-defined workflows, but as expressions of human language and processes that are inherently exploratory in nature. Content continues to be an underutilized asset in large organizations today, even after ten years of mainstream retrieval experience on the Internet and intranets. Search tools may help users find relevant content if they know precisely what they are looking for, but do not help with the work of understanding what is found. Content applications need to focus not just on retrieval, but also on routing, mining, and alerting services. Companies like Inxight provide taxonomy and visualization tools for knowledge workers to provide a conceptual and perceptual map of the content collection.

Information extraction technology (for entities and facts) has become mission critical in government intelligence and is quite common now in the publishing and pharmaceutical industries. Large organizations will need to pay special attention to content processes relating to mergers and acquisitions, corporate licensing of intellectual property, competitive intelligence, product-related content, marketplace feedback, supplier management, and regulatory compliance. Key lessons learned on this front include the importance of augmenting human skills with computational tools, factoring in natural use of language, the need for continually reprocessing text, and designing effective architectures in addition to algorithms.

internal memos, sales materials, patents and invention proposals, press releases, news articles, scientific literature, e-mail messages, and so on.

The causes for content underutilization are complex and varied. First, people, when overloaded by information, tend to "de-tune" and make simplifying decisions, often oversimplifying when considered from a broader perspective. Content often lacks sufficient "meta-data" characterizing the subjects, the sources, and other facets of the content to support effective access. Finally, the access tools of search and browse themselves often create problems, failing by being too brittle, imprecise, hard to use, or inefficient. All of these factors lead to users not using potential valuable content, which in turn leads to broader organizational problems of redundant work, costly mistakes, and missed opportunities.

This chapter focuses on a more intelligent approach toward content access and use. Access refers to not just finding relevant content, but also understanding what has been found. Furthermore, other kinds of content use applications beyond information retrieval, strictly defined, show great potential. As we approach ten years of mainstream retrieval experience on the Internet and intranets, the limitations of traditional search and browse systems are now quite clear, particularly in the face of the increasing complexity and competitive pace of the world.

The key insight marking the path forward is to respect the reality that content is not, in fact, unstructured data, as is characterized in the industry, but expressions of human language. The next section takes a look at shifting this perspective, following which we look at broader classes of content use applications, the underlying technologies of content analysis, and, finally, at specific examples of enterprise applications. We conclude with a few key recommendations.

Shifting Perspectives

Shifting our perspectives on the nature of content, the use of content in knowledge work, and the requirements for access technologies shows the path toward better leveraging of content.

From Unstructured to Richly Structured

The phrase *unstructured data* is meant to contrast documents to data as it is typically stored in relational databases in rows and columns. This characterization reveals a technology bias, since, in fact, to humans documents are nicely structured, whereas databases are generally unfathomable. The problem is that there is not enough time or money to access the structure within and across documents using humans. Thus, the game is now about finding ways to analyze and organize content using software-assisted processes that utilize human effort efficiently and effectively.

The content management paradigm tends to view documents as if they are records, with one big field or blob which is the content of the document. Content analysis is about drilling inside the boundary of the document to extract or analyze specific aspects of the content, particularly recognizing that content is linguistic in nature. This granular data then allows for a better contextualization of documents into conceptual spaces and connecting of the document with other documents. The shift in perspective is from regular tables of documents with minimal file system style meta-data to association networks across and within documents. It is this kind of rich, not impoverished, structure that any human quickly appreciates about the "hyper-structured" web.

From Transactional to Knowledge Work

More important than the stuff (i.e., content) are the work processes which the stuff serves. Could you imagine calling knowledge work, "unstructured work?" Indeed, it is much harder to characterize what is actually happening in knowledge work, but there is still an opportunity to better support these more open processes. The content management perspective here also limits the use of content: the focus has typically been on production and control processes defined as transactional, tightly scripted, repetitive workflows. Thus, it tends to be used in well-defined, late stage processes, for example, technical publication, insurance forms processing, and new drug submissions.

In contrast, knowledge work, by its very nature, cannot be tied down in strict workflows. The processes are inherently exploratory, creative, and analytical in nature. The challenges become evident even in finding documents, never mind using them. Search tools are brittle in that they provide almost no value when you do not really understand what you are looking for. Besides trying to repair this problem and open up the possibility of other applications beyond retrieval, there is also an opportunity to provide "loose coupling" in collaboration and communication processes that are critical in knowledge work. Content can be a bridge between people across time and space and social structure.

From Finding to Using

Search has been the focus of past efforts to leverage organizational content. Yet, besides the challenges of using search tools to find relevant content, the user is still left largely unsupported with the work of understanding what is found. In actuality, users are not typically interested in the documents per se, but rather what the documents say about the world. Here again, the key insight arises: content is made out of human language statements about the world. Right now, the use of the statements is left only to humans, which greatly limits the use of content.

Thus, fully utilizing content will depend on technologies that focus on processing the statements in the content, not just tools for the finding of documents. It is not just single statements that stand out for their uniqueness or relevance to our pursuits, but also patterns over entire collections. There is signal and meaning in the stocks and flows of content, and we unearth these with software. For many, this will conjure up the spectre of solving the grand scientific challenge of natural language understanding by machines, but there are sound and viable approaches that lie in a happy middle between leaving it to humans alone and relying on natural language understanding by machines.

Classifying Applications

All content use applications have something to do, not surprisingly, with content and with users. In particular, they all enable some kind of interaction between the information needs of humans and the meaning-bearing streams of content. Differences in the nature of interaction and handoff between the system and the user define distinct types of applications. First, activity may be driven by the user or, instead, by the flow of content. Second, the focus may be on providing documents to the user or rather on analyzing or processing the contents of statements contained in the documents. These two distinctions capture four basic types of applications:

- Retrieval—Users find and understand relevant documents.
- Routing—The system routes relevant documents to people.

- Mining—Users explore or analyze collections or flows.
- Alerting—The system generates events or reports sent to people.

In retrieval applications, activity is user initiated based on information needs that arise during tasks or projects. Retrieval applications are certainly the most widely deployed and understood type of application. Information retrieval has been an active field for almost the entire history of computing, and the Internet has catapulted it into the mainstream. Though the focus with retrieval is on finding documents, the requirement of relevance underscores the importance of knowing what a document is about. So, even here, the use of content analysis can dramatically improve retrieval systems.

Routing flips the retrieval paradigm by turning the pull of retrieval into the push of content-triggered delivery, for example, to an e-mail box. Routing makes sense when information needs are not just one time, but recur based on broader roles or organizational needs. A simple example is a syndication service that matches new documents against saved queries or users' profiles. Broader organizational applications include routing of documents to the right people for further processing, e.g., routing patents to examiners or support cases to relevant specialists. Because routing "pushes" content at people, it requires finer discrimination on what the documents are about, otherwise the push quickly feels like a shove.

While retrieval and routing applications can be improved by finer grained processing of contents, mining and alerting applications absolutely require such processing. Mining applications enable users to explore the statistics of content collections or flows looking for interesting patterns or occurrences. Mining applications turn text documents into structured data that can be combined with other data sources and integrated into statistical or business intelligence applications. Alerting applications are the routing style obverse of mining. They notify users when particular patterns or events occur in content flows or regularly route canned analysis (i.e., reports) to the users.

Analyzing Content

All the types of applications described above depend on technologies for analyzing content to "understand" some portion of the meaning of its statements. Somewhere between one extreme of completely depending on humans to extract meaning and the other extreme of expecting machines to fully understand content themselves (whatever that may mean), the approaches for extracting particularly useful aspects of meaning are now becoming quite viable.

Content analysis can be viewed as the processing of content into structured representations or databases that captures some aspects of the meaning of the content's statements. To get at meaning, we can ask what the statement is talking about, and what is it saying about it. These questions highlight the two basic mechanisms for meaning in statements. Statements "refer" to objects in the world and they "say" something about them.

A search index can be seen as a trivial example of such a structured database. It provides a table of where and how many times words are used in the documents of a content collection. Its model of the world is that the world has documents in it and that the words used in a document tell you what the document is about. At the other extreme is a rich semantic network typically found in knowledge-based systems in artificial intelligence. Such semantic networks try to model a more complete "meaning" of the statements to support machine reasoning systems.

In between these two structures, we can imagine a database, which, like the semantic network, truly is referring to objects in the world, but makes more limited types of statements. These statements are of high value in particular applications and can be reliably generated from textual content. Again, it is about looking for sweet spots that balance utility and viability.

For example, consider a collection of articles about company events. The world covered by the statements in the collections is familiar. It includes people, companies, roles people play in companies, corporate events (e.g., founding, bankruptcy, mergers and acquisitions), and so on. A structured database over this space of objects and relationships would capture more meaning than a simple word index, while not providing the structure to answer arbitrary questions that could be answered based on the articles.

Such information extraction technology is not yet applied in most industries, but it has become mission critical in government intelligence and is quite common now in the publishing and pharmaceutical industries. It includes what is called entity extraction (figuring out what objects in the world a statement is talking about) and fact extraction (figuring out what the statement is saying about them). It focuses on the meaning of statements in content and on the problem of graspability rather than that of findability.

Another key (and common) technology, Automatic Categorization, is really about the mapping of documents into conceptual spaces. Categorization is about the filing of documents into an organized classification structure (typically called a taxonomy), for example, the filing of books into the Dewey Decimal System or of Web sites into Yahoo!. The value here is in automating the filing process, so that enterprises can affordably and reliably categorize their private content. This can never be a fully automated process, because a dead taxonomy stops being relevant in the same way as a dead language does, but human involvement can be optimized to make the overall process effective and workable.

Supercharging Retrieval

Retrieval, search, and browse style applications can be improved dramatically using taxonomies and extracted information. In this section, we will illustrate this point using an application based on Inxight SmartDiscovery. In a new more powerful browse style interaction, a user accesses a collection by navigating across a taxonomy. In fact, this is a familiar paradigm, not just from the organization of physical information resources as in libraries, but also in the electronic world. The early popularity of Yahoo! demonstrates the appeal and usefulness of high-quality taxonomy, organized by human catalogers. Automatic categorization enables this style of interaction in settings where full human cataloging is not an option.

A visualization suited to large hierarchies is ideal for helping the user quickly understand the taxonomy as well as drilling down to categories of interest. The taxonomy and the visualization together are effectively operating as a conceptual and perceptual map of the content collection. As with real maps, these structures allow a user to get an overview of the territory as well as navigate to specific areas of interest. In Figure 32.1, Inxight Star Tree is used to show the structure of the taxonomy.

Also, as with maps, visualizations can provide a backdrop for showing search results. For example, a search for "war" shows that there are matching documents in numerous categories. By selecting one or more of the categories containing matches, the user can filter the results based on his or her understanding of the taxonomy. This kind of filtering is effectively equivalent to doing an advanced query, but the user sees what he/she wants rather than thinking of what he/she wants before he/she says it. Conversely, by looking at where there are matches in the taxonomy, the user learns about the taxonomy during the process. Thus, search teaches the user to browse better.

The right side of Figure 32.1 shows the documents of a selected category in a result list. In addition to a title and a link for matching documents as typically shown, the previews show "a little bit more but not too much" about each document. The previews include a query-sensitive summary of the document as well as a list of entities (e.g., organizations, people, places) mentioned in the document and all categories that the document matches.

This query returned a large number of documents, and it would still take a long time to look through all the results. The document list view, shown in Figure 32.2, provides additional tools based on extracted information. As with a book index, the additional indexes help a user understand an entire result set. In particular, three index types are shown. The first index shows the concepts related to "war" found in the results, the second index shows the matching categories from the taxonomy, and the third index shows the entities of different types found.

These indexes are live filtering tools that can be used to refine the query, which through the availability of metadata allow users to create advanced queries on the fly as they better understand what they are looking for and learn about the available content. As users narrow the search results list, the index/filter tools dynamically update to show the information about the refined result list. When the user finds a document of interest either by browsing the taxonomy or by refining a query, the user can then focus in on the document and continue to leverage extracted information within the boundary of the document itself, as shown in Figure 32.3. On the left side, an index of the people, places, dates, measurements, and the like, discussed in the document, provides a quick way of locating specific information in text. On the right side, the document is used as a springboard to find other documents by using a "more like this" or "relevance feedback" capability or by using the categories and entities of the document to start a new query.

Leveraging Content

The work in most industries can be characterized as a chain of activities starting with science or engineering or design or development at one end and ending with marketing and servicing at the other. For example, the work of a large pharmaceutical company starts with fundamental science and flows through drug discovery, drug development, clinical testing, drug approval, and commercial exploitation. These stages are typically seen as distinct, and often content from one is not leveraged in other stages. Better content analysis enables the repurposing of content across different stages in a number of applications that apply in many industries. Many of these applications address typical knowledge management concerns.

Mergers and Acquisitions

Mergers depend crucially on being able to integrate the content resources of multiple organizations, particularly because large mergers are usually followed by attrition and head count reduction. Meanwhile, the new organization typically has to handle all of the current workload, so it becomes all the more important to be able to understand what information is available and to use it after the merger.

Figure 32.1

A visualization can provide a perceptual map of a taxonomy, which in turn provides a conceptual map of a content collection

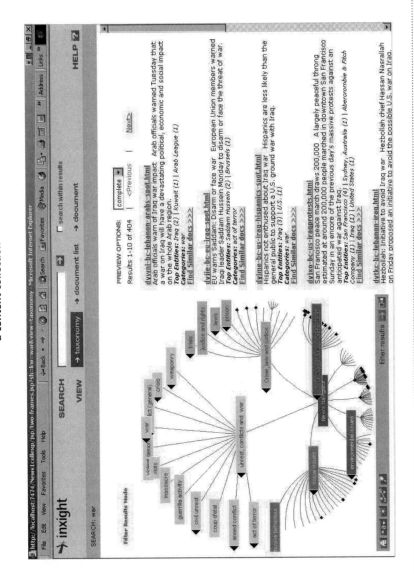

Figure 32.2

A search for the keyword "war" generated 404 "hits." The tools on the left are both views and filters that help users understand the entire result set and then focus on the portions of interest

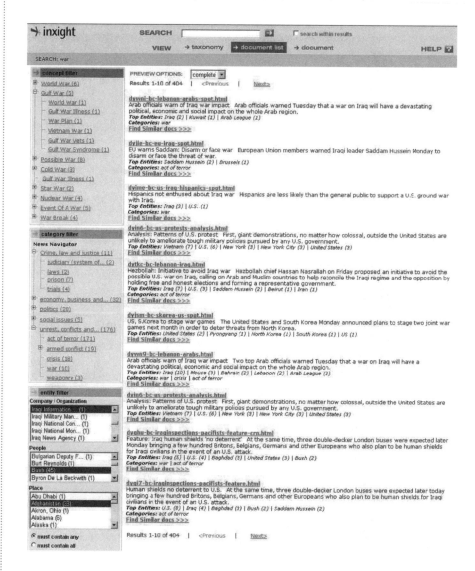

Corporate Licensing

Many large corporations accumulate large intellectual property (IP) portfolios through R&D as well as M&A. Increasingly, corporations look to external sources to license key technologies and look for revenue opportunities from licensing their own IP. Beyond the patents of a company, this activity requires dealing with other internal

Figure 32.3

The document level view allows quick grasping of the document content and uses the document as a source of queries back out to the collection

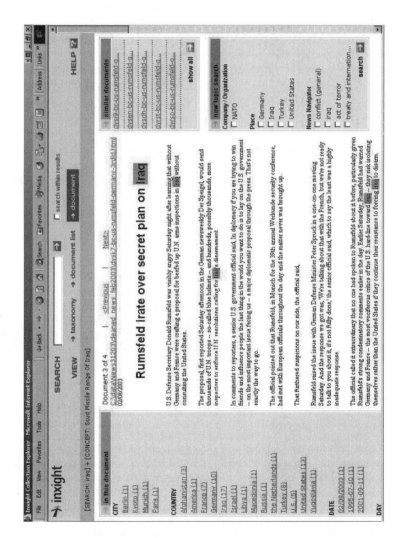

documents; the patents of others; and external scientific, technology, and marketplace documents.

Competitive Intelligence

Monitoring the market for competitive and marketplace dynamics is one of the oldest applications of search technology. Yet, this application is fundamentally about the fine-grained understanding of the interactions between the players, products, technologies, strategies, and actions in the marketplace. In the past, large companies tended to serve this function through small departments staffed with skilled research librarians and competitive intelligence specialists that followed well-defined methodologies. This approach has not been able to keep pace with the increasingly complex competitive and marketplace landscape, nor with the increasing variety or amount of available information and user needs across large global organizations.

Product Development

Companies produce large amounts of content during R&D as well as attain publicly or commercially available content. For example, life sciences companies leverage public content funded by government agencies (such as National Institutes of Health) as well as content from large electronic publishers. The pressures in the pharmaceutical industry are rapidly mounting to improve their drug discovery and development processes. Though work has gone into integrating and curating structured data sources (e.g., experimental data), internal textual content remains relatively underutilized.

Marketplace Feedback

Internet content sources and customer e-mail and surveys contain valuable feedback to an organization. Monitoring statements made about a company or its products in the press, on Web sites, in blogs, in discussion groups, and directly to the customer support organization can help evaluate brand perception and company reputation. Such monitoring can help tune corporate and product marketing activities, as well as help focus product development efforts on important areas for improvement or greater opportunity.

Supplier Management

Large organizations that provision products and services from a range of suppliers often struggle with product documentation and service level agreements. Internal users (e.g., product development) often must depend on an internal service department to figure out how to find necessary information. Suppliers and products and agreements are constantly changing, so manual organization efforts quickly fall behind.

A number of other applications, outside of knowledge management areas, are becoming important in large enterprises. These applications are well worth understanding because of their urgency.

Regulatory Compliance

Increasingly, large businesses or organizations are being regulated by laws or proactive policies to disclose various communications or documents to the public or to governmental agencies, to monitor or restrict certain communications with their customers, or to retain or destroy documents for some period of time or under certain conditions. Examples of regulations include the filing requirements on customer complaints related to pharmaceuticals; HIPAA in the healthcare industry; and, of course, the most visible of such regulatory acts, namely, Sarbanes-Oxley in the area of corporate accountability. A typical example of an application of extraction technology in this arena is to monitor e-mails between brokers and their clients for inappropriate messages and forward them to compliance officers.

Legal Discovery

In preparing for litigation, law firms, on behalf of their clients, dig through thousands or millions of documents looking for evidence to build their cases. Indexes of the people, organizations, and subjects and maps of the communications can help focus or prioritize discovery work. As a case develops, it also becomes important to search again based on new lines of thought. Because many of the documents are informal and are created by different people, it is important to be able to deal with vocabulary and name variation. These highlighted aspects of legal discovery also apply to many of the other collection-oriented applications below.

Customer Self-service

All successful product companies must ultimately focus on support costs for their products. One strategy that many companies are pursuing is to publish product and support information through interfaces that allow their customers to retrieve relevant support information directly. Besides mitigating costs for the company, a positive user experience that leads to solving the customer's problem can also enhance the company's brand.

Conclusion

The use of content analysis technology and deployment of content use applications beyond standard search or browse applications are just now starting to become viable in enterprises. Much can be learned from the experience of leading adopters in government intelligence and law enforcement agencies. The pressures on these organizations are extreme, and they cannot afford to not leverage available content in urgent missions.

A number of intelligence agencies are focused on the mission of counterterrorism, while law enforcement organizations continue their pursuit of criminals or, even better, their activities prior to the committing of their crimes. These missions have access to huge repositories of textual content gathered by multiple agencies and departments including field reports, collection summaries, immigration records, Web page content, e-mails, message traffic, open source news feeds, and the like. Though flexible and powerful user-driven retrieval applications are important, routing, mining, and alerting applications based on content analysis and information extraction are tantamount to directing human resources to consequential activities. In this arena, a number of important principles appear underscored:

- Humans matter—For the foreseeable future, it is unlikely that any automated approach is going to succeed in truly understanding natural language documents. Thus, the question is not about eliminating human intelligence, but rather about how to design overall systems that arm humans with effective computational tools at the end-user task and organizational levels. Years of investment in artificial intelligence have only clarified the absolute necessity of using human intelligence in government intelligence and law enforcement.

- Language matters—Content is, once again, made of human language. There is no avoiding the fact that language is made up of words in natural languages like German, Korean, Farsi, and English, but it goes beyond that to all the specialized languages we speak, from Terrorismese to Xeroxese to Medicalish. Furthermore, for the same reasons that there are so many languages, most terms have many surface forms. For example, consider the spelling of a foreign name in English or the same molecular compound in various scientific names and in drug/brand names. Any system that ignores this is missing the fundamentals of *natural* language.

- Architecture matters—Often there is great debate about algorithms and their accuracy, but since full text understanding is not around the corner, the focus should be on the overall effectiveness of the system. This real, bigger concern points at the importance of the architecture of systems. Systems must support the blending of human resource and computational processes and the overall management of multiple and various algorithms and their associated data.

- Speed matters—Again, since text will not be processed once and its full meaning captured forever, text will often be processed again and again for different purposes or projects or as new algorithms or language models are updated. Certainly, the actual text stream available to intelligence and law enforcement streams is torrential, but that same text stream is being processed over and over. Cascaded architectures based on sound and speedy processing at different levels can support overall efficiency, allowing simple changes to be made more aggressively, while still allowing for more complex updates.

As enterprises look to deploying content analysis infrastructure that can be used across a variety of content use applications, they should carefully consider the above principles. To distill this further, the key observation of this chapter is that we must keep our eyes focused on two essential realities if we are ever to truly leverage content. One reality, about content, is that content is text as well as language. The other reality, about leveraging or use, is that we have to think about the overall effectiveness of systems at organization and user levels, not the narrow level of algorithm accuracy or other technological virtues.

Structured Knowledge: The Key to Optimal Contact Center Efficiency*

Kent F. Heyman

An investment in knowledge pays the best interest.

Ben Franklin

KM in the Contact Center: The Care and Feeding of a Valuable Corporate Asset

The contact center has always been a key corporate asset. This has never been more true than in today's ultra-competitive business environment. As the first line of contact for most customer interactions, proper and efficient operation of the contact center has become indispensable to the mission-critical objectives of achieving customer satisfaction and maintaining customer loyalty.

Just as the importance of these mission-critical objectives has grown, the challenge of meeting them has increased. Many, if not most, contact centers are compelled by business circumstances to seek more efficient ways to deliver customer care, and budgetary restraints compel them to find ways to do more with less.

---

* *Editor's Note:* This chapter examines the key role that knowledge, and quick access to it, plays in today's contact center. It discusses the risks inherent in a contact center which relies on access to unstructured information (often mislabeled "unstructured knowledge"). This chapter also examines how specific information types impact the contact center in its mission-critical quest to achieve customer satisfaction and maintain customer loyalty, while also struggling with business demands to do more with less. A structured knowledge-base, used in conjunction with a powerful search tool, can enable efficiencies across multiple contact channels. Metrics are provided to assess contact center efficiency.

Three case studies are presented, based on KM solutions from ServiceWare. ServiceWare is a provider of Web-based KM solutions for customer service and IT support via contact centers and self-help on the Web; clients include Reuters, H&R Block, AT&T Wireless, Cingular Wireless, Green Mountain Energy, and Qualcomm. Its ServiceWare Enterprise™ solution allows for integration to a number of other business applications, including CRM, ERM, telephony, and help desk systems. Powerful search technology helps querying by phrases and also weights queries depending on how often they are asked.

At the operational level, there are several issues, virtually ubiquitous to all contact centers, which impact their ability to achieve optimal efficiency. First, agents fielding inquiries from customers, partners, suppliers, and/or employees must have thorough and extensive knowledge of the organization, its products, and its services. Without this knowledge or access to it, an agent will be hard pressed to efficiently deliver the right answers to inquiries. The challenge of imparting this "knowledge" to agents too often falls upon expensive training programs or, worse, trial and error.

In an environment where agent churn is common, the need to maximize access to answers and to minimize expensive training (or its low-cost equivalent, "baptism under fire") is acute. When agents are not completely conversant with the full array of products, services, issues, and solutions of the business, optimal efficiency can only be achieved through proper management of the information resident within the organization: its knowledge.

Sidebar
Case Study 1. Gelco: Improved customer satisfaction

Gelco Information Network helps over 1,200 global organizations manage their travel expenditures via automated expense management and payment solutions, based on enforcing policy compliance, supplier negotiations, and spending analysis. It decided on an innovative solution to help customers find answers on their own via a new self-service site. However, it faced internal challenges like knowledge possessiveness and job insecurity among its employees.

ServiceWare's KM solution in its call center was implemented with strict quality guidelines for contributed knowledge. For instance, expectations were set requiring all new knowledge in FAQs to be submitted with a 24-hour turnaround time. The solution integrated the call tracking system, phone system, and intranet. After just four months of utilizing 24 × 7 Web self-service, Gelco experienced a 17% decrease in the volume of calls coming into the call center. The company is now experiencing an average of over 500 customer sessions on the Web site each week, and, during peak support times, self-service usage increases. Agents are now able to get up to speed on new product knowledge in less than one week. Customer satisfaction has also visibly improved.

Structured Knowledge and Contact Center Efficiency

Whether used by an agent responding to a customer inquiry or by a customer using self-service, knowledge users need efficient access to the right data, information, or knowledge in order to obtain fast, accurate, and consistent answers. The information accessed by either audience can be knowledge, that is, information that has been collected, quality assured, and formatted for optimal search and retrieval, or it can be unstructured "information," that is, existing data and information found in document repositories or data warehouses or as disparate information accessible on a network.

In order to achieve optimal contact center efficiency, it is crucial to understand that information does not truly become knowledge until human experience is applied to it through usage. The only way to do this systematically and efficiently is to construct a true knowledge-base by transforming information into a structured format with proper validation.

Knowledge management (KM) tools allow the contact center to capture and categorize relevant information and make it readily available for retrieval by either agents or self-service customers. While both agents and customers can be given access to either *structured knowledge* or *unstructured information* or both, we will discuss below why true call center efficiency cannot be achieved through access to unstructured information alone.

Two contact center realities compel this conclusion: problem understanding and access to answers.

1. **Agents need to understand the issue or problem before they can deliver an accurate answer.** Agents not only need access to answers, they need the right knowledge to understand the questions that are being asked and the issues which are being posed. Agents will often spend as much as 70% of their time during a call in the problem diagnosis phase and 30% in the answer delivery phase of resolution of a customer issue. One of the key benefits of a structured knowledge-base is that agents can focus more on troubleshooting questions and minimize the diagnosis phase, enabling them to quickly get to the answer delivery phase of the customer experience. This is crucial to achieving efficiency (see discussion of First Call Resolution Section below). Since structured knowledge allows the agent to determine if he or she has properly diagnosed the customer's issue before delivering an answer, it is distinctly preferable to mere access to unstructured information, which can only help with the answer.

2. **Agents need access to proven answers.** Agents need fast access to accurate, proven information in order to provide consistent service. Agents often use informal methods to research inquiries and deliver answers to customers (e.g., "hey Joe," manuals, binders, sticky notes, case histories). However, these methods are not optimal because they do not promote knowledge sharing or knowledge reuse. Optimum contact center efficiency can only be achieved by capturing answers to previously asked questions and building structured knowledge from this experience.

The process of building knowledge does not necessarily require the presence of a formal knowledge engineer or subject matter expert. A well-defined process and tools that enable agents to contribute knowledge are recommended. In contact centers, questions often have already been asked before and are likely to be asked again. A KM system which is built upon knowledge contributed by skilled agents and based upon actual experience will facilitate efficient responses to customer inquiries by experienced and inexperienced agents alike. With such a system, a "new" agent has immediate access to all of the knowledge of even the most experienced agent. Also, in case experienced agents churn out of the contact center, legacy knowledge has been captured in a readily usable and accessible form.

Sidebar
Case Study 2. Wonderware: Cutting costs and boosting revenue

Wonderware is an operating unit of the production management division of Invensys and is a leading supplier of industrial automation software. Its global technical services department helps customers in over 30,000 plants worldwide. For its KM solution, the vendor was selected on the basis of criteria like self-learning and self-organizing search capability, robustness, ease of use, integration with other Microsoft and Siebel tools, and affordability. Twenty-two engineers provide support for Wonderware, and the technical support team reassigned two quality assurance technicians to create knowledge and administer the knowledge-base using ServiceWare Architect™.

Within nine weeks, the system had already generated a 34% reduction in calls compared to the same time period in the previous year. External customers conducted more than 500 unique searches per week on the support Web site. The case load went down 17% year over year. Wonderware was also able to reassign three support engineers to new consulting positions, selling technical services.

The company made it mandatory that agents contribute knowledge and new solutions each time they closed a case. KM has been made a regular part of the support process. Cultural acceptance grew quickly once the technical services group reaped immediate rewards, such as cost reduction and increased productivity.

Contact Center Efficiency Metrics

It is common for contact centers to measure efficiency through the implementation of certain metrics, most often *average handle time, first call resolution, escalation rates, training costs,* and *call deflection.* Appropriate tools can help bring about gains in each of these efficiency metrics via the use of structured knowledge as compared to unstructured information.

Average Handle Time

Structured knowledge enables agents to answer inquiries quickly and to avoid time spent searching, evaluating, or trying incorrect or unnecessary avenues of troubleshooting or questioning.

Unstructured information on the other hand typically requires extensive time to search, read, evaluate, select, and retrieve solutions. In many environments the use of unstructured information alone can actually increase the overall handle time.

First Call Resolution

Structured knowledge provides the correct problem diagnosis and therefore the correct answer at the time of the initial query. Thus, agents have an advantage because the answers have already been reviewed in a quality assurance process.

Conversely, agents relying solely on unstructured information run the risk of presenting inaccurate or untested solutions. The usefulness of unstructured information in this context is generally limited to experienced agents who are researching unique issues offline . . . certainly not while a customer is waiting on the phone.

Escalation Rates

Structured knowledge has the advantage of being a known and proven solution, likely to resolve the issue. This eliminates the risk of attempting unproven or inappropriate solutions, minimizing the need for escalation.

Unstructured information may or may not have the correct solution and may encourage, rather than minimize, the need to escalate to experienced agents. If such an escalation occurs and is not captured in a knowledge-base, it is likely to be repeated, often resulting in increased costs and unnecessary customer frustration.

Training Costs

Structured knowledge developed by experts or experienced agents, analyzed and quality assured, is considered proven and tested before it is published in the knowledge-base. Having a robust knowledge-base with proven solutions reduces the amount of information an agent must commit to memory before being deployed. Thus, training time is reduced.

By contrast, unstructured information is inherently unreliable and has not been quality assured. It is risky to give an untrained agent access to unreliable information, expecting him or her to do "quality assurance on the fly."

Call Deflection

Structured knowledge, based upon a validated and quality assured knowledge source, allows an organization to extend access of the knowledge-base to customers or end-users via Web self-service. When a properly structured knowledge-base is deployed for self-service, there is a high degree of confidence that the customer will find the correct answer quickly and easily and a minimal chance for an unsatisfactory customer experience.

By comparison, to deploy unstructured information via customer self-service is extremely risky, as it relies on the experience and analytical abilities of the customer to search, evaluate, and interpret information. This often leads to customer frustration and minimizes call deflection when the frustrated customer turns to the phone or, worse, seeks another provider.

Sidebar
Case Study 3. Made2Manage Systems: Award-winning web self-service

Made2Manage Systems is a provider of enterprise software for small and midsize manufacturers and distributors. It supports over 1,600 customers through service operations at locations in 4 countries. The complete solution (e.g., with SCM, CRM, BI) can be complex to support and needs a robust knowledge-base solution. With ServiceWare tools, Made2Manage dubbed its online support initiative "M2M Expert" and the online knowledge-base "Ask Expert."

Made2Manage found that in the year 2002–2003, over 95,000 individual searches were performed on the M2M Expert Web site, and 22% of calls were successfully deflected. Approximately 900 new knowledge-base solutions are being added to the system every month, and customers are also given the opportunity to suggest new knowledge for M2M Expert. The Association of Support Professionals has named M2M Expert to its list of "Ten Best Web Support Sites" for the second consecutive year.

Conclusion

In sum, in order to achieve optimal contact center efficiency, agents must be able to find the right answer quickly. To do so, they often cannot afford to conduct lengthy, repetitive searches for information through mere unstructured document repositories.

Structured knowledge, managed in conjunction with a powerful knowledge-base search technology, can consistently provide efficient access to correct answers, based upon the usage and experience of all users. This operates as a tremendous source of knowledge leverage, i.e., affording each agent the opportunity to draw upon the collective experience of the entire contact center. This eliminates much, if not all, of the need to read and evaluate irrelevant, incorrect, or misleading information.

Properly leveraged, the structured knowledge-base, used in conjunction with a powerful search tool, can also enable efficiencies across multiple contact channels, such as customer self-service, e-mail, and chat, as well as the more prevalent voice channel.

About the Contributors

Patti Anklam is an independent consultant with expertise in community of practice development, social network analysis, and KM. She was formerly director of KM for the Global Professional Services organization at Nortel Networks. In her 25+ years in the computer industry, Patti also held posts at IBM and Compaq. She is also a key contributor to the Gennova Group, a Boston-based network of consultants whose focus is on networked organizational forms.

Wilfried Aulbur is in charge of the office of Professor Jürgen Hubbert, Member of the Board of Management of DaimlerChrysler and Head of the Mercedes Car Group. He studied theoretical physics and computational material sciences in France, Germany, the United Kingdom, and the United States. After earning his Ph.D. degree in 1996, he worked as a postdoctoral researcher at the University of California, San Diego, and at Ohio State University. Since 1999 he has been at DaimlerChrysler, working on KM issues in Germany, the United States, and India.

Ritendra Banejee heads the organization practice at QAI India in Bangalore. He was formerly with Arthur D. Little. His consulting engagements include the National Remote Sensing Agency, Crompton Greaves, Kotak Mahindra, RPG, Clyde Blowers, and Commonwealth Secretariat. Ritendra is a frequent speaker on KM and is a contributing author to the book *Leading with Knowledge*. He graduated from Presidency College and Xavier's Institute of Management in India.

Darius Baria heads KM activities at Rolls-Royce Defence Aerospace Engineering in the United Kingdom. Darius continues to ensure that KM is implemented into all areas of the business. He graduated from Loughborough University (UK) and worked in training in an engineering company in Tokyo for over two years.

Steve Barth is editor and publisher of Knowledge Management magazine, now presented in electronic format by Line56 Media at www.destinationKM.com. An award-winning journalist, he has also written about everything from rainforests to trade wars, basketball teams to canoe paddlers! In 2002, he was a visiting scholar at the Learning Innovations Laboratory at the Harvard University Graduate School of Education.

Dan Carmel is Vice President of Marketing and Corporate Strategy for iManage. He has over 15 years of experience in marketing for IT companies. Dan has formerly served with Selectica, Sonnet Financial, The Vantive Corporation, and Savi Technology. He holds B.S. and M.S. degrees in Engineering from the University of Pennsylvania and an MBA degree from the Stanford Graduate School of Business (USA).

Heidi Collins leads Knowledge Management for Air Products and Chemicals Incorporated. She is the author of *Corporate Portals* and *Enterprise Knowledge Portals* (AMACOM). Heidi has over 25 years of experience as a business analyst and software developer. She has a Bachelor's degree from the University of Texas in Decision Information Systems and a Master's degree from Arizona State University in Computer Information Systems.

James Dellow is the Asia Program Manager for Ernst & Young's flagship extranet portal, Ernst & Young Online. He was formerly at Sydney's New Children's Hospital and the Australian Red Cross Blood Service. James is originally from the United Kingdom, but has lived and worked in Australia since 1995 after finishing his studies in Public Sector Administration at Sheffield Hallam University (UK). He is a member of the New South Wales Knowledge Management Forum.

Michele Egan, a French national, is the Knowledge Manager for the Human Resources Vice Presidency at the World Bank. She started at the World Bank 20 years ago in information management and then moved into human resources and corporate communications. Michele is a doctoral candidate in organizational processes and human systems at the University of Maryland and holds a Master's degree in Human Resources and a B.A. degree in Behavioral Sciences from the University of Maryland (US).

Svenja Falk studied political science, sociology, and philosophy at the University of Giessen, Germany, and the University of Southern California, Los Angeles. Svenja is now heading Accenture Research, Accenture's internal research center, with a responsibility for Austria, Switzerland, and Germany. She has published regularly on knowledge management (including as co-editor of the book *Knowledge Management in Networked Communities*) as well as on e-politics and e-democracy. Svenja lives in Frankfurt, Germany.

Ben Goodson is Knowledge Manager at easyJet, Europe's largest low-cost airline. He started working for easyJet in 1998 and became fascinated by the whole impact of the Internet on the company's business model. He eventually headed its intranet strategy and also worked on organizational development. Ben has an English degree from the University of Luton in the United Kingdom.

Roland Haas is Managing Director of DaimlerChrysler Research and Technology India (DCRTI). Roland worked with the KM team of DASA (DaimlerChrysler Aerospace) prior to moving to India. He has considerable experience in knowledge-based systems and has written extensively on the subject.

Susan S. Hanley is practice executive for enterprise collaboration and content management at Dell Professional Services. Her articles have appeared in *Knowledge Management Review*, *Management Consultant International*, and *Information Week*. She is also a featured author in the books *Knowledge Management and Virtual Organizations*, *Knowledge Management: The Foundation for Electronic Government* and *The Handbook on Knowledge Management*. Sue has an MBA degree from the University of Maryland and a B.A. degree from the Johns Hopkins University, Baltimore, MD.

Farida Hasanali is Program Manager for American Productivity & Quality Center's Knowledge Sharing Network (KSN), for which she led the design and development effort. Over the past eight years at APQC, Hasanali has led numerous consortium benchmarking projects. Farida is a frequent speaker on the KM conference circuit. She has co-authored three titles on KM from APQC's Passport to Success series. She holds a Bachelor's degree in Psychology from St. Xavier College in Bombay, India.

Anders Hemre is Director and Chief Knowledge Officer at Ericsson Research Canada. He has over 30 years of experience in the telecom industry in Europe, the Middle East, the Far East, and North America. He serves on the faculties of the Delphi group, KMWorld, IQPC, Braintrust, PDMA, Basex, and the Ark group. He graduated from the Chalmers University of Technology, Gothenburg, Sweden, with an M.S. degree in Electrical Engineering.

Kent Heyman is President and CEO of ServiceWare Technologies. He was a co-founder of Mpower Communications and also served as litigation department chairman and lead trial counsel for Dowling, Magarian, Aaron, and Heyman. He earned a Doctor of Law (J.D.) degree from the University of the Pacific's McGeorge School of Law and received a Bachelor's degree from California State University, Fresno (USA).

Arik R. Johnson is founder and CEO of Aurura WDC, a competitive intelligence and outsourcing bureau. He has extensive experience in consulting and has degrees from the University of Wisconsin–Madison in international business and history. Since 1999, Arik has served as the Wisconsin Chapter Chairperson of the Society of Competitive Intelligence Professionals (www.SCIP.org). He is a frequent speaker on the topic of CI and KM and is well published.

Bipin Junnarkar leads the KM efforts at the Hewlett-Packard Company. He has more than 20 years of experience in large-scale program management process transformation and KM. Bipin was formerly vice president of Knowledge Management for Gateway; he also held posts at Monsanto Company, Schlumberger, and Royal Dutch/Shell Group. He graduated from the Indian Institute of Technology in Bombay and Washington University in St. Louis, MO.

Gopika Kannan works in the Business Strategy department of DaimlerChrysler Research and Technology India. She consults, trains, and researches in the domain of knowledge management, strategy formulation, and business process improvements. Dr. Kannan is a consultant to the Airbus Knowledge Management team and is deeply involved in developing knowledge metrics and measures.

Peter Katz is Executive Vice President of Sales and Marketing at Entopia. He was formerly with iLogistix, Silicon Valley Networks, Micro Focus, Wells Fargo Bank/Crocker National Bank, and Price Waterhouse's Management Consulting Services. Peter holds an MBA degree from New York University's Stern School of Business and a B.S. degree from the University of Vermont in Burlington.

Beat Knechtli is currently Knowledge Manager for Asea Brown Boveri in Baden, Switzerland. He graduated from the University of Basel and served in management and IT positions in organizations like Hoffmann-La Roche. Beat lectures on KM in Basel and Bern in Switzerland. He is Vice President of the Swiss Knowledge Management Forum and a member of the European Knowledge Management Community.

Tharun Kumar is currently general manager of technology for ICICI OneSource, India's leading BPO company responsible for IT solutions. He was formerly country manager of technology for Cable & Wireless India, where he headed its Technical Centre of Excellence and was responsible for designing and implementing the "Phoenix" KM system. Tharun was also with Motorola and Hughes Network Systems in Malaysia. He has a bachelors in electronics from Bangalore University.

Stan Kwiecien is Best Practices Replication (BPR) Deployment Manager at Ford. He has been with Ford for 32 years and was an architect of Ford Motor Company's BPR process. He contributed 27 years of experience in manufacturing operations and an enthusiastic vision of the need to share and replicate knowledge. The process is now used to leverage the value of completed Six Sigma projects using the power of replication.

Laurence (Laurie) Lock Lee is Principal Knowledge Management consultant for CSC Strategic Consulting, Australia. He was formerly the practice leader for enterprise knowledge management with BHP Information Technology, prior to BHP IT's acquisition by CSC in 2000. He has published over 40 papers and reports and has been an invited speaker at public forums and conferences, both within Australia and internationally.

Joan Levers is Communications Manager for Hewlett-Packard Company's Knowledge Management organization. She has more than 25 years of experience in marketing communications, instructional design, and technical writing. Joan has also worked in the healthcare industry. She graduated from Texas Tech University in Lubbock and Oregon State University in Corvallis.

Manfred "Luigi" Lugmayr is Vice President of Product Management at Entopia. He was formerly with Hero Capital, Zadu, and Internet Media House. A native of Austria, Lugmayr also worked at C-Train GmbH and Siemens in Vienna and Cyberlab GmbH in Munich. Lugmayr received a degree in Electrical Engineering from HTBLA in Braunau, Austria and an M.S. degree in Computer Science from the Technical University of Vienna.

Hemant Manohar is the Chief Knowledge Officer of KPMG India.

Jon Mason is currently an executive consultant at education.au limited, an educational agency in Australia. He is also Assistant Director of IMS Australia and is active in e-learning standardization forums of Standards Australia, IMS Global Learning Consortium, IEEE Learning Technology Standards Committee, and Dublin Core Metadata Initiative. Jon is co-author of the book *Transforming E-Knowledge*.

Nel Mostert is Innovation Process Facilitator at Unilever Research & Development in Vlaardingen, The Netherlands. She has been active at Unilever in the field of cultural changes for more than 20 years. Nel graduated with an MBA degree from the Open University (UK); her specialization is identifiying barriers and enablers for creativity in an R&D organization.

Luke Naismith has been a senior policy analyst in Australia's National Office for the Information Economy since August 1999 and heads their Forward Strategy section. Luke is a member of the Standards Australia International Knowledge Management Committee and the Melbourne-based Knowledge Management Leadership Forum. He previously held senior positions in other government public service departments in IT, KM, and library services.

Takahiko Nomura is the Research Explorer at the Knowledge Dynamics Initiative (KDI) of Fuji Xerox, Japan. He is responsible for KM methodologies research and consultation services. His articles have been published in the *Annual Bulletin of Knowledge Management Society of Japan* and *IEEE WetIce*. Takahiko earned a Master of Engineering degree from Keio University, Japan.

Stephen Pao is Vice President of Life Sciences for AskMe Corporation. He was previously with Asta Networks and Latitude Communications. Steve is also a veteran of Oracle Corporation and is a frequent speaker at KM conferences. He graduated from the Massachusetts Institute of Technology in Cambridge with a Bachelor's degree in Electrical Sciences and Engineering and a Master's degree in Electrical Engineering and Computer Science.

Lynn Qu is a business consultant for AskMe Corporation. She was formerly program manager at Microsoft Corporation, in the Exchange, Explorer, and Expedia groups. Lynn graduated from the Massachusetts Institute of Technology in Cambridge with a Bachelor's degree in Electrical Engineering and Computer Science and a Master of Engineering degree in Electrical and Computer Sciences.

Ramana Rao is CTO and founder of Inxight Software and editor of the *Information Flow* e-mail newsletter. At Xerox Palo Alto Research Center [PARC] for ten years, Ramana has worked on intelligent information access, digital libraries, information visualization, and user interfaces. His work includes 25 patent filings and numerous refereed research papers. Ramana has a Master's degree in Computer Science and Engineering from the Massachusetts Institute of Technology in Cambridge.

Cynda H. Rushton is principal investigator for the National Nursing Leadership Academy and Assistant Professor of Nursing at the Johns Hopkins University School of Nursing in Baltimore, MD. She received her M.S. degree in Nursing from the Medical University of South Carolina and a Doctorate degree in Nursing at the Catholic University of America in Washington, D.C., with a concentration in bioethics. Cynda is a frequent speaker and nationally recognized expert in palliative and end-of-life care.

Christena Singh directs KM strategy at the Office of Small Business in the Department of Industry, Tourism and Resources in Australia.

Hilbert J. Bruins Slot is skillbase leader of the Knowledge Systems Group, part of the Knowledge & Information Science program at Unilever R&D in Vlaardingen, Netherlands. He graduated from the University of Utrecht and University of Nijmegen (UK). Hilbert was previously with the Dutch national expertise center CAOS/CAMM. His interests include knowledge structuring, inventive problem solving by TRIZ, and application of portal technologies for knowledge sharing.

Paul Spence is managing director of GeniusNet Limited, a niche management consultancy based in Wellington, New Zealand. GeniusNet manages the Innovators Online Network project. Paul is also chairperson of the SME task group of the ICT Capital business cluster. His background includes stints as a meteorologist and commercial pilot. Paul holds a BSc. and a diploma in business administration.

Sanjay Swarup successfully designed, developed, and launched common integrated processes for Ford operations in the United States, the United Kingdom, and Germany. He was a project leader and manager of manufacturing operations in Fortune 500 companies including Teledyne, John Deere, and Smith International. He currently guides Ford's Best Practice Replication System. He has an M.S. degree from the University of Michigan and an MBA degree from the University of Connecticut in Storrs.

Robyn Valade is currently Ford's Best Practice Replication Integration Manager. Her duties also include interfacing with the various Web support organizations within Ford to assure Web site availability, compliance, and performance. In her 20 years with the company, she has directed software development efforts within engineering and human resources, as well as led process improvement efforts in product development and marketing.

Dar Wolford is currently Ford's Best Practice Replication Manager. Her duties also include marketing this proprietary method outside the enterprise. Dar previously led the early entry of RAPID into Ford—a workshop-based methodology designed to drive out quick solutions to business issues. In her 27 years with the company, she has directed process improvement efforts in myriad business subjects from financials to logistics.

Eric Woods is Research Director for Knowledge Management and Business Intelligence at Ovum. Eric has been lead author on numerous Ovum reports on collaboration software, search, portals, and KM. He is also Service Director for Ovum's e-knowledge@ovum service. Eric is a consultant, conference speaker, and writer in the U.S. and European markets.

About the Editor

Madanmohan Rao, a KM consultant and author from Bangalore, is research director at the Asian Media Information and Communication Centre. He is the editor of two book series: *The KM Chronicles* and *The Asia-Pacific Internet Handbook*. Madan was on the editorial board of the book *Transforming e-Knowledge* and is editor-at-large of DestinationKM.com. He graduated from the Indian Institute of Technology in Bombay and the University of Massachusetts, with an M.S. in computer science and a Ph.D. in communications. He has work experience in the United States, Brazil, and India and has spoken at conferences in over 50 countries.

Index